SIGNS AND SOCIETY

SIGNS AND SOCIETY

Further Studies in Semiotic Anthropology

Richard J. Parmentier

Indiana University Press

Bloomington and Indianapolis

This book is a publication of

Indiana University Press
Office of Scholarly Publishing
Herman B Wells Library 350
1320 East 10th Street
Bloomington, Indiana 47405 USA

iupress.indiana.edu

⊗ The paper used in this publication meets the minimum
requirements of the American National Standard for Information
Sciences—Permanence of Paper for Printed Library Materials,
ANSI Z39.48-1992.

Manufactured in the United States of America

Cataloging information is available from the Library of Congress.

ISBN 978-0-253-02481-7 (cloth)
ISBN 978-0-253-02496-1 (paperback)
ISBN 978-0-253-02514-2 (ebook)

1 2 3 4 5   22 21 20 19 18 17

For Nancy Felson

Contents

Acknowledgments   *ix*

Part I: Foundations of Peircean Semiotics   *1*

1   Semiotic Anthropology   *3*

2   Charles S. Peirce   *24*

3   Representation, Symbol, and Semiosis: Signs of a Scholarly Collaboration   *36*

4   Peirce and Saussure on Signs and Ideas in Language   *42*

5   Troubles with Trichotomies: Reflections on the Utility of Peirce's Sign Trichotomies for Social Analysis   *48*

6   Semiotic Degeneracy of Social Life: Prolegomenon to a Human Science of Semiosis   *63*

Part II: Critical Commentaries and Reviews   *81*

7   Representing Semiotics in the New Millennium   *83*

8   The World Has Changed Forever: Semiotic Reflections on the Experience of Sudden Change   *101*

9   Description and Comparison of Religion   *107*

10   It's About Time: On the Semiotics of Temporality   *121*

11   Anthropological Encounters of a Semiotic Kind   *127*

12   Two Marxes: Evolutionary and Critical Dimensions of Marxian Social Theory   *136*

Part III: Comparative Perspectives on Semiosis   *161*

13   Money Walks, People Talk: Systemic and Transactional Dimensions of Palauan Exchange   *163*

14 Representing Transcendence: The Semiosis of Real Presence /
With Massimo Leone   192

15 The "Savvy Interpreter": Performance and Interpretation in
Pindar's Victory Odes / With Nancy Felson   208

References   239
Index   265

Acknowledgments

The essays in this volume were all written while I was a member of the Department of Anthropology at Brandeis University, and so I first thank my departmental colleagues who over the past quarter-century have made our hallway such a warm and supportive academic home. I have been fortunate to have had expert critical feedback on these essays by scholars from many different disciplines and institutions, especially Brigitte Miriam Bedos-Rezak, Stéphane Breton, Ward Goodenough, Nina Kammerer, Paul Kockelman, Kyung-Nan Koh, Janet McIntosh, Kathryn Morgan, Ryo Morimoto, June Nash, Sally Ann Ness, Nigel Nicholson, Susan Petrilli, Frank Reynolds, Peter W. Rose, Benson Saler, and Michael Silverstein. I particularly thank Nancy Felson and Massimo Leone, fellow members of the Editorial Board of *Signs and Society*, who coauthored two of these essays and kindly agreed to have them reprinted here. I gratefully acknowledge the support of Susan Birren, dean of Arts and Sciences at Brandeis, who approved my sabbatical leave for 2015–2016, which made possible the completion of two of these essays and the preparation of the volume. I also thank Asif Agha and Michael Silverstein, who replaced me as editor of *Signs and Society* during my sabbatical.

The chapters in this volume have been revised from their original presentation and publication forms and are reprinted here with permission.

SIGNS AND SOCIETY

PART I

Foundations of Peircean Semiotics

1   Semiotic Anthropology

Fields of Signs

The domain of semiotic anthropology is considered to be the results of empirical research carried out by anthropologists (in all subfields) that makes use of concepts and methods associated with the tradition of scholarship labeled "semiotics" or "semiology." Semiotic anthropology is not a formal subdiscipline of anthropology; it is not a "school" of anthropological thought; and it is not confined to researchers affiliated with particular academic institutions or national traditions. To some degree semiotic anthropology emerged as a correction and refinement of symbolic or interpretive anthropology or structural anthropology (Mertz 1985). In addition to the study of linguistic and written codes, anthropologists have employed semiotic notions in the analysis of cultural signs, such as pictorial representations and images, dress and bodily adornment, gesture and dance, spatial organization and the built environment, ritualized behaviors (taboo, divination, and performance), exchange valuables, and food and cuisine. Although anthropology has played a relatively minor role in the development of the larger discipline of semiotics, which is dominated by literary studies, it was an anthropologist, Margaret Mead, who coined the modern label at an interdisciplinary conference at Indiana University in 1962. In her summary comments Mead discussed the possibility of a new term:

> Which in time will include the study of all patterned communication in all modalities, of which linguistics is the most technically advanced. If we had a word for patterned communication modalities, it would be useful. I am not enough of a specialist in this field to know what word to use, but many people here, who have looked as if they were on opposite sides of the fence, have used the word "semiotics." It seems to me the one word, in some form or other, that has been used by people arguing from quite different positions. (Mead 1964, 275)

Like all aspects of contemporary research in semiotics, semiotic anthropology is heir to two dominant intellectual strands stemming from the work of American scientist and mathematician Charles S. Peirce (1839–1914) and Swiss linguist Ferdinand de Saussure (1857–1913). Peirce and Saussure did not know of each other; much of their writing on semiotics or semiology is fragmentary and took decades to become widely available, and neither discussed strictly anthropological topics with any specificity.

Peirce developed an innovative reformulation of valid scientific reasoning by viewing both human thought and natural processes as following the inferential logic of signs, or "semeiotic." For Peirce, the universe was perfused with signs that stand for or represent their objects and that determine further interpretant signs, which in turn represent the relationship between signs and their objects. Refusing to take natural language as the model semiotic system but recognizing the special character of conventional linguistic forms (which he called, following Aristotle, symbols), Peirce subdivided the opposed traditional category of natural signs (Greek *semeion*) into icons, which resemble their objects in some formal way, and indexes, which are spatially or temporally contiguous with their objects.

> A sign endeavors to represent, in part at least, an Object, which is therefore in a sense the cause, or determinant, of the sign even if the sign represents its object falsely. But to say that it represents its Object implies that it affects a mind, and so affects it as, in some respect, to determine in that mind something that is mediately due to the Object. That determination of which the immediate cause, or determinant, is the Sign, and of which the mediate cause is the Object may be termed the Interpretant. (Peirce *CP* 6.347)

Of the three Peircean grounds relating signs and objects, only symbolic conventionality requires the interpretant to supply the linkage between sign and object, although nothing actually functions as a sign unless it is interpreted to be a sign of some sort. Peircean symbols are, thus, irreducibly triadic; but symbols can communicate information about their objects only by embodying icons and can successfully point to the external world by embodying indexes, which anchor the contextual flow of signs (or semiosis) so that potential interpreters can bring their collateral knowledge to bear on the objects being represented. A scientist of international stature and a strong exponent of the pragmatic theory of truth, Peirce was not at all sensitive to the imperfections and limitations of cultural sign systems, even preferring to employ as a calculus for reasoning his own artificial system of existential graphs. In thinking about both the linguistic and graphic diagrammatization of inferential thought, Peirce insisted that the particular form of symbolization is irrelevant to the constitution of meaning and that a language is usable to the degree that its system of formal representation transparently mirrors the process of valid logical inference (Parmentier 1994c, 42–43). Of considerable impact in contemporary semiotic anthropology are passages in which Peirce suggests that, since all thought is in signs, a thinking person is not very different from a sign and, furthermore, that the interior process of thought does not differ in principle from dialogical communication between people.

There is no element whatever of man's consciousness which has not something corresponding to it in the word; and the reason is obvious. It is that the word or sign which man uses is the man himself. For, as the fact that every thought is a sign, taken in conjunction with the fact that life is a train of thought, provides that man is a sign; so, that every thought in an external sign, proves that man is an external sign. . . . Thus my language is the sum total of myself; for the man is the thought. (Peirce *CP* 5.314)

Saussure continued the classical and medieval tradition of viewing the linguistic sign (*signe*) as a dual entity, conjoining a perceptible expression or "signifier" (*significant*) with an intelligible concept or "signified" (*signifié*). The signifying relationships that bind the two levels of the sign fall along a continuum from radical arbitrariness, where there are no external constraints on the linkage between expression and conception, to relative motivation, where the relational, systemic complexity or the value of the linguistic forms—considered either in terms of linear sequence (the syntagmatic axis) or in terms of associative sets (the paradigmatic axis) —imposes a limitation on arbitrariness. In order to uncover the dynamic relationship between continuity and change in linguistic signs, Saussure adopted the methodological principle of separating actual events of speaking (*parole*) from the social conventions that stipulate the meaning of signs for members of a community (*langue*). Although his primary focus was on language as a semiological system, Saussure mentioned in passing a number of other cultural systems, such as maritime signals, religious icons, and gestural codes, where the component units that do not display the radical arbitrariness of linguistic signs are better called symbols. By replacing the view of language as nomenclature with the proto-structuralist notion that oppositional relations among signs constitute the system of *langue*, Saussure recognized that languages, and by extension other semiological systems, do not slice up conceptual space in the same ways.

A detailed comparison of Peirce and Saussure cannot be attempted here, but three points need to be made briefly. First, anthropological research following either Peirce or Saussure needs to take into consideration the terminological confusion stemming from the fact that the Peircean "symbol" correlates with the Saussurean *signe*, and that the Saussurean *symbole* is defined by the presence of iconic and indexical linkages. Second, there is a fundamental divergence between Peirce's keen attention to the token-level instantiation of general signs and to the contextual rootedness of semiosis and Saussure's omission of the referent from his basic notion of the sign and of events of speaking from his model of the linguistic system. And third, research in semiotic anthropology has begun to demonstrate clearly that Peircean and Saussurean approaches are in fact complementary, in the sense that the strengths of one theorist are matched by correlative weaknesses in the other (Parmentier 1994c, xiii–xv).

Foundations of Semiotic Anthropology

The Russian-born linguist Roman Jakobson (1896–1982) is certainly the pivotal figure in the development of semiotic anthropology. During summer holidays as a young student, Jakobson collected folklore (especially proverbs and epic tales) and recorded dialect data; with student friends (including the slightly older folklorist Petr Bogatyrev) he went on fieldwork expeditions in 1915 and 1916 in the Vereja region near Moscow. Jakobson's close association with Bogatyrev continued during their years together as members of the Prague Linguistic Circle, and in 1929 they published a short paper on creativity in folklore and literary language. Citing the Saussurean distinction between particular speech events (*parole*) and the set of conventions accepted by a community (*langue*), the authors noted that "like *langue*, the work of folklore is extra-personal and has only a potential existence. It is only a complex of certain norms and impulses, a canvas of living tradition, which the performers animate with the embellishments of individual creativity, just as the creators of *parole* do in relationship to *langue*" (Bogatyrev and Jakobson 1982, 38). But they then go on to point out an important distinction between oral and written traditions: A "work" appears as *langue* to the performers of folklore, that is, as extra-personal, whereas the author of a literary "work" regards it as *parole*. They warn, however, against the naive view that folklore can only be produced by a homogeneous society with a singular collective personality and that literary culture is totally isolated from the influence of legends, superstitions, and myth-making.

Bogatyrev continued his fieldwork among the Carpathian Ukranians (1923–1926) and his engagement as a scholar and performer of contemporary theater. In a series of papers written in the 1930s, he sought to synthesize Karl Bühler's functional approach to language and V. N. Vološinov's semiotic approach to language and material culture in arguing that tangible things become signs when they acquire meaning beyond the bounds of their existence as a practical thing, just as speech confers meaning on the phonemes of a language: "Some objects can be used equally as material things and signs; for instance costume with its several functions is a material thing and a sign at the same time. . . . Cases where costume is only a sign are quite rare. Even the Chinese actor's paper costume, which functions predominantly to signify that the actor is playing the role of a Chinese, is, after all, not only a sign but also something that covers the actor's body" (Bogatyrev 1976a, 14). Bogatyrev noted this same multifunctionality in the language of the stage: "In some cases, the dominant function of the speech of a dramatic character may lie not in the content of the speech as such but in those verbal signs that characterize the nationality, the class, and so forth, of the speaker. . . . A speech that is full of mistakes may designate not only a foreigner but usually also a comic character" (Bogatyrev 1976b, 36–37). From the point of view of the audience, then, the actor is a "system of signs" (Bogatyrev 1976b, 48). Bogatyrev was one of the first to apply semiotic and structural methods to cultural data beyond language, and his monograph on folk costume, which introduced the notion of the "function of the structure of functions," anticipated both French and British versions of structuralism in anthropology (Bogatyrev 1971, 96).

At the International Congress of Slavic Philologists in Prague in 1929, a steering committee from the Prague Linguistic Circle presented a unified text expressing its views on the nature of language and verbal art. A key point in these "Theses" is the definition of the "aesthetic function" (adding to the three functions identified by Bühler) as the focus on the level of signs or expression (also called the "message" in later formulations):

> From the thesis that poetic speech is directed at expression itself it follows that all the levels of a system of language that play only an ancillary role in communicative speech acquire a greater or lesser autonomous value in poetic speech. The linguistic devices grouped in these levels and the interrelation among the levels, often automatized in communicative speech, tend to become deautomatized in poetic speech. (Jakobson et al. 1982, 15)

A second influential idea involves the systemic nature of cultural phenomena:

> There can be no doubt that poetry is a self-contained entity set apart by its own signs and determined as an entity by its own dominant feature: poeticity. But it is also a part of higher entities, a component part of culture and the overall system of social values. Each of these autonomous yet integral parts is regulated by immanent laws of self-propulsion, while at the same time depending upon the other parts of the system to which it belongs; if one component changes, its relationship to the other component changes, thereby changing the components themselves. With the invention of photography, the goals and structures of painting changed; with the invention of the motion picture, the goals and structure of the theater changed. (Jakobson 1976, 180)

This broader ideological context can be a matter of a culture's semiotic ideology, as Jakobson notes in an analysis of the Hussites' rationalistic attack on the mystical symbolism of the medieval Gothic period: In challenging the symbolic nature of religious icons and liturgical rites, the Hussites rejected the "dialectical unity of form and content, of image and thing, of sign and object signified—the dialectical unity that forms the basis of medieval art and philosophy" (Jakobson 1976, 181). And a third idea is that Saussure's strict separation of synchrony and diachrony needs to be overcome by the recognition that language changes reflect the "needs of the system" and that phenomena such as stylistic archaism and unproductive forms are evidence of diachrony within synchrony.

Jakobson's extensive research on parallelism in both verse and prose has proven highly influential for comparative studies in linguistics and semiotics (see Fox 1977). Reflecting on his days as a student hearing a famous female story-teller recite epic verse and on his subsequent analyses of parallelism in syntactic constructions, grammatical forms, lexical identities, and prosodic schemes, Jakobson confessed, "Apparently there has been no other subject during my entire scholarly life that has captured me as persistently as have questions of parallelism" (Jakobson and Pomorska 1983, 100). These contributions exemplify his effort to take Saussurean concepts (here, the axes of selection and combination) and project them into veritable anthropological analyses of events of speaking and complex aesthetic constructions.

Anthropology Meets Semiotics

An early conjuncture of British anthropology and semiotics occurred in *The Meaning of Meaning* by C. K. Ogden and I. A. Richards, first published in 1923. The book includes an appendix containing extended excerpts from several of Peirce's published papers (1868–1906) and from his unpublished correspondence with Lady Victoria Welby (1904–1909) and a supplementary essay by Bronislaw Malinowski titled "The problem of meaning in primitive languages." This book, which went through five editions, is the first place that Peirce's ideas about semiotics received wide attention. Although it does not appear that Malinowski was aware of the Peirce texts when composing his essay (and he does not employ Peircean terminology), there are several points of convergence between Malinowski's view of the "essentially pragmatic character" (1938, 316) of language and Peircean semiotics, including the focus on the contextual grounding of linguistic signs, the multiple functions of acts of speaking, and the refusal to reify meaning as the inherent property of lexemes.

A much more direct and productive conjuncture of anthropology and semiotics occurred in 1942–1943 when Claude Lévi-Strauss and Roman Jakobson attended each other's lectures at the Free School of Advanced Studies in New York City. Lévi-Strauss's lectures dealt with comparative study of kinship systems, and Jakobson presented six lectures on sound and meaning and another series of lectures on Saussure. From his later reflections on these contacts, it is clear that it was the structural approach of Jakobson's phonological theory more than the general semiotic orientation that inspired Lévi-Strauss to found structural anthropology.

> It cannot be doubted that these lectures also make an important contribution to the human sciences by emphasizing the role played in the production of language (but also that of all symbol systems) by the unconscious activity of the mind. For it is only on condition that we recognize that language, like any other social institution, presupposes mental functions which operate at the unconscious level, that we can hope to reach, beyond the continuity of

the phenomena, the discontinuity by those "principles by which language is organized." (Lévi-Strauss 1978, xviii–xix)

From the premise that the invention of language is the defining development in the transition between the state of nature and the state of culture, Lévi-Strauss draws the inference that cultural analysis should follow the guidelines of linguistic analysis: "Because language is the most perfect of all those cultural manifestations which, in one respect or another, constitute systems, and if we want to understand art, religion or law, and perhaps even cooking or the rules of politesse, we must imagine them as being codes formed by articulated signs, following the pattern of linguistic communication" (Lévi-Strauss 1969, 150–51).

While Lévi-Strauss clearly grounds structuralism in language, he generalized this approach to encompass other codes of communication, some relying on articulate language as their primary code and others operating independently of the linguistic code. But each of these "languages" must meet the qualification of being a system of signs "transformable, in other words, *translatable*, into the language of another system with the help of substitutions" (Lévi-Strauss 1976, 19).

By synthesizing methods of structural linguistics from Saussure and Jakobson with the insights from information theory as formulated by Claude Shannon, Lévi-Strauss attempts to formulate the similarities and differences of systems of signs such as affinal exchange, economic transactions, religious rites, and mythological narratives, by employing semiotic concepts to differentiate these homologous communication systems. He puts speech and kinship alliance at opposite ends of a continuum, according to which the former exchanges words that are purely signifying signs (that is, mechanisms for the schematization of thought, without affective, possessive, or magical associations) and the latter exchanges women who continue to be both signs and values (Lévi-Strauss 1969, 496).

Two critical invariants are found in all these semiological systems: At the token level, all involve social activity mediated by the reciprocal exchange of messages, whether words, women, goods, or offerings; at the type level, the meaning of these messages is constituted not by motivated or analogous ties with isolated external referents but by the positional value of signs as part of systemic codes. The combination of these two fundamental invariants guarantees that cultural analysis will continue to be grounded in worldly realities functioning primarily as signifiers rather than as signifieds.

One cannot study gods while ignoring their images; rites without analyzing the objects and substances manufactured and manipulated by the officiant; or social rules independently of the things which correspond to them. Social anthropology does not confine itself to a part of the domain of ethnology; it does not separate material culture and spiritual culture. . . . Men communicate by means of symbols and signs. For anthropology, which is a conversation of man with man, all things are symbol and sign which act as intermediaries between two subjects. (Lévi-Strauss 1976, 11)

For Lévi-Strauss to prove his point that semiological value flows from the system and not from reference, he needs to analyze some cultural phenomenon in which the elementary units are not semantically motivated but rather are purely positional, that is, where the units resemble phonemes rather than lexemes. Myths serve this purpose well, since not only do mythic elements or "mythemes" acquire significance due to their position in paradigmatic sets that are not part of the narrative sequence, but myths as a whole are subject to constant transformation across spatial and temporal boundaries.

It is precisely this relationship between event and system that provides Lévi-Strauss with a primary mode of typologizing the cognitive worlds of various societies, which he divides into the "savage mind," a cognitive style that works to deny the impact of historical contingency on systems of cultural classification, and the "scientific mind," thinking that internalizes the historical process as the principle of development. This typological opposition is then expressed in terms of semiotic phenomena: The distinction between the dimensions of the sign as correlating a percept (that is, a sensory perception) and a concept (that is, a signified meaning) provides a metalanguage for comparison. Lévi-Strauss contrasts the engineer and the myth-teller as oriented respectively toward the intelligible signified and the perceptible signifier; the former tries to employ signs that are maximally transparent to known reality, while the latter forever generates new narratives out of the detritus of previous myths. He is careful to point out, however, that the distinction between mythological and scientific mentalities does not imply different degrees of rationality in contrasting types of societies, only different kinds of rationality. To further avoid the taint of evolutionary positivism, he notes that examples of each mentality are easy to find in the other kind of society: Just as the famous *bricoleur* or "handyman" who works by means of materials ready to hand manifests the savage mind within industrialized society, so the *churinga*, a sacred object that is the material embodiment of ancestral action in the past, indexes diachrony or pure historicity for Australian aborigines.

Peirce in Semiotic Anthropology

Just as Jakobson's revolutionary phonological theory and constructive critique of Saussure were providing Lévi-Strauss with a model for his semiological view of anthropology, Jakobson himself was making his first acquaintance with the writing of Peirce in the early 1950s. An eight-volume edition of Peirce's writings started to appear in print in 1931 under the editorship of Charles Hartshorne and Paul Weiss, both philosophy instructors at Harvard University, where Jakobson began teaching in 1949. Asked to summarize the results of the joint Conference of Anthropologists and Linguists held at Indiana University Bloomington in 1952, Jakobson prefaced his comments on specific papers with a general remark mentioning both Saussure and Peirce:

> In the impending task of analyzing and comparing the various semiotic systems, we must remember not only the slogan of F. de Saussure that linguistics is part of the science of signs, but, first and foremost, the life-work of his no less eminent contemporary, Charles Sanders Peirce. Peirce not only stated the need for a semiotic but drafted, moreover, its basic lines. His fundamental ideas and devices in the theory of symbols, and particularly of linguistic symbols, when carefully studied, will be of substantial support for the investigation of language in its relation to other systems of signs. (Jakobson 1971, 555–56)

The key to Jakobson's repeated efforts to combine the Saussurean definition of the sign as the correlative union of the perceptible signifier and the intelligible signified with Peirce's triadic model of the sign is his idea that meaning is essentially a translation of the sign into another sign. In his many comments on Peirce, Jakobson focused his attention on the triadic division of icon, index, and symbol, which for Peirce involves the complex relationship between sign vehicle and the object referred to, as a way to further distance himself from the Saussurean notion of the arbitrariness, which, in contrast, deals with the unmotivated relationship between sign and meaning—that is, with what Peirce calls the symbol (Jakobson 1980). Jakobson argued (incorrectly, it turns out) that the Peircean iconic sign is motivated by the similarity of the signifier and the signified, while the Peircean indexical sign is motivated by the contiguity of the signifier and the signified. (Saussure's signified is more accurately equated with Peirce's "immediate interpretant.")

An important next step in synthesizing Jakobson and Peirce was taken in 1976 by Michael Silverstein in a landmark paper that explicitly harnesses the Peircean trichotomy of icon, index, and symbol in order to contrast the decontextualized, referential value of linguistic signs (the subject of Saussurean analysis) with the contextualized, indexical, or pragmatic mode of meaningfulness that operates sometimes independently (e.g., deference forms) and sometimes conjointly with referential functionality (e.g., personal pronouns or other deictic forms or shifters) and is the real key to the linkage between acts of speech and the system of social life. Silverstein sees indexical meaningfulness rather than abstract semantic meaning as the true locus for the modeling power of language in anthropological theory:

> If language is unique in having a true symbolic mode, then obviously other cultural media must be more akin to the combined iconic and indexical modes of meaningfulness. In general, then, we can conclude that "cultural meaning"

of behavior is so limited, except for speech, and see a cultural description as a massive, multiply pragmatic description of how the social categories of groups of people are constituted in a criss-crossing, frequently contradictory, ambiguous, and confusing set of pragmatic meanings of many kinds of behavior. . . . Culture is, with the exception of a small part of language, but a congeries of iconic-indexical systems of meaningfulness of behavior. (Silverstein 1976, 54)

Having thus distinguished pragmatic or indexical categories and decontextualized or semantic categories, Silverstein proceeds to repeat this distinction at the meta-level by separating metasemantics, that is, talk about the semantic code (e.g., glossing), from metapragmatics, talk about the pragmatics of speech. There is a fundamental asymmetry between these two levels: Whereas metasemantic discourse is semantic, metapragmatic discourse is never pragmatic in the same sense that the object of that discourse is pragmatic. That is, metapragmatic characterizations never match the function being characterized: While language as a pure referential medium serves as its own metalanguage in metasemantic referential speech events, there can be no metapragmatic speech events in which use of speech in a given functional mode explicates the pragmatic structure of that very functional mode.

Language is the primary vehicle for people to understand the meaningfulness of their social action: It is the dominant expressive means of communication, facilitates the recording of cultural traditions across generations, and performs the metasemiotic function of interpreting other sign systems. But language can also block understanding, because speakers regularly misread pragmatic sign relations as semantic ones; and in the course of everyday life they have little awareness of the mediational role language plays in shaping their experience of the world, or they are regularly led to project a cultural ontology out of what Benjamin Lee Whorf called cryptotypic regularities and fashions of speaking. Speakers are also subject to the active regimentation of interpretations by institutionally powerful forces, from schools and the press to dictionaries and advertising commercials. Silverstein formulates the issue of awareness and lack of awareness in terms of the structural properties of language: "It is very easy to obtain accurate pragmatic information in the form of metapragmatic referential speech for segmental, referential, relatively presupposing indexes. It is extremely difficult, if not impossible, to make a native speaker aware of nonsegmental, non-referential, relatively creative formal features, which have no metapragmatic reality for him" (Silverstein 1976, 49). Silverstein's earliest prescription for a Jakobson-inspired *anthropologie sémiotique* in a short paper published in French in 1975 was followed a few years later by his University of Chicago colleague Milton Singer's Distinguished Lecture at American Anthropological Association meetings in 1978, which argued for a Peircean-grounded semiotic anthropology as opposed to a Saussure-inspired semiological approach:

Without wishing to deny the fruitful ingenuity of a semiological analysis of culture . . . I would urge the application of Peircean semiotic to the problems of culture theory and suggest that we call such explorations "semiotic anthropology." In one important respect, at least, a semiotic theory of signs has a distinct advantage over a semiological theory: It can deal with some of the difficult problems generated by acceptance of the complementarity of cultural and social systems. Because semiology limits itself to a theory of signification and linguistic codes, it cannot deal with the problem of how different cultural "languages" are related to empirical objects and egos, to individual actors and groups. The existence of such extralinguistic relations is, of course, recognized by semiologists, but the study of them is relegated to other disciplines— psychology, sociology, economics, geography, and history. They do not enter directly and essentially into semiological analysis. In semiotic anthropology, on the contrary, it is possible to deal with such extralinguistic relations within the framework of semiotic theory, because a semiotic anthropology is a pragmatic anthropology. It contains a theory of how systems of signs are related to their meanings, as well as to the objects designated and to the experience and behavior of the sign users. (Singer 1984, 50)

Following Peirce's key insight that conventional symbols embody iconic and indexical modes of meaningfulness, Singer made a comparative study of emblems of identity such as flags, banners, insignia, and heraldic devices. His ethnographic analysis of emblems in Newburyport, Massachusetts, in the 1970s (a restudy of Lloyd Warner's classic accounts from the 1930s) moved significantly beyond the theoretical positions of both Emile Durkheim and Lévi-Strauss by adopting a semiotic perspective:

A semiotic analysis of emblems as constructed signs will thus require an understanding of the characters they signify, of the objects they denote, and of the system of conventional signs ("symbols") they use to make statements about the relations of emblems, objects, and characters. Such understandings will be realized in the dialogues between the designers of the emblems (the "utterers") and the viewers (the "interpreters") in the context of ongoing social interactions. (Singer 1984, 108)

Singer uncovered a transformation in the social referents of the indexicality of emblems, from ethnic origin (*Yankee* versus *ethnic*) to residential duration (*local* versus *outsider*), accomplished by subtle reinterpretation of the latent identities signaled by formally continuous emblems. He witnessed a ceremony rededicating a bronze model (replacing an earlier stolen one) of the seventeenth-century ship *Mary and John* that brought early settlers to the area; this "replica of a replica" was reinterpreted in the 1970s as a symbol of collective identity beyond the lineal descendants of the earliest settlers. Singer also observed the "double or triple symbolism" in multi-ethnic family households, where emblems of identity from different countries of origin are juxtaposed on walls and mantelpieces.

Erik Schwimmer's parallel study of "icons of identity" (1986) among the Oro-kaiva of Papua New Guinea is a second example of the application of Peircean insights to an ethnographic topic previously treated by Saussurean-structuralist techniques. Whereas Lévi-Strauss attempted to replace a one-to-one metonymic relationship between social groups and totemic emblems by postulating a formal correlation between groups and totems as two systems of differences, Schwim-mer showed that particular plant emblems (*hae*) signal a person's membership in a nuclear social group because an ancestor became spatially attached to that tree (ate it, was born near it, used to sit on it, etc.) and, according to mythological nar-ratives, eventually was transformed into it. So when the person's descendants use a leaf of that same tree as a trail marker while walking in neighboring territory, they are in fact using a highly informational indexical sign that functions as a nonsemantic icon of group identity. As Schwimmer noted, "It is this shifting back between iconic and indexical that arouses our interest" (1986, 373).

A third example of the application of Peircean concepts in ethnographic de-scription is Valentine Daniel's path-breaking study of the Tamil culture of India, in which he finds semiotic relations at two levels. The first, more encompassing level characterizes the triadic relationship of the ethnographer's understanding (the sign) representing the informants' culture being studied (the object), and this necessarily imperfect or aniconic relationship in turn is represented by the resulting ethnographic writing (the interpretant). (Perhaps a more logical depic-tion would have the ethnographic writing as the representing sign, the total field-work situation as the object, and the increased scientific understanding of the culture gained by the community of anthropologists as the interpretant.) The second level characterizes the multimodal semiotic meanings manifested at vari-ous moments in the flux of mundane and ritualized social life.

> Most, if not all, signs are mixed. Signs, including symbols (especially sym-bols), are polysemic. . . . Some symbols, especially ritual and religious ones, tend to display their polysemic attributes with far greater élan than do others. The aspect of the sign that I have tried to bring forth is not its polysemy or its multivocality but its polychromy or multimodality. Iconic as well as indexical aspects may be concealed within the same sign. A sign runs in a bundle of cables, so to speak, not in a single strand. . . . A satisfactory cultural account must evidence a sensitivity to the multimodality of the signs in that culture, a sensitivity to the significant color that comes to be dominant to those who traffic in these signs in their daily lives, and a sensitivity to the partially or fully concealed modalities that refract the significance emitted by the domi-nant modal facet. (Daniel 1987 39–40)

Through close analyses of several interlocking sets of data (including house-hold organization, the relationship between bodily substance and human action and pilgrimage rituals), Daniel argues that iconism coding shared substance is the regnant or dominant semiotic style of the culture, in contrast to the pervasive style of symbolization in Western positivist culture (of which Daniel, surprisingly, sees Peirce's semiotic and pragmatist philosophy as representative). It is not accidental, given this postulation of the primacy of iconism in Tamil culture, that the consciousness of pilgrims is described (again using Peircean terminology) as a processual movement from triadic Thirdness to dyadic Secondness to nonanalytical Firstness, this last stage leaving the pilgrim "where there is nothing left to know either through analysis or synthesis. This is *pūrṇa*, perfect knowledge" (Daniel 1987 286).

Indexicality, Mediation, and Ideology

As these and other ethnographic works demonstrate, one of the great merits of a Peircean as opposed to a Saussurean approach to the semiotics of social life is that the category of meaningfulness labeled indexicality, that aspect of sign meaning linked to its context of occurrence, is fully recognized as a mode of signification analytically independent from semantic or symbolic meaning, which depends on decontextualized regularities stipulated by convention. Given that social life is largely concerned with human interaction and the objectification of meaning in material objects, any attempt to analyze the indexical dimensions of culture as if they were purely symbolic, as in the language of flowers or symbols of empire, would be misguided. Indexicality works in two directions: what Silverstein (1976) labels "presupposing," signs whose contextual anchor must be known prior to the instance of the sign, and "creative" or entailing signs whose very occurrence generates in reality or at least in cognitive salience the contextual matter.

Communicative events usually display some sort of construal by participants of the ongoing linguistic and nonlinguistic signs—either explicitly in metapragmatic/metasemiotic forms that describe, explain, or even rationalize the signs-in-context or implicitly in the cotextual organization of the "patterns of emergent entextualization" (Silverstein 2003, 196). Parallelisms or other kinds of diagrammatic forms that manifest an asymmetrical indexical pattern or moment seem to be widespread semiotic constructs that realize social power in culture (Parmentier 1997b, 37–42). Urban's semiotic analysis of origin myth telling among the Shokleng of Brazil shows this clearly. Origin myths are narrated by knowledgeable men in a highly marked speaking style at death ceremonies, involving two speakers rapidly echoing the individual syllables of the myth. Urban (1985, 1986) argues that, in addition to many dimensions of micro- and macro-parallelism in the myth text, the performance itself is a diagrammatic iconic sign of the production of cultural continuity, a function accomplished by the event itself.

The retrospective interpretation of indexicals in real time can distort their potential for multiple indexical mappings; and asking people after the fact frequently produces interpretations favoring presupposing over creative meanings, the product over the process of production. For example, since product is easier to see than process in the archaeological record, there is a tendency to read material remains in a presupposing rather than creative manner, so that, for example, differential grave goods are said to index degrees of social inequality, thus overlooking the possibility that material elaboration is designed to create an augmented afterlife status. In later reflection, actors tend to reread indexical multifunctionality either focusing on the most obvious indexical modality or by translating complex indexicals into decontextualized semantic regularities. Furthermore, multiple indexical meanings frequently piggyback on a single chain of signifiers, whose occurrence can signal spatial, temporal, and social indexicality all at once. And indexical meaning can intersect in complex ways with symbolic meaning, as in the case of duplex signs or shifters, where referential value can only be discovered after indexical calculation.

In order to clear up some confusion in applying analytical labels to processes that operate in distinct yet interlocking levels of semiosis, Mertz and Parmentier (1985) proposed the term "semiotic mediation," based on Peirce's approving citation of the word "mediation" as a summary description for all semiotic processes at the level of generality or Thirdness (Parmentier 1985a). They identified three levels of semiotic mediation: token mediation, code mediation, and ideological mediation. Token mediation involves the play of sign instances in the give-and-take of social life, viewed as a flow of signs in context. The circulation of material sign tokens involves various dynamics between the sign values and the social relations they mediate on a continuum ranging from the transactionally generated values of amulets to hoarded, noncirculating, inalienable possessions. Code mediation deals with the skewing, bias, or refraction that operates between perception and reality, much like a pair of colored glasses modifies sight. Without an alternative or comparative perspective, this mediational effect can easily go unnoticed: Members of a society regularly overlook the historical contingency and formal arbitrariness of their familiar codes, preferring to consider them products of transcendent wisdom or natural order. Cultural codes, like linguistic ones, rarely determine the limits of what can be signaled; rather, they work to facilitate certain expressible meanings and to prestructure equivalence relations by regular paradigmatic structures and syntagmatic parallelisms.

Ideological mediation has been the subject of much recent research into linguistic and semiotic ideologies, that is, by relatively presupposed, systematic sets of assumptions about semiosis in general. Folk ideas about the distinction between natural and conventional signs, notions about the universe as a book, and homologies drawn between linguistic and economic processes are a few examples of widely discussed semiotic ideologies. Analysis of these ideologies is difficult, since it is easy to erroneously substitute a passing articulated expression of an ideology (by a chief, king, or priest, for example) or a spontaneous rationalization prompted by our own metasemiotic inquiry for a truly pervasive, though largely unspoken, semiotic ideology. Semiotic ideologies are also hard to locate given the frequent lack of specific markers for metasemiotic signs in culture. In contrast to the sign processes in social life, artificial semiotic systems (e.g., computer programs) need to make a clear distinction between signs operating at the discursive level and signs operating at the metadiscursive level; the use of markers such as quotations or brackets serves to separate direct signification from comments on the signifying process. In human sign systems, on the other hand, these levels are often formally continuous, with little warning that a shift from use to mention has occurred. Linguistic terms that directly label various dimensions of semiotic functioning, ethnosemiotic labels, can be important clues to the operation of semiotic ideologies, although the ethnographer needs to be careful to not automatically assume that an elite or specialist vocabulary and awareness reflect the general population.

Under the general rubric of the "semiotics of dominance," Gal (1998) discusses various semiotic processes and devices through which any cultural idea gains the discursive authority to become dominant. A good illustration would be the process Gal calls iconization (relabeled more recently by Irvine [2004, 108] as rhematization), in which the situation in which linguistic features that indexically signal social differentiation is transformed into a situation in which some (iconic) quality of the linguistic feature is represented as parallel to some feature (behavioral, affective, moral) in the social group. Since these devices are accomplished largely through the use of language, and since an important subset of cultural ideas includes ideas about language, it follows that these semiotic processes can themselves be the object of debate and contestation. For example, in the late nineteenth century, Japanese intellectuals and educators identified certain linguistic forms (missing honorifics, phonological contractions of verb endings) in the speech of elite schoolgirls as lazy and vulgar. Their metapragmatic commentaries provided a rationalizing narrative of the origin of these forms in the schoolgirls' connection with impure *geisha* or corrupt Westerners. The commentaries, thus, collapse the temporal and causal relationship of indexicality between the index (the forms) and the indexed (the schoolgirls) into the relationship of iconicity, in which both forms and speakers simultaneously are lazy and vulgar (Inoue 2004). Herzfeld, similarly, shows how powerful iconicity, or the "illusions of iconic purity," can be as a rhetorical device in the promulgation of nationalist ideologies (1986).

Semiotics of Culture and the Culture Text

Since the 1970s, the so-called Moscow-Tartu School of semiotics has attempted to chart a synthetic theory, combining Saussurean, Peircean, and information-theoretic models, for understanding cultural sign systems, both historically and comparatively. In 1973 a group of scholars associated with this school issued a joint statement outlining a "semiotic-typological" concept of culture that examines both the hierarchically linked semiotic subsystems within a culture and the dynamic opposition of culture and an external, nonsemiotic space of non-culture. The basic unit of analysis is the culture text, which is a functionally integral sequence of signs that carries a coherent meaning.

> From the semiotic point of view culture may be regarded as a hierarchy of particular semiotic systems, as the sum of the texts and the set of functions correlated with them, or as a certain mechanism which generates these texts. If we regard the collective as a more complexly organized individual, culture may be understood by analogy with the individual mechanism of memory as a certain collective mechanism for the storage and processing of information. The semiotic structure of culture and the semiotic structure of memory are functionally uniform phenomena situated on different levels. This proposition does not contradict the dynamism of culture: being in principle the fixation of past experience, it may also appear as a program and as instructions for the creation of new texts. (Lotman et al. 1973, 73)

Yuri M. Lotman (1922–1993), the dominant member of the group, argued that the data for cross-cultural comparison are already at the metacultural level, since each culture displays specific metasemiotic constructs, such as instructional texts stipulating the norms of literary production or the artistic modeling of the universe. Systematic comparison is possible only because of the universal characteristic of cultural texts to be organized in spatial or topological schemes, such as center/periphery oppositions and boundary mechanisms.

> The central myth-making mechanism of culture is organized as topological space. With projection onto the axis of linear time and from the province of ritual play-action into the sphere of the verbal text, it undergoes important changes: in assuming linearity and discreteness, it acquires the characteristics of a verbal text constructed on the principle of a sentence. In this sense it becomes comparable with the entirely verbal texts arising on the periphery of culture. Yet it is precisely this comparison which makes it possible to discover some very profound differences: the central sphere of culture is constructed on the principle of an integrated structural whole, a sentence; the peripheral sphere is organized as a cumulative chain simply by the accretion of structurally independent entities. (Lotman 1979, 173)

And because every culture, whatever the particular shape of its textual models, understands itself in relation to nonculture, it is universally the case that culture appears as a hierarchical organization of semiotic codes, including natural languages as well as "secondary modeling systems," that is, complex semiotic languages built upon linguistic materials (Lotman et al. 1973, 76). From this premise, Lotman articulates the general goal of a typological approach to culture. Since the development of metalanguages within different domains or institutions of a culture will not all occur simultaneously, Lotman posits that, from a synchronic point of view, a culture needs to be seen as a cross-section of typologically distinct cultural epochs.

Lotman envisions a type of semiotic consciousness he calls mythological, in which signs (especially proper names) become so indexically linked with referents that the relationship appears asemiotic and thus there can be no hierarchical layering of language and metalanguage. Mythological texts appear to have symbols and metaphors only when translated into nonmythological categories. In the mythic world objects are seen as singular and integral wholes, signs are not ascribed but recognized (being synonymous with proper nouns), word and denotation are identified, text is isomorphic with the described world, understanding is based on recognition, identification, and transformation, and the entire system is monolinguistic. Lotman's typological approach does not require the unilineal succession of mythological to nonmythological to logico-scientific cultures, but rather speaks of the "prevalence of certain cultural models or of an entire culture's subjective orientation toward them" (Lotman and Uspenskij 1978, 226). Given the criterion of prevalence, a certain culture can display multiple types of semiotic complexity as a result, for example, of the penetration of mythological features into nonmythological periods (e.g., surrealism or symbolist poetry), the differential dynamism of center and periphery in incorporating new semiotic materials, the dialectical tension between motivated symbols and conventional signs corresponding to the opposition between a high sacred level and a low profane level, and the binarism of the symbolic activity of state elites and the putatively asemiotic, practical behavior of peasants. In his book *Universe of the Mind: A Semiotic Theory of Culture* (1990), Lotman constructs the concept of the semiosphere, by analogy with the biosphere (as coined by biologist Vladimir Vernadsky), to refer to the semiotic space that supports all the heterogeneous languages in a culture. "Across any synchronic section of the semiosphere different languages at different stage [*sic*] of development are in conflict, and some texts are immersed in languages not their own, while the codes to decipher them with may be entirely absent" (Lotman 1990, 126). At the metaphorical center of the semiosphere Lotman places the most structurally developed languages (including the natural languages of the culture); the peripheral boundary is the locus of innovation and metasemiotic reflection.

The research into the semiotics of culture by Irene Portis-Winner represents the fullest synthesis in contemporary semiotic anthropology of the Moscow-Tartu School, the Prague School, and Peirce.

> Semiotics of culture may . . . be viewed as more encompassing than a general semiotics glottocentrically conceived, since, while it attends to aspects of all sign systems in culture as they interrelate and does not overlook the more abstract level of underlying invariants and codes, it concentrates upon the infinitely variable and endlessly transformable concrete text in culture in relation to its highly variable context, human and nonhuman. The effect of these factors has been to free semiotics of culture from certain limitations historically dominating the broad field of semiotics, namely the emphasis on

langue or code to the detriment of *parole*, and the dominance of the linguistic model in the analysis of all sign systems whether verbal or not. (Portis-Winner 1986, 183)

Based on extensive ethnographic fieldwork both in Slovenia and among Slovenes in the Cleveland, Ohio, area (1973–1995), Portis-Winner finds that a subset of cultural texts (as defined by Lotman) dealing with ethnic groups, relations, and boundaries display two correlated levels of dualism. First, these ethnic cultural texts are dualistic in that the unique characteristics of a particular ethnic group are highlighted in opposition to the characteristics of other groups; second, ethnic cultural texts are dualistic in the two ways that they represent ethnicity, implicit montage and explicit montage, concepts drawn from Lotman's work on the semiotics of cinema. Portis-Winner generalizes the distinction between implicit montage, which involves the reorganization and transformation of images from the same semantic field, and explicit montage, which involves the juxtaposition of elements from different semantic domains and, by extension, the crossing of narrative boundaries. She then shows how one item, the *kosolec* (a large wooden hay rack in farmers' fields in Slovenia), can be an ethnic cultural text in both implicit and explicit senses:

> In the new ethnic culture the *kosolec* takes on various forms, such as a toy, a small carved trinket, or a landmark in the Cleveland farmlands. Here the compared elements, the different manifestations of the *kosolec*, form implicit montages, taking their origin from one semantic domain but inducing abstract, associative meanings as a set. Recollections of village activities, threshing, hay rides, and landmarks, are all brought together by the modality of the changing shapes of the *kosolec*. On the other hand, when the *kosolec* is covered with hay and juxtaposed to a truck on which it rides in a Fourth of July parade down Main Street in Cleveland, carrying a sign inscribed in large letters with the words "heartland of Slovenia," the *kosolec* suggests an explicit montage, namely the juxtaposition of elements from very different domains. (Portis-Winner 2002, 58)

Ethnic cultural texts (of either type) produced in a diasporic community can depict the origin village as timeless or mythological, enabling individuals who return for visits to overlook social changes; and in certain festive contexts, ethnic cultural texts can represent ethnic realities as liminal or even carnivalesque. The influence of Peirce appears in Portis-Winner's use of semiotic portraits of three generations of related informants from both Slovenia and Cleveland to construct an extended human sign, a concept that expands on Peirce's discussion of the parallelism between a "man" and a "word" and treats the individuals in these portraits as boundary-crossers, equivalent to the culture heroes in Lotman's narrative analyses.

Semiotics and Material Culture

If one of the advantages of a Peircean approach in semiotic anthropology is that its model of meaningfulness encompasses but is not based on language, then there will be obvious benefits for the ethnographic and archaeological study of material objects considered, as Vološinov suggested, as simultaneously things and signs. Certainly Peirce's concepts of indexicality (grounded in spatio-temporal contiguity) and iconicity (grounded in formal resemblance) would be essential to this project (Keane 2003, 415–17). And his distinction between individually occurring signs ("sinsigns") and instances of general regularities (tokens of types) immediately raises important methodological questions. Given the obvious role that material objects play in mediating individual and group relations, as trade goods and exchange valuables, for example, and as repositories of sedimented cultural values and historical experiences, Peirce's model of the sign is directly applicable to many ethnographic cases. Peirce's inclusion of the interpretant as a fundamental constituent of the sign relation, however, presents difficulties for archaeologists working without living informants, textual evidence, or possible ethnographic analogies. The relative permanence of material objects results in multiple layers of interpretants: Users of objects who are contemporaneous with the objects' production regard them differently than people reacting to them centuries later, and scholars treating objects as evidence of stylistic growth or of evolutionary development construct radically different interpretants than either of these two (Parmentier 1997b, 51).

On the other hand, a Saussurean effort to talk about the material world as directly meaningful has occasionally assumed a full or partial analogy between language and objects; the material record is analyzed in terms of grammar, speech acts, constitutive rules, denotation/connotation, and textuality. Several criticisms of this language analogy need to be made, including the absence of evidence that objects have the degree of relative arbitrariness found in linguistic symbols, that the meaningfulness of objects displays the double articulation found in all languages, and that the systematicity of patterning in the material record is driven by decontextualized referentiality. But the Saussurean concept of value as the positional meaning of a sign can play a positive analytical role, especially in situations where multiple objects display variation in quality aligning with differentiated spatial arrangement (Herzfeld 1992) or with a calculus of relative exchange value (Keane 1997, 72–75; Munn 1983, 302).

Semiotics and Diachrony

Peirce and Saussure have had only a modest impact on diachronic or historical work in semiotic anthropology. Marshall Sahlins, in charting new territory for a structural history based on the repudiation of the ahistorical disposition of classic structuralist theory (such as the notion of stereotypic reproduction), sees two critical dilemmas in the Saussurean project of general semiology (1985, 246): first, that the systematicity of signs requires that individual signs have no externally generated values (since their value is entirely positional), and, second, that the collective or social dimension of sign systems necessitates a strict separation of the system of signs from the implementation of sign tokens in discourse and interaction. Rather than throw away a valuable Saussurean insight, that "cultural categories by which experience is constituted do not follow directly from the world, but from their differential relations with a symbolic scheme" (Sahlins 1985, 147), Sahlins attempts its recuperation by demonstrating the role of "events" in revaluing sign, especially through the indexical relations between signs and their real-world objects in which "signs are set in various and contingent relationships according to people's instrumental purposes—purposes of course that are socially constituted even as they may be individually variable" (Sahlins 1981, 5). Social praxis puts symbolic systems in jeopardy, since the instantiation of cultural categories in social action implies the functional revaluation of signs: "No longer a disembodied or virtual semiotic system, meaning is now in contact with the original human powers of its creation. In action signs are subsumed in various logical operations, such as metaphor and analogy, intensional and extensional redefinitions, specializations of meaning or generalization, displacements or substitutions, not to neglect creative 'misunderstandings'" (Sahlins 1985, 151). In his extensive comparative research on Polynesian cultures, and especially in his reconstruction of the cultural impact of Captain James Cook's death in the Hawaiian Islands in 1779, Sahlins documents the performative quality of Hawaiian history:

> The Hawaiian order is more active historically, in a double way. Responding to the shifting conditions of its existence—as of, say, production, population, or power—the cultural order reproduces itself in and as change. Its stability is a volatile history of the changing fortunes of persons and groups. But then, it is more likely to change as it so reproduces itself. (Sahlins 1985, 250)

In a series of ethnographic studies dealing with Palau or Belau (Micronesia), Parmentier develops two semiotic angles implicit in Sahlins' theory of structural history. First, he finds deployed in origin myths and historical narratives a set of spatial models found in various contexts in the culture. These models are diagrammatic icons in Peirce's terminology, that is, complex signs that represent the relations among parts of some object by analogous relations among components of the sign vehicle. In Palau these ethnosemiotic schemata include the model of the "path" (*rael*), persons or objects moving or lined up in a linear order from a starting point to an ending point; "cornerposts" (*saus*), four coordinated elements supporting a quadripartite structure; "sides" (*bitang*), an oppositional pair of elements in which both halves are identical yet inverse; and "larger/smaller" (*klou/kekere*), a continuum of elements in a series ranked according to the degree or strength of a single dimension such as social rank, wealth, physical maturity, or sacredness. In contrast to a simple structuralist account, Parmentier argues that the narrative use of these four models in the present-day storytelling represents the history of the society as the logical unfolding of three of these models, that is, as the development of political organization from paths to cornerposts to sides. This sequence does not represent the actual development of Palauan society, as might be uncovered in archaeological research, but rather expresses a cultural logic grounded in the meanings of the semiotic models themselves: "Paths" imply the fundamental act of creating cultural meaning as the categorization of instances as tokens of general types; "cornerposts" express the hierarchically graded and functionally differentiated order found in mature or stable cultural institutions; and "sides" code oppositional, complementary, factional, or competitive units that presuppose a dyadic structure as a balanced whole. Whereas Sahlins concentrates on the revaluation or realignment of cultural values (male/female, chief/commoner, warfare/agriculture, foreign/indigenous) as a result of the engagement of these values in social action (especially in situations of culture contact), Parmentier focuses on the recategorization of cultural values in the rhetorical deployment of semiotic models that have a relatively constant meaning.

Second, Parmentier documents a particular category of historicizing signs in Palauan culture called *olangch*, meaning "commemorative or historical marker." These markers, including, for example, personal names and titles, gravestones and anthropomorphic stones, exchange valuables and money, ritual prerogatives and social routines, function as cultural shifters by articulating the organizational diagrams in contexts of social action and experience. *Olangch* are permanent signs that are present evidence of a significant past, but having been created in certain contexts in the past, they continue to undergo strategic manipulation in the present. Parmentier divides the functioning of these indexical symbols into "signs of history" and "signs in history": Signs of history represent the past as history in the sense of providing an explicit classification in terms of the four differentially valued diagrammatic schemata; signs in history are signs of history that, in addition, become objects of social interest and action because of their value as reified embodiments of historicity. "*Olangch* look in these two directions, toward the typifying role of schemata and toward the sedimenting role of practice" (Parmentier 1987, 308).

Note

This paper was originally published as "Semiotic Anthropology," in *Elsevier Encyclopedia of Language and Linguistics*, 2nd ed., ed. Keith Brown, *Linguistic Anthropology*, ed. Michael Silverstein. (Elsevier: Amsterdam, 2005), 199–212. Reprinted by permission of Elsevier.

2   Charles S. Peirce

Introduction

One of the puzzles of the intellectual history of the "pragmatic" turn in contemporary linguistics is the fact that the American mathematician and philosopher Charles S. Peirce (1839–1914), who developed a graphic formalism for evaluating the logical precision of scientific concepts, continues to be an important inspiration for the development of approaches to language that move beyond the synchronic, descriptive, and generative perspectives characteristic of the mainstream of linguistics scholarship. Many students of language first encountered Peirce's semiotic ideas in the early 1920s in the ten pages of excerpts printed as an appendix to Ogden and Richards's *The Meaning of Meaning* (1938 [1923]). The lengthy citations from Peirce's papers and letters in this widely read text include discussions of the nature of the sign, the classification of "interpretants" and "objects" of signs, and the distinction between general sign "types" and actual sign "tokens." Roman Jakobson's influential 1975 lecture, "A Few Remarks on Peirce: Pathfinder in the Science of Language," reprinted in *The Framework of Language* (1980) and echoing points made repeatedly in teaching and writing since the 1950s, brought Peirce's thought to the attention of general humanistic scholarship. Jakobson noted, in particular, Peirce's notion of "meaning" as a translation of one sign into a subsequent and further developed sign; that is, for Peirce, meaning is a process of interpretation rather than a fixed mental entity. Equally important for Jakobson, Peirce's analysis of the logical structure of sign relations harmonizes well with notions of "invariants" being simultaneously developed in European linguistic theory.

Following in the spirit of Jakobson, Michael Silverstein (1976) applied Peirce's semiotic typology more broadly to the study of linguistic signs in relation to their communicative functions. Peirce's trichotomous classification of kinds of relationships between "entity signaled" (Peirce's "object") and "signaling entity" (Peirce's "sign" or representation) yields "icons," where the relation is considered by sign users to be one of formal isomorphism, "indexes," where the relation is grounded in spatiotemporal contiguity, and "symbol," where the relation is the result of conventional rules for generating "semantico-referential meaning." Of critical importance for Silverstein is the complex interplay of indexical linguistic categories and purely symbolic ones; duplex referential forms or "shifters" (e.g., personal pronouns) combine both sign functions, whereas pure indexes (e.g., deference markers) do not contribute to reference as such.

Peirce's highly original way of linking a realist metaphysics with an experimental epistemology by means of "semeiotic" or the study of signs has, thus, provided the specific foundation for a variety of contemporary pragmatic perspectives. Taking pragmatics (see Parret 1983, 1986) to refer to any approach that considers language in reference to either (*a*) the concrete objects of experience (i.e., to *pragmata* in Aristotelian terminology), (*b*) the context-dependence or indexical character of linguistic meaning, (*c*) the strategic quality of speakers' intentionality, (*d*) speaking as human action, (*e*) the dialogic or interpersonal foundation of communication, (*f*) the sequential quality of interpretation as a continual process, or (*g*) the rhetorical, expressive, and connotative dimensions of meaning, it appears that Peirce has something to offer students of each of these aspects. But, as will be shown below, the specific philosophical doctrine of "pragmatism" developed by Peirce is expressly designed to nullify or avoid all seven of these pragmatic aspects of language. In fact, Peirce's brand of pragmatism and the contemporary pragmatics of language are roughly in complementary distribution.

An important task of this paper is to specify which aspects of Peirce's program need to be regarded with suspicion and which are potentially useful for modern scholars of language.

The Genealogy of Pragmatism

The historical genesis of Peirce's pragmatism (see Apel 1981; Eco 1995; Gallie 1952; Robin 1997; Rosenthal 1994) involves a double irony. First, it was the psychologist William James, not Peirce, who introduced the term into philosophical discourse, initially in a lecture titled "Philosophical Conceptions and Practical Results" (1967 [1898]) delivered at the University of California in 1898 and later incorporated into his book *Pragmatism*, reprinting other lectures from 1906 and 1907. In this lecture and book, James acknowledges the priority of Peirce, "the most original of contemporary thinkers," who first articulated the "principle of pragmatism" to a group of Cambridge intellectuals in the early 1870s:

> To obtain perfect clearness in our thoughts of an object, then, we need only consider what conceivable effects of a practical kind the object may involve— what sensations we are to expect from it, and what reactions we must prepare. Our conception of these effects, whether immediate or remote, is then for us the whole of our conception of the object, so far as that conception has positive significance at all. This is the principle of Peirce, the principle of pragmatism. (James 1975, 29)

In his many writings on pragmatism, James tried to give the principle a broader behavioral scope than Peirce's original conception (on the history of philosophical pragmatism see Thayer 1968; West 1989). Second, Peirce's earliest popular expression of the pragmatic maxim found in a paper "How to Make Our Ideas Clear" published in *Popular Science Monthly* in 1878 does not actually mention the term *pragmatism*:

> The essence of belief is the establishment of a habit, and different beliefs are distinguished by the different modes of action to which they give rise. If beliefs do not differ in this respect, if they appease the same doubt by producing the same rule of action, then no mere differences in the manner of consciousness of them can make them different beliefs, any more than playing a tune in different keys is playing different tunes. (Peirce W 3, 263–64)

To develop its meaning, we have, therefore, simply to determine what habits it produces, for what a thing means is simply what habit it involves. Now, the identity of a habit depends on how it might lead us to act, not merely under such circumstances as are likely to arise, but under such as might possibly occur, no matter how improbable they may be. What the habit is depends on when and how it causes us to act. As for the when, every stimulus to action is derived from perception; as for the how, every purpose of action is to produce some sensible result. Thus, we come down to what is tangible and practical as the root of every real distinction in thought, no matter how subtle it may be; and there is no distinction of meaning so fine as to consist in anything but a possible difference in practice (Peirce W 3, 265).

The historian Max Fisch cites a series of points in Peirce's writings from as early as 1868 that indicate that he was using the idea of pragmatism without naming it as a way of expressing his views on the character of scientific discovery. In an attack on Cartesianism published in the *Journal of Speculative Philosophy* in 1868, Peirce writes: "Finally, no present actual thought (which is a mere feeling) has any meaning, any intellectual value; for this lies not in what is actually thought, but in what this thought may be connected with in representation by subsequent thoughts; so that the meaning of a thought is altogether something virtual" (Peirce W 2, 227, cited in Fisch 1986, 290). Then, in a review of A. C. Fraser's edition of the British philosopher George Berkeley, Peirce notes a rule for avoiding the "deceits of language," namely, "Do things fulfill the same function practically? Then let them be signified by the same word. Do they not? Then let them be distinguished" (W 2, 483, cited in Fisch 1986, 290). Not only does Peirce fail to employ the term *pragmatism* in all these passages, but as late as 1900 he wrote to his friend and patron James, "Who originated the term *pragmatism*, I or you? Where did it first appear in print? What do you understand by it?" (cited in Brent 1993, 86).

Peirce's delayed admission that he was the creator of the pragmatic maxim is likely connected to the way James was applying the maxim in subjective, utilitarian, and nominalistic senses. Peirce not only rejected James's focus on "difference in concrete fact and in conduct consequent upon that fact" (James 1975, 30) and on the "practical cash-value" of words (James 1975, 32), but Peirce's profound conservatism on social issues—he believed in the power of the aristocracy, the benefits of slavery, and the infinite possibilities of the entrepreneurial spirit (Peirce in Hardwick, ed., 1977, 78)—also contrasts sharply with James's interests in moral development and social change. Indeed, sensing that his creation was being "abused in the merciless way that words have to expect when they fall into literary clutches" (Peirce *CP* 5.414), an exasperated Peirce decided to coin a new term, "pragmaticism," so ugly he thought no one would dare steal it.

For Peirce, pragmatism is a guide to clarifying scientific concepts by looking at significant differences in their rules of action, that is, different experimental procedures they stipulate. The true scientist can never have a personal stake in the practical outcome of these experiments and must operate "with the entire exclusion of the passions and emotional sensibility" (Peirce *W* 2, 337; West 1989, 46): "The true scientific investigator completely loses sight of the utility of what he is about . . . the investigator who does not stand aloof from all intent to make practical applications will not only obstruct the advance of pure science, but what is infinitely worse, he will endanger his own moral integrity and that of his readers" (Peirce *RLT*, 107). Toward the end of his life, Peirce wrote what is perhaps the clearest expression of his pragmatic maxim: "I maintain that the whole intellectual signification proper to any sign is summed up in the effects which it could rationally have upon our conduct" (Peirce *MS* 339, 347).

Pragmatism and Semiotics

Despite his formal training in chemistry and mathematics, and his professional scientific work in astronomy, geodesics, and physics, Peirce maintained a lifelong fascination with the semiotic nature of language (see Eco 1981; Habermas 1995; Halpinen 1995; Jakobson 1980; Kremer-Marietti 1994; Martens 198; Rethore 1994; Shapiro 1981), although he confessed at one point "I am neither an anthropologist nor a linguist" (*NEM* 3/2, 917). On the one hand, Peirce thought that the variety of linguistic signs in the world's languages served as readily understandable illustrations of his typological distinctions among sign processes (*RLT* 127; see Fisch 1986; Fitzgerald 1996; Parmentier 1994c, 2009; Savan 1987). Peirce's fundamental modal division of signs into signs of possibility (or Firstness), signs of actuality (or Secondness), and signs of necessity (or Thirdness) echoes, at least in overall organization, the classic Aristotelian distinction among words, terms, or rhemes standing alone, propositions or sentences binding together a subject and a predicate, and arguments or syllogisms linking three or more logical components. Finding the meaning of semantically rich words parallels the action of experimental composition:

> Find a man who has no idea of patriotism; and if you tell him that it is the love of one's country, if he knows what love is, and what a man's country, in its social sense, is, he can make the experiment of connecting these two ideas in his imagination, and noting the quality of feeling which arises upon their composition. Tell him this in the evening, and he will repeat the experiment several times during the night, and in the morning he will have a fair idea of what patriotism means. (Peirce *MS* 7, 9)

On the other hand, Peirce did not consider the usages of human language as the model of semiosis (*NEM* 3, 245), preferring, perhaps due to some peculiar configuration of his intellect (Brent 1996, 307), to construct an entirely artificial graphical system to better diagram the invariant nature of logical reasoning.

> It might be supposed that although such a study [of speculative semeiotic] cannot draw any principles from the study of languages, that linguistics might still afford valuable suggestions to it. Upon trial, I have not found it to be so. Languages never furnished me with a single new idea; they have at most only afforded examples of truths I had already ascertained by *a priori* reasoning. (Peirce *MS* 693, 191–92)

In thinking about both the linguistic and graphic diagrammatization of inferential thought, moreover, Peirce insisted that the particular form of symbolization is irrelevant to the constitution of meaning; or, to put it positively, a language is usable to the degree that its system of formal representation transparently mirrors the process of logical inference. (Late in life Peirce recalled that, as a child, he invented "a language in which almost every letter of every word made a definite contribution to its signification" [Hardwick, ed. 1977, 95]; this clear violation of the duality of patterning does, however, point to Peirce's early drive to develop a logical syntax.) So although languages are wonderfully useful semiotic systems, there is danger, as Peirce warned his English philosophical correspondent Lady Victoria Welby, "of falling into some error in consequence of limiting your studies so much to Language and among languages to *one* very peculiar language, as all Aryan languages are; and within that language so much to *words*" (Hardwick, ed. 1977, 118).

Recently, some scholars have attempted to read a theory of "speech acts" into Peirce's comments about logical propositions (see, e.g., Brock 1981; Martens 1981). Peirce thought that a general or type-level proposition does not imply any particular mode of expression. Indeed, he claimed that "one and the same proposition may be affirmed, derived, judged, wished for, doubted, inwardly inquired into, put as a question, wished, asked for, effectively commanded, taught, or merely expressed, and does not thereby become a different proposition" (Peirce *NEM*

4, 248). The actual assertion of a proposition in a particular linguistic form is a "replica" of it, but not in the usual sense that the general and particular levels (called by Peirce "type" and "token") are in any iconic relationship. But note that Peirce is not arguing, as some speech act theorists do, that there is a linguistically specific propositional sentence behind these various functional "acts," since a proposition is a general *logical* relationship without linguistic shape. His claim that all kinds of functionally distinct linguistic acts correspond to a single logical proposition reveals this purported "speech act" theory to be useless for contemporary pragmatic approaches to language.

As a scientist with international experience, Peirce knew first-hand the difficulties faced by experimentalists when the concepts employed within the scientific community are not clearly defined. Terminological vagueness can only be rectified for words lacking the cultural baggage of terms such as "nature" and "love" that are complex in contextual and historical overtones rather than in strictly sense-driven semantics. Such vague—because occasion-bound—signs can be subject to further exposition by an utterer or else can be open to multiple interpretations by the hearer. As Gallie explains, "The supreme value of Peirce's Pragmatism . . . is to show, once and for all, that the criteria by which we establish the meaningfulness of scientific statements cannot be applied in the case of other, e.g., historical and everyday practical statements" (1952, 69). In contrast, terms that have specific roles in deductive systems or that have clear perceptual implications are subject to the pragmatic maxim; but this is not to say that unverifiable propositions are entirely meaningless (Almeder 1983, 332). Conceptual clarity in scientific terminology involves the highly controlled, self-conscious, and deliberate elimination of all random, accidental, or contextual factors (Peirce *CP* 2.172).

Because many of Peirce's manuscripts dealing explicitly with the formal elaboration of his semiotic concepts were written well after the public articulation and defense of the pragmatic maxim, it is possible to underestimate the degree to which Peirce's pragmatism is the result rather than the source of his reflection on signs (Alston 1956–57). But, as Fisch wisely observes, "Pragmatism is a method for generating a particular kind of interpretant of a particular kind of sign" (1986, 373). Peirce considered signs to be any phenomena that transmit, translate, or mediate the connection between some object (what the sign is "about") and some interpreting sign (what the sign "means" to someone) in such a way that the "function of a sign, enables one who knows the sign, and knows it as a sign, to know [the object]" (c. 1902, *MS* 599, 31). In addition to signs that bear some formal resemblance to their objects ("icons") and signs that are in a "real existential relation" (*EP* 2, 276) to their objects ("indexes"), Peirce defines the most complete kind of signs ("symbols") to represent their objects only because some subsequent "interpretant" sign supplies the unmotivated or conventional "ground" between sign and object. All true symbols are "types," that is, abstract or general regularities, although to be experienced or communicated they must generate concrete instances or "tokens." Peirce then shows that all signs require apprehension *as signs* in order to be signs and that the meaning of propositions and arguments lies in future rule-governed actions determined by these signs:

> Now if in the acknowledgment of that truth he recognizes that that argumentation is a sign of that truth then it has really functioned as a sign of it; but if he does not then the argumentation fails to be for him a sign of that truth. Next consider, not an argumentation or statement expressly designed to lead to a given belief, but a mere statement of fact, a true proposition. That proposition may not be admitted by anybody. In that case, it does not function as a sign to anybody. But to whomsoever shall believe it, it will be a sign that, under certain circumstances, with a view to certain ends, certain lines of conduct are to be embraced, and the interpretant of it will be a rule of conduct to that effect, established, not in consciousness necessarily, but in the nature and soul of the believer. (Peirce *MS* 599, 43–45)

According to the pragmatic maxim, the "entire intellectual purport of any symbol consists in the total of all general modes of rational conduct which, conditionally upon all the possible different circumstances and desires, would ensue upon the acceptance of the symbol" (Peirce *CP* 5.438). For example, the meaning of a proposition formed in a language is subject to the pragmatic maxim when it is considered "not in these or those special circumstances, nor when one entertains this or that special design, but that form which is most directly applicable to self-control under every situation, and to every purpose" (Peirce *CP* 5.427). In other words, pragmatism involves eliminating the rich sensuousness of concepts and the contextual specifics of actual communicative utterances in order to deal only with their pure "rational purport" (*CP* 5.428):

> A concept is something having the mode of being of a general type which is, or may be made, the rational part of the purport of a word. . . . The method prescribed in the maxim is to trace out in the imagination the conceivable practical consequences—that is, the consequences for deliberate, self-controlled conduct—of the affirmation or denial of the concept; and the assertion of the maxim is that herein lies the *whole* of the purport of the word, the *entire* concept. (Peirce *CP* 8.191)

While the meaning of some signs—especially those of the indexical variety—lies in some actual existential resultant, the meaning of intellectual signs remains general, though none the less "real":

> Some signs, then, have existential meanings; but of course, no number of events could be adequate to the meaning of an intellectual concept, since such a concept is general; and no collection of individuals, however multitudinous, can be adequate to a general. For a general embraces all that are conceivably possible, when possibility is not restricted by any existential condition. (Peirce 1907, *MS* 318, 20)

This claim, that "general ideas are the true interpreters of our thoughts" (*CP* 5.3), puts Peirce's pragmatism directly at odds with subjective, behavioral, and nominalist versions of pragmatism that became popular in the wake of Peirce's original insights (Potter 1996, 96–97).

In searching for good examples of intellectual concepts clarified by the pragmatic maxim, Peirce deserted the world of everyday speech and formal prose and even passed from the language of the experimental sciences to the rarified world of mathematics:

> All grammarians find the conditional to be a modified future. At the time when I was originally puzzling over this enigma, I had reached somewhere about the point in my inquiry and was in a decided quandary, when I all at once said to myself, "Now if I only could find a moderate number of concepts which should be at once highly abstract and abstruse and yet whose meanings should be quite unquestionable, a study of these would undoubtedly show just why and how the logical meaning must be a conditional future, even for concepts quite unlike those." I had no sooner uttered this project to myself than I exclaimed, "Why, what am I talking about? There are plenty of such concepts! They are as plenty as blackberries in mathematics!" (Peirce *MS* 318, 29)

According to Peirce's complex semiotic terminology, pragmatism locates the fullest meaning in the "final interpretant," that is, the subsequent sign that expresses the "ultimate opinion" (*NEM* 3/2, 845) arrived at in a logical manner by the future scientific community. This ultimate logical interpretant of a concept is not a description of any immediate effects of the sign in operation (Robin 1997, 141) nor an account of where the community's discussion of it rests at one point in history; it is rather a "normative" notion that postulates the "habit that would correspond to that ultimate consensus on truth" (Apel 1995, 383), and as such will ultimately eventuate in some nonsemeiotic practical effects (Eco 1995, 218):

> It is evident that a definition, even if it be imperfect owing to vagueness, is an intellectual interpretant of the term it defines. But it is equally evident that it cannot be the ultimate intellectual interpretant, inasmuch as it is itself a sign, and a sign of the kind that has itself an intellectual interpretant, which is thereby an intellectual interpretant of the term defined. This consideration compels us to seek elsewhere than among signs, or among concepts, since they are all signs, for ultimate intellectual interpretants. This same consideration cuts off from searching among desires, expectations, etc. for ultimate intellectual interpretants, such intellectual character as desire etc. possess is due solely to their referring to concepts. At the same time, the ultimate intellectual interpretant must be some kind of mental effect of the signs they interpret. Now after an examination of all variety of mental phenomena, the only ones I have been able to find that possess the requisite generality to interpret concepts and which fulfill the other conditions are habits. (Peirce *MS* 318, 47)

While signs of any sort are capable of producing a series of interpretants, only intellectual concepts brought under the pragmatic maxim generate, in the end, an "ultimate" interpretant, that is, a particular habit of action, that "gives all members of the series their representational force without itself needing to derive that force from still another interpretant" (Alston 1956–1957, 86; Wu 1994, 74).

As Peirce's biographer Brent points out, this obsession with emotional neutrality and conceptual clarity takes on an ironic tone in light of the fact that Peirce was a helpless failure in his personal and practical life, a life full of physical pain, professional animosity, and uncontrollable emotions (Brent 1993, 1996; Fisch 1986). Indeed, as the extensive testimony of his peers reveals, Peirce lived "indifferent to consequences" (Brent 1993, 337).

Peircean Pragmatic Tools

Peirce's brand of pragmatism values the transparency of representational forms, entails an extreme form of propositional regimentation, and eliminates all contextual vagaries, rhetorical effects, and nonrational discourses from experimental reasoning. This pragmatism is "pragmatic" to one who would apply it only in the limited sense that the purposive goals and practical effects of signs are restricted to the universe of scientific discourse, logical inference, and rational communication. How, then, did Peirce manage to inspire so many inquirers into the contextual, strategic, and nonsemantic dimensions of language in context? The answer seems to be that, in clarifying the decontextualized nature of scientific discourse by means of the pragmatic maxim, Peirce constructed a framework for considering all sorts of variant, figurative, irregular, and nontransparent aspects of actual sign processes—aspects that are precisely privileged objects of contemporary pragmatic linguistics. Peirce notes, for instance, the importance of tonal color and facial expressions in human communication, though these would play no significant role in logical inference (*EP* 2, 391). Despite his focus on logical discourse, Peirce recognized that poetic or figurative expressions have their place in the gradual process of coming to know the truth: "Let one put up with figurative ideas rather than go without any, and perhaps by learning from them, one may advance to a stricter logical analysis after a prolonged study of the ideas that are to be analyzed" (1909, *MS* 634, 20).

Four concepts found in Peirce's writings that have been particularly influential need to be reviewed briefly: mediation, dialogue, indexicality, and collateral knowledge.

One of Peirce's most useful ideas is that the semiotic relation is a dynamic linkage of something signaled, the object, with some interpreting sign, the interpretant, by the "mediation" of the sign vehicle or representation (Parmentier 1985a). As Peirce somewhat cryptically put it about 1905:

A Sign may be defined as a Medium for the communication of a Form. . . . This Form is really embodied in the object, meaning that the conditional relation which constitutes the form is true of the form as it is in the Object. In the Sign it is embodied only in a representative sense, meaning that whether by virtue of some real modification of the Sign, or otherwise, the Sign becomes endowed with the power of communicating it to an interpretant. (1906, *MS* 793, 1–3)

The mediating role of signs is, for Peirce, a perfect instance of the irreducibility of triadic relations, or what he termed Thirds. To explain this, he often made reference to linguistic propositions involving a subject (nominative), a direct object (accusative), and an indirect object (dative); in the sentence "the boy gives the ball to the dog," the three possible dyadic relations cannot be separated if the proper understanding of the verb "give" is to be achieved. Similarly, in the syllogism, the mediating judgment, or second term, links the premise with the conclusion. Now this rather technical sense of semiotic mediation has been generalized by many linguists, philosophers, and social scientists to encompass the central idea that a culture's semiotic systems mediate individual cognition and the experienced world, although most modern theorists reject Peirce's goal of finding a totally transparent system of representation (Mertz and Parmentier 1985). Peirce has little interest in the code-level mediation of specific semiotic systems; certainly he would reject any hint of a Sapir-Whorf skewing dependent on systemic bias, and he would equally oppose a Saussurean notion that linguistic signifiers ("the arrangements of our language" [*CP* 5.409]) are correlated with conceptual signified ("the meaning of our ideas" [*CP* 5.409]).

Peirce's frequent observation that all thought is "dialogical" resonates with much modern analysis of the pragmatics of language, from George Herbert Mead's theory about the interpersonal communicative construction of subjectivity (see Caton 1993 to M. M. Bakhtin's (1986, 117–28) focus on the dialogic encounter as the fundamental character of the linguistic sign (see Urban and Smith 1998). While Peirce did admire human conversation as a "wonderfully perfect kind of sign-functioning" (*EP* 2, 391), his notion of the dialogic nature of thought did not require an actual interpersonal relationship; in thinking, one's mind enters into an internal dialogue with previous mental states (*CP* 4.7): "The ego of any one moment . . . is incessantly appealing to the ego of a subsequent moment, welded into the former one, to yield his assent and give his endorsement to the earlier instant's argumentation" (1907, *MS* 318, 13). And two minds, while communicating, become for analytical purposes one mind (*EP* 2, 390–91). This sequence of interpreting signs differs from interpersonal communication in that the process is governed by the systematic and necessary rules of logical inference rather than by the potentially conflicting struggle between two intentional strategies (*CP* 4.551). But Peirce's point that "cognition arises by a continuous process" (*W* 2, 214) of sign-to-sign relations remains as an important stimulus for various kinds of "processual" social analysis; this focus on process or sequence is, however, mitigated by Peirce's own development of an artificial graphical system that replaced the "line of speech" with a spatial representation of the "syntax" of all possible assertions (1910, *MS* 654, 6–7).

Peirce made many insightful observations about the operation of indexical modalities of linguistic meaning as distinct from purely symbolic linguistic categories (Sebeok 1995a; Silverstein 1976). In particular, he stressed the functioning of indexicals in anchoring sentences to the context of utterance (*CP* 4.56), of bringing the "general" down to the "case in hand" (*NEM* 2, 247). Deixis, for example, "stimulates the hearer to look about him" (*RLT*, 129). Various kinds of indexicals such as exclamations, pronouns, and proper names function to "force the attention to the occasion of the compulsive object" (*EP* 2, 172). Building on Peirce's typology of indexicals, linguistic anthropologists in particular have explored the interlocking of iconic and indexical signs in various kinds of "poetic" textualities (Silverstein 1981; Parmentier 1997a, 37–43). Complex discursive forms can both metalinguistically "diagram" their own rhetorical structure and, at the same time, powerfully recontextualize the discourse at efficacious moments. Comparative investigation reveals a telling asymmetry in patterning so that, when a vector of linearity places iconic orderings in a temporal context, the resulting combination of hyperstructured discourse and clear indexical grounding yields the potential for what Silverstein calls the "metaforces of power" (1981).

Especially useful for social analysis in the pragmatic mode is Peirce's concept of "collateral acquaintance" (EP 2, 496; Hardwick, ed. 1977, 72), that is, knowledge "understood by virtue of acquaintance with customs" (*NEM* 3/2, 840): "I think by this time you must understand what I mean when I say that no sign can be understood—or at least that no proposition can be understood unless the interpreter has 'collateral acquaintance' with every Object of it" (*NEM* 3/2, 843). Collateral knowledge supplies speaker and hearer with sufficient presupposed common ground so that deployed indexicals can pick out the relevant denoted objects (*NEM* 3, 247). If the sign in question, a noun for example, does not involve an indexical, then the "experience of the hearer" (*CP* 2.287) will be required to pick out the sign's object. In a sense, then, collateral knowledge includes everything necessary for communication *outside* the interpretant, which is the sign as it is creatively realized in acts of semiosis. A painting, for example, contains signifying elements that the painter wishes to express to the viewer, but since the painting is an instance of an artistic genre the viewer also needs substantial collateral information to establish basic things, such as the "subject" (as opposed to the "significance") of the painting (*NEM* 3/2, 841). Peirce's notion of mediate determination, that is, that the object determines the sign "relative to the interpretant" (1907, *MS* 318, 44), is a useful corrective to the vague idea that sign interpretation is unconstrained by any particular semiotic qualities of the object as transmitted through the sign. Peirce's insight is, clearly, grounded in his objectivist understanding of the nature of the physical world; transferred to the domains of language and culture, the implication is that not everything about an object is provided by the sign of that object, or as Peirce put it, "the Object of a sign then is necessarily unexpressed in the sign taken by itself" (*MS* 318, 34). Collateral knowledge shared by speaker and hearer is, thus, essential to contextualize the object in a locally appropriate "universe of discourse" (see Pape 1996, 106). Combining what contemporary scholars label "cultural knowledge" and "conversational presupposition," Peirce's notion of collateral knowledge blurs the distinction between knowledge shared by communicators *prior to* events of semiosis and knowledge obtained *in* the real-time process of fixing linguistic meaning.

Conclusion

Are contemporary scholars of the pragmatics of language who cite Peirce as a positive ancestor simply misreading Peirce, or perhaps reading into him their own ideas? To appreciate that the answer to these questions is "no" is to realize that Peirce's own pragmatic maxim actually predicts that the meaning of the term *pragmatic* would change over time, as indeed it has (cf. Silverstein 1997, 631, n.4). "A symbol, once in being, spreads among the peoples. In use and in experience, its meaning grows. Such words as *force, law, wealth, marriage* bear for us very different meanings from those they bore to our barbarous ancestors" (Peirce *CP* 2.302).

Like any symbol, the term *pragmatic* continues to develop and grow in the nurturing context of discursive communities (Merrell 1997, 137) and subject to the "openness of the living language for an enrichment of meaning by human experience" (Apel 1989, 47).

Note

This paper was originally published as "Charles S. Peirce," in *Handbook of Pragmatics*, ed. Jef Verschueren et al., (Amsterdam: John Benjamins, 1997), 1–18. Reprinted with permission of Benjamins.

3   Representation, Symbol, and Semiosis: Signs of a Scholarly Collaboration

I AM HONORED TO represent Brandeis University's Department of Anthropology at this gathering of scholars at Hankuk University of Foreign Studies.[1] My presence here today can also be taken as a representation of the seven members of the international editorial board of *Signs and Society*. And, in particular, I am pleased to be able to represent my Brandeis colleague, Professor Parmentier, the editor-in-chief of our journal, who sends his warmest greetings and whose words I will represent today.

It would seem that there is a lot of representation going on! In fact, representation lies at the heart of the sign processes or "semiosis" that are the focus of the multidisciplinary research published in *Signs and Society*. Two somewhat contradictory meanings of representation have been widely recognized: first, for one thing to represent another is for it to stand for or in place of something that is absent or unknowable, as a political representative does for a constituency; second, to represent can mean to *re*-present, that is, to make something present once again that was once absent, as a statue does for a deity (Leone and Parmentier 2014, S2). A third colloquial meaning that has developed in the past few decades involves the emphatic utterance of the quasi verb "represent!" to mean that the speaker affirms his or her existential solidarity and authentic stance with respect to some issue.

It is no doubt because of these multiple meanings that a group of distinguished scholars at the University of California at Berkeley called their journal simply *Representations*. In contrast, *Signs and Society* is based on the working notion that these basic "standing for" and "re-presenting" relationships need to be placed in at least five additional contexts: the "codification" or organization of signs into complex structures; the "communication" of signs across various transmission media; the fixing or "inscription" of signs in relatively permanent textual or material forms; the modalities of "interpretation" available to or prohibited for sign interpreters; and powerful restrictive or "regimenting" forces that specify or delimit meaning-making in all of these embedded contexts. So, following the lead of your own Semiosis Research Center, the journal is devoted to the study of sign processes or semiosis in all its manifestations. But in the announcement of our intention to investigate the multilayered relationships among representation, codification, communication, interpretation, inscription, and regimentation, we are only suggesting these six levels as heuristic or even provisional guides for research.[2]

It was, then, a remarkably appropriate example of semiosis when Professor Koh initially contacted Professor Parmentier—by e-mail, using the code of English—on April 26, 2012, to discuss the prospects of scholarly collaboration with Brandeis University.[3] We, too, had for a number of years—though in a much less formal manner—established a discussion circle we called the "Symbolic Form Study Group." And in our sessions over the years, we explored the nature of symbolic forms in fields such as linguistic anthropology, anthropological archaeology, comparative literature, classical studies, and art history with the help of a number of distinguished visitors such as Gregory Nagy, Irene Portis-Winner, and Irene Winter.

But it was not until we joined forces with Hankuk University's Semiosis Research Center in 2012 that we all became truly "symbolic"—in the etymological sense of that word. The English word *symbol* is based on the classical Greek word *symbolon*, which literally means "thrown together." It was originally used to describe two things, once part of a unity, broken apart, and then reassembled to constitute a unity again. Thus, the reuniting of two pieces torn from the same piece of paper or two fragments of pottery could be a "pledge" or *symbolon* for the persons holding them. Taken more broadly, *symbolon* came to stand for any agreement involving more than one party—thus a "conventional" arrangement as distinct from one occurring naturally. Note that the sense of symbol as a figurative, nonliteral, hidden, or mystical meaning is a later, derived, or secondary meaning.[4]

So in coming halfway around the world to be with you today, I am not only a multiple "representation," but, more importantly, I am one half of a symbol that has finally come back to regain its conventional unity, namely, the agreement between our two universities to produce *Signs and Society*.[5]

What are some implications of the title of our journal, *Signs and Society*? First of all, in this title we can hear distinct echoes of the famous words from the Swiss linguist Ferdinand de Saussure, lecturing in Geneva at the turn of the twentieth century, that a new science is imaginable, a science that does not yet exist but whose place is already reserved, that studies signs "at the heart of society." Saussure had in mind the relationship between various systems of codified symbols—material, gestural, pictorial, linguistic—that fuse a plane of expressive *form* with a plane of meaningful *content*. And, in a brilliant but frequently misunderstood move, Saussure showed that, rather than assuming that the signifying properties of these socially embedded codes derive essentially from human language, the more productive insight is to see in language features of these other codes, especially their "motivation." Motivation, or more precisely "relative motivation," describes some kind of rationale, connection, or externality (to use the economist's term) between the expressive plane and the content plane; in other words, some "limitation on arbitrariness."[6] Saussure railed against the illusion perpetrated by some philosophers that an isolated word can be adequately understood as an arbitrary hook-up between a sound segment and a conceptual segment, a relationship he termed *signification*. Rather—and this brings us back to the "and Society" of our journal's title—Saussure realized that signs never appear as isolated entities but as part of complex systems, including groupings of *co-occurring* signs, what he called "syntagms," the sequence of dishes in a fancy meal, for example; and *virtual* associative sets, what he called "paradigms," the classical orders in architecture, for example. Saussure labelled the positional contribution that these syntagms and paradigms make to the meaning of individual signs their "value"—a better translation would be "valence," alluding to the technical term in chemistry. And so, it is these complexes that provide the "systemic" motivation for both language and nonlinguistic signs of all kinds.

What is remarkable about language is that the arbitrariness of signification, that is, the absence of any necessary link between linguistic expression and linguistic meaning, makes possible the perfectly massive contribution of "relative," systemic or code-driven motivation—since nothing stands in its way—which, in turn, underpins the diachronic and cross-contextual stability of signification itself. So, for Saussure, symbolic codes are socially shared and historically transmitted, and every attempt to dislocate them from their sociohistorical grounding is a methodological derailment.

For all we can appreciate in Saussure's opening up the possibility of a "science of signs," he actually made only minor substantive contributions to its advancement. He left behind, for example, several notebooks documenting his rather bizarre investigations of the "anagrams" behind Latin poetry and mythology.[7] More to the point, Saussure never began the hard work of classifying or typologizing the relative motivation he so prophetically proclaimed. For this we need to cross the Atlantic Ocean and bring into the discussion the American scientist and philosopher Charles S. Peirce, who called himself a "backwoodsman" in the study of signs and symbols. Peirce's largely unpublished writings on "semeiotic," that is, the science of signs, predate Saussure's speculations on "semiology" by a couple of decades. Both scholars lived relatively reclusive lives, Saussure in his family's palatial homes in Geneva, Switzerland, and Peirce hiding from bill collectors in an enlarged farmhouse named "Arisbe" in Milford, Pennsylvania. As a result, the founder of semiotics—to use the more modern term first proposed by the anthropologist Margaret Mead in 1962[8]—and the founder of semiology never heard of each other,[9] although, as I will try to demonstrate, their work can be viewed as an example of unintended "complementary distribution."

Peirce's great insight was to realize that, in addition to investigating the nature of signification—signs and symbols taken in isolation—and the nature of codes—rules governing real or virtual complexes of signs—we need to add into the mix the *interpreters* of signs, not necessarily a physical person but some dynamic uptake, outcome, or effect signs have when viewed from the perspective of their processual deployment. This process he termed "semiosis," and in assuming the name "Semiosis Research Center" my colleagues at Hankuk University have fittingly honored that coinage. It was, by the way, St. Augustine, writing at the end of the fourth century, who first proposed the inclusion of the interpreter—a reader of Scripture or a listener to Augustine's sermons—in the study of signs.[10] But Peirce thought that any account of meaning that could include *both* laboratory-based scientific research and logically precise philosophical reasoning must recognize that, for both of these truth-driven enterprises, interpreters, or "interpretants," the technical term he invented, cannot be completely free to arrive at conclusions unconnected to the path stipulated or "determined" by the deployed signs—that is, by the necessary semiosis of either experimental science or syllogistic reasoning.

So, on the assumption that everyone is a truth seeker, signs and their objects must have definable or typologizable kinds of relationships; and their interpretants must form a representation of the *same* kinds of relationships that pertain between signs and their objects. And this is where we find Peirce's most used—and overused—distinction between sign relations based on formal resemblance or "icons," relations based on physical contiguity or "indexes," and relations based on arbitrary convention or "symbols": a painted portrait, as an icon, resembles the person depicted; a stop sign, as an index, at the side of the road tells us exactly where to stop the car; and the word *semiosis*, as a symbol, only exists because a community of speakers agrees on the range of its semantic meaning.

But now notice that, by assuming a commitment to truth, Peirce has actually uncovered the logical organization of Saussure's "motivation"! A keen scholar of classical and medieval writings on these matters, Peirce's triple division or "trichotomy" of sign-to-object relations roughly lines up with the more standard dual division between motivated "signs"—comprising icons and indexes—and unmotivated "symbols." Unfortunately, the word *symbole* in Saussure's French is equivalent to Peirce's English *sign,* and Peirce's English term *symbol* lines up with Saussure's French *signe*—not complementary distribution but complementary confusion![11]

And here I finally come to the point of this discussion of Saussure and Peirce: in insisting on sign process or semiosis as an essentially logical affair, Peirce necessarily abandoned the "and Society" dimension that was precisely the key to Saussure's fundamental discovery of the sociohistorical grounding of symbolic codes (see Parmentier 2014). Correlatively, without the constraint of the objective determination of interpreters and their interpretants through the mediational operation of signs as determined by their objects, Saussure could not come up with an adequate account of how signs and symbols function in real-time events and interactions, a realm he dismissed as utterly irrelevant to his semiology. And this, then, is the "motivation" for our journal: the "science of signs at the heart of society" may have been proclaimed in advance and explored by brilliant backwoodsmen on both sides of the Atlantic, but the real work of scholarship lies ahead—in the pages of *Signs and Society*, the inscribed textual symbol of a collaborative relationship crossing the even wider Pacific Ocean.

Notes

This paper was originally published as "Representation, Symbol, and Semiosis: Signs of a Scholarly Collaboration," *Signs and Society* 3 (Spring 2015): 1–7.

1. This essay was written for presentation on October 24, 2014, at "The History of HUFS Academic Journals: The Past, the Present, and the Future," a conference celebrating the sixtieth anniversary of the founding of Hankuk University of Foreign Studies (HUFS). It was delivered on my behalf by Javier Urcid, a member of the editorial board and former chair of the Department of Anthropology at Brandeis. I take this occasion to thank Javier for substituting for me on this occasion and to note that Javier also delivered his own paper titled "Semasiography and Writing Systems" during his visit to HUFS.

2. The journal's "mission statement," posted on its website, gives a fuller account of these embedded levels: *representation*: the "standing for" relationship between two things that come to be linked as signifying sign and represented object by virtue of some typologically specifiable motivation (Saussure), ground (Peirce), or reason; *codification*: code structures, including both presupposed patterned systems of signs that feature "mutual delimitation" (Saussure) between planes of expression and content and less coherently articulated systems of indexical and iconic signs characterized by formal gaps, overlapping signals, and referential opacity; *communication*: the flow of signs across face-to-face and technologically mediated channels, from speaker to hearer or performer to audience, along with mediational relays ([Richard] Bauman) of various sorts, by means of codes that, because of differential usages and stratified manipulation, serve additionally to demarcate social categories and groups; *inscription*: the entextualization (Silverstein) of signs and sign complexes in cognitively or historically fixed or sedimented forms, as distinct from the real-time interactional flow of signs, that can potentially become the focus on subsequent communicative interactions; *interpretation*: actions that read or misread signs by users who, taking sign/object relations as meaningful, generate additional chains of signs which variably naturalize ("downshift") or conventionalize ("upshift") the linkage between signs and meanings; *regimentation*: power-laden social actions that restrict, forbid, or shape interpretive meaning-making by explicitly or implicitly stipulating, constraining, or otherwise metasemiotically representing sign structures, text, and processes.

3. Kyung-Nan (Linda) Koh received her PhD in anthropology from the University of Pennsylvania; her principal advisor there was Greg Urban (a member of the journal's founding editorial board), and she studied semiotic anthropology with Asif Agha. Urban and Parmentier both received their doctorates in anthropology from the University of Chicago, were students of Michael Silverstein, were affiliated for many years with the Center for Psychosocial Studies in Chicago, and were the cofounders and coeditors of the Center's preprint series *Working Papers and Proceedings of the Center for Psychosocial Studies.*

4. The story of the development of concepts of symbol and sign in classical antiquity is well told in Manetti (1993) and Struck (2004).

5. Two scholars from HUFS, Linda Koh and Hyug (Andy) Ahn (representing Paig-Ki Kim, one of the two directors of the Semiosis Research Center), traveled to Brandeis to draft two memoranda of understanding, one with the Department of Anthropology (cosigned by Javier Urcid) and one with the Graduate Program in Global Studies (cosigned by Richard Parmentier). A larger delegation from HUFS came to Brandeis for an April 2013 working symposium titled "Global Semiosis," which coincided with a celebration for the publication of the first issue of *Signs and Society*.

6. In the wording of the *Course in General Linguistics* (Saussure 1959 [1915], 132–33), "Up to this point units have appeared as values, i.e., as elements of a system, and we have given special consideration to their opposition; now we recognize the solidarities that bind them; they are associative and syntagmatic, and they are what limits arbitrariness.... Everything that relates to language as a system must, I am convinced, be approached from this viewpoint: the limiting of arbitrariness." In the wording of Saussure's notes for the third series of these lectures, "Reduction in any system of *langue* of absolute arbitrariness to relative arbitrariness. This is what makes up the 'system.' If language were reduced to nothing more than denominating objects, all the terms in this language would be quite unrelated, would stay as separate from one another as the objects themselves" (2006 [2002], 233).

7. Saussure's biographer John E. Joseph interprets Saussure's extensive (and abruptly terminated) research into Latin anagrams in terms of his rigorous scientific standards, noting that Saussure expressed a healthy skepticism to his young research assistant: "I rather feel that you will finally remain perplexed, since I do not disguise the fact that I have remained so myself—, on the most important point, namely what one is to make of the reality of the phantasmagoria of the entire affair" (2012, 555).

8. Margaret Mead, taking part in a discussion among a large group of scholars at a conference at Indiana University on paralinguistics and kinesics, said that "the study of all patterned communication in all modalities" could be termed "semiotics," a coinage that seems to have gained general approval by conference attendees—despite Thomas Sebeok's complaint that the term was "overburdened" (Sebeok et al. 1964, 275)

9. Joseph (2012, 393) speculates that Saussure "encountered Peirce's sign theory" through a distant cousin named Flournoy, who had been in correspondence with the American psychologist William James, himself a close associate of Peirce. One might continue this line of speculation with two biographical "near misses": in 1856, Saussure's father Henri de Saussure, a distinguished naturalist, visited Cambridge, Massachusetts, to meet with Louis Agassiz, a close colleague and neighbor of Peirce's father, a professor of mathematics at Harvard University; and Peirce's younger brother René de Saussure received the PhD in mathematics at Johns Hopkins University in 1895, the institution where Peirce had taught logic in the department of mathematics from 1879 to 1884.

10. Augustine treated the hearer of verbal messages in chapter 7, "The Force of Words," of his treatise titled *On Dialectic*.

11. I avoid here the technical problem that Saussure's analysis of the linguistic sign (based on the Stoic division between the linguistic expression [*semainon*] and what is meant by linguistic expression [*semainomenon*], a correlative pair distinct from what the sign stands for in the external world), in terms of the linkage of expressive form ("signifier") and expressed concept ("signified"), differs significantly from Peirce's analysis of the three "grounds" (iconic, indexical, and symbolic) of the relationship between the "representamen" (roughly, signifying form) and the "object," whose properties "determine" the representamen (i.e., sign) as the mediator between object and interpretant. The closest approximation in Peirce's terminology to the Saussurean "signified" would be the "immediate interpretant."

4 Peirce and Saussure on Signs and Ideas in Language

CHARLES S. PEIRCE (1839–1914) and Ferdinand de Saussure (1857–1913) spent considerable effort trying to clarify and articulate what they meant by signs and the ideas, or concepts, associated with them. There are many attempts in the scholarly literature to align Peircean and Saussurean terminologies, as well as several valiant efforts to create new synthetic models encompassing their differences. My task here is different: to point out several ways in which Peirce, an American experimental physicist and logician (trained as a chemist), and Saussure, a Swiss linguist (trained as a philologist of Indo-European languages), have fundamentally opposed views stemming from different intellectual worldviews. While it is certain that Peirce and Saussure's understanding of sign systems matured over time, I think that it is also possible to find a unity in their respective developments, especially in terms of what each was fundamentally reacting *against*. For Peirce, this seems to be the philosophical position of "nominalism," that is, the denial of the reality of universals or generals in favor of individualism, sensationalism, and mechanism.[1] For Saussure, this seems to be the notion, common in many Enlightenment thinkers, that language is a "nomenclature," that is, a system of names for things or words for preexisting ideas.

One can only wonder what the conversation might have been if the young Saussure, finishing up his *baccalauréat* studies (including, to his father's delight, both physics and chemistry) at the local Gymnase prior to entering the university in Geneva, had only walked down the street during the month of October 1875 to witness the older Peirce swinging his pendulum at the observatory (Brent 1998, 97; Joseph 2012, 166–67).

For Peirce, ideas *are* signs, that is, whatever properties we can discover for signs "external" to the mind will also pertain to signs "internal" to the mind (*CP* 5.570)—the problem being that, while the latter are the more "perfect" kind of sign, we can only perform experiments on the former. Since we are entirely—unfortunately—dependent on these external signs, we might as well give preference to "forms of signs" that are "most easily examined, manipulated, preserved, and anatomized" (*MS* 637, 30). Just as much in logic as in metaphysics, "a pure idea without metaphor or other significant clothing is an onion without a peel" (*EP* 2 [1906], 397). If thoughts are already signs, then the "intellectual value" of our thoughts/ideas rest, first of all, on the "standing for" relation they have to "some object." All cognitions, that is, all ideas or thoughts, are "representations," first, because they stand for the "things they signify" (1986 [1873], 76) and, second, because, succeeding each other in time according to a general rule of inference, they must always appeal to *other* cognitions, or at least they must always have the capacity for being interpreted or translated into further cognitions (77). For Peirce, "meaning" is what is conveyed from one idea-sign to an interpreting sign ("interpretant") about some object of cognition—an inferential process the coherence of which is guaranteed by the intersection of logical form with properties of objective reality.[2]

This class of objects[3] that Peirce indifferently calls ideas-thoughts-cognitions-signs-representations can, in addition to these "standing for"("signification") and "translated into" ("interpretation") relations, be viewed from the perspective of their differential "material qualities," qualities they would have as objects *apart from* ("prescinded" from [*CP* 5.449]) these two relations: the distinctive sounds of words, the identifying shapes of printed letters, the colorful pigments of an oil painting.

Turning now to Saussure's lectures and notes dealing with signs and ideas, we can see that he repeatedly insists on the point that they can never be considered singular or isolated entities—that there is no "such thing as *a* meaning and a corresponding sign" (Saussure 2006 [2002], 24)—that is, there is no such thing independent of a *structure* of signs—and, more importantly, that "it is as pointless to try and approach ideas divorced from signs and signs divorced from ideas" (25). But this stricture against isolating sign/idea combinations and the notion of the unbreakable linkage between signs and ideas both only make sense, in this account, because of the essential heterogeneity of signs and ideas, as "*two different objects*" and not "simple homogeneous objects" (2006 [2002], 5, italics in original). Thus, "there are two grammars, one flowing from the idea and the other from the sign" (2006 [2002], 5), and "it is wrong to believe that there may be *forms* (existing in themselves, independently of their *use*) or *ideas* (existing in themselves, independently of their *representation*) (15, italics in original). Signs and meanings are, thus, both fundamentally dissimilar and fundamentally fused, as his famous paper analogy makes clear: "It is thus always quite vain to oppose sign and meaning. They are two forms of the same mental concept; signification would not exist without the sign, and constitutes an inverted experience of the sign, just as one cannot cut a sheet of paper without making an incision on both front and back with the same movement of the scissors" (2006 [2002], 66).[4]

And because, for Saussure, the linkage between segments of the plane of "acoustic image" and the plane of conceptual space[5] depends entirely on the conventional imposition by some collectivity functioning as the speech community, language at its core is irrational in the sense that there are no "internal" or structural reasons that might motivate the patternings of this linkage in various linguistic systems and no "external" reasons other than the conventions stipulated by and shared by members of the community. But for Peirce, while it is necessary to analytically separate, for every sign, those internal qualities the sign has from those qualities only imputed to the sign, in certain signs the material qualities "suggest" or even "point" to the mind what the signs stand for. Only in the special case of signs called "symbols" is there a complete disjunction between material and imputed qualities, resulting in a situation in which the qualities that distinguish the sign from other signs do *not* suggest or point toward the "meaning" of the sign.[6] Indeed, Peircean "symbols" depend entirely on the "*ratio*, or reason of the Object that has emanated from it" (1909, *MS* 637, 35).

So, for Peirce, the meaning of the conventional symbol ("as in the case of most words" [1986 (1873), 65]) is provided by the mind or "mental habit"—it will turn out to be the very interpreting sign that the symbol gives rise to—*completely independent* of the distinguishing marks that give the sign its particular identity. For Saussure, on the other hand, the arbitrary or unmotivated nature of the most elementary or simplex linguistic sign *depends completely* on the established bond between sound figure and meaning, the bond he describes as the front and back of a sheet of paper.

An important consequence of this contrast is that it leads to equally contrasting views about the role of consciousness in the functioning of semiological/semiotic systems. Given the fundamental principle of *la langue* that any two terms *a* and *b* are validated only by their "reciprocal difference," speakers are only conscious of the "difference *a/b*"; and, as a result, these two terms themselves are free to change "according with laws other than those which would result from a conscious influence of the mind" (Saussure 2006 [2002], 153): "Once the sign system belongs to the community nothing guarantees that an internal reason, a reason borne of individual reasoning, will continue to govern the relationship between sign and idea" (202).[7] But, in Peirce's account of signs, the key principle is just the opposite: the manipulation of signs is completely under the conscious control of the mind—a control that will eventually lead to the formation of "habits"—so "only if we are not conscious that the resulting belief is caused by one already adopted, we cannot watch the process nor control it, so that there can be no art of reasoning applicable to inference in that sense" (Peirce 2000, 354). Nothing could be farther from Peirce's view than Saussure's metaphor[8] of a ship at sea: "*Langue*, or indeed any semiological system, is not a ship in dry dock, but a ship on the open sea. Once it is on the water, it is pointless to look for an indication of the course it will follow by assessing its frame, or its inner construction as laid out in an engineer's drawing" (2006 [2002], 202).

Peirce illustrates his argument about the restricting or suggestive influence of "form" on thought by pointing out ways that "ordinary language" prevents us from grasping the nature of true logical propositions and valid syllogisms. For example, whereas in most European languages the common noun is a "distinct part of speech," and so those languages are required to use the copula "is" to express categorical propositions, in other languages (Peirce cites ancient Egyptian as an example) such words can also function—more logically, in his view—as verbs. And even in situations where grammatical forms *do* roughly correspond to proper logical distinctions—having, for example, legitimate indexical or deictic form as "stimulants for looking"—scholars still erroneously insist that these are "pro-nouns," that is, substitutes for nouns (*RLT*, 129).[9] And, finally, the discovery that patterns of ordinary speech can, in *some* instances, be translated into precise logical form is simply to say that these particular expressions *can* be analyzed into "the logical part of the science of the particular language" (*RLT*, 145).[10] Peirce even complained that the written register of "ordinary language" is more pictorial than diagrammatic, leading to writers' thoughts being "encumbered with sensuous accessories" (2010, 70); the remedy for this "vice" would be to develop a system in which "the different relations upon which reasoning turns may find their analogies in the relations between different parts of the expression" (70). Peirce bluntly concludes: "These languages do not represent the nature of thought in general, or even that of human thought" (*RLT*, 127), and so "the study of languages ought to be based on the necessary conditions to which signs must conform in order to fulfill their function as signs" (*MS* 693, 191).

Peirce then generalizes this "suggestion from form" argument to the even broader claim that "the forms of statements are not of the slightest consequence.... And the consideration of the ways in which the thinking of that matter is done is no more germane to the logical question than it would be to inquire whether the propositions were written in English or the Hungarian language" (*RLT*, 144, *pace* Thomas A. Sebeok). Not only must proper reasoners beware of the bias or nontransparency of their necessarily imperfect language constructions created to express propositions—and "propositions must be expressed *somehow*" (*RLT*, 144)—but the truth of reasoning, once carefully disentangled from "linguistic, or psychic considerations" (145), is ultimately completely independent from "how we think" (144).

I have tried to point out several important differences between Peirce and Saussure on the issue of the nature of the signs that make up a language. The first key difference concerns the importance of time in their accounts of signs and ideas. For Peirce, temporality lies at the heart of semiosis as a process, whether at the micro level of logical inference or at the macro level of the continuity of the universe. For Saussure, on the other hand, in the domain of *la langue*, there is no sequence in time: "The crucial element is the moment and *the moment* alone

(2006 [2002], 33, italics in original). Whereas Peirce requires "continuity" in every aspect of the universe "perfused with signs" (*CP* 5.449), Saussure argues for the methodological primacy of synchrony as the only way to picture the "state" of language from the perspective of interacting speakers at a specific time and place.[11] For Peirce, the ultimate interpretant of a sign is what the community will decide *in futuro*, while for Saussure that community has *already* "stated" its collective mind.

The other key difference concerns the necessity versus transparency of expressive form. For Saussure, the forms of language impose order on the flux of conceptual thought, while for Peirce the most "perfect" or "genuine" signs are those that transparently connect ideas to the subsequent ideas they determine, that is, without friction or noise from the distinctive qualities—perhaps naturally occurring—of the signs involved. If Saussure requires language to be a system of "differences without positive terms,"[12] Peirce pushes for a system of positive terms without any disturbing or refracting differences.[13] "Reciprocal delimitation," the defining discovery of Saussurean semiology, would be, for Peirce, the worst-case scenario for effective semiosis. Ultimately, then, what holds languages together are for Saussure the *systems* of relational differences between forms and meanings and for Peirce the logical *inferences* that govern the sequential relations of signs.

No doubt an amusing parlor game would be to try to align the various theoretical pieces of Saussurean semiology and Peircean semiotics, or at least to correlate those concepts that occupy relatively similar structural positions—to make, that is, a "Saussurean" analysis of this *a/b* relation:

Linguistic Sign	Symbolic Legisign
Value	Inference
Motivation	Degeneracy
Signified	Interpretant
Communication	Semiosis

But it seems to me more productive to clarify the significantly different analytical principles of the two approaches—to make, that is, a Peircean analysis of their relation.

Notes

This paper was originally published as "Peirce and Saussure on Signs and Ideas in Language." *Scienze dei linguaggi e linguaggi della scienze: Intertestualità, interferenze, mutuazioni*, ed. Susan Petrilli (Milan: Mimesis Edizioni, 2015), 293–300. Reprinted with permission of Mimesis Edizioni.

1. For Peirce, to think that general laws are merely conventional fictions—a view he attributed to Thomas Hobbes, John Locke, David Hume, and J. S. Mill, for example—is "antagonistic . . . to the spirit of science" (1978 [1894], 19).

2. Peirce did not come up with an account of *systems* of signs, that is, with a theory that would occupy the same place as Saussure's account of paradigmatic and syntagmatic axes of *la langue*. Peirce never considered that a distinct system of "valences" would be required for a theory of inferential discourse.

3. There are many strange aspects to Peirce's early account of ideas: that ideas are "objects"; that ideas have "material qualities." But when Peirce says that ideas are objects, he simply means that they are what we are *conscious of* when we think.

4. In trying to compare their views of the relationship between thoughts and signs, there does seem to be some level of parallelism between Saussure's metaphor of slicing a piece of paper and Peirce's metaphor of the rainbow, which is "at once a manifestation of the sun and of the rain" (*CP* 5.283).

5. Linguistically demarcated units of intensional space (*signifié*) are not really concepts in the philosophical sense; the linguistic meaning of the word *totality* is not equivalent to the philosophical concept of "totality."

6. Note that it is precisely the suggestive or "motivated" iconic and indexical signs that Saussure includes in the category of "*symbole*."

7. That language "does not depend on constant correction by the mind, because it does not originally derive from a visible harmony between the idea and the means of expression," is, for Saussure, its "crucial distinction" from other semiological systems, such as "religious ceremonies, political forms, customs . . . or even tools" (2006 [2002], 154).

8. Saussure also compared language to a symphonic composition (as distinct from a given performance), a game of chess, a monetary system, and a system of chemical valences.

9. Peirce's consistent and epochal distinction between signs and objects related by "associations of similarity" and signs and objects related by "associations of contiguity" enables a correlative distinction between "signification" and "denotation," a distinction completely missing in Saussure, whose dismissal of facts in the realm of *la parole* implies the absence of "shifters" (Jesperson) from his linguistic theory.

10. Peirce also complained that, while treatises on logic regularly profess to distinguish "logical forms and mere modes of linguistic expression," these same works consistently illustrate logical principles with examples drawn from particular languages, usually "Aryan" (*MS* 693, 178).

11. The methodological principle of separating out the synchronic "*état de langue*" does not mean that there is no temporality in language. As early as his lectures in 1891, Saussure discussed the "*continual transformation* of language in time," due to the "workings of analogy" and "phonetic changes" (2006 [2002], *111*).

12. "The language system is based on a certain number of *differences* or *oppositions which it recognizes* and is not essentially concerned with the absolute value of each of the terms that are in opposition, which may show marked variation without disrupting the status quo of the language" (2006 [2002], 19, italics in original).

13. Although Peirce often wrote about grammars as "iconic diagrams," formally equivalent to algebras (*CP* 3.418), he mostly viewed this diagrammatization in terms of the propositional rather than the morphological structure of languages.

5   Troubles with Trichotomies: Reflections on the Utility of Peirce's Sign Trichotomies for Social Analysis

The Trichotomies

According to the editors at the Peirce Edition Project, in 1903 Peirce composed a detailed "syllabus" in several sections for the eight lectures he delivered at the Lowell Institute in Boston. The fifth section of that syllabus, titled "Nomenclature and Divisions of Triadic Relations, as Far as They Are Determined" (*EP* 2, 289–99; *CP* 2.233–72), presents a detailed and systematic account of the 10 classes of signs generated by the intersection of three trichotomies and contains the famous (if perplexing) triangular table exhibiting the relations among these sign classes depending on the degree of shared characteristics. As Peirce explains:

> Triadic relations are in three ways divisible by trichotomy, according as the First, the Second, or the Third Correlate, respectively, is a mere possibility, an actual existent, or a law. These three trichotomies, taken together, divide all triadic relations into ten classes. These ten classes will have certain subdivisions according as the existent correlates are individual subjects or individual facts, and according as the correlates that are laws are general subjects, general modes of fact, or general modes of law. (*EP* 2 [1903], 290)

The First Trichotomy, which divides signs by their character as Firsts, Seconds, or Thirds, yields the division of qualisign, sinsign, and legisign. The Second Trichotomy, which distinguishes ways signs relate to their objects, yields the division of Icon, Index, and Symbol. And the Third Trichotomy, which looks at ways signs determine their interpretants to represent them *as* signs, yields the division of Rheme, Dicent, and Argument. Since, according to Peirce, no sign can determine an Interpretant to represent it as higher ranking than it is, icons can only be rhemes and indexes can only be rhemes or dicents. Since qualisigns, as Firsts, cannot have any degree of dyadic or triadic complexity, they can only be icons, and, by parallel reasoning, sinsigns, as Seconds, cannot be symbols, which are necessarily triadic. Of the resulting 10 classes of signs, positions 5 through 10 are legisigns, that is, general signs that exist only to govern the production of sinsigns that are their replicas; and the qualisign occupying position 1, can only exist as an embodied quality of some existing sinsign.

The power of Peirce's classic construction of 1903, which I will call the Three Trichotomies, is more fully appreciated when its obvious elegance is supplemented by careful attention to its embedded complexities. First, higher-numbered sign classes are composed of lower-numbered sign classes. An index, a weathervane, for example, is struck by the force of the wind, but since the direction of the weathervane and the direction of the wind resemble each other, this index contains an icon. Peirce is fond of saying that an icon provides information about what the index denotes. Propositions (position 9) join an index to indicate what the proposition is about and an icon (the "predicate") to provide information. For sign classes that are necessarily composite, Peirce adds the cryptic note, the "Syntax of these is significant" (*EP* 2 [1903], 296), suggesting that the ordering of these constituent elements is itself important. Second, as noted above, some sinsigns are replicas of legisigns (Peirce calls these "peculiar" sinsigns "tokens"), while others are "ordinary" or "normal" sinsigns occupying the same three sign classes (positions 2–4). While it might be empirically tricky to distinguish normal versus peculiar sinsigns, the difference is enormous: peculiar sinsigns (i.e., tokens or replicas) only do the semiotic work of the legisigns they are instantiating. A further complication, resulting from the combination of "composition" and "replication," is that certain sign classes can have multiple "varieties" of replicas. For example, a rhematic indexical sinsign (position 3) can be a replica of a rhematic symbol (position 8) or of a rhematic indexical legisign (position 6). One final refinement involves Peirce's use of the word "force" to describe a particular modality of determination of certain sign classes, distinct enough (for Peirce!) to identify additional "varieties" of the class. For position 6, for example, Peirce notes that some rhematic iconic legisigns exemplify the force of a word (position 8) in a proposition (position 9), while other rhematic iconic legisigns exemplify the force of a word in an argument (position 10).

Especially in view of Peirce's later semiotic writings, where he made repeated attempts to extend the number of trichotomies and, thus, the number of sign classes and where he enumerated finer distinctions for the Object and the Interpretant, it is perhaps understandable that some have sought ulterior psychological (if not neurotic) motives in this excessive pursuit of the "degree of distinctness of conception" (1910, *MS* 654, 4; Spinks 1991, 1–9).[1] Peirce even suggested a trichotomy of conceptual distinction, in his division of "precision," "discrimination," and "dissociation" (*W* 1 [1866], 518–19). Peirce defended his mode of reasoning: "My first argument in repelling the suspicion that the prevalence of trichotomies in my system is due purely to my predilection for that form, will be that were the predilection so potent, it would inevitably have made me equally given over to the trichotomic form of classification of whatever subject I might work on. But this is not at all the case" (*CP* 1.569 [1910]).

Viewing the ten classes of signs as the restatement of semiosis as a *logical process* is the key to understanding the relationship between the irreducible triadic character of the sign and the Three Trichotomies. The assignment of a representamen (that is, the sign vehicle) to a sign class is a positional evaluation relevant at a slice of time and from a particular point of view. At each moment in the chain of semiosis, a sign becomes the object of the next interpreting sign, which ideally will make the sign's reference less "indefinite" (1912, *MS* 12, 8). And the same representamen in a different context of semiosis can receive a different classification. In other words, the organizing principles underlying the Three Trichotomies are relational, functional, and contextual (Deledalle 2000, 19–20).[2] And given these characteristics, there is at least a *prima facie* positive potential for using the Three Trichotomies for understanding signs produced in the ebb and flow of social life.

Applications

Before examining this potentiality in greater detail, some general remarks about the use of the Three Trichotomies are in order. Like any complex analytical metalanguage with an esoteric technical vocabulary, the Three Trichotomies can unfortunately function as a tool to maintain rather than cross disciplinary boundaries, especially in the hands of scholars who would advocate the imperial expansion of semiotics/semiology as an overarching method. But, more positively, the trichotomies and the sign classes can be especially useful as a "translation check" for specialized vocabularies across many disciplines. I have been thinking recently about the term *style*, which appears in art history, archaeology, linguistics, and other fields, and have constructed a working semiotic definition that can be tested for adequacy and accuracy: *style* refers to nonreferential semiotic regularities that appear across contexts and across functions (i.e., the regularities must appear on different classes of objects) and that are not subject to formal segmentation (i.e., the semiotic features "wash over" objects in nonfunctional ways). Closely related to this, I have found semiotic vocabulary helpful for testing the consistency of arguments in the scholarly literature, where lack of care in talking about "signs" and "symbols" can often be easily remedied in the margins. Over the forty years I have been thinking about Peirce, I have internalized the sign classes so that, using just their numerical position, I can make efficient mental calculations about semiotic phenomena—calculations that are almost always premature. In teaching (and in some academic writing), I experiment by simply removing the terminological scaffolding and present research results as if my thinking was nonsemiotic. And, finally, I have found the ten classes of signs to function as a maximal etic grid that, when imposed on ethnographic material, suggests missing empirical possibilities.

Peirce frequently explained semiosis as a dialogic conversation, ideally an internal dialogue with the self from one moment to the next following principles of logical reasoning or among equally rational minds forming the scientific community. His apparent lack of attention to contested or ambiguous conversations characteristic of normal social interaction and to the shifting interpretive perspectives on cultural products across temporal or historical boundaries does not necessarily imply that aspects of the Peircean model are not useful for understanding the messy realm of social life.

Social analysis might usefully examine, for example, conflicting interpretations in terms of the semiotic reasoning behind the discourse of each participant. A claim based on some asserted factual or historical precedent might be trumped by a competing claim grounded on the assertion of an earlier precedent—thus both claim and counterclaim pursuing signs that are, say, dicent indexical sinsigns, with the differentiating dimension being an embodied qualisign of, say, age (extent of patina, for example). Contestants could, on the other hand, reinforce a counterclaim by making more subtle distinctions in sinsign status. One party might reinforce the claim that the evidential sign is actually a replica of an indexical legisign, while the opponent might counterclaim that the sign is indeed a replica but a replica of an iconic legisign, namely, an intentional forgery. Alternatively, one party to a legal conflict might base a defensive argument on the grounds that the opponent makes multiple, scatter-shot claims, each with semiotically distinguishable rationales, with the implication that none is especially confident. Note in this example the semiotic asymmetry in a legal proceeding wherein the defense is entitled to mount multiple possible grounds for reasonable doubt while the prosecution must advance a coherent theory of the case.

The Second Trichotomy (Icon-Index-Symbol), which Peirce himself declared to be the trichotomy he used most frequently, clearly has had the most impact for social analysis. This trichotomy has proved useful for scholars of ancient religious traditions to distinguish various kinds of representations of divinity. Halbertal (1998), for example, clarifies the nuances of Jewish theological arguments about idolatry in separating "similarity-based representations," such as cult-statues made from wood or stone, that are generally subject to the biblical prohibition against idols; "metonymic representations," such as cherubim and chariots, physically associated with and thereby indicative of divine presence; and "conventional representations" that describe the deity in linguistic metaphors that involve the mediation of an "idea." Two interesting theological moves engage this triple division: first, some theological rationalizations tend to transform the first, iconic, type into the second, indexical, type in order to deflect the charge of idolatry; second, other rationalizations argue that icons are really symbolic-conventional so whatever is permitted for language-based representations should also be permitted for images. The force of theological rationalizations can also be discovered in cases where these three basic sign divisions are undercut by the postulation of cross-cutting identities, as Janowitz shows in her analysis of Late Antique writers. When both Proclus and Pseudo-Dionysius say that "divine names are statues" (2002, 40), the theological point is to stress the nonarbitrariness (naturalness) of divine names, which resemble the essential iconism of statues as representational signs, which, in turn, implies that divine names manifest divine presence when uttered, just as statues do in ritual contexts.

The Second Trichotomy also informs several foundational texts by Silverstein, who draws on the "Peircean framework" (1985, 217) to distinguish two broad kinds of function in language, the pragmatic and the semantic, which roughly correspond to indexical and symbolic grounds of the Sign-to-Object relationship. The pragmatic(-indexical) function pertains to the meaningfulness of linguistic signs as they are connected to "ongoing usage in contexts of communication" (1985, 217), and the semantic(-symbolic) function labels the abstract context-free relations among senses, the regularity of which across uses constitutes the synchronic structure of language ("grammar"). Thus, again adhering closely to Peircean conceptualization, Silverstein quickly points out that, while semantic meaningfulness must be instantiated in spoken tokens of general types—resulting in contextually realized linguistic forms—the meaningfulness of these does not depend on indexical factors. Correlatively, linguistic signs functioning along the pragmatic plane, like their semantic counterparts, are legisigns in that spoken utterances are tokens of general types, even though their rule of use requires the calculation of parameters from their contextual realization. Additionally, Silverstein invokes the Third Trichotomy to distinguish dicent and rhematic types of referential functioning, noting that dicent or "true reference" presupposes the entity picked out without characterizing it in any way, which is the domain of rhematic or "attributive reference" (1985, 218). It is surely the case that Silverstein did not discover the distinctions between contextual and decontextual sign functioning and between definite and indefinite reference from an examination of Peirce's writings. But, having aligned linguistic functioning with semiotic distinctions, Silverstein's analysis suggests several critical advances. First, in stressing the plurifunctionality of linguistic signs, Silverstein provides an empirical challenge to the interpretation of Peirce that insists that different sign functions must correspond to distinct signs. Second, Silverstein's conceptualization of metapragmatics as encompassing metasemantics might be evidence of referential upshifting, since a pragmatic object is, technically, lower ranking than a semantic object.

Process and Complexity

Peirce's careful attention to the processual dimension of semiosis immediately raises hope for useful collaboration with several approaches in the social sciences, including discourse-based linguistic anthropology, processual and historical archaeology, and dramatistic models of cultural production. Many scholars have come to see Peirce's semiotics as a much-needed corrective to structuralism, where real-time events (exchange, for example) and the linearity of discourse (myth-telling, for example) are rephrased in terms of synchronic oppositions. This hope is, however, mitigated by several factors: first, the chain-like sequentiality of interpretants is constrained by semiosis's fundamental purpose, which is to better represent the object, or to put it in another way, to better transmit the object's determination through the chain of signs; and second, Peirce's idea that scientific knowledge is a constantly (if slowly) shifting representation is a statement about scientists and not about the nature of the laws of physics; and third, the Final Interpretant (at least in Peirce's late writings) is a nonsemiotic habit of action.[3]

So the question that arises is this: Are there any other aspects of Peirce's semiotics, the organization of the trichotomies, for instance, that might still save the day? Given the idea that Symbols are the most "developed" kind of signs (discussed in more detail below), is there a tendency for sociocultural phenomena to follow the upward numbering of the sign classes, as in accounts of the history of money that trace a path of increasing abstraction from barter to cowrie shells to gold coins to paper money to credit cards to modern financial derivatives, or as in evolutionary accounts (Henry Maine, for example) of social relations from the Secondness of status to the Thirdness of contract or from truthful reference to legal fictions? Linear projection of the sign classes—a kind of semiotic bootstrapping—has been enormously suggestive—for example, in Deacon's (1997) account of the acquisition of the human capacity for sign use in the evolution of the human brain, and in Silverstein's (1985) reconceptualization of the acquisition of language functioning in ontogenesis in terms of the Peircean sign classes. And scholars in many disciplines have documented historical shifts toward symbolization in cultural forms of many types, such as Monelle's (1991, 102) description of the "fading" awareness of the iconic motivation of musical signs, leading to the subsequent imputation of full conventionality. But every example of conventionalization seems to be countered by equally telling examples of processes working in the opposite direction. Irvine and Gal (2000) use the label "rhematization" to describe a semiotic process by which linguistic signs that once functioned as social indexes are reinterpreted in terms of iconic essentialism, which are in turn understood as natural rather than historical facts. This kind of "naturalization" has been noticed by scholars across the disciplines, perhaps most famously by

Roland Barthes and Pierre Bourdieu. There are even situations in which it seems that conventionalizers and naturalizers engage in a direct semiotic confrontation—the bottom line perhaps being that one who manipulates or regiments the flow of interpretants thereby indexes social power or cultural capital.

At first glance there might be particular benefit in looking at Peirce's account of the embedded, combinatorial, and hierarchical complexity of sign classes as an indirect or approximate model for studying the complexity of cultural products and events. Peirce uses a variety of terms, such as "perfect," "genuine," and "complete," that, together, support the view that sign classes form a ranked hierarchy. At the most general level, Peirce describes the "perfect sign" as one that does its job of transmitting qualities of the Object to the Interpretant in such a way that, first, the determination of the Interpretant by the Sign approaches the determination that might have been caused directly by the Object itself; second, that the Sign provides no other sort of determination that would be unnecessary and intrusive evidence of the Sign's own qualities; and third, that the perfect Sign never ceases to be acted upon by its determining object, which "brings it fresh energy" (*EP* 2 [1906], 391).

A perfect sign is, thus, a transparent sign (Parmentier 1985a). Peirce uses the word "perfect" in a somewhat related sense when he describes the shout of "hi!" to alert someone of imminent danger as a "somewhat more perfect kind" of index, relative to someone's gazing upward to look at something as a sign causing others to look up also (c. 1902, *MS* 599, 41). Second, Peirce establishes subclasses of signs by the degree of degeneracy in relation to the "genuine" subclass (*EP* 2 [1903], 162)—the concept of *degeneracy* is borrowed from the geometry of conic sections. "Taking any class in whose essential idea the predominant element is Thirdness, or Representation, the self-development of that essential idea . . . results in a trichotomy giving rise to three subclasses, or genera, involving a relatively genuine thirdness; a relatively reactional thirdness or thirdness of the lesser degree of degeneracy; and a relatively qualitative thirdness or thirdness of the last degeneracy" (*EP* 2 [1903], 162).

Higher-numbered sign classes have more possible degenerate subclasses, though any sign class can be genuine if it fulfills its proper semiotic function without falling to a lower-numbered subclass. Third, Peirce uses the word "complete" to describe signs (symbols, for example) that are completely semiotic in the sense that they would not have the properties they have without their being signs, and none of the properties they do have are dependent on the objects they might stand for. Note that the icon, which in another sense of the word is complete in itself, is said to not be a "complete sign" (c. 1903, *MS* 7, 14). Fourth, a sign class could be considered complex to the degree that it is defined by the intersection of the Thirdness of each of its trichotomies; thus, the Argument is a (triadic) Symbol which is a (triadic) Legisign which determines its Interpretant to be a Symbol.

Fifth, sign classes differ in their inherent degree of definiteness. Although some scholars have insisted that the numbering of the ten classes of signs in the Three Trichotomies should not be viewed as a hierarchical ranking, Peirce does note that the Argument (position 10) is a sign that maximally indicates the Interpretant it is intended to determine (*EP* 2 [1904], 307); that is, it leaves as little as possible to the vagaries of interpretation.

Now the phrase "culturally complex" could mean at least a couple of things: (*a*) a sign production that, either through historical accretion or artistic intention, is polyvalent—perhaps appealing to multiple sensory modes in the sense that a Wagnerian opera is more complex than a stop sign; (*b*) a sign production being subject to multiple conflicting interpretations, as is Shakespeare's *Hamlet* in comparison to a Post-It shopping reminder; (*c*) a sign production can be complex in the sense of being constructed of many parts, each of which has distinctive semiotic properties but with the totality exhibiting organizational properties not found in the component parts, as when an archaeologist speaks of an ancient city as a site complex; (*d*) semiotic phenomena that can be multifactorially complex in the sense of being the product of several interacting factors, such that it is difficult to line up particular determinations with particular semiotic qualities; and (*e*) cultural signs that are multifunctional, such as the utterance of a second person personal pronoun in a linguistic system in which this particular sign also marks the gender of the speaker as well as the social status of the hearer and, further, the utterance betrays a regional accent and the distinctive creaky voice of an elderly speaker, thus engaging semantic referentiality, referential indexicality, and nonreferential indexicality in the utterance of a single linguistic form.

Lining up these two roughly sketched lists reveals an almost total disjunction between Peircean semiotic complexity and cultural complexity. Indeed, it seems to me that Peirce's increasingly fanatical effort to expand the complexity of his trichotomies, culminating in the frenzied drafts and letters from 1908 to 1910, does not offer a proportional degree of direct assistance for the work of social analysis. In fact, the almost fractal proliferation of sign classes is intended to provide more precise delimitation of *single* signs by multiplying the number of relevant classificatory divisions. Cultural complexity, in the five senses mentioned above, would be for Peirce a nightmare requiring careful acts of "precission" (*EP* 2, 270) to impose order. But here it becomes crucial to distinguish Peirce's analyses (whether accomplished, hinted at, or anticipated) of semiotic phenomena and a social scientist's use of Peircean tools for the purpose of social analysis. To be sure, Peirce had some remarkable and path-breaking things to say about, for example, comparative grammar, scientific diagrams, and technologically mediated signs such as photography; but his analyses in all of these three areas are merely "valuable suggestions" that "illustrate" logical doctrines (*MS* 693, 6; 1910, *MS* 654, 4).

In a sense, then, all of Peirce's talk about empirical/ethnographic signs is designed to document semiotic evidence for the validity of the three phanero-scopic categories (First, Second, Third) and not to explain "psychological facts" or social realities (*EP* 2 [1904], 309). "[Modern psychology] can afford no aid whatever in laying the foundation of a sane philosophy of reasoning, albeit it has been and can still be of the most precious service in planning and executing the observations on which the reasonings depend and from which they spring" (*EP* 2 [1913], 471). Similarly, Peirce was especially careful to emphasize the danger in trying to generalize from linguistic facts to logical truths. For instance, he pointed out the almost complete disjunction between the role of common nouns in the grammars of the world's languages and the character of the propositional subject in logic (*CP* 2.354); only in ancient Egyptian does he find a similarity between psychological processes and logical forms. Even if there should be some potentially significant experiential regularity relevant to sign functioning, this would not be decisive for semiotic classification. "Let it be repeated that all the terms of the division must be strictly relevant to logic, and that consequently all accidents of experience, however universal, must be excluded. The result of this rule will necessarily be that the new concept of a 'sign' will be defined ex-clusively by the forms of its logical relationships" (*EP* 2 [1906], 389). The Peircean trichotomies, thus, can be seen to be themselves Interpretants of these pieces of semiotic evidence, all pointing to the ultimate phaneroscopic Object—the real-ity of Thirds.

Extensions

Having clarified that using Peircean tools is substantially different from engaging Peirce philosophically, a further option presents itself, namely, to use these tools for purposes that might run counter to strict interpretations of Peirce's writings. That Peirce constantly refined the details of his trichotomies and consistently warned against premature closure should not lead to the conclusion that the core principles behind the classification of signs are not carefully honed. On the other hand, social scientists should entertain no illusion that their creative extensions of Peircean tools will have any positive impact on the philosophical issues at stake. Several of these less than orthodox extensions will be discussed below.

In recent years I have been studying images of divinity from a comparative semiotic perspective. What is particular interesting to me is the "presencing ef-fect" whereby some image, statue, or icon is thought to bring into possible human experience power that is otherwise transcendent, invisible, or hidden. Now one of the quickest ways for a Sign to bring its Object into a specified spatiotemporal context is through creative indexicality—even better is through dicent indexical-ity. But, as the paired cases discussed below will show, dicent indexicality as a classification of sinsigns needs to be supplemented by metasemiotic ideologies of replication that stress the indexical relationship between sign type and sign token when the image becomes subject to widespread copying. In each of the two examples, one from Byzantium and one from medieval France, these two kinds of indexicality ride alongside each other in interestingly different ways.

In an only implicitly semiotic discussion of medieval Byzantium, Kessler (2000) argues that since the images carved onto a seal matrix or a coin die are reversed, they are actually unreadable, and so the resulting impressed images carry the obvious connotation of visibility. Painted images, similarly, achieve visibility when the sketched outlines are colored in. The most important sacred image is the Holy Face of Edessa, which Kessler calls a "relic-icon."[4] Even the distinction between the perfectly mundane handkerchief (thus the icon's later name, Mandylion, from the Arabic word for *towel*) upon which the Christ image was fixed and the divine prototype supported a metaphorical association of relic-images and the Incarnation, which similarly involves the miraculous conjuncture of the divine and the human. Against the iconoclasts (opponents of icons), iconophiles (advocates of icons) needed to carefully distinguish the divine image from the base materiality that received it; and both iconoclasts and iconophiles needed to distinguish their positions from pagan idolatry, which they claimed did not involve any truthful prototype at all. Multiplying the "original" image of the Holy Face certainly encouraged the separation between image and matter but also opened up the possibility of rejuvenating the image-material combination as embodying or presenting divine power. But replication could easily imply a cheapening of this power and a potential severing of the relic quality (dicent sinsign) from the icon quality (replica of an iconic legisign). Kessler shows that the solution to the tension between the "breadth" of the sign (its wide distribution) and the "depth" of the sign (the guarantee of divine presence)—these terms are used here metaphorically—is threefold. First, for the Byzantines the mechanical reproduction of copies equated the relative distance between prototype and all copied images; second, they creatively asserted the power of copies by treating them to the full ritual (liturgical, processual) attitude; and, third, displaying multiple copies alongside a purported archetype restated the indexicality characteristic of relics. And now even copies showing clear traces of artistic workmanship do not threaten the "protected" archetype.

> Mortal eyes contemplated the sacred Mandylion only in the replicas that differed from it in manufacture, medium, and size. In turn, these mere material images made by men postulated the ineffable source. Providing often "unpredictable artists" with an opportunity to apply their individual skills in configuring the invisible archetype in vivid, real forms, copies protected the Mandylion's essential inapprehensibility. Put another way, to the extent that the originary image was not invested in any *particular* realization, the issue of copying does not really arise; all copies are also authentic origins. (Kessler 2000, 87)

The alignment of theologically salient metaphors of replication, including the creation of humans in God's image, the incarnational imprinting of the Word into human flesh, and the transformation of the eucharistic elements, is even clearer in medieval Western Christianity, constituted as an "economy of the image" that did not face the challenge of iconoclasm (Bedos-Rezak 2006, 53). Perhaps because of this, Latin writers were free to advance arguments about the immanence, emanation, or participation of the divine prototype in images of various sorts in such a way that the distinction between experienced sign (*signum*) and signified truth (*res*) is not thereby blurred. Key to these arguments in the twelfth century, Bedos-Rezak shows, is the widespread application of the metasemiotic metaphor of sealing, with the triple distinction of the substance of the matrix, the matrix image (*sigillum*), and the waxen imprint (*imago*), corresponding to God, Christ, and the human soul. One way an "essentialist" relationship among these components is maintained is by noting evidence for unavoidable indexicality, as in the direct physical "filiation" between model and image, like the traces left in the imprint by the matrix. But to avoid any misunderstanding, royal seals included bodily marks and attached explanatory textual materials. Bedos-Rezak suggests that, by the thirteenth century, the dominance of the theological interpretation of sealing metaphors declined, while the use of replicated seals actually increased, leaving writers with a challenge to rationalize the authority and authenticity of seals by shifting from their indexical grounding to their "conventionality"; that is, copies that identically replicated the model were viewed as generated tokens of a general type (i.e., as rhematic indexical legisigns). "Seal images, bound by and meaningful through conventions of similitude, formed a referential system in which one image referred primarily to another. Here again, reference to an origin and to an originator was obscured. Rather, cultural templates were highlighted as generative models, and each use of a conventional and replicated image instantiated these templates as both natural and normative" (Bedos-Rezak 2006, 55).[5] The acceleration of mechanical reproducibility in these two cases had contrasting implications, especially given that the semiotic object in the Byzantine East was divinity while the semiotic objects in prescholastic France were civil or religious authorities. But both holy icons and politico-religious seals are replicas of indexical legisigns, with the difference being that the East came to stress the indexical dimension and the West the legisign aspect.

A second case study of an extended application of the Three Trichotomies is Preucel's effort to apply the full panoply of sign classes to archaeological situations where evidence of Interpretants must be reconstituted from surviving material signs. In many cases archaeology is hampered, in my view, by the obvious fact that the analyst is not present at the moment of the creation of the material artifact (though production processes can often be observed either in laboratory simulation or through ethnographic analogy) or at the original moment of interpretation, that is, when the artifact is first put into play in social life. And the fact that an artifact has survived through time is itself a mixed blessing— first, since it is always difficult to know the import of that survival, which could be entirely contingent on the result of some positive preservational intention, and, second, since the flow of time can alter the contextualization of the artifact, which might *now* be cospatial with other objects (natural or human-made) from multiple distinct time periods and might have been dislocated (again, either randomly or systematically) in ways that violate the relative temporality of stratigraphy. This double distantiation implies that the archaeologist faces an uphill battle on two semiotic fronts, corresponding to the two correlates of the Peircean Sign—between the Sign and the Interpretant (the distantiation of the analyst) and between the Sign and the Object (the distantiation of the artifact); or, to put it another way, between the nonexistence of evidence for local interpretive ideologies and the relative noninterpretability of indexical regularities.

Preucel valiantly attempts to turn both of these methodological problems to his advantage by *relocating* them back into the archaeological record. First, he argues that the persistence of material objects through time is not lost on their original creators and interpreters: "Material signs, by virtue of their material qualities and associations, have the potential to *fix* meanings and create a sense of stability and timelessness" (2006, 258, emphasis added)—thus making the reasonable assumption that past peoples project ideological discourse *from* selected materially embodied qualisigns. Second, he observes that changing interpretive contexts can alter the meaning of material signs, which, once distantiated (in both senses noted above), cannot continue to regiment themselves: "The openness of signs to alternative interpretations perpetually threatens to *destabilize* existing semiotic ideologies" (2006, 258, emphasis added; the sequence of these two quotations has been reversed).

Preucel's analysis of pottery and architecture before, during, and after the Pueblo Revolt of 1680 suggests that revitalization is a semiotically complex stance that combines a future-looking, creative response to current threatening circumstances with a desire to anchor that response in traditional cultural forms. Thus, the iconization of cosmologically salient images, values, and practices simultaneously indexes those cultural traditions as both present and relevant. For example, innovation in pottery design that replicates traditional motifs carries a supplementary meaning in this revolutionary context: a depicted war shield on a pot is open to interpretation as both a call to arms and an invocation of culturally specific powers (ancestral and spiritual, in this case) to guarantee success. And the replication of other pre-Spanish motifs indirectly indexes the temporal disjunction between pre- and post-contact worlds. Similarly, the construction of new dual-plaza pueblos on outlying mesas presupposes an iconic link to the mythological White House and creatively indexes the *difference* between this design and the layout mandated in Spanish-dominated villages as well as those layouts found in pueblos that did not join in the revolt. It is even possible that, taken as a *set* of "indexical icons," material signs generated in the context of the revolt might be interpreted by the Pueblos back then as a semiotic Argument, that is, as a constructed syllogism whose conclusion mandated military action: *in hoc signo vinces.*

Now the question remains whether Preucel's account would be possible in the absence of two things: textual depositions of captured individuals compelled by the Spanish and rich ethnographic analogies provided by contemporary Pueblo societies, which combine to make possible Preucel's counter-intuitive observation that traditional replication signals revolutionary intent. This in turn permits Preucel to generalize about the potential for a specifically Peircean approach to the archaeological record:

> Peirce's sign typology permits the discrimination of different sign modalities with reference to different interpretants. It allows important distinctions to be made between signs that mean something to the analyst (such as a sequence of pottery styles to represent a historical process—a symbolic argument), signs that mean something unique to a past actor (such as a particular pottery design used to represent a social affiliation—a dicent indexical sinsign), and signs that mean something that is widely shared within a past community of actors (such as a particular pottery design used to refer to a specific ideology— a rhematic indexical sinsign). It distinguishes between laws and generalities (legisigns) and specific instances of their realization (sinsigns). In some cases, the meanings of the analyst and past actor may converge, but this is not necessary and the degree to which this is the case will depend on the goals of research. (2006, 250)[6]

This appeal to the full use of the sign classes derived from the Three Trichotomies raises an important question: Is it a positive contribution to have found, within a single discipline's approach to its data, instances of all of the ten classes of signs? (The same question could fruitfully be raised in musicology and art history.) I would hazard the following opinion: that all 10 classes have been located is not in itself significant, but that the effort to locate them might indirectly clarify some important issues, especially including identifying the "syntax" of varieties of sinsigns and distinguishing actors' and analysts' perspectives, makes the effort at least useful.

Lessons

Are there lessons to be learned from this highly selective review of applications and extensions of the Three Trichotomies? One would certainly be the discouragement of "butterfly collecting" of signs, that is, the unsystematic assignment of some cultural phenomenon to some particular sign class without further analysis of other important issues flowing from the relational, functional, and contextual character of the trichotomies mentioned above. Analyses in terms of what Tarasti (2002, 173) calls "intermingled sign classes" are allowed—such as his "symbolic-indexical improvisation"—even though they technically violate the design of the Three Trichotomies, *but only* if that violation is recognized as itself significant. There is a difference between an iconic index and an indexical icon, since only the first is typologically expected—and usually uninteresting. Next, it is important to keep in mind the difference between ethnosemiotic typologies and the Peircean sign classes, since it is the disjunction rather than the conjunction between these two perspectives that is informative. Another lesson might be expressed as: take only what you need, that is, avoid building an elaborate Peircean (or other) semiotic model only to find a high percentage of the analytical tools left in the toolbox.[7] And, finally, semiotically informed social science research must always be careful not to assume that similar configurations of cultural signs from disparate times and places have some consistent cultural meaning.

Notes

This paper was first presented to the Michigan Semiotics Work Group at the University of Michigan (May 5, 2007). It was originally published as "Troubles with Trichotomies: Reflections on the Utility of Peirce's Sign Trichotomies for Social Analysis," *Semiotica* 177 (2009): 139–56.

1. Peirce's explorations of trichotomies beyond the Three Trichotomies have had limited impact on scholars in the social sciences, perhaps because many of these writings remain unpublished.

2. Short (2004, 235) makes a clear argument that, strictly speaking, one thing may be many different signs "relative to different bases of interpretation and relative to different purposes. A foxy odor is a sign of danger to the rabbit but of dinner to the cougar." According to this reading of Peirce, there can be no duplex signs or shifters, but rather, a single substrate has distinct referential and indexical signs. I am not sure what difference this makes for social science research.

3. Neither of these observations denies the important claim that the trichotomies of interpretants "refer to stages of semeiosis" (Short 2004, 235).

4. According to legend, this icon was created when Christ pressed his face into a piece of cloth. It is the most prominent member of a class of images labeled "not made by human hands," a class that includes, for some, the Shroud of Turin.

5. From the evidence Bedos-Rezak provides, it is clear that the term *conventionality* here refers to the status of being a legisign and is not meant to invoke the Peircean definition of a Symbol as a conventional sign. It also resonates with the notion of *convention-N* (for normative) in Parmentier 1994a, 107.

6. This programmatic conclusion echoes Parmentier's earlier recommendation of a Peircean approach to the archaeological record first published in 1994 (corrected in 1997b):

A pottery style, for example, rarely functions symbolically; rather, style is an indexical legisign embodying an iconic legisign, and a particular pot in that style is an indexical sinsign, a 'replica,' in fact, since it is generated from a template which it (trivially) indexes. To be sure, it is important to keep in mind that style frequently appears as a matter of indexical signs, but the observation that stylized pottery or carved stone images can be employed by their users to mark group affiliation or to set boundaries or can be employed to signal that the makers/users follow a pattern promulgated by a dominant regional center or 'horizon' corresponds to Peirce's distinction between a 'dicent' indexical sinsign . . . and a 'rhematic' indexical sinsign. . . . In some cases the producers' or users' intention might even be the same as the archaeologists, although more usually these will diverge. Pottery interpreted by an archaeologist using, for example, neutron activation analysis or magnetic intensity dating in order to establish absolute or relative chronology or spatial origination based on an analysis of the materiality of pot *fragments* is functioning as a dicent indexical legisign . . . whereas a pottery style studied by an archaeologist as a sign of group identity or cultural influence functions as a rhematic indexical legisign. A *sequence* of pottery styles would function as a symbolic 'argument,' that is a general regularity representing its object (which is itself a generality) by convention interpreted as a convention, because the archaeologist is using a diachronic pattern of pottery types to construct a representation of [the regularity of] an historical process. (1997b, 50–51, brackets added)

7. Daniel's (1987) detailed enumeration of the ten sign classes, which are not then fully exploited in the subsequent pioneering ethnography, does not fall under this stricture, since his clearly announced intent is for his listing to suggest possible tools for others.

6   Semiotic Degeneracy of Social Life: Prolegomenon to a Human Science of Semiosis

Prelude

Twenty years ago, Ketner (1993) published a groundbreaking paper proposing "semiotic" as a cure for what ails "social science" and "literature" (by which he means literary studies, not the artistic production of literature). His key point is as follows:

> We must analyze triadic relations by means of triadic relations. In particular, if there is a matter about which we lack understanding, we can use a set of triadic relations we already comprehend reasonably well to model the relations in the areas of relative ignorance. Once such a model is constructed, we can study or manifest it to discover new things about the relations within it, hoping that the newly discovered relations there will be analogous with undetected relations in the area modeled. If they are analogous, then we will have increased our understanding of the area modeled. Stated in a very abstract fashion, that is Peirce's general method of diagrammatic thought. (Ketner 1993, 51)

That is, social science and humanities disciplines cannot be based on the reduction of activities such as "understanding, interpretation, promising, narrating, or inheriting" to dyadic or mechanical models based on causal or functional relations. The "cure" Ketner proposes is the application of Peirce's ideas about triadic relations or thirdness as the best model for these essentially human processes, models which are themselves "formulations of abstractive observation and reasoning of the truths which *must* hold good of all signs used by scientific intelligence" (Peirce, quoted in Ketner 1993, 52, emphasis in original). The hypothesis of the present paper is that Ketner's semiotic cure can too easily become itself a dangerous virus and that it is time to reopen the question, *not* whether human thought and action—which is embedded in social institutions and cultural meanings—can be studied as causal dyads, but rather of the claim that Peirce's semiotic *method* is the royal road to reveal the "human science of semiosis."

This paper explores three interrelated ambiguities or perplexities in Peirce's ideas about semiotic modeling: first, an apparent confusion in the definition of the sign as something that determines further signs or as something that produces replicas of itself; second, an apparent contradiction in the source of what Peirce calls "degeneracy" in certain sign relations; and third, an apparent puzzle about the role of logically necessary modeling systems in guiding the path of experimental (quantitative and probabilistic) hypothesis testing. Seeing—in some detail—how each of these "apparent" problems get resolved will be key to comparing Peirce's method of semiotic "exemplification" to possible alternatives, the details of which lie beyond the scope of this prolegomenal paper.

Vectors of Exemplification

The properties of Peircean sign trichotomies are a logical consequence of the scientific need to construct systems of representation consisting of conventional signs that allow the maximally efficient *discovery* of scientific truths and the maximally perfect *diffusion* of those truths within a scientific community. The properties and operation of such conventional systems of representation, whether some graphic form of diagrammatization (such as Peirce's Existential Graphs) or some other semiotic construct (geometrical figures or algebraic notations), must not only be consistent with his foundational ontological categories of First (quality, feeling), Second (relation, reaction), and Third (representation, mediation), as everything must, but should also ideally be *exemplary* in revealing the subtle implicational interactions of manifestations of these very ontological categories. To achieve these three goals of discovery, diffusion, and exemplification, the system of representation must, to the degree possible, facilitate the "efficient"[1] determination[2] of subsequent signs (the "interpretants") by preventing any hindrance or blurring due to its own inherent properties (principally: inconsistency, incompleteness, and inefficiency), since without such "transparency" (Parmentier 1985a) the signs that mediate represented objects and determined interpretants will not be able to determine the latter to perfectly represent the way (the "ground") signs stand for the former.[3]

But these artificially created systems of representation need not manifest the properties that characterize either existing systems of signs created for discovery/diffusion purposes *other than* the progress of scientific knowledge (human languages, for example) or to facilitate the untutored psychological processes of individual human cognition (the "everyday reasonings" [Peirce *NEM* 4, 185] found in habitual or traditional thinking). Of course, the act of placing human languages and psychological processes up against the model of logical systems of representation can reveal interesting regularities of nontransparency, where distinct types of culturally relative "semiotic mediation" (Parmentier 1985b) are at work, as well as telling failures of self-referentiality, where interpretations actually mask their own logical impropriety.

What, then, would be the point of the scientific study of *precisely* these zones of nontransparent signs (that is, culture) and improper logic (that is, human cognition)? What would be the point, that is, of creating some logically rigorous system of representation to represent less-than-perfect examples of semiosis? To study by means of semiotic modeling, say, the varieties of syntax in human languages, or the ritual sequence of magical practices, or the historical growth of legal fictions by means of the Peircean trichotomies would, at the very least, violate the principle of exemplification noted above, given the disjunction between the apparatus of scientific reasoning and the subject matter under investigation.[4] On the positive side, however, such an effort might uncover patterns of parallel "degeneracy" (discussed below) if it were found that the ranked relationship *between* transparent systems of representation and nontransparent systems of representation resembles the ranked relationship between "genuine" and "degenerate" signs *within* transparent systems of representation.

And what, additionally, might be an alternative to this asymmetrical modeling exercise? One could see, for instance, the hermeneutical circle of Paul Ricoeur and Clifford Geertz as a good example of such an alternative, in its rejection of the imposition of all "positivist" systems of representation in favor of acts of interpretation by analysts that exactly mirror the all-too-human semiotic forms and processes being studied; that is, in which the "model of the text" provides a weak claim for exemplification: we make texts about their texts (Ricoeur 1971) and we make interpretations looking over the shoulder at their making interpretations (Geertz 1973). The Peircean model of exemplification can also be clearly contrasted with "ordinary language" approaches to philosophical questions. Considering the word *because*, Peirce warned against paying any attention to "how men feel" or "how they think," even to the etymology of the word; rather, the significance of *because* is its logical function, and that can be discovered (that is, exemplified) by contemplating an "ideal construction" that will hold in every possible world (*W* 6, 355).

It might then be asked (to attempt a Peircean pun), is there a "third way," that is, a way between using scientific systems of representation to model social life, the properties of which undoubtedly fall short of perfect semiosis, on the one hand, and matching the vagaries of nontransparency with a model of interpretation just as messy, on the other hand? It can be argued that possible third ways would require the *reversal* of the vector of exemplification, so that the explanatory metalanguage reflects, in some respects, the properties of its represented objects (namely, social life) and not the other way around, and that this reversal requires a research method roughly equivalent, for example, to the analysis of "indexical orders" (Silverstein 2003) in which both the mode of analysis and the social processes being studied are subject to the same unavoidable pragmatic, that is, indexical, constraints.

Reasoning with Signs

A common misunderstanding of Peirce is to assume that he views signs primarily as the representations *of* thoughts or cognitions. His proposal is a bit more radical than this since he believed that cognitions *are* signs, namely, the signs of those cognitions that were present to the mind just before that stand for the same object: "A thought is a special variety of sign. All thinking is necessarily a sort of dialogue, an appeal from the momentary self to the better considered self of the immediate and general future" (Hardwick, ed. 1977, 195). So it might be possible, given high mental powers, to come to understand how the flow of cognitions in the mind is patterned by just thinking carefully about that flow. But Peirce recommends that mere mortals can carry out this investigation more conveniently by examining "external signs," as long as we keep in mind, first, the *absolute identity* of internal and external flows and, second, the paradoxical fact that the external signs that best exemplify the operation of the rational mind are ones created *just for that purpose* by rational minds:

> These principles might be evolved from a study of the mind and of thought, but they can also be reached by the simple consideration of any signs we please. Now the latter mode of studying them is much the easiest, because the examination of external signs is one of the most simple researches which we can undertake, and least susceptible of error, while the study of the mind is one of the most difficult and doubtful. We shall therefore proceed in the remainder of the work to *compare signs*, and generalize our results. (*W* 3, 83, emphasis added)

So in thinking about the modeling function of Peircean conventional systems of representation[5] it is important to distinguish the various levels at work: (*a*) *signs* themselves can range from tiny to huge, for example, a splash of color on a painting, an abrupt sound that commands our attention, a proposition playing some role in a logical syllogism, or the theory of natural selection; (*b*) the three (or more) *trichotomies* that figure in much of Peirce's mature speculation on signs outline a complex typological architecture of signs; and (*c*) the principles of *reasoning* best suited for scientific work include necessary deduction, experimental induction, and hypothesis-forming abduction or retroduction.[6] Standing apart from all these three semiotic levels of sign, trichotomy, and reasoning is *reality* itself, which Peirce considered as that which is as it is *apart from* all of our representations, though reality itself can be divided into the triad of First, Second, and Third.

But abstract reasoning that uses signs as constituents of conventional systems of representation and that follows a logically necessary path does not, by itself, tell us anything about the "truth" of the propositions it models—the truth of a scientific formula consisting in its really being a sign of the objects involved (*NEM* 4, 253).[7] So in this sense, Peirce's semiotic model is formal or normative rather than substantive. To know the rule of interpretation for weathervanes, for instance, that they face in the direction in which the wind blows and are turned by that same wind, does not tell us which way the wind is blowing today. To heighten the sensitivity of researchers to the need for methodological delicacy in distinguishing "regular" sinsigns as existent Seconds that could possibly function as signs from replicas of legisigns whose very being depends on a general rule that governs their experienceable instantiation does not *in itself* provide a surefire guideline for separating the two subtypes in an archaeological test pit. In Peirce's words:

> Logic is a science little removed from pure mathematics. It cannot be said to make any positive phenomena known, although it takes account and rests upon phenomena of daily and hourly experience, which it so analyzes as to bring out recondite truths about them. . . . The logician has to be recurring to reexamination of the phenomena all along the course of his investigation. But logic is all but as far remote from psychology as is pure mathematics. Logic is the study of the essential nature of signs. (*NEM* 4, 248)

In constructing and manipulating conventional systems of signs, the laboratory scientist and the mathematician/logician can both be said to engage in experiments that produce new knowledge. The "hard sciences" such as chemistry and physics are, at heart, no different from logic or mathematics in that all are "experimental," the difference being that logic experiments on some "array of signs" designed to represent the premises of arguments (*NEM* 4, 276):

> Every inquiry is carried on by means of experimentation, External or Internal. The chemist mounts an apparatus of flasks and tubes, places certain substances in the flasks, lights a Bunsen burner underneath, and watches to see what the result will be. The mathematician constructs a geometrical diagram according to a certain prescription and then looks out for new relations, not thought of in the construction. The chemist relies on the laws of nature; the mathematician on the associations and laws of the mind. (*W* 5, 381)

Peirce thought that one of the distinct benefits of experimental reasoning by signs as part of coherent systems of representation is that the deliberately conscious framing of problems enables us to overcome the blindness with which we tend to regard regular, repeated occurrences of everyday life—the beat of our own heart, the sound of our own voice, the style of our own writing: "What is the most obvious characteristic of the universe we live in puzzles me to answer otherwise than by rote" (*W* 6, 383).

I suspect that at some deep level, Peirce thought that his two commonest definitions of the essential "being" of a sign are identical despite their apparent difference. The first definition is that the proper "being" of a sign is to generate replicas of itself, that is, to clothe general Thirds in some experienceable Seconds (sinsigns "of a peculiar kind" [*CP* 2.256]), all of which, for the purposes at hand, are equivalent:[8] "You can write down the word 'star' but that does not make you creator of the word" (*CP* 2.301). The second definition is that the proper "being" of a sign is to determine or cause an interpretant, this interpretant being in fact a further determination of itself.[9] How can the generation of replicas and the determination of interpretants *both* be part of the definition of the sign or both be *equivalent* definitions of a sign? On the one hand, these definitions seem to involve radically different processes, since the replicas generated in the first definition are "*not signs*" to the same degree that their general templates are, while the interpreting signs in the second definition are *more complete* representations of the original sign. On the other hand, in addition to the fact that Peirce repeatedly stated these two definitions (suggesting that they functioned as replicas of each other and thus of some other even more general definitional sign), Peirce actually equates them in a passage written in 1903: "For it can be said, without dispute, that no sign ever acts as such without producing a *physical replica* or *interpretant sign*" (*EP* 2, 271, emphasis added). Now since Peirce is quite clear, in his writings on logic, that "or" means one thing or another thing *or both*, this sentence is inherently ambiguous as written, especially in light of the claim, just a few sentences later, that "A Sign is a Representamen with a *mental* Interpretant" (*EP* 2, 273, emphasis added). Another passage, also from 1903, even more strongly suggests that Peirce saw not only the power of replication (called here "repetition") to be consistent with the sign's power of determining interpretants, but also that the first *implies* the second:

> A representamen which should have a unique embodiment, incapable of repetition, would not be a representamen, but a part of the very fact represented. This repetitory character of the representamen involves as a consequence that it is essential to a representamen that it should contribute to the determination of another representamen distinct from itself. . . . Every conclusion from premisses [*sic*] is an instance in point; and what would be a representamen that was not capable of contributing to any ulterior conclusion? I call a representamen which is determined by another representamen an *interpretant* of the latter. (*EP* 2, 203, emphasis in original)

One possible route to resolving this (real or apparent) ambiguity about the sign would be to look to passages in which Peirce talked about the function of signs in the most general way, but this, alas, doesn't offer much help. While he insisted that all sorts of formal reasoning require the diagrammatic manipulation of signs ("diagrams" being mental images designed to aid the imagination [*NEM* 4, 219n]), the very being of signs is to generate replicas, the particular expressive realizations of which (whether lingual, graphic, gestural, or even silent thought) are of *no concern* to that same reasoning,[10] whereas the determination of more perfect interpretants is the *goal* of semiosis at the most general level. Now this telling ambiguity goes a long way to helping explain another one, at least for the modern reader of Peirce. When we expect him to say that the key thing is for a sign to be a representing power, he actually says the reverse: that the key thing is for a sign to "be represented." Thus, being a representation and being capable of being represented are equivalent notions for Peirce (*CP* 8.269).

Having come up with an outline of the necessary properties of a system of representation adequate for logical reasoning, the analyst's next task is to place this template up against various kinds of physical or mental processes (abstract as well as concrete) to discover the degree to which they do or do not conform to the exemplar when considered as sign processes.[11] Peirce often uses the word "criticism" for this comparative act, especially in situations where the whole point of the effort is to advance, refine, or develop the signs under examination. "Here all must be voluntary, thoroughly conscious, based on critical reflection. Logic is wanted here to *pull inferences to pieces*, to show whether they be sound or not, to advise how they may be strengthened, to consider by what methods they ought to proceed" (*W* 5, 328, emphasis added). And in another passage, Peirce writes about drafting correspondence: "The critical attitude consists of reviewing the matter to see in what manner corrections shall be made. This is what one does when one reads over a letter one has written to see whether some unintended meaning is suggested. The criticism is always of a process, the process which led to the acceptance of the idea" (*NEM* 4, 41–42). In other instances he is content with taking note of the discrepancies uncovered, from the fallacies of philosophers to the inadequacies of human languages. Peirce does acknowledge that constant criticism is suspended in the "ordinary business of life" (*W* 5, 327) thanks to involuntary or autonomic biological processes and to habits no longer subject to continual voluntary, conscious, and critical reflection. Peirce devoted substantial energy to this effort to "pull inferences to pieces," both in his extensive reflections on the divisions of syllogistic reasoning and in his careful dissection of "genuine" and "degenerate" subdivisions of sign types.

Modeling Semiotic Degeneracy

It would be a serious abuse of what Peirce called the "ethics of terminology" to simply say that, in his semiotics, the class of "genuine" signs best models logical inferences and scientific law, while the category of "degenerate" signs models a residual class of incoherent, irrational, or incomplete sign-like phenomena of mental and social life. For one thing, the term "degenerate" has nothing to do with moral evaluation; it is merely a term Peirce borrowed from the geometry of conic sections to refer to figures whose mathematical properties are capable of being reduced to simpler figures.[12] Applied metaphorically to signs, the term refers to those signs whose constitution and operation, when carefully grasped, differ from the typological position they pretend to assume at first glance. At least, in this sense, they are less "genuine" signs in comparison to those signs whose proper functioning is consistent with their typological position. So in speaking of the degenerate signs of mental or social life, the word is doubly metaphorical.

An easy way to grasp the distinction between genuine and degenerate signs is to compare different readings of an instance of social interaction. In the first, Jack gives a cookie to Jill. There are clearly three things involved: Jack, Jill, and the cookie; but the meaning of the verb "give" demands that the event be understood as essentially triadic (and thus a Third) in that it is not possible to *reduce* a valid act of "giving" to a second reading of sequential dyadic acts: Jack's placing the cookie on the table and then Jill's picking up the cookie. Peirce calls this paired dyad an "accidental third" (*W* 5, 301) and gives a colorful example: "'How did I slay thy son?' asked the merchant, and the genie replied, 'When thou threwest away the date-stone, it smote my son, who was passing at the time, on the breast, and he died forthright'" (*W* 5, 301). To illustrate a second degree of degeneracy for three elements tempting us to regard them as Thirds, Peirce uses an example of comparison: Philadelphia lies between New York and Washington. Note that in this case of "comparative thirds" (*W* 5, 301), Philadelphia would continue to exist in the same place even if one or both of the other two cities burned down—their triadic relation being merely a mental synthesis of disparate facts. Just as in the case of the accidental Third, Jill could really eat the cookie, but it would not have been given to her by Jack—and if accused of stealing, Jill would need to *invent* a characterization of the event as gift-giving—a "transfer of the right of property" (*CP* 1.345)—when in fact it was nothing of the sort.

Peirce uses these kinds of illustrations of the two degrees of degeneracy in Thirds to clarify—by "comparing signs," as noted above—what would constitute a "genuine" Third. And his principal discovery is that, in both degrees of degeneracy, some incorrect mental operation is in play, namely, the creation of a "relation of reason" (*relatio rationis*). What is equally if not more interesting would be to ask: Why would these two triadic relations (two dyads and three separate terms) tempt us to regard them as triadic in the first place? Perhaps the urge to correct our modeling of some kinds of quasi-semiotic relations by comparing them to the exemplary template of "genuine" relations is the ultimate source of degeneracy!

Another example presents a telling contrast. Peirce presents an elaborate analysis of the degeneracy of indexes, that is, of signs that are in some spatial or temporal contiguity with what they stand for and that function primarily to alert the interpretant to be aware of this relation of secondness. This example needs to be contextualized (indexically!) in terms of a higher-level ranking according to which conventional signs (called "symbols") are genuine in necessarily engaging irreducible triadic relations (object, representamen, interpretant), while indexes and icons are degenerate to the first degree and second degree, respectively. So *within* the already-degenerate class of indexes, Peirce separates a genuine index (a man punches me in the face) from two varieties of degenerates:

> Degenerate secondness has two varieties, for a single object considered as second to itself is a degenerate second, and an object considered as second to another with which it has no real connection, so that were that other taken away it would still have those same characters which are implied in the relation, is also a degenerate second. Genuine secondness is dynamical connection; degenerate secondness is a relation of reason, as a mere resemblance. (*W* 6, 211)

What is important to note is that, just as in the first example of degenerate degrees of thirdness, the immediate cause of the degeneracy of indexes is the overactivity of a "relation of reason," that is, a relation that subsists between two facts only one of which would disappear if either of the other two vanished.

The perplexing problem—and the point of this section of the discussion—is that these two cases involving the imputation of relations of reason ("semiotic fictions" might be a good label for the pair [cf. *W* 1, 312]) differ from the gradation of symbols as genuine signs and indexes as degenerate signs of the first degree (and, to fill out the picture, of icons as degenerate in the second degree), because in the case of the symbol-index-icon gradation, the source of degeneracy lies in the absence rather than the presence of mental activity. Symbols, recall, are signs only because they are understood to be signs, that is, by virtue of the interpretant's furnishing a "ground" based on some conventional association between the representamen and the object. The reason that symbols offer the best chance of exemplifying genuine thirdness in the universe and in the functioning of the human mind is that, to the logical mind, they appear to maximally reveal the same "intelligibility" (*W* 6, 178). A symbol stands for what it represents both "necessarily," in that it would not exist apart from its representational function, and "accidentally," in that nothing in its inherent character makes it the sign it is; or, as Peirce puts it, a symbol derives the actuality of signification only from its interpretant (*NEM* 4, 261). So "relation of reason," distinct from "real relation," is for Peirce the surest indication of a maximally developed sign: "Now what is true by virtue of a relation of reason is representation, that is, of the nature of a sign" (*CP* 5.448n).

What can be made of the comparison of these three different cases and of the observation that mental activity can be the source of genuineness *and* also of degeneracy? It seems to me to reveal, once again, Peirce's insistent effort to place all sign processes up against perfect exemplars, specifically, against perfect exemplars at different grades of semiotic relation. For a sign to be an index is for two things to be in a real relation (*relatio realis*); to be a Third requires real, not imaginary, triadic interconnection; to be a symbol involves imputed mental association. To be sure, degenerate signs are extremely useful in ways that genuine signs (that is, conventional symbols) are not: the icon is "perfect" in respect to signification and the index is "perfect" in respect to denotation (*NEM* 4, 242), but failure to match—by whatever criteria—the designs of these exemplars is the surest way to degeneracy.

Peirce as a Quintessential Quant

In a personal letter written in 1901 to President Remsen of Johns Hopkins University, Peirce comments on the declining path of his own health and remarks that he expects to live for thirteen years (Fisch and Cope 1952, 294); he did in fact live exactly thirteen more years, dying as predicted in 1914—the ultimate "final interpretant" for a "quant."

It is obviously unfair to judge Peirce's contribution to what we would today call the "human sciences" (that is, a combination of social sciences and humanities), first, because many of the modern disciplines had not obtained their institutional or intellectual identities during his lifetime, and second, because Peirce's scientific training, research, and writing did not center on these nonquantitative fields. But the fact remains that Peirce did make systematic forays into fields such as history, psychology, theology, linguistics, economics, and literature and less systematic comments on anthropology, sociology, music, archaeology, and architecture. Taken together, these texts offer a sideways glance at his habitual mode of thinking, a view especially informative for readers (like the present author) unable to follow his technical writings about oscillating pendulums, Boolean algebra of relations, quincuncial map projection, and the speed of light through the ether. For a man of science who modestly claimed to be "desperately negligent" in "non-logical matters" (*NEM* 4, 57), Peirce actively transgressed disciplinary boundaries in proudly disclaiming on research projects that appear to him to demonstrate the universal applicability of his quantitative and logical skills: "For me . . . upon the first assault of the enemy, when pressed for the explanation of any fact, I lock myself up in my castle of impregnable logic and squirt out melted continuity upon the heads of my besiegers below" (quoted in Murphey 1961, 406). A brief sketch of several such projects will be sufficient (not statistically!) to illustrate Peirce's approach to the study of the "objects of human creation" (*NEM* 4, 57) and to test the notion that, for Peirce, logically constructed systems of representation are exemplary explanatory models.

In 1901 Peirce composed a paper titled "On the Logic of Drawing History from Ancient Documents" which criticizes several different views of philosophically inclined historians about the validity of historical testimony. On one view, for example, we should reject as untrue testimony that narrates events "in any degree unlikely" and also as untrue narratives the events of which are so highly probable that there is a strong likelihood of it all being invented (*EP* 2, 77). Peirce cut to the heart of this paradoxical stance: "They preserve a noble freedom in

manufacturing history to suit their subjective impressions" (*EP* 2, 77). More sophisticated are historians who try to decide questions of fact by weighing the
algebraic value of the subjective impressions of testimonies for and testimonies
against some matter. Peirce admits that, while there is something naturally appealing to this "theory of balancing likelihoods," its naturalness is no defense
against error: "There is no kind of fallacious reasoning to which mankind is liable
to which as much as that might not be said" (*EP* 2, 79). He then points out, more
substantively, that in most cases the separate testimonies for or against are not independent, for not only do testimonies on both sides usually conform for reasons
other than a "mere tendency to truth," but they both show a preference for recording marvelous instances in favor of routine events and a tendency for hypotheses
to agree with the "preconceived notions" of the persons believing them. Is there,
then, any hope of resolving conflicts in historical testimony? Peirce points out
that, in almost every case when archaeological excavations have actually tested
historical hypotheses (in Egypt, for example), the previous conclusions based on
the method of balancing testimony "were found to be more or less fundamentally wrong" (*EP* 2, 84).[13] So in this first example of disciplinary boundary crossing can be seen Peirce's insistence of the value of the abductive method against
pseudo-logical or pseudo-probabilistic efforts.[14]

In 1883–1884 during his brief tenure at Johns Hopkins University, Peirce
organized a group of students to study the psychology of "Great Men" as an
outside-of-class project. He prepared a detailed question-sheet and then divided
up the labor of consulting biographies in order to fill in information about their
ancestry, physical characteristics, work habits, productivity, and cultural mi-
lieu. In addition to these obviously relevant kinds of questions, he included less
obvious questions such as sleep habits, appreciation of contemporaries, use of
stimulants, cause of death, weather conditions during childhood, and tendency
to hallucinate. An initial list of one thousand names was whittled down to a more
manageable 288, and from this list the group selected every sixth name for careful
study. The students then assigned to each name their opinion on relative greatness using a scale of 1 to 6, derived from the scale astronomers use for describing
the apparent magnitude of stars. A perusal of the few tabulation sheets and rank-
ings by category that are published (*W* 5, 25–106) reveals quickly the messiness
of this pedagogical experiment, in the large amount of missing data and in the
noncomparability of the answers. But this was precisely what Peirce intended, as
he explained later in a draft introduction to a newspaper article about the project:

> I wished it to be a subject susceptible of mathematical treatment, since an in-
> ductive investigation so treated may throw abundant light on the proper logical
> procedure where mathematics is not available, while the converse can hardly
> be true. Yet there were several reasons for selecting a subject concerning which
> no exact observations could be made. Much more logical caution is requisite in

such a field; and it was desirable to explode the ordinary notions that mathematical treatment is of no advantage when observations are devoid of precision and that no scientific use can be made of very inexact observations. (*CP* 7.256)

A member of the group commented much later that nothing much came of the project, although Peirce himself continued to be fascinated with the ranking of brilliant men [sic] long after his teaching days.

A final example of Peirce's mode of thinking about nonscientific matters involves several independent lines of discussion which might suggest that he is a hidden historical sociologist. In his 1891 paper "Man's Glassy Essence," Peirce turned around an earlier aphorism, that a person is a "symbol involving a general idea," to claim that, due to the tendency of feelings to spread to organisms in intimate contact, "every general idea has the unified living feeling of a person" (*W* 8, 182). On this basis he speculates that crowds, religious congregations, and citizens sharing *esprit de corps* might be seen as "corporate" personalities and that these "greater persons" can have a powerful influence on individuals. The influence of social collectivities on individuals can also be seen in Peirce's habit of celebrating the thinking style of New England "Yankees," his own family stock. He repeats a joke, not entirely in jest, about a Frenchman, an Englishman, and a German assigned to write a book about the camel. The Frenchman makes minute measurements of a particular camel in the local zoo and writes up a "spiritual account" of the animal; the Englishman outfits a multiyear expedition to Arabia and writes a multivolume work consisting entirely of "undigested facts"; and the German retires to his study and produces a treatise on the "pure idea" of the camel (*W* 1, 455–56). Now Peirce objects to these specific characterizations of the three authors but *not* to this way of describing the intellectual tendencies of nations.

These discussions of corporate persons and regional character are not at all inconsistent with Peirce's well-known ideas about the collective nature of scientific investigation, arguments which posit the "community" of scientific researchers as the locus of the growth of knowledge, since it is this community that will reaffirm, "at a time sufficiently future" (*CP* 5.311), its conception of the real. And that these conceptions *change* is what distinguishes scientific knowledge from other varieties of human opinion. For example, Peirce drew a firm line between the modern scientific method of "fixing belief" according to which beliefs could not be caused by anything "human" but only by "external permanence," namely, reality (*W* 3, 253), and the earlier "method of authority" according to which powerful institutions such as priesthoods and political regimes control individual thought, violently suppress alternative ideas, and ensure the perpetuation of beliefs by "ruthless power" (*W* 3, 251):

> Let all possible causes of a change of mind be removed from men's apprehensions. Let them be kept ignorant, lest they should learn of some reason to think otherwise than they do. Let their passions be enlisted, so that they may regard

private and unusual opinions with hatred and horror. Then, let all men who reject the established belief be terrified into silence. (*W* 3, 250)

Peirce is quite clear that both of these arrangements of method have two things in common. First, "the ultimate conclusions of every man shall be *the same*" (*W* 3, 254, emphasis added), the only difference being that the conclusions resulting from the scientific method are true, that is, they "coincide with fact" (*W* 3, 256). And second, both methods are *essentially social*, whether the despotic, inquisitional state "from the earliest times" (*W* 3, 250) or the open rationality of the modern community of scientific investigators.

In several passages, Peirce argues that different "methods" of investigation are appropriate for different classes of phenomena under study—an idea that might be seen to counter the drift of my argument that Peirce systematically held up all inquiry to the model of logical reasoning, itself the evolutionary product of the consilience of internal (thought) and external (nature) semiosis. For example, he distinguishes within the field of historical research methods for studying "monuments" (archaeology) and methods for studying "documents" (philology).

> For if there are two different methods, both of them sound and scientific, which are applicable to the same problem, they ought to be employed jointly; or if not, they at any rate are too closely associated to make different families of science. Nothing, for example, can be in stronger contrast than the method of investigating ancient history from monuments and from documents. But the only proper course is to use both methods conjointly. It is true that one man may not be strong enough to work in both ways to advantage; but still he will thoroughly know that his own work is only the result of the division of labour and that it has to be joined to another man's work by a third workman, before anything can be settled. (*CP* 7.375n)

I think that in this passage Peirce is referring to different research "techniques" and that this does not alter his commitment that *all* inquiry aimed at "truth" needs to follow the method of "science" and that discourse in all fields of inquiry need equally to "pass through the fire of scientific revision" (*N* 1, 141). And so, despite his keen attention to different "families" of science, Peirce viewed all rational activity as unified, as illustrated in his comments on the dominance of the theme of "growth" in the sciences of his own times. Reflecting on the general tenor of his own researches across the disciplines, Peirce discerned a trend in late-nineteenth-century thinking in general:

> As this Century is drawing to a close, it is interesting to pause and look about us and to ask ourselves in what great questions science is now most interested. The answer must be that *the* question that everybody is now asking, in metaphysics, in the theory of reasoning, in psychology, in general history, in philology, in sociology, in astronomy, perhaps even in molecular physics, is the question *How things grow*; and by far the most interesting aspect of the history

of science, is that it shows how an important department of human thought has been developed from generation to generation, with a view of comparing this growth with the historical development of art, of religion, of politics, and of institutions generally, and not only with historical development but also with the growth of the individual mind, and not only of mind, but of organisms both in their geological succession and with the gradual coming into being and crystallizations of the fundamental laws of matter and mind—from all of which facts taken together we are to expect in the future a grand cosmogony or philosophy of creation.[15] (*CP* 7.267n, emphasis in original)

To these illustrations of Peirce playing historian and sociologist can be added a group of more familiar passages in which he brings human languages and psychological processes under the scientific microscope. While it is true that he uses elements of language as wonderfully clear examples of signs of various types, with words exemplifying symbols, pronouns indexes, and syntax icons (*CP* 2.280), Peirce also writes extensively about ways in which actual languages *fail to line up* with the standards set by the trichotomies.[16] A Peircean science of language, thus, bears little relationship to the discipline of linguistics, whether as the synchronic study of grammatical systems, the historical study of sound changes, or the anthropological study of how people talk in social circumstances. In fact, a Peircean linguistics would be subject to the same objection that Franz Boas (and Peirce himself [*CP* 2.211]) raised against attempts to hold all grammatical systems up against the model of Latin (or "Aryan" languages).

> It happens to be true that in the overwhelming majority of languages there are no general class names and adjectives that are not conceived as parts of some verb (even when there really is no such verb) and consequently nothing like a copula is required in forming sentences in such languages. The author (though with no pretensions to being a linguist), has fumbled the grammars of many languages in the search for a language constructed at all in the way in which the logicians go out of their way to teach that all men think (for even if they do so, that has really nothing to do with logic). The only such tongue that he has succeeded in finding is the Basque, which seems to have but two or three verbs, all the other principal words being conceived as nouns. (*CP* 2.328)

To focus on how languages are *not* the sign systems they could be if only governed by logical reasoning is equivalent to constructing a logical language "*de novo*" (*CP* 2.290n) to replace actual languages, which for Peirce are a "haphazard lot."[17] A parallel set of passages develops this insistence on the total irrelevance of actual psychological processes.[18] Peirce is not saying that it would be impossible in principle to study "facts of that description from which are supposed to be ascertained by the systematic study of the mind" (*CP* 2.210), only that he is ultimately uninterested in how people actually think, being already convinced he knows how people *should think* and what "sentiments we ought rationally to entertain towards matters and things in general" (*N* 2, 139).

This sketch of a few of Peirce's often amusing adventures outside the laboratory has had several serious purposes. First, taken together, these examples demonstrate that, for Peirce, the production of *new* knowledge requires the diligent application of logically necessary systems of representation, and for two tightly related reasons: to reveal unanticipated inferential consequences that can be put to observational tests and to guarantee that the resulting propositional expression of this newly acquired knowledge is properly regimented. Second, these examples show that, despite the obvious arrogant intellectual imperialism, the method of semiotic exemplification requires a rigorous *delimitation* of the range of its application. That is, what cannot be modeled cannot be known to be true, and the semiotic features of particular models determine their field of operation. Thus, Peirce notes that his system of Existential Graphs cannot model either a musical composition or the imperative command "Ground Arms!" of a military officer because neither is subject to propositional representation (Hardwick ed. 1977, 197). The maximal distance between possible and impossible semiotic modeling would be between mathematics and poetry, since, while both mathematician and poet create semiotic forms that express mental constructs, they differ in that the former is interested in the necessary deductions from possible hypothetical inferences from these forms while the latter is principally interested "in the creation itself" of these forms (*NEM* 4, 268).

Coda

It should be apparent, after this rapid-fire journey through Peirce's construction of systems of representation that model semiosis by exemplifying it, his efforts to rank divisions within the resulting exemplary model that help predict less-than-genuine applications, and, finally, the imperialism of his own intellectual adventures into unfamiliar realms of mental creation and social action, that in this essay Peirce functions as a sign, that is, as standing for certain trends in social and cultural analysis that doggedly refuse to admit the reversal of exemplification with which I began. Between the pole that exemplifies semiotic models of the universally valid syllogism guiding abductive inference and the pole that substitutes distantiated texts or performed dramas as the mode of analysis lie third ways that need to be sensitive to the pragmatic dimensions of research in both data and theory and that refuse to take the semiotic degeneracy of the former as evidence for the genuineness of the latter.

Notes

This paper was first presented at the Working Symposium on Global Semiosis, Brandeis University (April 26, 2013). It was originally published as "Semiotic Degeneracy of Social Life: Prolegomenon to a Human Science of Semiosis," *Semiotica* 202 (2014): 1–20. The writing was supported by the National Research Foundation of Korea Grant funded by the Korean Government (MEST) (NRF-2010-361-A00013).

1. "It appears to me that the essential function of a sign is to render inefficient relations efficient" (Peirce *CP* 8.332).

2. Peirce equated the term "determined" with other terms such as "specialized" (*CP* 8.178) and to "render definitely" (*CP* 8.361). He clarified that the interpreting sign does not usually do its job merely on the basis of the determining vector of the representamen, since at the same moment the interpretant needs to bring into view a whole range of "collateral" experiences technically separate from the action of the sign (*CP* 8.178).

3. Transparency does not mean that signs do not have "material qualities" that serve the necessary function of distinguishing one sign from another; it only serves as a warning not to confuse these qualities with the meanings conveyed: the word *white* is printed in black letters even though the quality of blackness is no part of the significance of the sign.

4. Parmentier (2009) provides an analysis of "troubles" encountered in the social sciences and humanities using Peirce's three trichotomies that generate the ten-fold classification of signs; Parmentier (1994c) provides an introductory account of the organizing principles of the trichotomies. The present paper's topic falls between these two.

5. When Peirce says that the system of representation best equipped for scientific and logical reasoning consists of "conventional" or "arbitrary" signs, he does not mean to imply that researchers can pick any mode of representation they like, or that the rules of operation of such a system are open to a wide range of alternatives, for like any good signs they need to determine interpretants to represent how these same signs stand *truthfully* for their objects, though the choice of algebraic, geometrical, or graphic designs is only constrained by the goal of transparency.

6. Peirce clarifies this triadic relation involved in scientific research:

> A phenomenon having been observed in a laboratory, though we may not know on what conditions it depends, yet we are quite sure that it would make no difference whether the number of degrees of the longitude of the planet Eros just one week previous were a prime or composite number. The third way of reasoning is *induction,* or experimental research. Its procedure is this. Abduction having suggested a theory, we employ *de*duction from that ideal theory a promiscuous variety of consequences to the effect that if we perform certain acts, we shall find ourselves confronted with certain experiences. We then proceed to try these experiments, and if the predictions of the theory are verified, we have a proportionate confidence that the experiments that remain to be tried will confirm the theory. (*CP* 8.210, emphasis in original)

7. "There is, then, to every question a true answer, a final conclusion, to which the opinion of every man is constantly gravitating. He may for a time recede from it, but give him more experience and time for consideration, and he will finally approach it" (*W* 2: 469).

8. Peirce's notion of the replica is so broad as to be practically useless for guiding research into sign processes that might resemble replication. From the narrowest examples of type-token replication, the ten instances of the word *the* on the page of a text, Peirce glides easily to examples of isomorphisms across registers (replicas of the same sign in spoken, written, or pictorial notation) and of isofunctional regularities (different propositions being the "same" if their logical implications are identical). And much scholarly ink has been spilled over the question of how indexical legisigns and iconic legisigns produce their replicas, since in these two classes of signs the power of the interpretant in creating the ground of the representation is relatively restricted in comparison to the class of symbols.

9. This second definition of the sign is a consequence of the more basic idea that all thought takes place in time; from this follows that not only are all thoughts in signs but that "every thought must be interpreted in another" (*W* 2, 208).

10. Peirce (*NEM* 4, 255) further comments that two symbols can also be said to be replicas of the same symbol, as in two words whose only difference is in the grammatical expression of case (*he* and *him*, for example) or two words whose only (insignificant) difference is "rhetorical."

11. No doubt this comparison will lead to subsequent refinements in the system of representation, a feedback loop evidenced by the sudden explosion of the trichotomies in the last decade of Peirce's life.

12. Although the term *degeneracy* is not used as a term of moral approbation, it does have an evaluative tinge, as when Peirce writes of "weak" secondness (*CP* 5.67) and the "maimed conditions" of degenerate Thirds (*CP* 5.70).

13. Peirce notes that his own published conjecture that ancient Babylonians had high scientific genius was later confirmed by archaeological discoveries of their astronomical accomplishments (*CP* 7.182n); he also notes that Babylonians were keen archaeologists (*N* 2, 52).

14. Peirce is notoriously quick to point out, on the other hand, the presumptuousness of nonscientists employing pseudo-mathematical reasoning in their work, as the sociologist who, in writing that "impulsive social action varies inversely with the habit of attaining ends by indirect and complex means," incurred Peirce's condemnation: "The language is to a mathematician repellent. Is any more meant than the truism that when men are in the habit of acting reflectively, they are less under the domination of impulse? If so, why should it not be expressed nonmathematically?" (*N* 3, 70). The criticism does not apply, however, to philosophers who are valiantly trying to think clearly and who *should,* therefore, adopt a writing style "as closely as possible to a self-explaining diagram or a tabular array of familiar symbols" (*N* 3, 129).

15. In another passage from 1898, Peirce writes that the one word that characterizes the age is "accuracy" (*N* 2, 169).

16. Parmentier (1997a) compares Peirce's views on language with contemporary approaches in linguistic anthropology.

17. In a 1909 letter to Lady Victoria Welby Peirce describes his boyhood effort modeled after Wilkins' "real character" to "invent a language in which almost every letter of every word made a definite contribution to signification. It involved a classification of all possible ideas; and I need not say that it was never completed" (Hardwick ed. 1977, 94).

18. I find it predictable that the collection of distinguished papers from the Harvard Sesquicentennial Congress published as *Charles S. Peirce and the Philosophy of Science* (Moore 1993) makes almost no reference to the social sciences either in terms of Peirce's direct contribution or in terms of the impact of his methods in various disciplines. An exception is Hendrick's (1993) essay on the relevance of Peirce for psychology, which generalizes from the perfection of Thirds to claim that "most cultures are uneasy about prostitutes," perhaps because they expect loving sexual relations to manifest thirdness in which participants treat each other as "symbolic natures"—a generalization that would no doubt intrigue Peirce, who was apparently terminated from his teaching position at Johns Hopkins University due to concerns about his second marriage to a French actress. More to the point, why would the relation "John pays Mary for sex" not be equally triadic, and why would a threesome not be even more "genuine"? In fact, Peirce used the "lover" relationship as a perfect example of a dyadic second (*CP* 1.363).

PART II

Critical Commentaries and Reviews

7 Representing Semiotics in the New Millennium

Analyzing Cultural Meanings

The appearance of *Analyzing Cultures* by Marcel Danesi and Paul Perron (1999), bearing the modest subtitle *An Introduction and Handbook*, is both a welcome addition to the growing literature on the application of semiotic methods to the study of human cultures and a mark of the maturity of the discipline of cultural semiotics. It also provides me with an opportunity to reflect critically on several key notions in semiotic analysis and to discuss several recent research projects studying material and linguistic signs. In what follows I will be particularly concerned with several troublesome points in cultural analysis that need to be held constantly in mind as the interdisciplinary field of cultural semiotics moves confidently into the new millennium.

Rather than pursuing a narrowly defined theoretical perspective or relying on a limited number of academic disciplines, Danesi and Perron consider a range of approaches, many exemplified with illustrative cases from types of cultural data. Entire chapters are devoted to the semiotic study of the body, language, metaphor, space, art, material objects, narrative, and mass-mediated images. Neither Peirce nor Saussure and neither language nor the material world merits a privileged position in these clearly constructed chapters. Curious, at least in my view, is the absence of reference to whom I regard as the foremost exponents of the semiotic approach to culture, Yuri Lotman and Michael Silverstein. The authors also generally neglect both the Moscow-Tartu School and, with a few exceptions, the subdisciplines of linguistic anthropology and semiotic anthropology. On the other hand, the authors possess an enviable grasp of continental semiotics from Vico to Barthes (especially in regard to language-based phenomena) and of the burgeoning field of biological semiotics. *Analyzing Cultures* is not an "introduction and handbook" to semiotic theory, although rudimentary expositions of several important theorists are provided, nor a comprehensive original theoretical exposition (see now Sebeok and Danesi 2000); rather, it is designed to orient the student reader to the broadest possible conception of culture. As they put it:

Culture is seen by semioticians generally as a communal system of meanings that provides the means for human beings to translate their instincts, urges, needs, and other propensities into representational and communicative structures. The primary goal of semiotic analysis is to document and investigate these structures. (Danesi and Perron 1999, 14)

Danesi and Perron recommend the semiotic approach to the study of all aspects of human activity. To clarify this comprehensive perspective, they present a triadic model in which *semiosis* is defined as the innate capacity for sign comprehension, *representation* labels the mind's ability to use signs to refer to the world and to other signs, and *signifying order* denotes the collective sign systems of a culture. The biological capacity and the cognitive processing are both subject to the "mediation" of cultural sign systems: "The signifying order thus provides the means for the developing human being to organize the raw information that is processed by her senses into meaningful wholes. But as a consequence, the understanding of the world is not a direct one. It is mediated by signs and, thus, by the referential domains that they elicit within mind-space" (Danesi and Perron 1999, 68). Fortunately, these idiosyncratic definitions of semiosis and representation are not strictly followed throughout the book; and the more usual sense of semiosis as the real-time, processual chaining of interpretants and of representation as the most general "standing for" or "substitutional" relationship between sign and object are both mentioned.

Late in the discussion, the concept of *macrosignified* is introduced as a mechanism to assist semiotic analysis at what Danesi and Perron call the "global" level of integration, that is, semiotic order found in a single culture viewed as a totality. The way toward macrosignifieds has, however, been paved throughout the book by the authors' repeated attention to the "interconnectedness" of codes and texts within a signifying order. In particular, the previous discussion of conceptual metaphors suggests that they are the "conceptual glue" that keeps the "system of culture" together (1999, 181), not only by serving as an overarching set of meanings but also by being subjected to layering at several levels. Two brief examples cited from our culture illustrate this point: the semiotic structure "up/down" functions to integrate linguistic, cognitive, and pictorial representations, and the schema "love is a sweetness" as a macrosignified linking visual, ritual, and narrative signs. The quest for a characterization of cultural integration as a coherent linkage of sign systems does not discriminate between small-scale societies, where many analysts have discovered high degrees of coherence or even systematicity, and complex industrial societies, where mass media in particular ensure the spread of shared meanings.

The interconnectedness of meanings in a culture is the reason why, from tribes to advanced technological societies, signifying orders impart a sense of wholeness and, thus, of purpose to the activities that people carry out. Macro-signifieds are distributed throughout the network of meaning pathways that define a culture. (Danesi and Perron 1999, 294)

The notion that cultural codes are patterned or ordered is certainly familiar in contemporary anthropological analysis, from Clifford Geertz's (following Max Weber) "webs of significance" (1973), to David M. Schneider's "galaxies of regnant symbols" (1976), to Michael Herzfeld's "metapatterns" (1992), where the systematicity of culture at the level of symbol meanings is regularly used as a theoretical weapon against adaptive or infrastructural reductionism. But there has also been, more recently, a strong backlash against attempts to claim too much systematicity for culture (Hannerz 1989), focusing instead on chaos (Friedrich 1988), ambiguity (Battaglia 1999), multiple voices (Abu-Lughod 1991), dialectical apprehension (Fabian 1985), difference (Gupta and Ferguson 1992), and resistance (Ortner 1995).

I want to make three points in reference to macrosignifieds that might clarify and advance the authors' potentially fruitful concept. First, analysis of specific cases is required to ascertain if a high degree of semiotic systematicity is the product of creative, artistic, or reflexive traditions operating in relative social isolation (as, for example, in an island society or an ethnic isolate), or the result of the spread of officializing, hegemonic, or "closed" ideological constructions characteristic of stratified societies (Sarangi 1995, 12). The former could be called a systematicity of integration and the latter a systematicity of regimentation (Parmentier 1994c, 127–28). Second, in *Analyzing Cultures*, metasignifieds are defined within the context of a single culture. But a comprehensive account must also investigate the historical transformations of patterns of semiotic integration; intercultural processes such as regional patterns (style horizons, for instance), transnational flows (Appadurai 1991), and interactions at the boundary of the semiosphere (Lotman 1990, 136); and comparative regularities found in unconnected societies. In other words, the authors' term *global* is in serious need of globalization. And, third, the search for macrosignifieds needs to be sensitive to the methodological problem that the complexities, ambiguities, and openness of cultural meanings can easily be ironed out by the act of analysis itself. Merely asking questions in a decontextualized frame will tend to produce a textual artifact that, for example, renders nonisomorphic indexicals as purely "symbolic" meanings (Silverstein 1996).

Of Types and Tokens

One of the basic distinctions in semiotic theory is between sign tokens, what Peirce (CP 2.245) named "sinsigns," that is, actually occurring sign instances anchored in spatio-temporal contexts, and sign types, or "legisigns," that is, general regularities that stipulate the systematic linkage between form and meaning and that delimit the parameters for the production of recognizable sign instantiations. Western metaphysics has long debated this distinction, with some, like Plato, insisting that the truer reality lies in the permanent realm of sign types (what Plato called "ideas" or, in its later Latin translation, "forms"), and others, like Aristotle, insisting that only concrete or material entities are worth worrying about in discussing the signifying element of semiotic relations. The theoretical discovery of the necessity of including type-level signifieds rests with the Stoics, who talked about the *lekton* as what is meant by regularly occurring linguistic expressions (Glidden 1983). Social research faces a particular dilemma that follows from this dichotomy: our only data come from sign *tokens*, what actually gets said, built, pictured, or worn, while the cross-contextual regularities that constitute culture are actually sign *types* that never show themselves at an empirically measurable level. As Peirce saw so clearly, erasing all the tokens of a word does not eradicate the general template that defines the word's phonological shape. On the other hand, it is nearly impossible to measure significant absences, silences, or ellipses in social life, since "nothing" is difficult to record.

One methodological implication of this type-token distinction is that it is difficult to know if a particular occurring sign is a "sinsign" pure and simple or an instance of a legisign, what Peirce called a "replica," since they both look alike at the level of experienced reality, what Peirce labeled "secondness" (Daniel 1998, 85–86). An archaeologist comes upon a group of stones that look like they were artificially shaped to meet some evident technological demand; that is, each stone appears to be a replica of a legisign since it is an instance of a recurring class of intentionally shaped stones (Bednarik 1992, 39). But the expedition's skeptical geologist insists that the stones are merely naturally shaped sinsigns pointing not to human intention but to the forces of volcanism and erosion (Herzfeld 1992, 70). Note, however, that as soon as naturally occurring stones are regarded as evidential signs of volcanism or erosion (rather than as pointing to a cultural pattern) they become instances of legisigns again, since the physical processes that produced them are subject to law-like regularities. Nature as well as culture can create legisigns (Short 1989, 129).

Even more perplexing is the observation that social life regularly involves the spontaneous creation of replicas out of sinsigns: accidental or singular occurrences become repeated customary performances. As my informants in Palau (Micronesia) put it, in following a singular occurrence, social action lays down a "path" that grows in strength with each repetition; only a brave person or a titled chief has the power to risk striking out on a course never traveled before (Parmentier 1987, 109). Social research in societies with hierarchical social organizations has provided rich documentation of the manipulation of the process of creating types, or "typification," as both a tool and an index of social power.

Alternatively, technically effective design features can become standardized in other nonutilitarian contexts where the absence of instrumental explanation promotes folk rationalizations, as people search for some cultural principle or historical motivation to explain otherwise inexplicable features.

A final point about replicas is a warning that there exists a potential for terminological confusion, since the term *replication* has recently been applied to the generative process of the production of interpretants in a semiotic system. Evolutionary semiotic theorists, Deacon for example, speak of the power of replication of signs as an adaptive mechanism not constrained by biological or genetic reproduction (Bouissac 1998, 746). But replication is also still used in the sense of the production of sign tokens modeled by some type, mold, or pattern.

A Context for Indexicals

One of the great merits of a Peircean, as opposed to a Saussurean, approach to the semiotics of social life is that the category of meaningfulness labeled indexicality is fully recognized as a mode of signification analytically independent from semantic or symbolic meaning, which depends on decontextualized regularities stipulated by convention. Given that social life is largely concerned with human interaction and the objectification of meaning in material objects, any attempt to analyze the indexical dimensions of culture as if they were purely symbolic—as in expressions like "the language of flowers" or "symbols of empire"—is misguided in the extreme (Silverstein 1976, 53–54). Unfortunately, a great deal of ethnography produced in the subdisciplinary domain of "cognitive anthropology" mistakenly attempts to analyze indexical regularities in terms of complex semantic typologies (e.g., Boyer 1990), or worse, attempts to downgrade indexical legisigns to ad hoc contextual reactances.

Indexicals present an especially difficult area for social research for several reasons. Indexicality, that is, aspects of sign meaning linked to the contextual occurrence of sign vehicles, is a rather messy business, both in formal composition and in norms of interpretability. Formal problems stem from the power of indexicals to operate in two logical directions, what Silverstein (1976) labels "presupposing" signs whose contextual anchor must be known prior to the instance of the sign and entailing or "creative" signs, indexicals whose very occurrence generates in reality or at least in cognitive salience the contextual matter. The trouble is that the analyst or outside observer, lacking full acquaintance with a foreign culture's sign processes, will have an almost impossible task figuring out what is presupposing and what is creative. Note that the word *creative* here is not restricted to some aesthetic impulse: creative indexicals can be generated to have ideological effects not correlated with any preexisting contextual realities. The retrospective interpretation of indexicals in real time always distorts their potential for multiple indexical mappings. That is, asking people after the fact frequently produces interpretations favoring presupposing over creative meanings or, to use the terms of Bourdieu (1990, 86), favoring the completed "product" over the process of "production." Since product is easier to see than process in the archaeological record, there is a tendency to read the material record in a presupposing rather than creative manner, so that, for example, differential grave goods are said to index degrees of social inequality. Aware of the methodological problems of this tendency toward mechanical reflection, Kuijt (1997) proposed that the lack of differential funeral goods and the presence of similar death masks at the prepottery Neolithic site of Jericho can be interpreted as a creative effort to ward off encroaching hierarchy by asserting an ideology of equality at death.

In later reflection, actors tend to reread indexical multifunctionality either focusing on the most obvious indexical modality or by translating the whole mess into decontextualized semantic regularities. Think for a moment about legal and popular discourse concerning the semiotic status of the American flag—a legisign stipulating the production of replicas, with iconic and indexical layers of significance riding (or flying) along with the official referential value. For some, burning the concrete emblematic embodiment of the nation should be a crime, while for others the flag points not to the nation but to the constitutional principle of the freedom of political expression, a principle that guarantees our right to destroy replicas without undermining the enduring type. Furthermore, multiple indexical meanings frequently piggyback on a single chain of signifiers, whose occurrence can signal spatial, temporal, and social indexicality all at once. Finally, indexical meaning can intersect in complex ways with symbolic meaning, as in the case of duplex signs or shifters, where referential value can only be discovered after indexical calculation. Despite their being bidirectional, multifunctional, nonisomorphic, and regularly misconstrued, the study of indexical signs lies at the heart of social semiotic research.

Contextual semiosis or indexicality is more than an analytic quagmire; it is the systematic coding of the fact that cognition and social interaction take place in real space and time. One of the ways that cultural sign systems have evolved to make up for the cognitive and developmental limitations of the human species is using this interaction between code and context to generate efficiencies in the encoding-decoding process (cf. Deacon 1997). "Markedness" is perhaps the most distinctive of these strategies: instead of matching sign vehicles and sign meanings in a one-to-one relationship, cultural codes regularly use two formal patterns to signal a general, decontextualized, or "unmarked" meaning and a more specific, contextual, or "marked" meaning (Waugh 1992, 31). And then the unmarked value can be interpreted either as an overarching category encompassing both values (the "zero interpretation") or as some value standing in opposition to the positive mark (called the "minus interpretation") (Waugh 1982, 303). The disambiguation of these two interpretations of the identical sign form is possible only by the recognition of contextual factors, including the previous occurrence of another sign in the syntagm or some agreed-upon pragmatic rule of appropriateness (Newfield and Waugh 1991, 234). While some semioticians, notably Shapiro (1981), have tried to construct a model for markedness using Peircean categories, I have always felt that Saussurean principles, which speak more fully about code structure, offer a more fruitful approach. The methodological trap, obviously, is that from a single sign instance or an occurrence accessible only from after-the-fact reporting it is never sufficient to know if the general or specific meaning is being signaled. Only the habit of erroneously reinvigorating dead metaphors vexes the ethnographer more than misreading markedness relations. Many attempts to display the semantic organization of various cultural fields have been torpedoed by markedness values that upset the neatly ordered taxonomic diagrams, since the same formal label can appear at a given node and also at one node lower in the hierarchy.

But even having mastered the pervasive markedness values in a culture's sign code, the analyst is caught in a related difficulty: markedness values can themselves be resources for strategic or rhetorical creativity, as in the familiar process of norm violation in the aesthetic domain so well documented by Prague School theorists (Mukařovský 1979). Markedness proves to be the mechanism through which stylistic innovations in usage, construction, or belief enter a culture's semiosphere, as Lotman (1990) persuasively showed. For instance, in his book *Musical Meaning in Beethoven*, Hatten (1994) documents the historical shift in the markedness relationship between major and minor keys in Western music history: as the Classical style developed out of the Baroque, minor keys came to express a tragic mode, leaving major keys as more general, multifunctional, and thus unmarked.

The markedness asymmetry of relationship categories is, finally, useful in establishing the developmental sequence or historical evolution of sign systems, since, generally, the marked or contextual value of a privative opposition is mastered later than the functionally more general or statistically more frequent unmarked value (Kuryłowicz 1949). Care, however, needs to be taken not to read into the formal expression of what looks like an unmarked term the differentiation of markedness values that arise developmentally or historically only later. If propositionality is the unmarked linguistic function of well-formed sentences for adult speakers, translating a baby's monosyllabic utterances into condensed propositions on the grounds of their ubiquity is to misunderstand the unfolding of linguistic functions (Silverstein 1985). Sebeok (1997, 114) applies markedness values to the evolution of semiosis itself: the development of the biosphere is *marked* in relation to the *unmarked* protosemiotic world of prebiological chemistry.

Context also plays a creative role putting systematic regularities into flux in the use of the poetic principle to establish meaning equivalence relations that, while looking like code-driven definitional glosses, pertain only for the moment. Jakobson (1987) points to the various ways that parallelisms in sequential unfolding of the syntagmatic order, whether in poetic genres, mythological narratives, or ritual actions, place two terms or compositional units not otherwise identified into what Silverstein (1981) named "pseudo-equivalence" relations. When Incan people of the Andes said that their mummified ancestors are "seeds" planted in the ground, they were not making a semantic gloss but rather asserting a complex metaphysical principle grounded in the opposition between wet and dry (Gose 1993). Indeed, many cultural processes obtain their performative power by convincing participants that the presented equivalence applies more widely than in just the constitutive context. This is quite easily done, given two observations. first, poetic or contextual equivalences look exactly like code-stipulated ones: "God is love" has the same syntactic shape as "God is the unmoved mover." Second, emotionally charged contexts, like those in the ritual realm, work to render contextual sign processes as if they were immutable, naturally motivated, or transcendently authored (Rappaport 1999, 232).

Performing Signs

Verbal art has been widely recognized as a prime territory for the play of signs at a high level of complexity; creations in genres such as chants, myths, poems, and proverbs display an overall sign structure that compels the interpreter to resist the transparency or confusion of expression and referent (Morris 1939, 137) and to build up a total response by a "connected tissue of references" (138) internal to the work itself. An exemplary semiotic study of the rhetorical uses of indexicals, parallelism, and performativity is Felson's path-breaking analysis of Pindar's *Pythian Four* (1999). Pindar, a Theban poet of the fifth century BCE, was commissioned to write odes praising athletic victors at the four Panhellenic Games, including the Pythian Games held at Delphi. Many of these works were originally performed before hometown audiences or the Games themselves by a principal speaker (perhaps the poet himself or the chorus acting as the voice of the poet), a chorus, musicians, and dancers. Later, these poems may have been reperformed in secondary contexts without music and dance; and eventually they became part of the canon of classical literature.

Pythian Four is especially interesting for its dynamic manipulation of various deictic forms to create a fictional world in which the audience is drawn into the spatial and temporal movements of the characters (cf. Auer 1995, 12). Felson explores several rhetorical devices, including deictic ambiguity, where a pronoun's unique referent is not clearly presupposed (such as the EGO form referring to the poet both as author and as performer [cf. Irvine 1996, 143]); sudden dramatic shift in time reference; narrative embedding, where a smaller section is framed by a surrounding section with different spatial and temporal parameters; and the "coalescence of place," where different characters occupy the same space (especially Delphi) at different narrative times. Generally, the textual task of representing the indexicals of speech faces the logical problem that the contextual meanings of the original (now unrecoverable) utterance can never be grasped *once repeated* (Pape 1999, 548). On the other hand, the poetic use of similar deictics and shifters in the framing language can rescue, to some degree, the vividness of the represented indexicals.

Even more remarkable is Pindar's ability, in just under three hundred lines, to *simultaneously* anchor the poem in these fictionalized and performance contexts and ensure this poem's power to transcend the original context as an eternal work of art. At the overt level, *Pythian Four* celebrates Arcesilas, king of Cyrene (North Africa), who was victorious in the chariot race at Delphi in 462 BCE. This is largely accomplished by drawing an extensive and overt parallel between Arcesilas's journey to the Games, his athletic victory, and his reception as a returned hero and the exploits of the mythical Jason, who sailed with the crew of Argonauts to Colchis to gain the magical golden fleece. A second poetic function, introduced only at the very end of the ode, is to praise a certain Damophilus, an aristocrat from Cyrene living in exile, and to directly petition King Arcesilas and his court to repair the political fabric by repatriating the exile.

Jason, robbed of the throne of Iolcus at birth by the treachery of his cousin Pelias, is taken away from his homeland to be raised in the caves of Philyra; his reclamation of the kingship is delayed by the ruse of obtaining the golden fleece, an impossible task intended to lead to his death. Note that Arcesilas, Jason, and Damophilus are all engaged in parallel journeys, but only Damophilus's round-trip is yet to be completed. One additional character needs to be mentioned: Battus, the heroic founder of Cyrene and lineal ancestor of the current king, mediates between the mythic and contemporary time frames. Eight generations before the present, Battus also journeyed to Delphi in search of a cure for his stammering. But the oracular priestess responded to this request by prophesying that Battus would leave his homeland of Thera and found the new city of Cyrene in fulfillment of an earlier prophesy of Medea, daughter of the king of the Colchians, to Jason's Argonauts sixteen generations before.

I want to discuss three ways that the ode accomplishes its multiple poetic goals: structural parallelism, indexical linkages, and asymmetrical metapragmatics. And here I am following Felson's detailed analysis but refocusing in semiotic terms her theoretical insights. The most obvious parallelism has already been mentioned: the heroic journey and successful return home of Jason, Battus, Arcesilas, and (potentially) Damophilus. A second structural parallel concerns instances of powerful verbal performances, including Medea's prophecy to the Argonauts ("chanting in oracular verses"), two Delphic prophecies delivered to Pelias ("cries of the Delphic priestess"), Jason's powerful address to the people of Iolcus ("in mild intonations" and "a wise appeal"), Aphrodite's instructions to Jason in the verbal skills needed to seduce Medea ("prayers and charms"), the Delphic oracle's pronouncement to Battus, Oedipus's proverb about the disfigured tree that maintains functionality in new contexts of use, the Homeric saying about the good messenger ("a message rightly phrased"), and the successful performance of one of Pindar's odes at Thebes ("a fountain of ambrosial words") (translations from Nisetich 1980, modified by Felson). All these instances of the performative use of language anticipate the final one, the performance of the poem itself, designed to cure the alleged political ills of Cyrene.

Having established these two major parallel structures that provide the diagrammatic argument of the poem, the poet weaves these parallels together with a series of indexical signs in various media. Like the objectified words of an oracular priestess or skillful poet, certain other semiotically potent objects provide these intertextual linkages: a clump of earth presented to the Argonauts by Euphamos as a "token of hospitality" and as a portent that, having this earth in their possession, the sailors would someday found a new city in the sandy deserts of North Africa; and a group of magical objects, such as the wryneck that charms an already willing Medea to betray her father, the olive-oil-based pain killer that enables Jason to withstand the fire-breathing oxen, and the golden fleece kept in a sacred grove in Colchis the possession of which promises to be a cure for death. The poem is also unified by several references to the genealogical ties indexically linking various characters, most especially by the connection between Battus, the stammerer, and Arcesilas, the victorious hero, and between Euphamos, whose offspring by the Lemnian women eventually reach Cyrene, and the people of Cyrene.

All these diagrammatic and indexical devices are synthesized by a series of metapragmatic statements by the ego-figure in the poem that monitor the ongoing state of the poem and end up guaranteeing the performative effectiveness of the ode (cf. Briggs 1993, 200; Silverstein 1993, 51). After introducing the genealogical link between Battus and Arcesilas and having foreshadowed the role of Medea in the narrative, the poet announces the topical parallelism of the ode: "Of him [Arcesilas], then, will I sing, and of the Golden Fleece." Then, in the middle of the quoted speech of Jason upon his return home, the poet represents him saying to his internal audience, "But now you know the highlights of the story" (line 116). But clearly that audience at Iolcus would not know the "highlights" yet, and so the poet's metapragmatic comment serves to insert into Jason's audience of Iolcans Pindar's contemporary audience, who are indeed very familiar with the myth of the Argonauts. The poet momentarily halts his lengthy recounting of the myth of Jason to reassure his audience that he knows where this narrative journey is leading: "I know a certain shortcut, for I am guide to many in the turns of song" (line 248). Toward the end of the ode, the poet digresses briefly just before his final encomium to Damophilus to repeat two pieces of traditional verbal lore, both of which have metasemiotic import (cf. Parmentier 1994c, 92). The proverb from Oedipus states that a strong tree cut down by a woodsman's axe no longer has its original beauty or fruits, but can still be used as firewood, to make furniture, or in house construction. Damophilus, like the tree, once cut off from his original land, can come home to new political usefulness. The poet reinforces this political point by stating directly to Arcesilas, "I have spelled out these graces here for you to be the author of them" (line 275). A Homeric proverb is then quoted: "A good messenger furthers any enterprise," which the poet then immediately glosses: "And the Muse rightly prospers through a message rightly phrased." Note the "asymmetrical" linearity of these instances of metapragmatic discourse (Parmentier 1997b, 37–42): from announcing the topical parallelism of the code, Pindar then reminds the audience that he is master of the highlights. He then claims that his poetic skills are the model for other poets. Next he indirectly suggests that, like a rehabilitated political exile, a poem can have different functions in different contexts. And, finally, he makes reference to an ode, perhaps the very ode being performed here, that when sung at Thebes proved to be a "fountain of ambrosial words." Ultimately, then, rhetorical virtuosity—the poetic skill to combine indexical, diagrammatic, and metapragmatic elements—is essentially linked to contextual performativity, and both work together to guarantee the immortality of poetic form.

Semiotic Ideology and Levels of Awareness

That cultural sign systems do not float about in some abstract realm of meaningfulness but are anchored in the textual products and social relations they serve implies that, in addition to asking about the function of a sign as a fact about its code and as a fact about its context, we must always ask questions about social function. What social functions drive the semiotic forms and in whose interests does the sign system operate? Every society, no matter how egalitarian its ethos, shows some stratification in its ability to know about, interpret, and record sign phenomena.

This knowledge or awareness of semiotic regularities can be conveniently divided into three components: breadth and depth of grasp of the basic sign units or lexicon of a code, differential delicacy in the manipulation of code alternatives in various contexts, and degrees of metasemiotic apprehension. Metasemiotic awareness of the qualities of the sign system is often available to those with comparative or intercultural experience or those whose social privilege allows leisure for philosophical reflection. Ethnographers are familiar with the phenomenon of border-crossing outsiders or esoteric specialists whose metasemiotic skills make them particularly useful informants. There is always danger, however, of accepting indigenous metasemiotic discourse as the final description of the semiotic codes, rather than as a particularly insightful yet situationally restricted perspective, that is, as metasemiotics with its own pragmatics (Silverstein 1993).

Knowledge and awareness, however decontextualized at first glance, are often useless without the practical skill in performing signs in context: whether in fashion, cuisine, gesture, or language, status accrues to those who can exploit the available codes for rhetorical effect—which in some cultures might even require a studied underperformance or a boastful neglect of norms required of lesser mortals. Those positioned more toward the middle of the social field need to expend more energy to perform to the norm or else to exceed it in hypercorrect behaviors. The positional nature of semiotic awareness is evident in situations where a given sign phenomenon is interpreted differently by differently positioned actors, as in the case of ritual masking in New Guinea discussed by Schwimmer (1990, 14, n.9), where the already initiated know the symbolic or conventional quality of masks, while those undergoing initiation are convinced they embody real spiritual powers.

Cultural sign systems vary in their openness to metasemiotic interpretation (Watt 1984, 119). Legal codes, for example, require trained elites to impose interpretations, often by declaring some potential sign vehicle to be a token instance of an offense type or by stipulating an acceptable chain of precedents (Mertz 1996, 236). Traffic codes, similarly, exist in codified handbooks with explicit interpretive instructions. At the other extreme, mantic systems like divination and aesthetic systems like pictorial art allow greater flexibility for personal interpretation. The institutionally endowed authority to impose closure of interpretation, what I have written about elsewhere (Parmentier 1994c, 1997b) under Silverstein's (1992) concept of "regimentation," often involves several indirect or nonexplicit techniques, such as controlling the metasemiotic resources available to interpreters or promoting a general semiotic ideology that becomes a presupposed grid for acts of interpretation. Taken together, these highly regimenting metasemiotic discourses offer the analyst tempting, convenient, and coherent summaries of a culture's semiotic systems. The danger, of course, is that they distort as much as they inform, both by presenting the view from the "top down" as the cultural system and by tending to iron out contextual variation and indexical multifunctionality into smoothly shaped principles.

Types of Mediation

In order to clear up some confusion in applying analytical labels to processes that operate in distinct yet interlocking levels of semiosis, Mertz and Parmentier (1985) proposed the term *semiotic mediation*, based on Peirce's approving citation of the word *mediation* as a summary description for all semiotic processes at the level of thirdness (recall, the sign-object relation is linked by a mediational interpretant in all fully triadic signs). Alas, the term semiotic mediation did not actually catch on in either semiotics or anthropology, despite a most welcome recent effort by Sebeok (1995a) to revitalize it, I suspect because of the very complexity of the mediational processes it sought to encompass (Keeler 1990). We intended to include at least three levels of semiotic mediation, which I can gloss here as "token mediation," "code mediation," and "ideological mediation"—the levels, of course, are purely analytical and in themselves make no claim to any empirical regularities.

Token mediation involves the play of sign instances in the give and take of social life, viewed as a flow of signs in context. Without buying into structuralism as a general method, we can appreciate Lévi-Strauss's role in reminding social researchers that people exchange words (e.g., in reciprocating marriage vows), gifts (e.g., in giving beanie babies at birthday parties), and siblings (e.g., in marriage alliance systems), and the ethnographer who fails to chart this sign flow has missed most of social life. The circulation of material sign tokens involves various dynamics between the sign values and the social relations they mediate on a continuum ranging from the transactionally generated values of amulets (Tambiah 1984) to hoarded, noncirculating "inalienable possessions" (Weiner 1992, 1994).

Code mediation, what is usually considered a Whorfian issue, deals with the skewing, bias, or refraction that operates between perception and reality, much like a pair of colored glasses modifies sight. Note, importantly, that without an alternative or comparative perspective, this mediational effect can go unnoticed. Members of a society regularly overlook the very arbitrariness of their familiar codes, preferring to consider them products of transcendent wisdom or natural order. Cultural codes, like linguistic ones, rarely determine the limits of what can be signaled; rather, they work to facilitate certain expressible meanings, to prestructure equivalence relations by regular paradigmatic structures and syntagmatic parallelisms.

Much recent social analysis has pursued the topic of mediation by "semiotic ideologies," that is, by relatively presupposed, systematic sets of assumptions about semiosis in general. Folk ideas about the distinction between natural and conventional signs, notions about the universe as a book, and homologies drawn between linguistic and economic processes (Rossi-Landi 1973, 1983) are a few examples of widely discussed semiotic ideologies. Analysis of these ideologies is most difficult, since it is easy to erroneously substitute a passing articulated expression of an ideology (by a chief, king, or priest, for example) or a spontaneous rationalization prompted by our own metasemiotic inquiry for a truly pervasive, though largely unspoken, semiotic ideology.

Semiotic Replication

An especially sophisticated study of medieval seals by Bedos-Rezak (1992) provides an elegant illustration of the changing relationship between semiotic ideology and semiotic practice. In the medieval West it was common from at least the sixth century for kings to affix personal seals to documents (especially charters). The image and legend of medieval seals were carved into a matrix that was then pressed into hot wax, leaving an inverse of the carving on the document. At the basic level, the presence of the wax seal provided evidence that the document was not a forgery and, for the unlettered masses, served as an impressive nonlinguistic accompaniment of the charter. While Merovingian kings used the seal as a sign of the person (i.e., the king) responsible for the document's production and issuance, the Carolingian kings formulated a theory of the royal seal as a manifestation of the power of kingship. As particular seals became regularly associated with the identity and discursive power of the king, the use of seals generated an image of kingship as a permanent institution standing apart from the physical individuality of the king and from the contextual vagaries of historical changes. "The seal was not his, belonging to the royal office of which it constituted a ritual appendage, from which it derived the power of representing royal authority, and for which it constituted a semiotic field of practice and significance" (Bedos-Rezak 1992, 31).

Bedos-Rezak traces several linked changes in the practice of sealing in subsequent centuries. The eleventh century witnessed a sudden rise in the production of charters, documents attesting to the gift of land to religious institutions made for the benefit of the donor's eternal soul. Ecclesiastical officials not only assisted in the production of these Latin texts but further sanctified the authenticity and permanence of the gift by various liturgical acts and graphic additions. The anonymous scribes who produced the charters followed the convention of constructing the donor as a first-person ego. Although that individual was not the direct author of the text, the ego indexes the donor as the source of the gift. In order to anchor written documents to the original act of giving and to the empirical person of the giver, charters were inscribed with various graphic signs with spiritual import (knife, rod, cross, etc.). Now it turns out that individuals closely associated with the "writing bureaus" producing the charters are the same individuals engaged in a lively discourse about the general semiotic properties of linguistic and nonlinguistic texts.

Two points are relevant to stress here. First, there is a gradual diffusion or extension of sealing, starting from the king to the nobility, and then to ecclesiastical officials, and finally to nonroyal personages and institutions (scriptoria and chanceries). Second, prescholastic writers of the eleventh and twelfth centuries increasingly reflected on the parallelism between the immanence of the person iconically represented in the seal and the "real presence" of Christ manifested in the eucharistic elements.

> That a seal represents by being an object whose marked matter has become graven form is crucial in terms of prescholastic semiotics. The seal metaphors . . . suggest that an imprint, by virtue of containing the trace of an origin in its very matter, is a sign forever indicating a radical presence, for instance, that of God in human beings. (Bedos-Rezak 2000, 1527)

Bedos-Rezak argues that the semiotic revolution of the prescholastic period involved crucially this feedback relationship between the practice of sealing and the theology of immanence. This fostered the development of a high degree of awareness of semiotic problems in many cultural spheres; lively debate about the role of signs in aesthetic expression, eucharistic ritual, and linguistic structure; and a corresponding expansion of the systematicity of official semiotic doctrine. It does not appear that anyone thought that seals were "creative indexicals" in the strong sense that a token seal could bring into existence an official personage; but the presencing effect of seals did contribute to the production of an abstract system of social differentiation parallel to other representational systems, such as heraldry.

> Through signs, the individual acquired definition and was constituted as an effective site for the production of symbolic activity. Ultimately, individual identity was subordinated to signs because, in terms of the prescholastic dialectics . . . signs had greater and more stable powers of representation, their modes of representation involving less personality than typology. . . . Seals did not construct social relationships, but they did catalog them as a hierarchical set, serving as a formal system for the indication of social status. (Bedos-Rezak 2000, 1532)

What is striking in this analysis is Bedos-Rezak's perception that, in this particular case, there is no necessary contradiction between semiotic awareness and an ideology of immanence in the signifier/signified relationship. Semiotic beliefs at this moment in the medieval period, that a referent is made ontologically present in the sign or that the bar of signification is erased in special contexts, are part of a highly rational and literate debate and are not the result of a nonreflective "mystical participation" so many analysts impose on the "tribal" world. As Peter Abelard, the innovative prescholastic philosopher, noted, when the mind (*intellectus*) is presented with a statue of Achilles, the statue is regarded as a representation and not as Achilles himself (Guilfoy 2004, 210–11).

A fascinating project would be to compare the theologically informed discourse and practice of type-token replication in Eastern and Western Christianity during the Middle Ages. In a perceptive article on the copying of religious icons and other images in Byzantium, Vikan (1989) confesses that in earlier studies he considered the widespread phenomenon of near-exact copying over a range of centuries to be understandable in terms of the convenience of the production context (with many scribes looking at the same "original") and of a "democratic" impulse to distribute mass-produced tokens to pilgrims. But subsequent reflection convinced him to look more deeply at the theological context, noting first of all that in Byzantine theory and practice power and holiness are embodied equally in *all* copies of an icon, since every icon in whatever style or material condition is the "mediating vehicle between supplicant and the deity or saint represented" (1989, 50). This is the case not because of some idea that the materiality of the token is specially transformed but by the opposite idea, that in looking at a religious icon the believer gazes transparently at the archetypal referent. Vikan quotes Saint Theodore:

> Every artificial image . . . exhibits in itself, by way of imitation, the form of its model . . . the model [is] in the image, the one in the other, except for differences of substance. Hence, he who reveres an image surely reveres the person whom the image shows; not the substance of the image. . . . Nor does the singleness of this veneration separate the model from the image, since, by virtue of imitation, the image and the model are one. (Cited in Vikan 1989, 50)

In the case of religious icons, the archetypal referent is the sacred model that guides the process of reproduction. But, Vikan asks, what about objects that are produced as a result of the reproductive imprint of a "forming agent" that is itself holy, as a saint's relics, a piece of the True Cross, or the Shroud of Turin? Note that, for relics, indexicality replaces iconicity as the dominant semiotic modality. The veneration of icons and the transaction of relics in Byzantium can both be grounded in the theological metaphor of the "imitation" of Christ and the saints, a metaphor not at all unlike the semiotic metaphors discussed by Bedos-Rezak for Western Christianity. As Saint Basil wrote:

> [In the scriptures] the lives of saintly men, recorded and handed down to us, lie before us like living images of God's government, for our imitation of their good works. And so in whatever respect each one perceives himself deficient, if he devotes himself to such imitation, he will discover there, as in the shop of a public physician, the specific remedy for his infirmity. (Cited in Vikan 1989, 57)

And, to bring this discussion back to medieval seals, Saint Theodore draws an explicit connection between the role of images of Christ and images of the emperor:

> Or take the example of a signet ring engraved with the imperial image, and let it be impressed upon wax, pitch and clay. The impression is one and the same to the several materials which, however, are different with respect to each other; yet it would not have remained identical unless it were entirely unconnected with the materials. . . . The same applies to the likeness of Christ irrespective of the material upon which it is represented. (Cited in Vikan 1989, 51)

The notion, then, that religious minds fear pictorial representation (Brandt 2000) must be seen as relative to the mediating cultural ideology of images (Berndt 1983; Davis 1986; Gero 1973; Kitzinger 1954; Ladner 1953; Leroi-Gourhan 1986; Preston 1985; Valeri 1985; Winter 1992).

Semiotic ideologies, like the ones informing the production of seals, icons, and relics, are often hard to locate given the frequent lack of specific markers for metasemiotic signs in culture. In contrast to the sign processes in social life, artificial semiotic systems need to make a clear distinction between signs operating at the discursive level and at the metadiscursive level. The use of markers such as quotation marks or brackets serves to separate direct signification from comments on the signifying process. In human sign systems, on the other hand, these levels are often formally continuous, with little warning that a shift from use to mention has occurred. The frequent absence of explicit markers to distinguish levels of semiosis creates many opportunities for misunderstanding, as the artist Duchamp learned when the urinal he placed in an exhibition (under the title "Fountain"), which he intended to be a metalevel comment on the futility of an aesthetic based on beauty, was received by viewers as pointing out the previously unrecognized beauty of the urinal's lines (Danto 1997, 84). This ambiguity of levels is partly responsible for the flowering of various "double-voiced" genres such as irony and parody, which enrich discourse beyond the explicit or inherent metadiscursive forms such as verbs of speaking and quotative inflections (Bakhtin 1981, 360–61). And the metasemiotic character of irony and parody points to the fact that not all metasemiotic discourse is an expression of powerful elites: cultic practices invert dominant rituals, carnivalesque dramas challenge existing social norms, and fringe artists comment on the status quo of a society (Babcock 1978, 296). This implies an additional analytical complication, since the presence of "subaltern" discourses cannot be taken as direct evidence for the social power of those voices; often, institutional authority allows a degree of discursive opposition as a means of deflecting more dangerous revolutionary activity. And inversely, extreme efforts by dominant groups to silence the sign production of subordinates can be taken as evidence for the potential power of subversive forces (Nash 1997, 347).

Conclusion

This rapid survey of troublesome points and exemplary work in cultural semiotics is intended to suggest that in this new millennium theoretical advances will be made by detailed empirical research that clarifies and expands a delimited number of concepts—as Felson's focus on deixis and Bedos-Rezak's on replication. Careful study of these kinds of state-of-the-art projects can, then, lead to hypotheses and generalizations worthy of testing. It is not important, in my view, to impose a single regimenting analytical metalanguage, although my own research and thinking have found the Peircean tools useful in suggesting certain distinctions in sign functioning and in allowing cross-case comparison. But even the Peircean model does not predict the way signs in social life are structured or interpreted. And it is not yet clear that the hierarchical "syntax" of Peircean sign types (Parmentier 1994c, 18–19) corresponds to any developmental, historical, or evolutionary processes.

One implication of this view is that there is danger in trying to study "semiotics itself" as an independent or even hegemonic discipline if that involves abandoning the empirical territory of traditional disciplines. The proliferation of semiotic encyclopedias, dictionaries, handbooks, and introductory texts, not to mention the numerous journals, conferences, monograph series, and web sites, should not tempt scholars away from their primary disciplines. On the positive side, if semiotics can remain free of the institutional and intellectual constraints of more established disciplines, then researchers might continue to "enjoy a greater degree of speculative freedom" (Bouissac 2000, 18).

Note

This paper was originally published as "Representing Semiotics in the New Millennium," *Semiotica* 142 (2002): 291–314. Reprinted with permission of Walter de Gruyter.

8 The World Has Changed Forever: Semiotic Reflections on the Experience of Sudden Change

Having spent more than twenty-five years thinking about social change in Oceania, in particular about the historical changes reflected in the mythological narratives of Palau (Belau), I did not anticipate how difficult the challenge would be to consider—prompted by the invitation to participate in today's panel—sudden, rapid, or traumatic change. Would this mere augmentation of the rate of acceleration necessitate a dramatic reformulation of the almost canonical post-Sahlins model for studying the "anthropology of history" as the transformation of the structures of reproduction? That is, is sudden change (let me use the word "sudden" to stand as a shorthand for my more elaborate earlier phrase "sudden, rapid, or traumatic") on a continuum with change? While it is obvious that a sudden disaster can *trigger* a period of rapid social change, there is something in suddenness itself that uniquely reveals underlying social regularities (or irregularities). And where do we place sudden change in relation to the Braudelian triumvirate of event change, conjunctural change, and changes of "long duration"?

Part of the dilemma seems to me to rest on the addition of the phrase, "the experience of" sudden change, since there is considerable evidence from Oceania, as well as anecdotal evidence from our own contemporary world, that people do not in fact experience unanticipated, unprecedented, epochal upheavals *as change*; and, in a nontrivial sense, it could also be said that in these situations people don't *experience* anything. This accounts for the occurrence of words like "speechless," "incomprehensible," and "unfathomable" used in the aftermath of crises whose primary cognitive impact is that they surpass understanding. From a sociological perspective, there is talk of the inability of a group to "frame" or "encompass" the changes confronting them. And from a more semiotic perspective, we can think of the nonexperience of trauma in terms of the opposition between the systematic suppression of evidence indexing the event, which generates an *excess* of signs, and the incapacity of people to form representations or expressions of the event, an outcome that leads to an *absence* of signs.

I was struck the other day the historian van Dijk's remark that, after the overthrow of Pharaoh Akhenaten's short-lived monotheistic reign at Amarna in eighteenth-dynasty Egypt, "nothing would ever be the same" (2002), since I had just read similar words recorded by Linenthal after the Oklahoma City bombing that "life . . . may be forever altered" (2003). That the "world has changed forever" has certainly become a major rhetorical trope and ideological slogan in the contemporary United States. What interests me most about these expressions of apocalyptic finality is the underlying cultural self-understanding: that the social orders of Egypt and Oklahoma do not anticipate sudden change as, to be paradoxical for a moment, a regular feature of collective experience. But my reading of ethnographic and ethnohistorical accounts from Mesoamerica, South America, and Melanesia has reminded me that there are in fact cultures that have built-in models of transformation and also built-in models to deny transformation, and so the analytical task of exploring "the experience of sudden change" surely requires attention to the contrasting cultural models of change.

My own field of Oceania is certainly a good place to start thinking through these issues, since this broad expanse of cultures spread out across the Pacific Ocean has universally experienced literal and metaphorical "waves" of sudden change at the hands of natural forces—volcanic eruptions, tsunamis, infestations, and typhoons—and at the hands of cultural forces—European (and, it now appears, Asian) exploration, colonialism, missionization, and warfare. Disaster, again literally and metaphorically, comes from over the horizon, which in many Oceanic cultures is a mythical location that conjoins the "heavens" with the "foreign." Recent anthropological and historical scholarship has laid to rest the assumption that Oceanic societies are "peoples without history" by demonstrating, first, that there are semiotic modes for representing the past other than written narrative; second, that in the often dramatic encounter between indigenous and foreign powers the former are equal to the latter in agency, though often not in potency or efficiency; and third, that, *pace* Obeyesekere, more than practical or utilitarian rationality underpins the motivations and intentions of both parties to these interactions across what Dening labels "islands and beaches" (1986).

In my book *The Sacred Remains: Myth, History, and Polity in Belau* (1987), I attempted to introduce a fourth advance, already anticipated by many specialists in the field and especially stimulated by my teacher Bernard Cohn's (1961) work on India, that there are multiple temporalities and multiple histories informing this archipelagic nation, and that there are interesting linkages between these multiplicities and the types of material embodiments of history (*olangch*, principally, stones) and the hierarchical qualities of the sociopolitical system (principally, untitled vs. titled roles, low-ranking vs. high-ranking vs. villages). I pinpointed, for example, several parallel processes or trajectories that are found repeatedly in narratives, such as the gradual consolidation of a local polity around a focal capital village, at which moment that polity is described as an integrated and mature system of "four cornerposts"; the dynamic tension between the lateral dispersal of kinship affiliation (due in part to Palau's being a "disharmonic regime") and locally grounded lines of political authority; and sequential waves of externally imported symbols of sacred power, especially pieces of bead money that are the coin of the realm and a class of gods called the Ruchel who populate myths about innovation and who provide a narrative model for the historical appearance of foreigners "from the west" (*a rechad er a ngebard*).

But in focusing my attention on what I called "models of transformation," I did not directly address the issue of the experience of *sudden* change. Indeed, one of the principal arguments in the book is that there is an inverse relationship between social rank and the sedimentation of change: high-ranking titleholders from high-ranking villages ground their legitimacy in relatively permanent historical markers and, more interestingly, in markers that are no longer "in play" in the dynamics of social life. The title of the book translates a key ideological expression (*a meang a medechel*) of this denial of "event-time" in the capital village of Ngeremlengui, since once the "sacred" has come to "remain" in one place, mythological narratives function to perpetuate the fiction that historical contingencies (assassinations, usurpations, wars, economic competition, and intra-island migration, for example) do not have the power to alter the traditional order. It is not so much that Ngeremlengui's ideology of history denies change—even the district's name, "Place of Molting," suggests otherwise—but that the epochal flood that overturned the political order, bringing into existence the lithically grounded "cornerpost" organization of capitals, did not establish a precedent that this kind of change would ever occur again. The question becomes, then, will the experience of sudden change, in contrast to gradually sedimented transformations, also vary according to the stratified ideology of temporality?

So, to rethink the Palauan case, I have turned my comparative attention recently to articles and books that treat the experience of sudden change. Let me review a couple of insights that have been helpful in this project. Turner (1988) has written about how the Kayapó of the Amazonian rainforest confronted the destructive advent of Brazilians, not as a singular experience, but belonging to a pattern established in previous dealings with regional groups. Brazilians, he writes, were "not seen by the Kayapó as presenting special problems from the standpoint of their mythic system as a whole" (205). In a related ethnographic case from South America of the "inclusions" of the external, Hill finds that the Wakuénai's experience of periodic state-level expansion along the Rio Negro, including dramatic loss of population due to disease, allowed for recovery periods during which "ethnogenesis" actually flourished (1996, 152). In mythological narratives, contact with "whites" was encompassed by locating this change at the "center of mythic space" (157).

In a series of almost incredibly detailed studies, Porter Poole (1994) shows how the Bimin-Kuskusmin of the Upper Sepik area of Papua New Guinea came to understand anomalies attendant on the "great destruction" of the 1940s (caused by mining operations digging into sacred ground) by arguing that strange events that could not be accounted for by existing cultural metaphors did not, in fact, "leave a scar" on their ritually charged "center place"—at least until these changes proved so dramatic that another interpretive model came to the fore that read events as analogous to various transformations, destructions, and weakenings mentioned in myths. In another case study of the Duna, also from the New Guinea highlands, Stürzenhofecker discovered that, in a situation where the culture's interlocking metaphors were decisively upset by externally derived change (again, mining), practices that did remain in place metonymically took on the "weight" of all the other metaphors and that certain cultural values that had been part of the presupposed cosmological grounding (primarily, gender asymmetry) now became highly politicized topics for discussion (1998, 32–33). Together, these two developments led to a more general alteration in the Duni ideology of history, from the concept of "ground ending/completing" to the evangelical concept of the "end of the world." Schwimmer documents a parallel response by the Orokaiva to the volcanic eruption of Mount Lamington in 1951, after which the people started to accept the missionaries' ideas about the end of the world (1969, 73). The coincidence that the "Lord of the Dead" was thought to live in this very mountain, Schwimmer points out, was certainly a factor contributing to the belief that this god's anger was responsible for the four thousand deaths. McDowell (1988) argues that the Bun, a people in the East Sepik Province of Papua New Guinea, have an "episodic" ideology of history, according to which *all* change must be "dramatic, total, and complete" (rather than gradual, cumulative, or evolutionary). The fundamentally discontinuous nature of change is modeled by the Bun in their rites of passage, where status transitions are sudden and irrevocable (1988, 124).

What, then, do these comparative examples add to my methodological reflection on sudden change in Oceania? While it might seem to be a serious cop-out, I think that analysts must be sensitive to contingency, accident, and coincidence in studying responses to change. That Captain Cook arrived at the "big island" of Hawaii at the exact time and from the exact direction (and with an appropriate last name, if "Ku Ku Ku Ku" sounds like "Cook Cook Cook" when chanted by tens of thousands of islanders on the shore) is certainly significant in the ritually enacted identification of the English captain as a Hawaiian high god. In 1963, President Sukarno of Indonesia attempted to ritually launch the "New Order" by means of the Eka Dasa Rudra ceremony held on top of Mt. Agung on the island of Bali. But the ritual climaxed on the very day that the mountain erupted, throwing out mud, rock, smoke, and dust; and although the ritual specialists continued the process, Sukarno decided to stay home. A journalist on the scene wrote at the time, the "Balinese interpreted this as a divine judgement on the Sukarno regime" (Lansing 1983, 137).

Contingency can also play a role in the disambiguation of alternative interpretive framings of a situation. A culture might entertain, at the level of model, multiple possible readings of "first contact" with, for example, European explorers as returning malevolent ancestral spirits (ghostly white skins tend to encourage this interpretation) or as returning fraternal relatives. Which model is applied in a particular situation sometimes comes down to whether bullets or trade axes are exchanged first. Similarly, a suddenly changed circumstance that is taken to be a generalized threat to order can be viewed either as a singular anomaly or as an opening to chaos, depending on a variety of contingent factors.

Contingencies can be not quite so dramatic, as in the case of Raroia in the Tuamotus Islands in Polynesia, where the typhoon that devastated the island in 1901 not only destroyed houses, farms, and trees but many items of material culture, including the "family books" in which, at the behest of the missionaries, people had entextualized their genealogies and chants. With the books lost, only a few specially trained elders held on to the memory of the traditional past, and so the typhoon ended up have far more drastic consequences than those dictated by nature (Danielsson 1952, 136–37). The original copies of transcribed and translated traditional narrative collected by the Palau Community Action Agency were lost in a fire that destroyed the building; fortunately, the archive had been microfilmed for storage at the Sinclair Library at the University of Hawaii.

These last two examples help to identify a second generalization, that the distinction between change and devastation might depend on the simple fact of what semiotic markers a society chooses to be loci of memory.

A third generalization that emerges is that, while sudden changes might not be comprehensive (let alone endurable), it does seem that dramatic events cause a heightened consciousness or awareness of some aspects of the situation, if only of massive suffering—New Orleans would be a perfect example. This observation might be another application of the concept developed by Prague School linguists that any deformation of a norm (linguistic, aesthetic, moral) involves a reference to the very norm being violated. Societies in Oceania have responded to Western contact in many cases with an increased ritualization of behavior, perhaps best known from the "cargo cults" that developed throughout Melanesia in response to the trauma of World War II. Garcia-Acosta (2002) provides a fascinating illustration from Mexico, in which long-term socioeconomic trends in an area went under the radar until an earthquake prompted a house-by-house survey by a damage assessment team; only then did the residents come to realize the true extent of the Catholic Church's real estate holdings in the area. Another possible response in consciousness would be an increase in rule-governed conventionality or new strictures against heteropraxy.

A fourth generalization would be that responses to sudden change might not be self-evidently about change at all. The historian of religion Jonathan Z. Smith has written insightfully about Melanesian cargo cults as ritual instantiations of the larger issue of the "confrontation of native and Western economic systems" (1993, 305). His analysis of a myth involving the failure of traditional reciprocal exchange is a good reminder that cultures often produce self-understandings that, like the dream-work in the Freudian model, represent only by symbolic indirection (Smith 1976, 18). Modekngei, a local revitalization movement in Palau, provides another illustration of the "indirection" of symbols of change: wearing a red loincloth (*saker*) by an elder male is taken to be a symbol of traditional sacredness and esoteric wisdom (I had only one memorable encounter with the famous chanter Spes so dressed back in 1978). But it turns out that twenty yards of red cloth came to the islands as trade goods in 1871, and, as a prized object from a foreign ship, red cloth became a way to translate externality into sacredness.

While I would not conclude that I have advanced a theory of responses to sudden change, I do think that research methods that probe the roles of contextual contingency, historical markers, elevated consciousness, and symbolic indirection may be steps toward such a comprehensive theory.

Note

This paper was first presented at the meetings of the American Society for Ethnohistory, Commemorating Encounters: Reenactments and Reinterpretations, Williamsburg, Virginia (November 3, 2006). It was originally published as "The World Has Changed Forever: Semiotic Reflections on the Experience of Sudden Change," *Semiotica* 192 (2012): 235–42. Reprinted with permission of Walter de Gruyter.

9 Description and Comparison of Religion

In 1947, a young anthropologist named Ward Goodenough arrived at Chuuk (formerly Truk), a group of atolls and high islands in the Caroline Islands of Micronesia, as part of the Coordinated Investigation in Micronesian Anthropology (CIMA), funded by the Office of Naval Research and supervised by George Peter Murdock of Yale University. More than a half-century later in 2002, Goodenough, by then a university professor emeritus at the University of Pennsylvania, published the results of his research on the pre-Christian religion of Chuuk in *Under Heaven's Brow*, a book that represents the lifework of the most distinguished Micronesian specialist in this country. Its authoritative status derives from three factors. First, Goodenough is an expert on the Chuukese language and is, in fact, the coauthor of the standard dictionary (Goodenough and Sugita 1980). He is also a scholar of the comparative linguistics of the Micronesian region. His translations, retranslations, and derivations, therefore, carry great weight. Second, Goodenough has mastered all the available evidence on Chuuk, including early German ethnographic studies, archaeological site reports, and unpublished field materials from a number of other scholars. And third, Goodenough is one of contemporary anthropology's eminent theoreticians, cofounder of the method of componential analysis, and author of widely read treatises on social change, language and culture, and the comparative method (1956, 1970a, 1981a, 1983).

Chuuk is a group of seventeen high islands and numerous low-lying atolls surrounded by a reef encompassing a central lagoon with an area of 822 square miles.[1] Limited archaeological evidence points to human habitation of Chuuk in the first or second centuries BCE; widespread evidence of habitation dating from the fourteenth century CE provides a baseline for understanding precontact Chuukese culture. In addition to plentiful marine resources, the islanders rely on breadfruit and taro to sustain life. The language spoken on Chuuk belongs to the Nuclear Micronesian subdivision of the Oceanic division of the Austronesian language family. Data from related languages suggest that the inhabitants of Chuuk migrated from atolls to the east; this westward expansion across the central Pacific continued for centuries, and the entire region was linked by interisland trade.

In contrast to other high islands in Micronesia, including especially Palau and Pohnpei, Chuuk remained isolated from Western contact until well into the nineteenth century. Palau and Pohnpei were regular ports of call for traders, whalers, and missionaries, but Chuuk has experienced sustained contact only since the 1880s (Hezel 1973). The project of reconstructing the pre-Christian religion of Chuuk is greatly facilitated by the ethnographic studies of Augustin Krämer in 1906–1907 and the missionary Laurentius Bollig in 1912–1914. Goodenough makes full use of these German works, and, given his mastery of the Chuukese language, he is able to clarify, correct, and augment their often imperfect translations. By 1947 only some of the traditional rituals were still being practiced; still fewer were observed in 1964–1965 when Goodenough returned to Chuuk for additional fieldwork. Today Chuukese are members of Protestant and Catholic churches, a subject not treated in *Under Heaven's Brow.*

According to traditional Chuukese cosmology, the home of the spirits of human ancestors is Achaw, the expanse of sky somewhere far to the east, a place that is also the origin point for the Chuukese people. The vault of the heavens was viewed as a huge inverted bowl, with different layers corresponding to various celestial phenomena, such as winds, birds, and stars. Above these tiers was "Under Brow," the home of the pantheon of sky gods. Communication between the spirit world and the human world was possible when spirits took on human form, when spirits took possession of human bodies, or when "effective spirits" of the dead intervened through spirit mediums (Goodenough 2002, 113). The world of human experience was populated with local spirits dwelling, for example, in rainbows, mountain peaks, reefs, caves, fishing zones, trees, and driftwood. Like many Oceanic peoples, Chuukese had a concept of "effecting power" (*manaman*, cognate with Polynesian *mana*), which provided efficacy for persons, spells, knowledge, and medicine.

Chuukese folklore makes reference to a line of high chiefs who founded a cult site on Achaw Peak, the highest spot on Weene Island. Bearing the title Sowuwooniiras ("Lord of Upper Side of Cult Site"), these chiefs were "human gods" and the purported founders of the important chiefly lines of Chuuk. Other oral narratives as well as archaeological and ethnohistorical data point to persistent warfare between and within districts, causing repeated changes of chieftainship. By the nineteenth century these struggles coalesced into warfare between two competing political leagues led by opposed "political priests" (*itang*), military leaders who had mastery of rival "schools" of traditional knowledge and rhetoric. "Their knowledge gave legitimacy to chiefs and provided a system of sanctions upholding the political and social order. They were the orators at assemblies, where they expounded on public morals, preaching on the proper way for people to behave to one another and to the chiefs. They were the principal players in the competitive politics through which chiefs sought to gain renown. They competed with one another to enhance their own reputations as men who had rhetorical skill, historical knowledge, and access to the most efficacious and formidable spirit power" (Goodenough 2002, 290).

Using evidence from philology, ethnohistory, and archaeology, Goodenough draws a connection between names, events, rituals, and structures on Chuuk with those on Pohnpei (formerly Ponape), a high island hundreds of miles to the east. On Pohnpei, the rule of the Saudeleur dynasty was anchored at Nan Madol, a massive megalithic complex built on artificial islands off the southeastern coast. The power of the dynasty was sedimented in four stone "corners," each representing a political district on the main island. The fourth stone corner was associated with Daukatau, a political-religious cult in the Wene district, said to have come to Pohnpei from Katau in the east. The sacred place at Daukatau in Wene, accessible only to the high priests of the ranking matriclan, was a complex of basaltic pillars, the same building materials used at Nan Madol. Pohnpeian folklore describes the overthrow of the Saudeleur dynasty by Isokelekel, said to have come to Pohnpei from Katau in the east to support the high priests of Daukatau.

Similarly, on Chuuk the summit of the volcanic plug Tonaachaw (Achaw Peak) on the island of Weene is the "most sacred place in Chuuk" (Goodenough 2002, 295), a cult site where rituals were addressed to the high god Sowukachaw by priests of the Sopwunupi clan. Sopwunupi means "District of the Sacred Stone Structure" (echoing the name Pohnpei, which means "On the Stone Structure"). As the cult of Sowukachaw spread from Tonaachaw to other regions of Chuuk, variations of the *itang* tradition became codified into regional schools, each with a unique style of political rhetoric. Originally all linked by genealogical ties to the foundational cult at Tonaachaw, the schools eventually broke away to become political rivals. Ultimately, these divisions led to warfare and to the abandonment of the cult center at Tonaachaw toward the end of the eighteenth century.

Goodenough's compelling synthesis of the available evidence from Pohnpei and Chuuk leads him to conclude that the *itang* cult of Chuuk spread from Wene in Pohnpei. Of critical importance for this reconstruction is the symbolic association at both places of basaltic stone structures with sky gods (in particular, thunder gods). But since, like most residents of high islands in Micronesia, Pohnpeians were not seafarers and since similar stone structures have been found on atolls such as Namu and Aur, Goodenough hypothesizes that the transfer of the cult between high islands was actually facilitated by skilled sailors from the atolls, particularly from the Mortlock Group one hundred eighty miles to the southeast (2002, 295). This argument has enormous implications for the study of the cultural history of Micronesia, for, as Goodenough writes, "Instead of thinking of high islands as having empires, we can think of them as centers of influence, their influences being spread by the atoll dwellers who came to them to trade and to seek refuge" (1986, 562)

And this, in turn, has important ramifications for Goodenough's broader comparative concern to ground the study of "phylogenetically related cultural traditions" in a methodology as sound as that found in historical linguistics and evolutionary biology (1997, 16–26). Earlier attempts within anthropology to establish the "genetic" history of cultures floundered primarily because attention was focused on often superficial resemblances of isolated traits. Goodenough proposes the methodological stricture that analysts of cultural traditions look "not simply to the similarities of their parts but also to the similarities of the place of the parts in the larger system, the similarity, that is, of the structural arrangement" (17). The difficulties of actually doing this are well known to biologists, who distinguish between anatomical features that are structurally homologous and features that are merely functionally analogous—only the former offering solid evidence of evolutionary connection.

Illustrating his argument with linguistic data, Goodenough shows that his principle of "structural arrangement" can lead to detecting a phylogenetic connection even in cases where cultural features appear not to have any obvious similarities. Suppose two languages show obvious systematic sound change, such as Gilbertese *tama-na* 'his father' and Chuukese *sama-n* 'his father.' If this sound change appears regularly in semantically parallel forms, then clearly Gilbertese /t/ corresponds to Chuukese /s/. By carrying out this comparison more broadly, it becomes possible to establish cognate words in the two languages in cases where all the constituent phonemes have been modified. "If such comparison is productive of cognate words that no longer look (sound) alike on the surface at all but whose differences conform to the pattern of corresponding differences already worked out and whose meanings (functions) remain reasonably similar—or reasonably derivable from ones that were similar—powerful confirmation of the hypothesis of genetic relationship is provided" (Goodenough 1997, 19). Thinking now about cultural rather than linguistic data, Goodenough argues that a history of connection can be established only in situations in which the "amount of change in the cognate traditions has not been very great and there are other kinds of evidence that corroborate relationships" (21). It is important to note here that cognate traditions need not be labeled by semantically cognate terms. Goodenough cites the case of the Samoan *fono* and the Gilbertese *mwaneaba*, two cognate political assemblies. Of course, the presence of similar semantic labels is highly suggestive of cognate institutions, such as the Tahitian and Maori religious structures both called *marae*.

Another difficulty in moving from the solid realms of language and biology to that of culture is that there is no necessary connection between the genetic identity of a population and its cultural practices. Kansas farmers can practice Buddhism just as easily as the son of a Micronesian fisherman can earn a degree in physics. Goodenough is, of course, fully aware of the variety of historical processes of change that can lead to structural similarities without genetic connection. A society can, for example, borrow a cultural trait or complex from another society that may or may not be phylogenetically related at some earlier node. One society can imitate cultural practices of another society without any exchange of genetic material. Or a society can be changed by the migration of people with different cultural practices—Anatolian farmers bringing their Neolithic culture with them as they migrated into Europe, for example (1970b, 262). Migrating peoples can, of course, fully adopt the cultural practices of their host societies, leaving only genetic markers as evidence of population movements. In other words, the whole problem of "phylogenetic" connection is much more complicated in anthropology than in biology.

Goodenough suggests that "Remote Oceania," that is, the Pacific islands settled by people with Lapita pottery, speaking Austronesian languages, provides an excellent research case precisely because, since we already know that these cultures bear a phylogenetic relationship, the study of functionally related phenomena that do not evidence physical similarities might still be fruitfully compared by close attention to the parallel structural arrangement of component parts. In a brilliant piece of comparative sleuthing, Goodenough proposes that the structure of the village dance ground in Malekula (Vanuatu), with its opposition between "male" and "female" ends and the carefully graded positioning of sacred stones, clubhouses, and residences, can be compared to the structure of the Tahitian *marae,* despite their distinct dissimilarities:

> If we remove the dwellings from the end of the dance ground associated with women, if we remove the club house, if we construct some kind of stone platform along the "sacred" end, and if we arrange the effigies in the form of upright stone stabs or carved wooden boards that represent former chiefs and ancestral gods along the platform, we come up with a Tahitian *marae.* . . . What I am suggesting . . . is that the Malekula dance ground and the way it is organized as a ceremonial place is a cognate institution with the Tahitian and Maori . . . *marae* and, presumably, with the ceremonial grounds or centers associated with communities in other Oceanic societies. (1997, 105)

Although in this discussion of phylogenetic traditions Goodenough wisely separates the study of language from the study of culture, in his treatise *Description and Comparison in Cultural Anthropology* he insists on their fundamental methodological similarity (1970a). Namely, he supports the premise that there is a direct analogy between phonemic/phonetic analysis in linguistics and between emic/etic analyses in anthropology. The distinction between emic and etic dimensions of analysis in the study of religion is usefully explained by Armin Geertz: "The *emic* perspective involves explanation, interpretation, and understanding in relation to the rules or assumptions of the religion and culture itself. These rules or assumptions are found as a) explicit rules or statements, b) implicit assumptions that local thinkers and foreign scholars can analyze in a variety of ways: ethno- analysis, textual and iconographic analysis, historical analysis, etc., and c) expressed through behavior such as pilgrimage, dance, trance, prayer, meditation, drama, ritual, and so on. The *etic* perspective involves the explanation, interpretation, and understanding in relation to on-going interests in the global and comparative study of religion" (2000, 71). Although Goodenough repeatedly discusses the distinction between emic and etic dimensions in terms of "particular" and "general" perspectives, that is, between culturally salient discriminations and universally applicable scientific generalizations, it is vital to appreciate Lincoln's keen observation that, in the study of religions, the "particular" religious system may in fact insist on its "eternal, transcendent, spiritual, and divine" truth while the "general" analytical perspective must engage the "temporal, contextual, situational, interested, human, and material dimensions" (2000, 118–19; cf. Smith 2001, 141–43).

Goodenough's enthusiasm for this analogy between linguistic and cultural phenomena seems to me to be misplaced, particularly in consideration of the problem of the "domain" of analysis. The domain of language can be easily established, since in every culture language is a system of meaningful speech, a "kind of tool for implementing intentionality in social interaction" (Goodenough 1990, 608). But this is not paralleled by other cultural domains, for example, kinship and religion, where the definitions of the two domains are much less clear. Comparison of many particular languages is obviously needed to establish the universal etic tool kit that can provide the metalanguage general enough to encompass the known evidence of particular sets of distinctions. But comparison of kinship and religious systems involves two distinct tasks: first, defining by multiple emic analyses the maximal set of formal distinctions of the domain and, second, defining the domain itself as a result of the first operation and then justifying or confirming that definition in terms of functional universals grounded in the species-being of humans and the requirements of social life. The trouble is that the first operation seems to presuppose the second; that is, there is no principled way to collect, for example, the "varieties of religious experience" as a means toward defining the domain "religion." What data would one collect and what would one overlook?

Now it may be the case that certain domains are easier to define than others. One might assume, for instance, a gradation from language to property to religion, defining the first quite simply as the accepted rules for articulate speech and the second as the individual and collective ownership of material and immaterial objects. But what—"simply"—is the domain of religion? Goodenough seems to have two answers to this thorny question, answers that might turn out to be incompatible. First, at several points he makes the commonsense argument that, as scientists based in the "Anglo-American" culture and language, we should define a given domain in another culture by its "functional analogue" to the local construction of that domain in our own culture: "We label 'property' in Truk the cultural forms that seem to be the functional analogues of what we already label 'property' in Anglo-American culture" (Goodenough 1970a, 120). Chuukese might make distinctions among types of property or property relations that are unfamiliar to us—indeed it does, as Goodenough demonstrated in his classic monograph (1951)—but the domain of property is self-evidently similar. Second, Goodenough claims that domains are established by "functional universals," that is, cultural rules and practices that answer to requirements common to all human societies. For example, all human societies need (*a*) to determine when a woman is eligible for sexual relations and eligible to bear children, (*b*) to know when a man is eligible to engage in sexual relations and to beget children, (*c*) to determine who has sexual privileges with whom, and (*d*) to determine the membership rights of children and the maintenance obligations of adults (Goodenough 1970a, 8). While some societies may accomplish these "transactions" with two kinds of institutional arrangements ("marriage" and "family," for example), others may use entirely different social forms.

As Goodenough expresses this shift from form to function: "So let us ignore the kinds of social groups involved and look at the kinds of human social problems the transactions are intended to solve" (1970a, 9). Marriage, in this reasoning, is universally about "sexual access," and as such it reflects several "general human characteristics," including the tendency to form affect-laden relationships, the prolonged dependency of human children, the combative attitude of males regarding sexual access to females, and the tendency of coresidential siblings to avoid sexual liaisons. In short, cultural domains can be defined by showing how "they relate to the handling of problems of social living that arise from human nature," or put even more succinctly, showing "the concerns with respect to which people maintain culture" (1970a, 17, 38).

It is clear that Goodenough does not see the "Anglo-American functional analogue" argument to be inconsistent with the "functional universal" argument. Indeed, he explicitly links the two: "The definitions I offer are not presented as the best definitions in any absolute sense. They are the best definitions I have been able to find that simultaneously serve two purposes. One is that they be universally applicable and provide fixed reference points for general comparison. The other purpose is that within the limitations imposed by universal applicability the definitions retain as much as possible of the considerations we have traditionally had in mind when we have identified something in another culture as the analogue of what we call marriage, family, and parenthood in our own culture" (1970a, 37). A useful exercise, then, would be to examine closely Goodenough's theory of the domain of religion by focusing on his definitive treatment of Chuukese religion, to see if it is possible to characterize that unfamiliar religious system both in terms that fall within some asserted human universal "concern" and with reference to "what we call" religion.

In a series of articles that appeared from 1974 to 1999, Goodenough articulates a consistent anthropological approach to religion that forcefully rejects the "Anglo-American functional analogue" argument he used so successfully in his work on property and kinship in favor of the "functional universal" argument. Indeed, the definition that Goodenough comes up with after the twin tasks of "description" and "comparison" is one that renders the domain of religion decidedly unfamiliar to our own tradition. And, ironically, the attainment of this universal definition requires a substantial and self-conscious effort to overcome the familiar understanding of our local religious traditions.

In these papers Goodenough notes that, during his initial fieldwork in Chuuk, he dutifully pursued his assignment as part of the research team of collecting information on pre-Christian religious beliefs and practices. Initially following the "functional analogue" premise of taking "our own cultural assumptions" as a first guide to defining religion, he went about looking for symbolically laden ritual practices and beliefs in supernaturals. This research, he informs us, centered on four major areas of ritual elaboration—divination, harvest rituals, disease diagnosis, and rituals for the dead—and was guided by the "*a priori* assumption that it belonged to the domain of religion" (1981b, 412). But, he observes in retrospect, "I became increasingly uneasy about what I was to make of it" (411). This unease generated two questions: Why did Chuukese continue certain beliefs and practices even after conversion to Christianity, and why were there many other areas subject to ritual elaboration that were not within the assumed bounds of "religion"?

The answer to both questions, and the ultimate stimulus for Goodenough's mature theory of religion, was the recognition, years after his initial fieldwork, of a remarkable empirical consilience between his research results and those published by Gladwin (1953, with Sarasan) in *Truk: Man in Paradise*. Gladwin was a member of the original CIMA (Coordinated Investigation of Micronesian Anthropology) team, and his work reported on the psychological and emotional concerns of the Chuukese people, based on field research and on Thematic Apperception Tests administered to local residents. Not only did these results confirm the "religious" practices Goodenough had already noted, but they suggested that other cultural practices were similarly "vehicles for expressing and managing emotional problems relating to the maintenance and/or realization of the self, as each self develops and matures in the matrix of social relationships in which they are embedded" (1981b, 411).[2]

At this point Goodenough clearly identifies the function of "self-maintenance," which proved useful in analyzing ethnographic and psychological data from one case, as the universal function of religion.[3] There is, evidently, no need to build up an etic tool kit through the careful comparison of cases. "Given this approach to religious life in Truk," Goodenough writes, a universal definition of religion appears: "Beliefs, customs, and institutions may be considered religious to the extent that people use them as vehicles for managing the emotional and other psychological problems relating to the maintenance and/or realization of the self" (1981b, 414). Because the concern for self-maintenance must be present in every act that is to be deemed religious, the same event can be religious for one participant and not religious for others (e.g., a funeral for a mortician) (1988, 121). Similarly, a rite that becomes routinized through time and thus only engages the perfunctory attention of participants is no longer religious, while compulsive behavior in many domains of life, say, business or sports, is religious. And since self-maintenance is largely a matter of solidifying one's place in a social group, many activities that increase a sense of group solidarity are religious, including rock festivals, spring break, campus sit-ins, and health club workouts.

The focus on self-maintenance does not, for Goodenough, imply an individual- or personality-centered understanding of the "religious" function, for the simple reason that "Who we are as persons derives from our relationship with others and from how we perceive ourselves in terms of the socially defined categories of age, sex, competence, group affiliation, etc. . . . Acceptance by others as members of both formal and informal social groups is critical in the maintenance of ourselves as social and thus as human beings" (1992, 288–89). An important implication of this relational view of the self is that it supports Goodenough's desire to move away from "belief" as the defining feature of the religious attitude. Indeed, he argues that participation in the traditional ritual practices of a community does not imply the conscious or reflective attention to the "truth" of the surrounding worldview. In fact, Goodenough finds the opposite to be the case: questions about the "truth" of dogma or about the "existence" of supernatural beings rarely disturb religious experience, except in situations that force the religious "background" into the problematized foreground. And even in the context of the "forced acculturation of ideas" (to use Taussig's [1980, 40–43] phrase), such as in Christian missionization, the people of Chuuk managed to maintain a degree of continuity between traditional and Christian beliefs and practices. For example, the Christian God was equated with the traditional "Great Spirit" and heaven with the abode of spirits in the sky; Christian ritual practices were viewed as a useful additional tool for self-maintenance; missionaries were conceptualized as parallel to traditional mediators with the spirit world; and family and clan continued to be more important loci of social identity than affiliation with either pagan or Christian systems (Goodenough 2002, 293).

Not only does this universal definition of religion seem, at first glance, not to characterize the religions familiar to members of the Anglo-American tradition, but it also appears to open up the label "religion" to institutions that are clearly outside that tradition's accepted domain. Both of these points are explicitly accepted by Goodenough. Indeed, he claims that, under his functional definition, communism is "one of the great, competing religions of modern times" and that the American Philosophical Society "serves religious needs for those of us who religiously attend its meetings" (1981b, 414, 415). If obviously political and scholarly institutions are religious by virtue of their linkage to "people's major emotional preoccupations, especially their concern with the cultivation and maintenance of the self in the social and symbolic milieus in which they live" (Goodenough 1974, 182), then cross-cultural comparison of structural arrangements becomes useless, as does the construction of etic tool kits.

Following the broad definition that any aspect of human culture that helps people manage "certain problems of existence is, to that extent and for those people, serving religious ends" (2002, 329), Goodenough is certainly permitted to include in *Under Heaven's Brow* data that would not normally be found in an ethnographic description of a culture's religious system—courtship rites, warfare chants, and ceremonial food exchange, for example. The definition does, however, provide only a patina of coherence for a book assembling data from so many diverse historical and ethnographic sources. Basically, Goodenough's argument is that Chuukese social life, in the context of an island environment, led people to feel very much at risk of damaging their physical, emotional, and relational well-being. Every individual was dependent upon the lineage for support and identity; and young people and women were additionally dependent on their male elders. "Complete dependence on one's lineage promoted emphasis on lineage solidarity and the obligations of mutual support among its members, and, with this, a tendency to let other lineages worry about their own affairs on their own. Indications of lack of solidarity, such as failure to render to one another the amenities of rank and the obligations of lineage membership, threatened the individual members' feelings of solidarity, given their dependence on that solidarity" (2002, 78). Risk threatened individuals in positions of authority as well as individuals in subordinate roles, since their decisions could turn out badly. Divinatory rites, Goodenough argues, provided one mechanism to shift decision-making responsibility to a higher, blameless authority. Similarly, everyday activities such as fishing, canoe building, and healing were highly ritualized. "This emphasis on strict adherence to proper procedure was also evident in the emphasis on strict observance of proper behavior in social interaction so as not to give offense and become liable to retaliatory action, especially by the powers of specialists and sorcerers" (2002, 331).

In linking aspects of Chuukese social life and psychological dynamics to "religious" rituals, Goodenough is also proposing a general theory of ritualization that counters other ideational, structural, and political approaches found in the anthropological literature. First articulated in 1974 and repeated in *Under Heaven's Brow,* this theory states that "people tend to be unable to leave alone what is symbolic or expressive of their emotional conflicts—what is expressive or symbolic, that is, of their major ego concerns. Being unable to leave such things alone, being compulsively drawn to them, people tend to elaborate them and to keep coming back to them over and over again" (1974, 171). Rituals are "vehicles for man aging the emotional and other psychological problems relating to the maintenance and/or realization of the self" (1981b, 414). And "as long as performing the rite brings emotional relief or helps people manage their concerns, it will be compulsively performed whenever the feeling of need reaches a crucial level" (1988, 121). Rituals are symbolic condensations of emotional concerns that externalize these concerns in the same collective arena of social life that caused the concerns in the first place: "Ritual not only helps people meet concerns relative to the state of their selves, it can also evoke such concerns in order to relieve them" (2002, 11).

So, discovered as the unifying feature of Chuukese religion, self-maintenance becomes, for Goodenough, the universal religious function. But he goes one step further, constructing a prescriptive argument that divides the world's religious traditions into two camps, those that accept the criterion of self-maintenance and can therefore feel comfortable with the scientific results of his study and those that continue to insist that the "God question" is relevant to people's lives and, thus, problematically confront the findings of science.

> But the tradition of belief in the existence of a divinity as the source of enlightenment or salvation persists—however that divinity is to be conceptualized, if at all—as does its corollary that without such belief no genuine enlightenment or spiritual self-fulfillment can be attained. For people who have grown up within this tradition and for whom this tradition has provided the terms and symbols of vitally important aspects of their self-hood, how to understand the nature of divinity in the light of modern science is inevitably an important religious concern. But the "God Question" cannot be such a concern for people who have grown up in traditions where the emphasis has been on observance rather than on belief or on the quest for harmonic attunement within oneself. For these people, acceptance of the understandings of modern science need not detract from the value of the observances through which they maintain cherished aspects of self and seek personal salvation. (Goodenough 1992, 294)

The final stage in the argument appears in a 1999 article where Goodenough argues that religious traditions that do have concepts of "God or gods" are themselves produced by "the human concern with achieving and maintaining experiences of the self that are satisfying and emotionally fulfilling. . . . Thus we see conceptions of God and the divine as among a larger set of human devices for dealing with certain kinds of problems of human existence" (1999, 276). According to this, the relevant distinction is not between belief-based religions and observance-based systems but rather between cultural traditions, whether beliefs or observances, in which individuals are under the illusion that their religions are about spiritual beings and traditions that recognize the truth that self-maintenance is the universal religious function, despite the fact that the historically well-grounded domain of "religion" has little empirical correspondence with those enlightened traditions—other than perhaps our own religion of healthy mindedness. In other words, not only are religious traditions universally about self-maintenance, but the awareness of this universal claim is the real key to emotional salvation.

In terms of the earlier discussion of the twin programs of "Anglo-American functional analogue" and "universal function" articulated especially in *Description and Comparison* and exercised in Goodenough's many writings on kinship, property, and social structure, it is clear that, in the articles on religion and in *Under Heaven's Brow*, Goodenough has come full circle. Declaring his inability to understand religion in Chuuk until he jettisoned his preconceived ideas based on his own Anglo-American tradition, Goodenough elevates the particular discoveries of the logic of the Chuukese system to the status of functional universal, and then he reinserts this universal function as an analytical wedge to turn the Anglo-American tradition upside down, with its emically standard religions ruled out of bounds.

One of the problems with this trajectory is a curious contradiction between Goodenough's work on religion and his highly elaborate methodology for studying language and kinship, namely, that etic comparison requires previous emic description and that emics is always a matter of locally recognized or at least salient distinctions. Generally, "the expectations one has of one's fellows may be regarded as a set of standards for perceiving, believing, evaluating, communicating, and acting. The standards constitute the culture that one attributes to one's fellows" (1970a, 99). According to the Goodenough of *Description and Comparison*, the test of the adequacy of a systematized set of etic concepts is its "ability satisfactorily to describe all the emic distinctions people actually make in all the world's cultures" (129). The trajectory I have outlined for Goodenough's work on religion rejects these solid methodological principles.

One issue remains to be addressed: Is there an even more general contradiction between the study of functional universals and the study of cultural phylogeny, discussed earlier? A reader of *Under Heaven's Brow* is struck by the persistent interweaving of these two methods of analysis, although much of the discussion of linguistic derivation, historical borrowing, and areal comparison is relegated to technical footnotes. (I focused above on the analysis of the *itang* cult as perhaps the fullest textual discussion of phylogenetic issues.) One must respect an author's declared aims, and Goodenough is insistent that his monograph is not a comparative work. Its comprehensive treatment of a vast array of ethnographic topics makes it, however, an essential source for anyone attempting to do a comparative study of Micronesian religion. Goodenough recognizes that comparison based on universals (either on the painstaking construction of etic typologies or on the direct identification of requirements of human nature and sociality) and comparison based on genetic or historical relationships are done for a "very different purpose" (1970a, 126), and he also recognizes the differential potential for phylogenetic reconstruction for different cultural domains. In language and technology, for instance, analysts have been fairly successful—in language because of the regularity of its patterning, and in technology because of the evident linkage between form and function. To advance phylogenetic analyses into other realms of culture, Goodenough insists that emic/etic work is essential in identifying functional analogues that, in turn, must be the starting point for the comparative study of cultural form (128).

While this seems at first glance to be an unexceptionable principle, I do not see how, in practical terms, a strongly grounded conclusion about a functional universal of some domain (e.g., self-maintenance for religion, sexual access for marriage) will assist in the phylogenetic comparison of a limited set of particular ethnographic cases. Comparison based on function can establish that several geographically dispersed phenomena are instances of the universal (i.e., that they fit within the defined cultural domain) but can say very little about their specific cultural-historical linkage, which is only accessible by the careful study of "structural arrangement." Indeed, it was one of Goodenough's insightful methodological observations that a lack of evident formal similarity does not rule out the possibility of phylogenetic linkage. But there is no principled way to construct an etic typology broad enough to encompass the entire set of empirically discovered emic distinctions if local forms *without* resemblances are also deemed possible instances. It seems to me more logical to carry out cross-cultural comparison in contexts of likely phylogenetic linkage directly from emic, that is, locally salient, structural arrangements. If positive linkages result, these can then be added to the set of cases accepted as instances of the domain.

Notes

This paper was originally published as "Description and Comparison of Religion," *History of Religions* 43 (3) (2004): 233–45.

1. Although some reference will be made in this article to the details of Chuukese ethnography, the central focus will be on the methodological aspects of Goodenough's work on religion. The evaluation of Goodenough's ethnographic contributions needs to rest in the hands of scholars of the Central Caroline Islands.

2. Goodenough articulated this attention to religious phenomena as solutions to emotional problems as early as 1963: "The functions we designate as religious relate largely to individual emotional needs and problems, which may or may not be widely shared. Furthermore, what is religion in the life of a given people is only going to have partial resemblance to what our own cultural values have normally led us to conclude under the term" (1983 [1963], 477).

3. Goodenough may also have been encouraged to think in terms of universal functions of religion by the writings of his father, Erwin Ramsdell Goodenough, who was the John A. Hoober Professor of Religion at Yale University and a distinguished historian of Jewish and Christian religions in the Greco-Roman period. E. R. Goodenough viewed the function of religious phenomena as "giving man security from the *tremendum* by an illusion that he is controlling it" (1967, 9), and wrote "we are stabilized in our emotions when we come to feel we are not helpless in a hostile universe, but that we can do something to control our destinies, so that, insofar as religion increases our hopes for crops and income or success in examinations, it quiets psychological unrest and so increases man's power and happiness" (1965, 74).

10   It's About Time: On the Semiotics of Temporality

THE INVITATION TO comment on this set of papers in linguistic anthropology dealing with temporalities and texts (first presented at the American Anthropological Association's 2005 meetings in Washington, DC) has prompted a moment of personal reflection, since it was exactly twenty years ago, in 1985, that I published my first application of semiotic categories to the ethnographic analysis of time and history. My paper, "Times of the Signs: Modalities of History and Levels of Social Structure in Belau" (Parmentier 1985b), tried to synthesize Fernand Braudel, Meyer Fortes, and Marshall Sahlins by using Charles S. Peirce's sign theory to argue that the social uses of three classes of stones—bead valuables, grave markers, and anthropomorphic megaliths—engage three levels of social structure—roughly, social roles, kinship-based houses, and hierarchical polities. Correspondingly, each social action involving these classes of stones marks three modalities of time—biographical, sociocentric, and historical—with the highest-ranked element in each class functioning as the linkage to the next-highest class. I should point out that this trichotomous argument, though elegant, turned out to be premature and was mostly abandoned in my subsequent ethnography, *The Sacred Remains* (1987), in favor of the more fruitful embedded pair of "signs of history" and "signs in history," concepts that several of the authors in this journal issue have usefully resurrected.

In the years since that early paper, my thinking on time has been nourished by a number of papers across several disciplines, including Bakhtin's often-cited borrowing of relativistic space-time in "Forms of Time and Chronotope in the Novel" in *The Dialogic Imagination* (1981), cited by a number of contributors to this issue; Marin's discussion of intertextual time in "Depositing Time in Painted Representations" in *On Representation* (2001a); Ginzburg's historical account of indexical inference in "Clues: Roots of an Evidential Paradigm" in *Clues, Myths, and the Historical Method* (1992); and Koselleck's schematic history of the semantics of time in "History, Histories, and Formal Structures in Time" in *Futures Past* (1985).

My study of the papers in this issue and of the introductory comments by the coeditors has persuaded me that "it's about time" to take semiotic stock of the growing body of literature that analyzes varieties of language-based signaling of temporal and historical relations in order to explore a possible linkage between the pragmatics of temporality in language and the largely nonlinguistic signs originally described as "signs of" and "signs in" history. I made this analytical distinction at the beginning of *The Sacred Remains*, and throughout the ethnography I develop the argument that, for a class of "historical signs" Palauans call *olangch*, it is helpful to distinguish two hierarchically linked functional planes: "signs of history" can be anything in any medium that represents the past (e.g., a monument, a history book, a name, a specific spatial arrangement of objects, a historical painting); and "signs in history" are those signs of history that, additionally, become token players in the dynamics of social life *because* of the first representational function. So if a commemorative plaque represents a historical moment in a country, then to seize (or deface or reinscribe) that plaque is to make it into a sign *in* history. In other words, there is an inclusion hierarchy to these two concepts, not a binary opposition: all signs in history are first signs of history.

A short review of Peirce's approach to signs will help clarify the nature of this inclusion relationship. Fundamental to a Peircean view of signs, linguistic or otherwise, is the notion that three elements need to be kept in sight at all times: (*a*) the quality of the expressive semiotic vehicle (what he calls the Sign), (*b*) some aspect of physical, social, or psychological reality brought into play by these means (what he calls the Object), and (*c*) the semiotically determined state of affairs that results from and objectifies the interplay of Signs and Objects (what he calls the Interpretant). It might turn out in a given slice of semiosis, especially in the perfectly transparent world of scientific investigation that Peirce preferred, that Signs, Objects, and Interpretants asymptotically line up in terms of mutually reinforcing temporalities. Since for Peirce rational thinking and communication by signs are ultimately identical, temporality is a basic dimension of all semiosis: "Time is a system of relationship in most intimate analogy with the consecution of thought" (2000, 397). And at the most complex level of his tenfold classification of signs, the Symbol (a conventionally grounded general sign [i.e., type-level] representing a general object) has a particularly well-defined temporal dimension, since the "growth" of the Symbol reflects both the progressive quality of the scientific community's understanding and the evolutionary quality of reality itself: "Reality, therefore, can only be regarded as the limit on the endless series of symbols" (1976, 261). But in the less-than ideal world more familiar to linguists and ethnographers, an important task is to describe the temporal inflections of Signs, Objects, and Interpretants *independently* and only then to recompose the particular semiosis under study in light of a comparative understanding of the implicational relations among the three elements.

One possible typological construal of Sign-Object-Interpretant relations for linguistic signs indexing temporality would distinguish four analytic planes. The first plane involves the context-specific linguistic marking of time as a property of either real-time events of speaking or the interactional dynamics of participants' behaviors. Included in this first plane would be temporal "shifters," clarified by Otto Jesperson and Roman Jakobson, such as verb tenses, and also turn-taking norms and participant roles so carefully analyzed by several related disciplines.

A second plane groups together ways in which time is organized by textual or "entextualized" (Silverstein 2003, 51) properties of language, such as the "tropical" narrative or historical present discussed by Emile Benveniste, and the metrically driven parallelisms uncovered by Prague School poetics. An irony of this plane, as Silverstein (2005, 8) notes, is that, while it takes real durational time to reveal the iconic-indexical structure of texts, the regimented interpretation of entextualized forms is often that their coherence is static or frozen.

A third plane includes diachronic changes at the level of linguistic code (noted by Jakobson [1985, 30] as the source of "dynamism" in synchrony), such as the historical processes of the entextualization of texts (as in the account by Nagy [1985] of the standardization of the Homeric canon from oral to written registers), temporal valorization of speech registers that invoke ideological or political regimes (such as the Bakhtinian "chronotopes"), lexicalization or grammaticalization processes, and stylistic changes in genres.

Finally, the fourth plane encompasses the vast field of the cultural construction of time and history, including ideologically laden concepts of evolutionary progress, periodization, and calendrical systems. Here linguistic phenomena often link up with nonlinguistic signs that represent and actualize history. So, roughly speaking, this initial typology of analytical planes distinguishes contextual time, textual time, code time, and cultural time. The empirical task is to find out, first, what kinds of linguistic means are more frequently used to generate various temporal meanings, then to study the various complex intersections of temporalization in all four planes (context, text, code, culture), and, finally, to investigate consistencies in the noncoincidence of temporalization in the semiotic moments of Sign, Object, and Interpretant.

After a brief review of the four papers in this section of the journal issue and an attempt to organize their collective contribution to the study of the pragmatics of temporality, I will return to the issue of the relationship between linguistic and nonlinguistic semiotic markers of time and history.

Davidson's (2007) paper "East Spaces in West Times: Deixis, Heteroglossia, and the Post-Socialist Chronotope in Eastern Berlin" investigates several layers of indexical meanings of spatial and temporal adverbs. In contrast to the unmarked, mainstream discourse of contemporary "unified" Germany, East German residents of the former German Democratic Republic use temporal and spatial adverbs in marked sense in private speech. For them, "here" and "now" connote the postsocialist state of insecurity, alienation, and expense, rather than the unmarked sense of "wealth" and "freedom" connoted by mainstream speech. But, since these marked usages also index speakers who use them in this special way as former East Germans, they are forced to confront this second-order indexicality in public or official contexts by complex management strategies, including double-voiced forms ("so-called West times") and studied deictic disfluency, both designed to distance the speaker from the force of these indexicals by suggesting the presence of another author.

In Perrino's (2007) paper, "Cross-Chronotope Alignment in Senegalese Oral Narrative," in which Mr. Ndome, a Senegalese (Wolof) storyteller, departs from the "normal" tropic use of narrative present and momentarily inserts the researcher/hearer as a sympathetic participant/observer in the narrated event, the pragmatic effect is to further decontextualize the real-time event by endowing it with a "general and hypothetical quality." He constructs an interactional text (implying that the ethnographer, Perrino, is a mediocre student) by means of a denotational text (about a smoker) in which an interactional participant is projected into the world of the denotational text. First, inserting the present participant ethnographer as a witness to the past event being reported deauthorizes her potential for insisting on an alternative construal of the current interactional text by literally decontextualizing her into the reported past world; and, second, having successfully neutralized her as a potential interpreter, Mr. Ndome asserts his own construal of their interactional history by arranging carefully designed analogical parallels between the reported and the discursive planes whose metapragmatic implications are both obvious and unchallengeable. Note that this pragmatic strategy appears to be the inverse of the subtle pedagogical ploy employed by Peter McGuff in the Kiksht storytelling session with Edward Sapir analyzed by Silverstein (1996). Although the Wolof and the Kiksht conversations both rely on elaborate iconically encompassed indexical chains to anchor their metapragmatic effects, the Kiksht example mystifies the cross-plane participant identities (so Sapir hasn't a clue that he is actually being referred to), whereas Perrino's participant identification is all too explicit.

Wirtz (2007), in her paper "Enregistered Memory and Afro-Cuban Historicity in Santería Ritual Speech," points to register-shifting in Lucumí (words, pronouns) and the Creole-like Bozal (accent, pronunciation, etc.), both opposed to the unmarked Spanish, as being potentially "electrically charged" only when these linguistic alternants are deictically anchored by ritual speakers. One of the resulting ironies is that, when the form *ara o* 'land' is taken to be a metaphorical deictic for the present ritual moment, it also simultaneously indexes the culturally constructed space-time of a mythic past. As she goes on to argue, both mythic transcendence as well as historical transformation need to be performatively grounded. As a coda to her own ethnographic analysis, Wirtz reports on a previous linguist's informant who, unintentionally, went into a glossolaliac trance when asked to reproduce in a formal elicitation session forms that might have been used by African slaves. The power of even the "mention" of these nonstandard "bozalisms" to induce trance provides a beautiful example of the change from presupposing to creative indexicality. Note, finally, that in all these examples, at the moment a speaker's trancing voice shifts to being perceived as the embodied voice of either historical or transcendent personae, the metapragmatic function also switches from being entextualized as "reportive" to "reflexive" (Silverstein 1993, 50), generating the predicted power-potential of the coincidence or alignment of participants on the denotational and interactive planes.

Lempert's (2007) paper "Conspicuously Past: Distressed Discourse and Diagrammatic Embedding in a Tibetan Represented Speech Style" analyzes the quotative clitic-*s* used by debating Buddhist monks, both in India and in the United States. Despite the often obvious lack of authoritative and traditional knowledge (and perhaps *because* of this lack), these monks use this quotative marker with high frequency to stamp their own speech as canonical by virtue of the represented speech of tradition. But the saturation or "lathering" of the marker that constructs a creative—if only temporary—diagrammatic relationship between (actually ill-informed) debating speech and authoritative Buddhist exemplars also serves to indexically flag the speakers' incompetence. The persistent invocation of "tradition" signals the necessity for substituting reported wisdom for interactional wits, especially when the event itself occurs under the uncomfortable glare of cultural objectification (i.e., recording).

Taken as a set, these four papers illustrate Peirce's suggestive observation that indexical signs in language have "very peculiar powers" (1976, 172), indeed, powers well beyond the primary function he identifies for them, namely, as "stimulants for looking" (173). In all four of the papers, pragmatic forms are used in speech to index and refer to another dimension of language increasingly distant from the utterances, participants, and contextual parameters of the plane of discursive interaction: the heteroglossic others' voices (Davidson), the historical story about the smoker (Perrino), embodied historical and spiritual voices (Wirtz), and transcendent Buddhist tradition (Lempert). But in each of these four cases, aspects of the interactional text metapragmatically conspire to reinsert the creative power of the seemingly distanced denotational text back into the discursive axis. Again, taking the papers in sequence: the second-order indexicality of spatial and temporal deixis mark East German speakers as politically nonnormative; the mention of archaic forms by a linguistic informant propels the informant unwillingly into trance; the rhetorically constructed parallelism between story and interaction asserts the rhetorical identity of the hearer and the smoker; and the iconic repetition of the reportative clitic changes this indexical from presupposing to creative in labeling its users as incompetent masters of the very tradition they are quoting. Note in all four papers the consistent use of "reflexive" calibration of metapragmatics (Silverstein 1993, 50)—double-voicing, possession, parallelism, and repetition—to undo the "reported" noncoincidence of interactional and denotational frames and the resulting release of creative indexical power in ways unintended, unnoticed, unwanted, and unavoidable by some participants in the speech event.

What light can these four excellent papers in linguistic anthropology shed on the relationship between language-based indexicals of temporality and material objects seized on to be signs in history? At first glance the two topics seem to have one thing in common and one thing in sharp contrast. What they appear to have in common is the functional stratification of a plane of denotation (the represented or indexed denotational text) or representation (signs *of* history) and a plane of real-time discourse (as regimented in the interactional text) or social action (signs *in* history). Where they appear distinct is the relationship between these two planes. In language, indexing the past implies a relative differentiation between the time of speaking and some other time frame; to recover this other time frame in order to reconnect some aspect of it back to the discursive time frame requires special effort, either through some marked "poetic" construction or some "reflexive" calibration device that manages to erase the original "mechanical" indexed noncoincidence. On the other hand, seizing in real time some material object because of its already regimented potency to represent the past implies some degree of embodied transparency between the representational axis and the interactional axis. The present is indexically "charged" with the aura, patina, sedimented value of the distanced past only to the extent that the representational plane is *not* subordinated to the interactive plane.

Note

This paper was first presented at the meetings of the American Anthropological Association, Washington, DC (November 27, 2005). It was originally published as "It's About Time: On the Semiotics of Temporality," *Language & Communication* 27 (2007): 272–77. Reprinted with permission of Elsevier.

11 Anthropological Encounters of a Semiotic Kind

I AM HONORED TO be able to contribute the two texts below to this journal's survey of semiotic approaches within the discipline of anthropology. Delivered originally as "performance" pieces, these two texts reflect on the methodological implications of semiotic analyses from two other fields of inquiry, classics and medieval studies, that continue to have enormous relevance for anthropology. The first was presented as a formal response to Brigitte Bedos-Rezak's lecture titled "Imprint: Ontology and Christian Theology in the Western Middle Ages," which was given as the keynote address at the symposium "(Re)constructing Religions: Evidence, Methods, and Disciplines," held at Brandeis University on October 23, 2003. Ever since her ground-breaking 2000 essay on the semiotics of medieval identity, Bedos-Rezak, now at New York University, has almost single-handedly advanced a "semiotic anthropology" of the high Middle Ages, particularly the period just prior to the systematization known as "scholasticism." An authority on the theological and political dimensions of the practice of "sealing," she has produced nuanced readings of the historical trajectory of various sorts of practices and ideologies that constitute a veritable "culture of the imprint." My response to her lecture focuses on a Boasian question, namely, the difficulty of discovering a history of social practices from the writings of elite or "esoteric" agents of these same practices. Readers of this journal will want to study with care Bedos-Rezak's most recent expression of her semiotic approach to the Middle Ages in her 2010 book *When Ego Was Imago*.

The second text is a "welcome song" performed at the beginning of a highly productive meeting of the Symbolic Form Study Group at Brandeis University on May 3, 2006, when our "semiotic circle" was joined by Gregory Nagy of Harvard University. Thanks to the collegial intervention of Leonard Muellner, Nagy agreed to lead a general discussion of the relationship between text and society, with particular reference to the Homeric epics. A scholar of all aspects of ancient Greek poetics, Nagy has developed a number of concepts—especially his notions of "diachronic skewing," "multiformity," and "poetry as performance"—that have important consequences for recent anthropological efforts, particularly by Richard Bauman, Michael Silverstein, and Greg Urban, to expand the notion of "textuality" to include forms of oral discourse. The key "political" point of my remarks was to bring into conscious articulation Nagy's brilliant work on the semiotic qualities of the Greek epic tradition and anthropological work in the tradition of the "natural histories of discourse."

The two texts below are presented unchanged from their original delivery. I hope that, being "entextualized" here for the first time, anthropological readers will be informed that significant semiotic work in classical and medieval studies speaks profoundly to our own subdisciplinary concerns.

First Encounter: Methodological Reflections on Medieval Metaphors of Semiotic Mediation

Robert Fitzwalter, an imperious early thirteenth-century English earl, attempting to lease a valuable wood from the Abbey of St. Albans, colluded with one William Pigun, a resident of the abbey. William noticed that the abbey's official seal, kept in a box with various documents and charters, was carelessly looked after. And so when Robert sent him a forged charter William "furtively and rapidly sealed it under his sleeve; though done hastily, yet [the impression] was amazingly clear, elegant and exact, though the seal had been snatched away by trickery," so reports the chronicler Matthew Paris (1986, 17). Fortunately the equally clever Abbot John deduced that the charter was a forgery and that it was an inside job; William, his trickery being revealed, was banished to a solitary cell in Tynemouth. From then on the seal, now kept under several keys, was brought into the chapter whenever deeds were drawn up and sealed in everyone's presence, and then returned to a strong chest in the safest possible place.

In Abbot John's dying days, a delegation of monks (including Alexander of Appleton, the "bearer and guardian of the seal") brought the charter into his presence to argue against the abbot's practice of arbitrarily exiling monks to distant cells. But the abbot refused to seal the charter; and the members of the delegation took his silence for assent and sealed it themselves. The abbot died three days later, and so the charter seal was broken and then resealed by no less than Stephen, the Archbishop of Canterbury. Alas, the monks of St. Albans enjoyed their chartered protection for only a short while, since almost immediately after his installation as the new abbot, William of Trumpington—a buddy of the king—refused to honor its terms, prompting a visit by the Cistercian papal legate Nicholas. Upon reading a copy of the charter the legate denounced the monks for renouncing their vows of obedience. "And with these words . . . he tore the charter into pieces with his front teeth, and, smashing the seal attached to it, threw it onto the floor" (Paris 1986, 37).

I retell these tales to reinforce the point that seals were principal semiotic mediators in the life of medieval elites and that, by the beginning of the thirteenth century, the normative role of seals as "signs of history" had already become manipulated as "signs in history," to use phrases I have applied to the engagement of historical markers in the dynamics of social life (Parmentier 1987). That is, seals not only represented the identity and authority of the absent sealer but were also focal objects of social praxis.

Reflecting on these stories, stories that describe events over a hundred years after the Prescholastic period focused on Bedos-Rezak's papers on medieval semiotics, suggests several issues related to the general themes of forms of evidence and methods of reconstruction in historical semiotics. Sealing is a social practice that leaves little evidence of its contextual and processual aspects; what remains physically are seal matrices, wax imprints, and copies or casts of both, each providing information about the substances involved, such as gold, bronze, wax, etc. and the inscribed words accompanying the figure. Seals are additionally, as Bedos-Rezak shows, the object of metasemiotic discourse, as writers refer to seals and sealing directly in historical narratives and metaphorically in theological texts. In her scholarship over the past twenty-five years Bedos-Rezak (1993, 2000) has rightly insisted on the necessity of studying the iconography of seals *and* the discourse about sealing in order to produce a semiotic account of medieval society as the "culture of the replica."

Thanks to Bedos-Rezak's research, medieval sealing joins the ranks of material technologies that have been identified as providing semiotic metalanguages in culture: weaving for ancient Greeks, metallurgy for the Inca, pottery for Native Americans, and printing for early modern Europe. In each of these cases, aspects of the technology stimulate metaphorical association and philosophical speculation that, in turn, offer the analyst a privileged "ethnosemiotic" window for reconstruction.[1] While not doubting the importance of seals, weaving, pottery, metallurgy, and printing, I want to suggest that the analyst should always be careful not to overlook alternative metasemiotic metaphors,[2] especially alternatives that seem to form a paradigmatic set at a given period of cultural history. In the medieval period alternatives would include "covering" (*integumentum*) (Stock 1973, 50), macrocosm/microcosm analogies, the mirror image, organic bodily metaphors (Le Goff 1989; Bynum 1991, 254), hierarchical orders (Duby 1980, 66–69), the "Porphyry's Tree" (Vance 1987, 86; Piltz 1981, 56), light as divine emanation (Panofsky 1979, 21–24; Eco 1986, 43–51; Duby 1981, 97–135), the book (Gellrich 1985, 41; Petrucci 1995), and typological transfer (*translatio*) (Nichols 1983, 20). And sealing seems to be a member of a paradigmatic subset having to do with molding relatively plastic substances, such as minting coins, pottery, sculpture (Morrison 1990, 65), model construction (Abelard in Tweedale 1976, 171), and stamping on an anvil. So the twin methodological tasks become, first, finding contextual regularities governing the use of all these alternative metaphors and, second, deducing the "intensional" core (that is, the specific meaningful features) of paradigmatic sets. (Note that Bedos-Rezak argues that "imprinting" is the key to the plasticity subset.)

Standing back from these objects and texts, we can see that the political use of sealing is a perfect exemplification of the triadic process of Peircean semiosis—whether or not anyone in the twelfth century realized it as such!—in which, initially, the sealer (normally a person with some authority who directs that a seal be affixed) creates a seal matrix (consisting of a metallic substance and some unique inscribed design) capable to impressing into wax (or some other soft medium) an impression of the matrix design (often leaving some material residue of the very sealing process), in order that the document so sealed will be interpreted (at some removed temporal and spatial context) by an interpreter as having authenticity and, thus, as conveying authority grounded in the transmittal of the sealer's identity and, thus, power. In more technical Peircean vocabulary, a medieval seal (matrix) operates as a dicent indexical legisign generating identical imprints, which are rhematic indexical sinsigns of the special class called "replicas." (The matrix generates potentially many identical replications, so, while as a real thing it is not a true Peircean legisign, it operates like one.) The semiotic "ground" between seal matrix and original sealer is indexical because the sealer actually presses (or has pressed on his authority) the seal into the wax. And the sealing process is dicent, that is, intended to be interpreted as authenticating a specific document authorized by the presence of the sealer at some previous definite moment, although this is made possibly largely on the basis of the similarity of the seal impressions stemming from a single authority.[3]

That seals simultaneously engage iconic and indexical modes of signification provided medieval thinkers with material for more general theological and philosophical reflection. The seal, for example, mirrors the triadic commonplace that God creates the human soul through the imprint of the Son, who is the figure of God's substance.[4] Abelard then brilliantly realized what Bloch (1983, 35) calls "imbrication of signification and generation" in postulating a parallel triad for language: verbal signs (*verba*) standing for signified objects (*signatum* or *res*) and producing significant concepts (*dicta* or *sermones*) or what are "said about things" in the mind of the listeners.

Critical to Bedos-Rezak's account of the medieval semiotic landscape is the argument that the generalization of this triadic semiotic model provides elites with an intellectual explanation for the "presencing" of divine realities in human experience. In the context of any dualistic religious worldview that strictly separates transcendent, eternal, and unknowable divinity from the mundane, temporally bound, and changeable world, mediating processes and phenomena have been regularly noted—Lévi-Strauss's (1974) study of rain and mist as mediators in Pueblo mythology is the classic example. In the specific context of the medieval period the problem of mediation was often expressed semiotically as bridging the gap between experienced signifiers and divine signifieds. In other words, the issue of the immanence or presencing of transcendence parallels the issue of what Saussure calls the "motivation" of signification and what Peirce calls the "ground" of the sign. Anthropologists are justly wary of crude typological generalizations about cultures grounded in some "mystical participation" in which the levels of sign and referent are blurred because of some evolutionary cognitive deficit (Berger 1968, 282; Parmentier 1997b), but the problem I want to raise here is the *historical* dimension of mediation.

If it is true that mediation was especially problematic in the twelfth century due to the simultaneous expansion of monastic spirituality and the birth of a science of nature, then several hypotheses are possible to explain the proliferation of imprinting metaphors (Grant 2001; French and Cunningham 1996). Given that these metaphors occur regularly in the context of theological reflection on the Trinity, the Incarnation, and the Eucharist, it might be, first, that the seal metaphor spread because it provided a metalanguage to understand these three privileged mediational moments as a paradigmatic set, as evidence for the normative "presencing" of the signified in the world of experience. Second, it might be the case that all this theological focus on semiotic mediation reflects a *crisis* in the religious life of elites of the period, as a defense against the growing spiritualization of *natura* (called a "genitive force," a "crafting fire," the "mother of all things," and the "instrument of divine operation" [Gregory 1988, 64]), that is, a mediation from the ground up. Alternatively, it spread as a way to counter the declining power of the Platonic "dialectic of participation" (Gregory 1988, 74) or the Augustinian linkage of likeness and participation (Bell 1984); or as a hyper-rationalized account of divine presence that maximally distances the Schoolmen and monks from the *illiterati* ("unlettered") or *idiotae* ("simpletons") (Gurevich 1992, 97) for whom relics and images—and miracles and magic—provided a steady stream of opportunities for "blending the spiritual with the physical world of events" (Gurevich 1985, 85; Brooke and Brooke 1984), like a child, notes Anselm, fearful of a sculpted dragon, who "does not yet know how to distinguish clearly between a thing and the likeness of a thing" (quoted in McKeon, ed. 1930, 1, 161).

Still another possibility might be that the expansion of sealing practices and metaphors signals the actual distance or even absence of the sealer (God or king) whose presence, transparent in an earlier world of "orality," can only be created though semiotic projection (Vance 1986, 52). As Jaeger (1994, 347–48) has recently argued, the plasticity and humanism of Gothic art might be a nostalgic representation of a period of moral discipline that has already passed. The methodological consequence of this argument from "envy" is frightening: if there can be such a temporal disjunction between iconography and mentality, how can the analyst ever trust any kind of semiotic data as positive evidence for the operation of cultural categories?

Many scholars have pointed out the increasing reflexivity and systematicity of twelfth century religious thinking and artistic programs as prelude to the monumental summative works of the next century (Southern 1995, 49–58; Colish 1988). At this time everyone seems to be asking a "superfluous novelty of questions" (Goswin of Mainz, quoted in Jaeger 1994, 367) about everything. "Even on public streets" writes Stephen of Tournai, "the indivisible Trinity is taken apart and wrangled over" (quoted in Chenu 1968, 294). Anselm even asked the self-reflexive question: whether a grammarian is a substance or a quality! (Colish 1983, 76). Systematicity anywhere in culture outside language immediately summons the spirit of Franz Boas, who used religious phenomena to illustrate the difference between fundamental or primary cultural categories and "secondary elaborations" generated by esoteric specialists. What a people consider independent objects and what they consider aspects or attributes of objects varies cross-culturally; some people, for example, view the luminosity of the sun to be an object the sun can put aside. What if twelfth-century theological reflection on the doctrine of the Trinity is really just a secondary elaboration attempting to explain the independence and/or identity of attributes of divinity?

Furthermore, Boas argued that it is often the historical fact of breaking or violating relatively unconscious or deeply patterned cultural associations—often stimulated by acculturation or borrowing from neighbors—that results in the coming into consciousness of these patterns, making the categories and associations open to rationalization and eventually to systematization. Boas seems to describe a medieval Schoolman and his seal as he "ransacked the entire field of his knowledge until he happened to find something that would be fitted to the problem in question giving an explanation satisfying to his mind" (quoted in Stocking, ed. 1974, 254).

Two methodological paradoxes are implied by the Boasian argument: first, the more substantial the textual evidence of, for example, the seal metaphor, the greater the probability that this consciously articulated discourse *conceals* the fundamental and integrating classifications of a culture; and, second, the greater the systematicity of, for example, theological doctrines, the greater the probability that this achievement reflects the work of an "esoteric specialist" far removed from the operating principles of the culture—described reflexively by Abelard, whose "excellent knowledge . . . cannot be attained by long study, but only by genius."

Second Close Encounter: A Welcome Song for Gregory Nagy

In pursuing this semester's interdisciplinary exploration of the topic "societies and texts" we first examined a set of exemplary literary studies denominated "the new historicism" centered on the work of the Renaissance scholar Stephen

Greenblatt. Today we turn our attention back about twenty-eight hundred years to the period of the entextualization of the Homeric poems and, specifically, to the contributions of our distinguished guest Gregory Nagy. In 1998 another Homeric scholar, Richard P. Martin (1998, 108), wrote, "Cultural anthropology will mold the shape of classical studies for this generation. . . . To be fully and honestly philologists, we must now learn our Geertz along with Greek, absorb Lienhardt as well as Latin, undertake ethnography after epigraphy." Those of us here who share cultic identity with Geertz and Lienhardt certainly appreciate Martin's comment, but an inverse remark by Nagy (1992, 23) is perhaps more directly appropriate for today's discussion: "Ironically, the field of anthropology has as much to benefit from the currently construed field of Classics as the other way around." Let me try to briefly sketch at least one of these benefits.

Nagy's account of the diachronic stages of the entextualization of the Homeric oral epic is the best exemplification I know of the analytical model for the anthropological study of texts proposed by the authors in *Natural Histories of Discourse*, a collection edited by Silverstein and Urban (1996)—although I am not aware of any reciprocal citations. As heir to the Parry-Lord discovery of the orality still evidenced in the fixed Homeric canon, Nagy honors that intellectual heritage by exposing its fundamental weakness: of not taking oral performance seriously enough to realize that the texts of Homer that we have don't just evidence the contexts of their performance but are *fully constituted* by those contexts. Parry and Lord saw vestiges of orality in the systematicity of formulaic expressions fixed in specific metrical contexts; and they accounted for the internal coherence and Panhellenic uniformity of the two poems by postulating an enregistering moment of dictation whose "external impetus" is the exact opposite of performance in context. Nagy, on the other hand, rethinks the whole matter. He locates the coherence and uniformity of "texts" and "textuality" in the diachrony of their contextual enactments and in the centrality of their focal performance sites. The textual uniformity of the Homeric poems even at the spatial extremities of their diffusion is the result of parallel performance contexts, *not* of the replication of text-artifacts (Nagy 2001). That these texts were eventually written down in a Phoenician-derived alphabet and then subjected to "cultural consolidation" (Nagy 1997, 178) does not compel us to take this historical contingency as an all-powerful retrodictive interpretive key.

Alas, Nagy's position actually makes the whole analytical task much *more* difficult, for the simple reason that the two epics don't seem to reflect in any obvious or direct way either the societies or the contexts of archaic eighth-century Greece. The world represented in the texts is the Mycenaean period four hundred years earlier, and the texts' very monumentality makes it unlikely that wandering singers went around performing the complete *Iliad* and *Odyssey* at festivals and competitions. But Nagy turns these challenges into weapons in a set of precisely interlocking theoretical moves involving what Silverstein names the "pragmatics" of the "metapragmatics" of texts, and helping to reinsert what Bauman (2004a, 128–58; cf. Nagy 2004, 43) labels "mediational relays" as the cultural mechanisms for the constantly changing enactment of tradition.

While it is both true and interesting that these poems are richly self-reflexive, that is, contain numerous examples of explicit and implicit metapragmatics or discourse about discourse, Nagy (2003) postulates in his concept of "diachronic skewing" an encompassing disjunction between the texts' reflexive metapragmatics and the pragmatics of texts as performed. In many publications Nagy (1990c) brilliantly explores, for example, the ethnosemiotics of the conventional index (*sêma*), signs requiring mental acts of recognition (*nóēsis*). Note, by the way, that the Homeric *sêma* is a perfect Peircean Third: Odysseus is the semiotic Object, the scar is the Sign, and the recognition is the Interpretant. More relevant for the study of textuality more globally are the metapragmatic references to weaving (Nagy 2002, 79), sewing, the chariot-wheel, and carpentry, in which the poet creates the cohesive and unified fabric of song (Nagy 1995, 179, n. 122). The poet himself is metaphorized as a varied-throated nightingale; the resourceful hero is likened to the performer of poetry who adjusts each performance to the needs of the local context; and even the name "Homer" etymologically exemplifies a semiotics of coherence. Furthermore, embedded in the epics are accounts, "mirroring" real-world performance events, of singers taking turns at song, storytellers reciting epic tales to enthralled audiences—indeed, telling the very tale of Troy—and other contextually anchored speech-acts such as praising, blaming, prophesying, lamenting, and praying.

It would be a serious mistake, Nagy implies, to read off from these textual metapragmatics the "natural history of discourse," that is, the actual pattern of mediational relays (e.g., rhapsodic sequencing) that enables these oral poems to crystallize into the Homeric epics, since in almost every moment and at every level the Homeric testimony "belies" (1990b, 24) both the history of their entextualization and the contextual parameters of their performance. The creation of the poems is "viewed as happening at a remote point in time, not over time" (1996, 76). As Nagy (1979, 16) puts it, "The immediacy of performance . . . is counterbalanced by an attitude of remoteness from composition." In a related discussion of sympotic songs, he echoes, "The song proclaims that its own unchangeability is a prerequisite for its own perpetuation" (2004, 29). (The comparativist Foley [1999, 20] makes a related point: "The referent of the concrete signs in the performance or text lies outside the immediate performance or texts.") Perhaps the fact that the *Iliad* and the *Odyssey* stand in complementary distribution might be seen as a global refusal of intertextuality.

Now this strategy of radical decentering—the ideological regimentation of a text as being distantiated or decontextualized—is typical of many authoritative cultural texts in the archaic world and, again ironically, seems to correlate with an "ideology of mimesis as re-enactment" (Nagy 2004, 27), with an esoteric hermeneutic in which power is demonstrated in the privileged discernment of hidden signs (Ford 2002, 74), and with a mythological surround that presents a "coherent system" (Muellner 1996, 51) precisely at those moments of normative violation requiring immediate recalibration. Ritual performance is culturally powerful to the degree that contingencies of performance are *masked*. As Nagy cites Homer, "the poet only hears" (*Iliad* ii. 485).

Clearly the political function (that is, the pragmatics) of performing epic poems changes through time, especially in this period of massive social upheaval prior to the emergence of classical Greece. Songs about Troy sung as hero tales before royalty in Mycenean citadels, sung in dispersed and autonomous city-states for aristocratic pleasure and reassurance, sung by professional rhapsodes in Panhellenic competitive festivals on behalf of tyrants "diligently searching through the legendary past to find precedents" (Snodgrass 1980, 70), and sung by school children as feats of pedagogical memorization are all radically different in their encompassing pragmatics. We might say, then, that there is a *diachrony* to diachronic skewing! And this vital lesson about the changing pragmatics *of* texts reinforces the related (and entailed) methodological necessity of being constantly attuned to the revaluation of markedness asymmetries in the cultural categories *within* texts. As Nagy (2003, 40), following the master Kuryłowicz, writes, "A diachronic perspective reveals a shift in meaning from category to subcategory or from subcategory to category."

"Benefit" to anthropology? Context; diachrony; comparison; textuality; tradition. What's not to like?

Notes

This paper was originally published as "Anthropological Encounters of a Semiotic Kind," *Recherches Sémiotique/Semiotic Inquiry* 32 (2012): 187–99. Reprinted with permission of the Canadian Semiotics Association.

1. The essentially semiotic nature of seals can be traced back to Greek terminology: the royal ring seal was *symbolon* (Vance 1986, 129); seals are *semeia* in Plato (Carruthers 2008, 21).

2. As Geoffrey of Vinsauf notes, "Such a metaphorical use of words serves you like a mirror, for you can see yourself in it, and recognize your own sheep in a strange countryside" (quoted in Leupin 1989, 25).

3. On this terminology see Parmentier (1994b, 3–22).

4. Peter Abelard says that the Father is the wax (substance) and the Son is the waxen image (Buytaert 1974, 137). He also comments that the bronze seal, though a single thing, has both matter and form, that is, the carved figure (Luscombe 1992, 297).

12 Two Marxes: Evolutionary and Critical Dimensions of Marxian Social Theory

THIS LECTURE EXAMINES several fundamental concepts in Marx's social theory, with the goal of showing how they fit into a coherent whole.[1] For the contemporary anthropologist, however, this conceptual unity can easily appear divided, for there seem to be *two* Marxes, a first belonging to the world of nineteenth-century evolutionism and a second belonging to the world of contemporary reflexive or critical social theory. Evolutionary writers such as Lewis Henry Morgan and Herbert Spencer describe an inevitable rise from "primitive" society through a stage of "barbarism" to the glories of "civilization" as found in Britain, Europe, and the United States. Part of Marx's theory of society shows that he is heir to this developmental or evolutionary point of view, although he ultimately transforms this perspective into a revolutionary one when he postulates a future state of society transcending capitalism (and, ironically, returning to a "communal" simplicity resembling the beginning of the evolutionary process) that all should work toward.[2]

The second Marx is the forerunner by almost a hundred years of the very kind of critical, immanent, or reflexive approach to social analysis that is much in vogue in contemporary anthropology, particularly in work deriving inspiration from Jürgen Habermas and Pierre Bourdieu. The word "critical," often used to label those theorists who have been influenced by this second Marx, does not mean that they necessarily "criticize," in the sense of providing a negative commentary or evaluation on some aspect of society—though many critical theorists do just that. The word is used in its German sense (*Kritik*), as in Kant's three "critiques" of pure reason, practical reason, and judgment, of a theory being committed to the exploration of the self-grounding of its own concepts. So a critical social theory takes as a basic question: how is it possible for a theory of society to be historically grounded or analytically contextualized in the very society it is trying to understand?

Anthropologists share in this critical stance whenever they consider the reflexive or dialogic character of their own fieldwork, in which the subjectivity of the anthropologist is treated as essential to the fieldwork process. But more importantly, theoretical constructs built up by the analyst have to be deconstructed or unpacked, given the society in which the analyst is a member. In this sense, Marx's writing about nineteenth-century society can be seen as an early critical ethnography of capitalism, as if he were an ethnographer studying a foreign society—although Marx lived much of his life as a "stranger" in Paris and London, he was studying the basic institution of his own society. So there are "two Marxes," the evolutionary Marx looking backward and the reflexive or critical Marx looking forward.

A Materialist Philosophy

Marx defended his doctoral dissertation on Democritus and Epicurean philosophy in 1841, after turning away from training to be a lawyer—much to his father's dismay. Marx rejected both Kantian and Hegelian idealism and the tendency toward metaphysical abstraction in the study of law. Rather, as he wrote to his father in 1837, "The concrete expressions of a living world of ideas, as exemplified by law, the state, nature, and philosophy as a whole, the object itself must be studied in its development; arbitrary divisions must not be introduced, the rational character of the object itself must develop as something imbued with contradictions in itself and find its unity in itself" (2010b [1837], 12). His father replied in a prophetic understatement: "Your ideas of law . . . are very likely to arouse storms if made into a system" (2010b). In particular, Marx complained that modern liberal legislation has a tendency to elevate to universal status the legal conditions found in particular historical contexts. Marx's attention to the "concrete" coincides with his change from legal studies to political economy, corresponding to his move to Paris and to his involvement as a journalist with the *Deutsch-Französische Jahrbücher.*

Rather than beginning the analysis of a society by studying phenomena such as symbolism, language, worldview, and religion, Marx begins with the principle that one of the subsystems of society, the economy, has "functional primacy." By that he means that the economy is that subsystem around which the fundamental and pervasive groups of society crystallize; that is, social groups form themselves around their economic interests rather than around, say, their ethnic identity or religious beliefs.

> In direct contrast to German philosophy which descends from heaven to earth, here we ascend from earth to heaven. That is to say, we do not set out from what men say, imagine, conceive, nor from men as narrated, thought of, imagined, conceived, in order to arrive at men in the flesh. We set out from real, active men, and on the basis of their real life-process we demonstrate the development of the ideological reflexes and echoes of this life-process. . . . Morality, religion, metaphysics, all the rest of ideology and their corresponding forms of consciousness, thus no longer retain the semblance of independence. They have no history, no development; but men, developing their material

production and their material intercourse, alter, along with this their real existence, their thinking and the products of their thinking. Life is not determined by consciousness, but consciousness by life. (1973 [1857–1858], 47)

This is a forceful expression of a "materialist" perspective on social analysis, which moves from the earth to the heavens rather than from the heavens to the earth.

But Marx's principle of the primacy of the forces of material production must be seen as part of a more general view of human subjectivity and history. First of all, for Marx the world of human existence is the historical product of human activities, rather than the result of passive, philosophical reflection:

> But life involves before everything else eating and drinking, a habitation, clothing and many other things. The first historical act is thus the production of the means to satisfy these needs, the production of material life itself. And indeed this is an historical act, a fundamental condition of all history, which today, as thousands of years ago, must daily and hourly be fulfilled merely in order to sustain human life. (Marx and Engels 1970 [1845–1846], 48)

This human activity is geared toward the functional prerequisites of life, namely, obtaining the goods and services necessary for material existence, but this activity of making history through productive acts is not completely unconstrained in a given society, and for two reasons. First, nature imposes limitations on the character of productive activity, on the labor that people exercise in the world. Those living in a desert obviously cannot grow fruit trees unless they have an oasis, while those living near flowing rivers are likely to benefit from irrigation enterprises. So nature imposes limitations and possibilities on the making of human history. But second, and more interestingly from the anthropological point of view, this labor activity is constrained because it takes place in the socially inherited circumstances anthropologists call "culture." What is done in an industrial workplace or in a fishing community or on a farm takes place in the context of traditional modes of livelihood inherited from the past.

The radical quality of Marx's fundamental belief in the centrality—indeed the dignity—of human labor is difficult for us to appreciate today. In Marx's time, as in earlier times, labor was viewed as a post-Edenic curse, as a painful burden imposed on humanity to provision life; and those who toil to enable their masters to be free from this necessity are essentially slave-like or even animal-like. But for Marx, human fulfillment was not to die young in glorious combat, nor to philosophize in physical comfort, nor to transcend the experience of the real world in search of salvation, but to willingly engage in the "metabolism between man and nature" (Arendt 1977, 39; cf. Marx 1973 [1857–1858], 489).

Given these two sorts of constraints, the category of production for Marx is not simply work or the sheer expenditure of human energy, since it involves two related processes. The first is "the appropriation of nature on the part of the individual within and through a specific form of society" (1973 [1857–1858], 87). So people do not go out and till the earth, collect berries, or work in an industrial factory other than through a specific form of society. Second, production is not simply work, since it involves enacting definite socioeconomic relations among individuals. These relations Marx called "relations of production," and it is these relations—management to worker, plantation owner to slave, hunt leader to band member—that satisfy the goals of production for a given social system. So industrial labor, plantation labor, and hunting labor are all human actions mediated by particular forms of social relations. The consequence of this, of course, is that mechanical technology is relative to particular historical conditions. The invention of new technologies such as fire, the wheel, and the steam engine only makes sense if the social system that surrounds that invention can make use of it. We know, for example, that the Chinese invented the wheel and used it for making toys, and that they invented gunpowder and used it for making fireworks and only later for launching military projectiles.

This double process of production can be considered along two dimensions. The first is Marx's theory of "objectification," and the second is Marx's notion of "reproduction." In the act of production, human abilities and needs are given objective form in the products of labor; and these products, though they are objective things, have a socially defined utility, what Marx will come to call a "use-value." In acting productively human beings give their needs material forms in the things they produce. To the degree that they produce things useful to themselves as members of society, those objects have qualitatively different use-values. A product as a use-value is always the bearer of a set of practical rules, and both the need and the proper use of the object are socially specific. The use to which a piece of chalk can be put is a socially derived use, whether people use it to write on a classroom blackboard or to paint their faces white in preparation for a ritual dance. So a product like chalk is the material embodiment of the needs and uses of people, what Marx calls the "social repository of subjective activity."

> It is only when the objective world becomes everywhere for man in society the world of man's essential powers—human reality, and for that reason the reality of his *own* essential powers—that all *objects* become for him the *objectification of himself*, become the objects which confirm and realize his individuality, become *his* objects: that is, *man himself* becomes the object. (1964 [1844], 140)

This is the first dimension: we obtain our humanity and individual subjectivity through embodying ourselves in the goods we produce as members of a society. For Marx, quite simply, the history of the world is the history of the progressive enlargement of this world of objects through the production of wealth. Marx's insight here goes beyond the trivial claim that members of the human species are tool users, *homo faber*; significantly, the fashioning of inorganic nature is proof that humans are thereby conscious of their being this kind of species. Our "species being" is, thus, completely different from that of hard-working animals (bees, beavers, ants, etc.), whose lives are identical with their activity. Only a human, in contrast, "can contemplate himself in a world he himself has created" (1964 [1844], 329). Alluding to Aristotle's famous phrase in *De Politica*, Marx writes: "Man is in the most literal sense of the word a *zoon politikon*, not only a social animal, but an animal which can develop into an individual only in society" (1904, 268).

Second, not only do people realize themselves in objects, but in doing so they reproduce themselves and their society. For Marx, appropriating nature in productive activity is only one side of the process of production, since the producers are simultaneously consumers. What do they use up? First, they use up natural resources like water, air, and soil; second, they consume the products produced; third, they exhaust the individuals who produce the products. As Marx says, "Production itself aims at the reproduction of the producers within and together with these, his objective conditions of existence" (1973 [1857–1858], 495). That is, in production we aim to reproduce the producers of the goods and to continue the same kind of social system that produced the goods in the first place. Primary among these goals is to reproduce the workers, the people who do the production. So there is a pun on the word "reproduction": society only exists historically if it reproduces itself through the reproductive fertility of its own members (since people die), but this kind of productivity is only one half of Marx's argument. He says we also reproduce the very structures of the relations of production that exist in the first place. If we are a slave society, like the conditions found in the nineteenth century in parts of this country, productive activity on the cotton plantation also reproduces the slave system that guarantees the production of cotton.

For Marx, the environment is essentially unstable: since resources get used up, it can be stabilized only by human action taken to ensure the reproduction of the productive resources, which include natural as well as human resources. In addition, and more importantly, Marx argues that in production we also reproduce the inherited cultural tradition that defines the uses of the objects we make. This is cultural reproduction: forms of ideology—language, art, literature, for example—are also reproduced to reinforce the possibility of continuing the same kinds of productive enterprises.[3]

Evolutionary Stages

I note that Marx's basic view of society was evolutionary—in fact, revolutionary, and it is necessary at this point to chart briefly what he thought the stages of human society were. Marx vigorously read ethnographic materials from early youth to right before his death (sitting, in those years, when his overcoat was not in the pawn shop, in the reading room at the British Library). His practice was to make exhaustive and critical annotations from writers such as Tylor, de Brosses, Bachofen, Maine, Kovalesky (a Russian sociologist), and Lubbock. But it is Marx's relationship with Morgan that deserves our closest attention. Kovalesky apparently brought a copy of Morgan's *Ancient Society* back with him from a trip to America and lent it to Marx in the late 1870s. Marx accepted Morgan's theory of the primitive "gens" (clan) and his account of the evolution of the family; he was, however, suspicious of Morgan's tendency to view social matters in organic or biological terms (recall that Morgan is fond of terms such as "blood" and "germs"). He was also conscious of the fact that Morgan was a friend of powerful Washington insiders, a conservative Republican defender of the status quo, and a highly paid upstate New York railroad lawyer. Marx was sympathetic to social evolutionary writers especially since, as a group, they generally rejected the individualism of compact or contract theories of the origin of society. He particularly objected to the notion that the "social" aspects of human life could be stripped away, either theoretically or historically (as in Hobbes, Locke, and Rousseau) to reveal the essence of human nature. He agreed with Morgan's depiction of the stages of the development of culture and especially with the notion that property becomes a critical agent of change only in the later stages of that development. Marx thought that capitalism was a form of society that developed or evolved in very particular circumstances.

What did it evolve from? Marx has a residual category, what he labels archaic or "precapitalist" society, that is, forms of society prior to capitalism. He writes in a letter draft from 1881, "The archaic or primary formation of our globe contains a number of strata of different ages, one superimposed on the other. Just as the archaic formation of society reveals a number of different types which characterize different and successive epochs" (1989 [1881], 363). In precapitalist society, including tribal societies often studied by anthropologists, Asiatic states with their "oriental despots," "Germanic" societies of isolated and independent farmers, and urban societies of the classical (Greece and Rome) and medieval worlds, productive forces are restricted because of the natural ties people have as members of a community, especially natural ties of kinship. Labor activity in these societies is subsumed by ties of kinship and directed by political roles such as patriarchs, chiefs, or kings. Second, nature itself, rather than being a productive resource, is seen as a quasi-religious object, an object of worship. If people are tied by bonds of kinship and bound by political subordination to kings and rulers and do not have an exploitative relationship with nature, Marx says that their productive activity is not going to get them very far, historically. Their society stagnates. Marx thought that these precapitalist societies, particularly the ones found in India, South America (the Inca), classical Greece, and China—what he called the "Asiatic societies"—are static or just cyclical, since they cannot make the transition to capitalism by realizing productive resources. This fundamental triple division into precapitalist, capitalist, and (future) communal states of society can be broken down further by dividing the first epoch into three economic formations: the Asiatic, the Antique or Classical, and the Feudal. Marx notes that labor is unfree in all three of these formations, whether as collective bondage, slavery, or serfdom (of course, wage labor in capitalism is free in form only). Note that the Asiatic and the capitalist stages are global in scope, while the Antique and Feudal are restricted to the European context: the Asiatic mode is global in that the transition to civil society occurred around the world; capitalism is global in its unstoppable expansions from its original European roots.

The next great evolutionary stage, then, is the rise of capitalism, where human labor gets emancipated from bondages of social relations, from the family, and from political power, only to become itself a commodity to be bought and sold in the marketplace like other goods and services. If you want to work, you have to sell your labor, and the chief of your village is not going to say, "You must work for me," since you can say, "No, I will work for whomever I want." Second, nature in capitalism is no longer regarded as the object of a religious attitude but rather as the object of a practical-rational attitude. Nature is to be exploited. And third—a point I will explore in more detail later—in the capitalist world, because of the nature of markets, capital itself acts as a quasi-necessary force in determining the social relations that people have. In other words, economic activities come to determine social activities, rather than the other way around, as in the precapitalistic regimes. In fact, Marx says that the social character of human interactions disappears and becomes for members of the society like things. Marx calls this "reification" (from the Latin word *res*, "things") or "thing-ification": our social relations become things. Think of the process of getting an education: parents might think that a year in college is not "worth" $50,000, and so the educational opportunities of their children are given a monetary value. Or think of people who get mad at their friends and say, "It is not worth hanging around with you, since you borrow my possessions and never return them." Both of these examples involve transforming a social relationship into a quasi-economic relationship; in fact, they both involve a cost-benefit analysis of social life, much like Benjamin Franklin criticized the way his contemporaries "spent" their leisure time, as if it was an economic resource too easily frittered away. In capitalist societies the sociability of people is subordinated to instrumental, economic rationality. That is the bad news; the good news is that history really takes off at this point; there is progressive development of global resources, which for Marx is a never-ending process: "It must nestle everywhere, settle everywhere, establish connexions everywhere" (Marx and Engels 2002 [1848], 223).

To repeat: although certainly evolutionary, Marx is also revolutionary. Marx dedicated all his writings and political activities to actually bringing about a third and final stage of human history—the communal or socialist stage—that would be characterized, first of all, by the abolition of reification, that is, by getting rid of these instrumental dealings among human beings so that people can come to treat social relations as they are, namely, as social. Decision-making in the economic sphere in this socialist phase would be determined not by economic forces, not, that is, by instrumental rationality, but rather by deciding what is good for the society at large. People would decide socially what goods to produce and who should be working in what jobs. In other words, the management of things would become subordinated to the social goals established by people. Marx and Engels write: "[Communism], for the first time, treats all natural premises as the creatures of hitherto existing men, strips them of their natural character and subjugates them to the powers of the united individuals" (1970 [1845–1846], 86). This is, of course, a utopia that would maintain all the tools, the factories, and the technologies of capitalism but would get rid of a certain form of rationality. (Marx and Engels regularly excoriated utopian writers such as Saint-Simon, Fourier, and Owen, who hoped to achieve the end state without the "overcoming" of capitalism.) In this socialist phase, living activities in the present become much more important than the inherited cultural patterns, the patterns of productivity and reproductivity from the past. This is a free-for-all society in which people are able to constantly rechart its direction without feeling the weight of inherited tradition. It is kind of a society without a culture—of course, an anthropological impossibility. So in this third and final stage of human history, technical decisions become separated from social decisions; legislation replaces police power; although, as I pointed out, the existence of this final stage presupposes both absolute abundance and technological inventiveness. Marx was, as ironical as it may seem, enthusiastic about the latest in industrial machinery.

The Asiatic Mode of Production

Now let's go back and look more carefully at Marx's analysis of the Asiatic form, not because we are particularly interested in precapitalist societies for themselves, but because there is an important analogy between the way Marx handles Asiatic societies and the way he handles capitalism. Recall that the Asiatic form is a subtype of the "forms which precede capitalist production." Marx was very interested in giving these early social and economic systems their due historical weight, not as an abstract exercise in ethnohistorical analysis but as a necessary prelude to his larger arguments that capitalism has specific historical preconditions and that basic concepts such as property, appropriation, reproduction, and labor have very different meanings and interrelationships in noncapitalist contexts. Despite the fine gradations of subtypes Marx proposes (Asiatic, Roman, Germanic, etc.), all of these precapitalist forms reveal two fundamental qualities. First, as human workers appropriate the surrounding natural resources, whether hunting areas or irrigated farmlands, their goal is to reproduce themselves and their communities and not, as will be the case later under capitalism, to produce a surplus of value by exchanging their labor for money. Second, although individual ownership of certain classes of property does exist in precapitalist systems, the individual's relationship to the land, that is, to the objective conditions of labor, is always mediated by some social form, whether a band, a tribe, a commune, or a town: "But this relation to land and soil, to the earth, as the property of the labouring individual . . . is instantly mediated by the naturally arisen, spontaneous, more or less historically developed and modified presence of the individual as member of a commune—his naturally arisen presence as member of a tribe, etc." (1973 [1857–1858], 485). I mentioned that in these Asiatic state formations individual activity is subordinated to strong political leadership, to kings and despots of all sorts. Marx argues that, in the case of the oriental despot, whether the "father of the nation" or some benevolent ruler, the unity of society, the self-consciousness of people as a society, is largely the result of a unity imposed from the top down. He says, "It is not in the least a contradiction to it that, as in most of the Asiatic land-forms, the *comprehensive unity* standing above all these little communities appears as the higher *proprietor* or as the *sole proprietor*" (1973 [1857–1858], 472). This resembles the familiar situation in the Middle Ages where the king is the titular owner of all the land or the lord of the manor owns the land that the serfs simply work.

Thus, these states, whether kingdoms or chiefdoms, provide the *higher unity of society*. But it is precisely this kind of oppressive centrality that creates the stagnation of these societies. Dynasties come and go, but the basic economic resources are reproduced again and again in what Marx calls "the unchangeableness of Asiatic societies" (1976 [1867], 358). Marx was fascinated by the growing ethnographic information on Asiatic societies, and he used this data to reinforce two general theses about societies: first, that each historical phase of society rests on a particular economic system (in the Asiatic forms, this was largely irrigation technology and farming), and second, that systems of production are always mediated by existing social relations: "But the fact that prebourgeois history, and each of its phases, also has its own economy and an economic foundation for its movement, is at bottom only the tautology that human life has since time immemorial rested on production, and, in one way or another, on social production, whose relations we call, precisely, economic relations" (1973 [1857–1858], 489). This clearly expresses the basic materialist principle noted before.

There is, in fact, a telling analogy between these Asiatic societies and capitalism, that is, a parallelism between what Marx calls "appearance," the way things seem, and reality, the ways things are. In the Asiatic societies, under the bracket of appearance, the despot appears as the creator of the wealth of the community, blessing the fertility of crops, being the recipient of tribute. Under the reality bracket, it is really the local communities who are laboring mightily to provide taxes or tribute. But in their ritual phase, they might say, "O great king, you are the source, the guarantor of our existence," while of course the people themselves are doing all the work. Can we examine capitalism analogously under these same brackets of appearance and reality? To anticipate: Marx thought that in capitalism the appearance is that the capitalist is the source of all productivity, the person who is running the business, but in reality it is the labor of workers on the production lines that is the source of productivity.

I explored the Asiatic argument to show the analogy of appearance and reality: that workers not only fail to realize the reality but "buy into," to use a reified expression, especially through certain forms of religion, a myth of appearance: that the king is the source of fertility of Asiatic societies and that the capitalist is the locus of productivity in capitalist societies.

The Commodity Form

We are now prepared to turn to Marx's ethnography of capitalism. Marx wrote a book, *Capital*, which today appears as a three-volume work, although Marx himself lived to edit and perfect only the first volume (some scholars claim that, before the publication of the first volume in 1867, Marx had already drafted all three volumes of *Capital* and three separate volumes on surplus value). The other volumes were edited by his coworkers, Engels especially. I will look at the first volume of *Capital* as a self-analysis by a participant-observer in mid-nineteenth-century European society, just as an anthropologist or sociologist would analyze a society during fieldwork.

Readers of *Capital* are often struck by how much time Marx spends talking about the *theorists* of capitalism, that is, famous writers like Malthus, Ricardo, and Smith. He spends almost as much time deconstructing previous economic theorists and their attempts to understand the logic of capitalism as he does analyzing the machinery and productive relations of nineteenth-century England. Why did he spend so much time looking at other theorists? He did so because they did not realize that the very categories of their economic analyses, concepts such as capital, value, money, price, and labor, beg the most important questions. Marx sets his task as trying to uncover the hidden or essential relationship of these categories, especially by developing a coherent model of the logic linking all these concepts. For Marx, these categories in the hands of economic theorists are like "native" or "emic" models anthropologists are fond of elevating (wrongly, alas) to explanatory status. But rather than taking them as accurate scientific reports, Marx tries to figure out *why* these writers thought the way they did: "The categories of bourgeois economics consist precisely of forms of this kind. They are forms of thought which are socially valid, and therefore objective, for the relations of production belonging to this historically determined mode of social production, i.e., commodity production" (1976 [1867], 169). The theoretical ideas, thus, are completely appropriate given the forms of commodity production these theorists are trying to understand. Our task is now to see how Marx provides the *same explanation* for the mistakes of economic theorists and for the misapprehensions of workers in capitalism.

Marx begins with an examination not of the historical origin of capitalism, but with a long discourse on something he calls the "commodity form," which for him is the (Durkheimian) "elementary form" or the (Morganian) "germ" of capitalism. Put simply, a commodity is something produced by capitalist industry, privately owned by its producer, and destined for sale in the marketplace. A productive good is just an object, but when it is for sale in the market it becomes a commodity. Marx thought that this basic category of capitalism could be looked at in terms of two "forms of appearance," two ways that commodities appear to us. One has already been mentioned, use-value. If shoes are produced for sale in the marketplace, the use-value of shoes has to do with the qualitatively different utility these products of human labor have for the people who wear (or dance, jog, hike, etc., in) them. Different shoes are produced by qualitatively different kinds of human labor, and those qualitative differences among shoes are realized in the variable consumption of shoes: running shoes, boat shoes, snowshoes, and so on. The use-value, then, depends on the sensuous, natural form of a commodity as a useful thing, combining specific human labor with the natural qualities of objects. But it should not be forgotten that a useful thing is determined to be useful by a determinate social context.

The commodity, Marx goes on to say, can appear in a second way, as "exchange-value." A commodity as exchange-value has to do with the fact that qualitatively different products become equated, the value of one expressed in terms of a quantity of another. In moments of exchange, a certain number of yards of silk is equated with a certain amount of gold, or with a certain amount of boot polish, or with a certain amount of sugar. This is because the marketplace is a mechanism for establishing the relative value of commodities. For a seller of a commodity, that commodity has no use-value at all; in fact, Marx argued that the value of a commodity is only a relationship with the value of its market equivalent. But if we have sugar, silk, boot polish, and shoes, what abstract essence do these have in common so that they are equilibrated at a given price in the marketplace? Only the fact, Marx thought, that they are products of the same amount of real human labor, that is, the labor necessary to produce them. If it takes three hours to make a shoe but only one hour to produce a piece of silk, Marx says that the silk will cost a third as much as the shoe simply because it took less labor time to produce it.

When, in this "language of commodities," the value of commodity A is expressed as equivalent to a certain quantity of commodity B, the specific kinds of labor used to produce A and B are reduced to being "human labor in general" (Marx 1976 [1867], 142).

> In order to tell us that labour creates its own value in its abstract quality of being human labour, it says that the coat, in so far as it counts as its equal, i.e., its value, consists of the same labour as it does itself. In order to inform us that its sublime objectivity as a value differs from its stiff and starchy existence as a body, it says that value has the appearance of a coat, and therefore that in so far as the linen itself as an object of value, it and the coat are as like as two peas. (1976 [1867], 143–44)

When a quantity of linen (twenty yards of commodity A) is equated with a number of coats (one of commodity B), the two sides of the equation are nonsymmetrical in this respect: the commodity A whose value is being expressed is in the "relative form of value," while the commodity B that is being equated to A is in the "equivalent form of value." Additionally, the quantitative ratio of this expressed equivalence depends on the specific circumstances operating at the time: change could affect either side of the equation, as when flax becomes less fertile (twenty yards of linen now equals two coats), or when the technology of looms improves (twenty yards of linen now equals half a coat). What remains constant in the midst of these changes is labor time, the "third commodity" that lies beneath the equivalence of A and B.

In a particularly perplexing series of paragraphs, Marx explains this nonsymmetry by saying that the relative form (commodity A) expresses its value in the use-value, a "natural form" of commodity B; that is, in this relation of exchangeability between A and B a number of commodity B expresses the magnitude of value of A. Thus, the use-value of B becomes the "form of appearance" of its opposite, the value of A, which Marx now claims is a "supra-natural" property because it conceals a social relation, whereas the equivalent form seems to consist of a form endowed "by nature." The exchangeability that endows commodity B with the ability to be used to express the value of a magnitude of commodity A *appears* to belong to it as a property, just like its weight and temperature.[4] This analysis needs to be inspected very carefully. This is no longer just qualitative labor, the kind of labor that went into producing a kind of shoe, but rather what Marx calls "abstract labor," the average hours of work plain and simple. So the only thing commodities have in common when placed in a relation of exchangeability is the amount of abstract labor, this homogeneous work time in the factory put into the objects. As a result, he argues that exchange-value is the form of appearance of the value of commodities abstracted from their use-value. He is no longer looking at them qualitatively—what is good for me, how can I use it—but in terms of how capitalists make deals in the marketplace. A person who goes to Chicago and buys grain futures or pork belly futures cannot use these purchases to make breakfast. What is for sale is not the actual commodities but the relative value of the commodities.

> If we leave aside the determinate quality of productive activity, and therefore the useful character of the labour, what remains is its quality of being an expenditure of human labour-power. Tailoring and weaving, although they are qualitatively different productive activities, are both a productive expenditure of human brains, muscles, nerves, hands, etc., and in this sense both human labour. They are merely two different forms of the expenditure of human labour-power. Of course, human labour-power must itself have attained a certain level of development before it can be expended in this or that form. But the value of a commodity represents human labour pure and simple, the expenditure of human labour in general. . . . It is the expenditure of simple labour-power, i.e., of the labour-power possessed in his bodily organism by every ordinary man, on the average, without being developed in any special way. (Marx 1976 [1867], 135)

In exchange-value, then, the specific differences between the labor of weaving linen and the labor of tailoring a coat are completely ignored, since we are only talking about the abstract nature of human labor. A product of labor taken in isolation can only have use-value or utility, but when these are put into the marketplace a new system emerges, a system of commodities, and a new form of appearance emerges, namely, exchange-value. And what do these commodities have in common? Only the fact that a certain amount of "socially necessary labor" was used to produce them. If the real "worth" of a commodity, thus, is simply the "congealed" human labor required to produce it, this "value" appears to market participants as an exchange-value.

This process is an excellent illustration of Marx's concern for the relationship between historical realities and the theoretical reflection they make possible. Enlightenment philosophies of universal human equality can be seen, for example, not as a potential source for the liberation of individuals from all forms of social oppression, but rather as the ideological counterpart of the homogenization of qualitatively diverse labor into the abstract equivalence of undifferentiated labor due to the mechanism of market exchange. Human equality mirrors the equivalence of all human labor time.

> The secret of the expression of value, namely the equality and equivalence of all kinds of labour because and in so far as they are human labour in general, could not be deciphered until the concept of human equality had already acquired the permanence of a fixed popular opinion. This however becomes possible only in a society where the commodity-form is the universal form of the product of labour, hence the dominant social relation is the relation between men as possessors of commodities. (Marx 1976 [1867], 152)

It is important to note that that this differentiation of use-value and exchange-value is not only a logical distinction but a historical one: "Exchange-value . . .

only arises where at least some part of the labour-products, the objects of use, function as *commodities*; however, this does not happen at the beginning, but only at a certain period of social development, hence at a determinate level of historical development" (Marx 2010a [1879–1880], 551). Note that in strictly separating exchange-value from use-value, Marx's theory of value is almost exactly the opposite of modern economic theory, which is based on calculating the ratio of market availability (supply) and consumers' judgments about utility (demand).

Marx offered a hypothetical scenario for the emergence of the exchange-value of commodities as a form of value distinct from natural properties and human utilities. First, two objects are brought into a "simple" relationship by an accidental occurrence of exchange. Second, in the "expanded" form, the value of one commodity is expressed in terms of an innumerable series of other commodities (e.g., coffee, tea, corn, gold). Since there are numerous potential equivalences in this series of equations, the *particular* kind of use-value of the equivalent becomes irrelevant, and, note, the equations themselves are no longer reversible. And finally, the value of all possible commodities is expressed in terms of a single equivalent form (e.g., cattle), which becomes thereby the "general" form of value. Or, put negatively, the one commodity that is used as the universal equivalent is thereby excluded from being a relative form of value. This exclusion, in turn, signals the "fixity" and "validity" of a universal money form, characteristically, gold. This progression from "simple" to "expanded" to "general" forms of value exactly mirrors the stages of the revelation of the character of value:

> It is thus that this value first shows itself as being, in reality, a congealed quantity of undifferentiated human labour. For the labour which creates it is now explicitly presented as labour which counts as the equal of every other sort of human labour, whatever natural form it may possess, hence whether it is objectified in a coat, in corn, in iron, or in gold. The linen, by virtue of the form of value, no longer stands in a social relation with merely one other kind of commodity, but with the whole world of commodities as well. (Marx 1976 [1867], 155)

More importantly, at the end of this process the true character of the linkage between exchange and value is revealed: "It becomes plain that it is not the exchange of commodities which regulates the magnitude of their values, but rather the reverse, the magnitude of the value of commodities which regulates the proportion in which they exchange" (1976 [1867], 156). And since the "general form" potentially anticipates the role of money as the "universal form" of value, Marx can summarize the entire historical sequence by saying that "the simple commodity form is therefore the germ [note!] of the money-form" (1976 [1867], 163).

The development of the commodity form, thus, begins with the "simple" or accidental relative equation of the value of two commodities and then moves to the "expanded" form in which an endless series of commodities is equated with a single commodity. But in capitalist markets an additional entity, money, is used as a third object to equate *all* goods and services. It is not just that a certain amount of linen equals a certain number of shoes, but they all in turn are equal to a certain quantity of money, namely, the price. They have a dollar value attached to them: coat, linen, silk, and shoe all can equal $22.85. So money is a very peculiar cultural object or institution. When we barter products, I have something you want and you have something I want, and we are both taking into account the qualitative difference between products. But when money becomes the universal equivalent form of all products in the marketplace, it in fact becomes the "form of appearance" of the value of commodities. My car *is* $30,000; my house *is* $400,000, rather than a fast vehicle or a charming place to live. But more importantly, money is not just a mechanism of market exchange, since in capitalist society *money itself* becomes a commodity that can be bought and sold in financial markets. So money as a commodity is a very strange one, since unlike all other commodities it has no sensuous qualities; it has, Marx observes, "no smell."

> Money is the absolutely alienable commodity, because it is all other commodities divested of their shape, the product of their universal alienation. It reads all prices backwards, and thus as it were mirrors itself in the bodies of all other commodities, which provide the material through which it can come into being as a commodity. . . . Since every commodity disappears when it becomes money it is impossible to tell from the money itself how it got into the hands of its possessors, or what article has been changed into it. *Non olet.* (1976 [1867], 205)

"It does not smell" because it does not leave any sensuous trace of its true origins. Marx thought that the market exchange of different commodities mediated by money can easily turn into the entrepreneurial use of money to produce commodities with the goal of making more money and that this, in turn, predicts the possibility of investing in financial markets to make money *without* the messy intervention of any goods and services at all.

This raises a question: Why does Marx claim that the "social" character of labor only emerges when commodities are maximally separated from the qualitative, sensuous labor that created them in the system of capitalist exchange? I think it is because the exchange-value system puts commodities into mutual relationships and thus mediates the producers of the products, whose private labor appears to have social characteristics only in acts of exchange:

> Men do not therefore bring the products of their labour into relation with each other as values because they see these objects merely as the material integuments of homogeneous human labour. The reverse is true: by equating their different products to each other in exchange as values, they equate their different kinds of labour as human labour. They do this without being aware of it. (Marx 1976 [1867], 166–67)

But note that, coming to grasp "after the feast" the social character of commodities, Marx quickly points out that this reflection is actually a *miscognition* of the nature of the "social": the bourgeois mind considers the social dimension as arising from the relationships among commodities and *not* between real workers, managers, consumers, and the like. These real social relations are especially "concealed" when human relations "appear as relations between material objects" (Marx 1976 [1867], 169). This categorical misapprehension that characterizes the world of commodities is not found, Marx claims, in either "primitive" or medieval contexts, since in these two earlier epochs "the social relations between individuals in the performance of their labor appear to all events as their own personal relations, and are not disguised as social relations between things, between the products of labor" (1976 [1867], 170).

The "Very Mysterious Being" of Capital

Marx makes a further argument that this dual aspect of commodities, qualitative use-value and quantitative exchange-value, accounts for the "mysterious," mystical or enigmatic character of capitalism. Capitalism involves a double inversion of the categories, first of social characteristics and second of natural characteristics or relationships among people and things. Social characteristics are, of course, things people do as social beings, and natural characteristics are qualities objects have in the world. But in capitalism there is a double inversion of these relations. The key to this discovery is that once market exchange is set in full motion, the measurement of human labor by its quantitative duration becomes expressed as an inherent natural characteristic of commodities, namely the price of a commodity. In other words, something entirely social, that is, work, which is how people express themselves individually as humans and as social beings, becomes abstracted in terms of labor time. I spent five hours making this; my skill as a craftsman is not important, only the abstract hours expended by anyone. And that quantitative measure is seen to be a natural characteristic of the commodity, that is, the price.

> We have already seen that the commodity must acquire a two-fold mode of existence if it is to be rendered fit for the circulation process. It is not enough for it to appear to the buyer as an article with particular useful qualities, i.e., as a specific *use-value* which can gratify specific needs whether of individual or of productive consumption. Its exchange-value must also have acquired a definite, independent, *form*, distinct, albeit ideally, from its use-value. It must represent both the unity and the duality of use-value and exchange-value. Its exchange-value acquires this distinctive form independent of its use-value, as the pure form of materialized social labour-time, i.e., its *price*. For the price is the expression of exchange-value as exchange-value, i.e., as *money*, and more precisely as *money of account*. (Marx 1976 [1867], 955)

The price of a commodity appears to be part of the characteristic of the commodity, embodied in it naturally. The value of a commodity is an attribute of commodities, something *in* the commodity. Shoppers going to the store think that the price is somehow *in* the commodity rather than in the social relations of production. What is, in fact, merely an abstraction or an appearance has become a natural part of the commodity: "The mysterious character of the commodity-form consists therefore simply in the fact that the commodity reflects the social characteristics of men's own labour as the objective characteristics of the products of labour themselves, as the socio-natural properties of these things" (Marx 1976 [1867], 164–65). This is what Marx calls "fetishism." To describe this peculiar nature of commodities in capitalist society, he had recourse to an analogy from the domain of religion:

> We must take flight into the misty realm of religion. There the products of human brain appear as autonomous figures endowed with a life of their own, which enter into relations both with each other and with the human race. So it is in the world of commodities with the products of men's hands. I call this the fetishism which attaches itself to the products of labour as soon as they are produced as commodities, and is therefore inseparable from the production of commodities. (1976 [1867], 165)

So, put negatively but in reality, the values of a commodity put into exchange have absolutely no connection to the physical nature of the commodity; put positively, the commodity form in reality is a social relationship, an activity among people in the marketplace. But in capitalism, these social relations of production and sales take on the "fantastic form of a relation between things." So in fetishism, what was in fact an artificial, humanly created relationship—production of goods and the acts of buying and selling—becomes an autonomous reality: the market has forces, what economists in Marx's time called the "invisible hand," to regulate itself.

What are the social consequences of this? The relationships among commodities, as soon as they appear as the necessary result of their "natural" relations, start to control people by appearing to be subject to natural laws, taken to be objective, abstract, immutable, and totalizing, such as the law of supply and demand, the law of cost-benefit, or the law of maximizing resources. Economic theorists who purport to study the economy in fact only reaffirm this very analytical inversion of use-value and exchange-value.

> The forms which stamp products as commodities and which are therefore the preliminary requirements for the circulation of commodities, already possess the fixed quality of natural forms of social life before man seeks to give an account, not of their historical character, for in his eyes they are immutable, but of their content and meaning. Consequently, it was solely the analysis of

the prices of commodities which led to the determination of the magnitude of value, and solely the common expression of all commodities in money which led to the establishment of their character as values. It is however precisely this finished form of the world of commodities—the money form—which conceals the social character of private labour and the social relations between the individual workers, by making those relations appear as relations between material objects, instead of revealing them plainly. (Marx 1976 [1867], 168–69)

The double inversion is clear: human labor becomes an object, a thing sold in the marketplace at a wage, rather than a qualitative embodiment of our activity; the objects we produce become fetishes, alive somehow as a total universe acting outside of our social consensus. And social relations, originally the source of all economic values, return only as *mediated* by the commodity form—everything from personal and group identity to noneconomic relationships is expressed in the "language of commodities."

But objectification is only one way of looking at the realities of human labor under capitalism. As early as 1861, Marx's economic notebooks describe the "subsumption of labor" in terms of the reality/appearance duality: workers really do not create commodities, but, under capitalism, "living labor" is compelled to work beyond the needs of individual workers. The differential between actual, productive laboring and compensated, wage labor necessary to live Marx labels "surplus value," that is, the amount of appropriated unpaid labor.

Since living labour is incorporated into capital—through the exchange between capital and the worker—since it appears as an activity belonging to capital, as soon as the labour process starts, all the productive powers of social labour present themselves as productive powers of capital, just as the general social form of labour appears in money as the quality of a thing. Thus the productive power of labour, and the specific forms of it, now present themselves as productive powers and forms of capital, of *objectified* labour, of the objective conditions of labour, which—as such an independent entity—are personified in the capitalist and confront living labour. Here once again we have the inversion of the relation, the expression of which we have already characterized as *fetishism* in considering the nature of money. (1994 [1861–1863], 122)

Marx's political attitude toward capitalism focused on this opposition of appearance and reality: in capitalism and in appearance, profit is generated by the efficiency of machinery and the ingenuity of capitalists; but in reality, profit comes from a concealed differential between the wages paid to laborers and the true costs to capitalists for having the goods produced. This is what he called "exploitation." There is a differential between what capitalists have to pay laborers (just enough to enable them to purchase the goods minimally necessary for their survival as workers) and the real costs of producing the product. And this superabundance or profit appears to be the result of the capitalist's genius, while in reality it is the result of the exploitation of workers, who are not paid the full wage.

> The product—the property of the capitalist—is a use-value, as yarn, for example, or boots. But although boots are, to some extent, the basis of social progress, and our capitalist is decidedly in favour of progress [Marx is joking here], he does not manufacture boots for their own use.... Use-values are produced by capitalists only because and in so far as they form the material substratum of exchange-value, are the bearers of exchange-value. Our capitalist has two objectives: in the first place, he wants to produce a use-value which has exchange-value, i.e., an article destined to be sold, a commodity; and secondly he wants to produce a commodity greater in value than the sum of the values of the commodities used to produce it, namely the means of production and the labour-power he purchased with his good money in the open market. His aim is to produce not only a use-value, but a commodity; not only use-value, but value; and not just value, but surplus-value. (Marx 1976 [1867], 293)

Why, then, do workers have difficulty seeing the reality of their own oppression, *exactly the same* difficulty economic theorists have in conceptualizing the true or essential interrelationship among economic categories? Marx links these two instances of "transposed consciousness" to the general inversion of subject and object:

> Yet the way that surplus-value is transformed into the form of profit, by way of the rate of profit; is only a further extension of that inversion of subject and object which already occurs in the course of the production process itself. We saw in that case how all the subjective productive forces of labour present themselves as productive forces of capital. On the one hand, value, i.e., the past labour that dominates living labour, is personified into the capitalist; on the other hand, the worker conversely appears as mere objectified labour-power, as a commodity. This inverted relationship necessarily gives rise, even in the simple relation of production itself, to a correspondingly inverted conception of the situation, a transposed consciousness, which is further developed by the transformations and modifications of the circulation process proper. (1981 [1894], 136)

Marx argues that it is precisely this totalization of the commodity form that becomes the whole world for people, a world tied together by "natural" laws rather than historical circumstances. Not only do products produced by specific qualities of labor for particular uses become commodities exchanged in the marketplace through their price, and not only does money become the measure of all the commodities, but money itself can become a commodity to be invested to create additional surplus value.

What is the source of the surplus value of money? Interest rates. If the "fetish" quality of the commodity consists in its mystical potency to generate value by obscuring the social relations that make value possible, this magic is only ex-aggerated to an infinite degree by what Marx calls "interest-bearing capital." Instead of the actual transformation of money into capital, here, "in its pure form, self-valorizing value, money breeding money, and in this form it no longer bears any marks of its origin" (1981 [1894], 516). (This power of money to generate money through interest rates resembles, Marx writes, "the property of a pear tree to bear pears" [1981 (1894), 516].) Not only does interest-bearing capital mask its origin, but it ultimately asserts a reversed chronology, since this "simple form of capital" is taken as "logically anterior to its own reproduction process" (1981 [1894], 517)—a "capital mystification in the most flagrant form" (516).

The fact that lending out money at interest existed, in the form of usury, long before the capitalist mode of production offers Marx an excellent opportunity to demonstrate one of his key methodological principles of analyzing economic phenomena at historically specific junctures of the "mode of production and the social arrangements corresponding to them" (1981 [1894], 730). In the ancient world, the usurer was universally hated, precisely because, for both peasant and lord, the weight of debt attacked the production process itself—in the "precapitalist" period, the worker is still "the proprietor of his conditions of labor," who relates to the money-lender's capital "as a producer." While usury "sucks it dry" (1981 [1894], 731), it does not itself change this mode of production.

> Usury has a revolutionary effect on pre-capitalist modes of production only in so far as it destroys and dissolves the forms of ownership which produce a firm basis for the articulation of political life and whose constant reproduction in the same form is a necessity for that life. In Asiatic forms, usury can persist for a long while without leading to anything more than economic decay and political corruption. It is only where and when the other conditions for the capitalist mode of production are present that usury appears as one of the means of formation of this new mode of production, by ruining the feudal lords and petty production on the one hand, and by centralizing the conditions of labour on the other. (Marx 1981 [1894], 732)

Marx then comes to his methodological point: "What distinguishes interest-bearing capital in so far as it forms an essential element of the capitalist mode of production, from usurer's capital is in no way the nature or character of this capital itself. It is simply the *changed conditions* under which it functions, and hence also the totally transformed figure of the borrower who confronts the money-lender" (1981 [1894], 735, emphasis added).

For Marx, then, the basic fact of labor in capitalistic societies is that the self-realizing process we mentioned at the beginning becomes blocked, since labor is sold as homogeneous units, working hours. And people's human essence is given a price, a wage. Workers lose their individuality and must join the marketplace subject to its laws. Even when they go on strike, they are subject to the laws of the market. He calls this inevitable situation of human labor "alienation," where people put themselves into the products but no longer see them as *their* products. Their job is to put the third bolt on the left fender of a car, but they have no pride in the fact that the car is the objectification of their human subjectivity. In fact, workers may not even buy the cars they produce.

Reflexive Analysis and Critical Theory as Methodologies

Given that Marx himself makes reference to the tribal world in adopting the term *fetishism* to describe a characteristic of commodities in capitalism, a reasonable question would be: To what degree can fetishism, as an analytic concept in social analysis, be applied to these noncapitalist systems? As was demonstrated in the previous discussion of the parallelism of appearance and reality in the Asiatic and capitalist modes of production, there is certainly plenty of illusion going around at every stage of social development. One important difference would be the source of illusion or misrecognition: in precapitalist societies, the source might be called the "politico-religious" sphere that produces ideological constructs tying the social order to transcendent claims; in capitalism, in contrast, the engine producing fetishism is the economy itself. No longer required to directly produce illusion, the sphere Marx calls "superstructure" in capitalism takes on a related function: generating sets of ideas that ultimately support or reinforce the class-based interests of the ruling capitalists. Taking things like the arts, law, philosophy, religion, and other cultural arenas together, Marx claims that they generate largely symbolic forms that are closely tied to the interests of the ruling class, and in several ways. The ruling class may, first, actually directly *produce* items in the superstructure (advertising, for example). Or it may, second, *commodify* cultural forms produced by nonelite members of the society. It may, third, appropriate and *refunctionalize* certain cultural forms. And, at the most abstract level, it establishes or approves a language code that delimits the universe of discourse in the public sphere. The ultimate efficiency is reached when the working class so internalizes superstructural cultural forms that they reproduce them by their own activities and beliefs—this is the "hegemony" that modern social theorists make so much of. An ideology, as Arendt points out, articulates what someone pretends to be for the sake of their active role in the world. Speech, especially, is ideological talk whose chief function is to conceal the truth.

In a particularly telling methodological aphorism, Marx writes: "Reflection on the forms of human life, hence also scientific analysis of those forms, takes a course directly opposite to their real development" (1976 [1867], 168). The development of capitalism from primitive forms of economic activity follows a trajectory of increasing *opacity* of reflection by participants in the various epochs. Isolated on his deserted island, Robinson Crusoe is able to keep accurate records of his useful objects and the labor time necessary to produce them; the forms of his self-created wealth are fully "transparent" and, of course, involve no barter or exchange. Even the medieval serf understands that, in the performance of labor, the hierarchical social relations of feudalism are undisguised personal relations, just as the communal labor of peasants in the Asiatic mode of production are "in their natural form social functions" (Marx 1976 [1867], 171). In contrast, bourgeois capitalism works to conceal the principles of its operation, despite the persistent attempts at scientific explanation by economists who, first, refuse to see its historical character and, second, miss the social basis of economic value.

In order to reverse this trend, Marx argues that the economist needs to utilize a number of conceptual tools shown to be useful in the "hard" sciences. The first chapter of volume one of *Capital,* as I noted, begins with a discussion of the commodity form as the "cell" of capitalism, followed by chapters on exchange and money. But in these three introductory chapters Marx intentionally strips capitalism of many of its complexities, leaving aside, for example, various important topics such as merchants, money-lenders, and interest-bearing capital. This "method of abstraction" mirrors the scientific method, as, for example, when Galileo "thinks away" friction in explaining the laws of falling bodies. Another method used by Marx is "saving the phenomena," used brilliantly by Newton, according to which inconsistencies and paradoxes are explained by bringing them within a revised conceptual scheme. Marx is also fond of "thought experiments," in which purely logical or conceptual operations are used to isolate contradictions in a theoretical model. For example, Marx disproves Ricardo's argument that capitalists make profit by selling commodities for more than their value; while both Marx and Ricardo agree that labor constitutes value, Marx points out that, since all sellers become buyers, no real profit would ever be gained if profit was artificially tacked on to value. The goal of all these methodological devices is to separate the essence of some phenomenon from its appearance. Just as in science it is necessary to distinguish the truth that the earth revolves around the sun from the everyday experience (as Wittgenstein famously reminds us) that the sun circles the earth, so in economics it is important to counter the appearance that workers' labor is fully rewarded in wages with the reality that capitalists extract surplus value from this unpaid labor.

What, then, can we conclude about Marx's ethnographic accomplishments? The first point is to realize that Marx is a native observer, for these developments were going on at the time in nineteenth-century European capitalism, though Marx himself never personally set foot in any of the factories he was studying in the library at the British Museum, even the factories run by his partner Engels. (Marx thought that certain social legislation passed in England signaled that that country was in fact moving slowly beyond "pure" capitalism.) Second, the categories of Marx's analysis (value, money, price, wage, labor, etc.) derive from the language of the economic theorists read at that time. But he takes these labels, these "emic" or indigenous categories, and tries to reveal the ways in which they themselves predictively masquerade as scientific descriptions of capitalism. They are scientific descriptions that must be unpacked to reveal the reason why people have such a hard time understanding the realities: because of the *systematicity* of the appearances of the market. Marx says, "Economic categories are only the theoretical expression, the abstraction of the social relations of production" (1963 [1846–1847], 109). That is, the ideology of the economic theorists is precisely designed to legitimize, justify, and mask true social relations, which is a situation of exploitation and alienation.

> Thus, just as production founded on capital creates universal industriousness on one side—i.e., surplus labour, value-creating labour—so does it create on the other side a system of general exploitation of the natural and human qualities, a system of general utility, utilising science itself just as much as all the physical and mental qualities, while there appears nothing *higher in itself*, nothing legitimate for itself, outside this circle of social production and exchange. Thus capital creates the bourgeois society, and the universal appropriation of nature as well as of the social bond itself by the members of society. Hence the great civilizing influence of capital; its production of a stage of society in comparison to which all earlier ones appear as mere *local developments* of humanity and as *nature-idolatry*. For the first time, nature becomes purely an object for humankind, purely a matter of utility; ceases to be recognized as a power for itself; and the theoretical discovery of its autonomous laws appears merely as a ruse so as to subjugate it under human needs, whether as an object of consumption or as a means of production. (Marx 1973 [1857–1858], 409–10)

The principles of Marx's analysis derive, thus, immanently from the social system he is analyzing; and he insists again and again on the historical specificity of capitalism, which is not just another social system that might be analyzed using other than these categories. These *are* the categories to analyze capitalism, since there is a relationship between the analysis and the local justification (by economists, especially) of the very system. That is, the system reproduces itself in an ideology, which is economic theory.

The scientific analysis of the commodity form in the hands of political economists is capable of revealing only a portion of the "mystical character of the commodity," because to the degree that their discovery of economic laws echoes the invariant laws of nature, the true historical contingency of capitalism is hidden, and to the degree that economic laws are thought to be embodied *in* the commodity (like gravity in a falling apple), the social reality of human labor is masked.

> Even its best representatives, Adam Smith and Ricardo, treat the form of value as something of indifference, something external to the nature of the commodity itself. The explanation for this is not simply that their attention

is entirely absorbed by the analysis of the magnitude of value. It lies deeper. The value-form of the product of labour is the most abstract, but also the most universal form of the bourgeois mode of production; by that fact it stamps the bourgeois mode of production as a particular kind of social production of a historical and transitory character. If then we make the mistake of treating it as the external natural form of social production, we necessarily overlook the specificity of the value-form, and consequently of the commodity-form, etc. (Marx 1976 [1867], 174)

In contrast to both Enlightenment and Evolutionary thinkers, for Marx the exercise of individual rationality (e.g., making "compacts" or reforming "survivals") results in the end in the destruction of the collective system. The capitalist cannot prevent the trend toward a "falling rate of profit" that results from rational competition among capitalists in different economic sectors: as capitalists intensify their quest for profit, the workers get poorer and poorer and then have less available cash to purchase the goods that their exploitation is making. Of course, Marx is not rejecting rationality (i.e., free decision making) but only showing that our economic activity actually *prevents* the fulfillment of full rationality: the capitalist ends up destroying capital, and the worker must sell his/her labor in the marketplace. We can vote (thus, political rationality) and we can debate (thus, civic rationality), but we cannot work rationally in the modern world. Thus, the worker is alienated, even though many workers try to realize their humanness in activities outside of the workplace (in hobbies, sports, entertainment, clubs, etc.).

I cannot end without pointing out the final step of Marx's argument, which was revolutionary, not just analytical. He intended his ethnography of capitalism to be the ultimate example of "action anthropology," to, in fact, overthrow the system he is analyzing! Marx identified what he saw as the immanent—in two senses of belonging within and expected in a moment—factor, namely "class." People organize themselves fundamentally around their economic interests, so Marx identifies class as the unit of struggle that was going to overthrow the capitalist world. He could not overthrow it theoretically by just writing a book, *Capital*; he thought that social groups themselves would see to it that this world was overthrown.

> Economic conditions had first transformed the mass of the people of the country into workers. The combination of capital has created for this mass a common situation, common interests. This mass is thus already a class as against capital, but not yet for itself. In the struggle . . . this mass becomes united, and constitutes itself as a class for itself. The interests it defends become class interests. But the struggle of class against class is a political struggle. . . . An oppressed class is the vital condition for every society founded on the antagonism of classes. The emancipation of the oppressed class thus implies necessarily the creation of a new society. (1963, 173–74)

So this is the ultimate subjective involvement of the analyst in the society being studied: namely, to overthrow the injustices found by the act of social analysis. And that overthrowing will not be imposed from without, but generated by real contradictions in the society itself, namely, class struggle.

Notes

1. This pedagogical piece is the edited transcription of a lecture to students in my graduate course on the history of anthropological ideas, which I taught from 1989 to 2014.

2. Marx sent Darwin a dedicatory copy of the first volume of *Capital,* which Darwin left uncut.

3. We are very close here to the concept of "hegemony," that is, a society reproducing forms of ideology that guarantee the commitment of its members to the perpetuation of the existing status quo, no matter how oppressive.

4. The impact of this nonsymmetry will be revealed in the next section of chapter 1 of *Capital,* where Marx charts the expansion of the language of commodities from a singular equivalence relationship to an expanded series of equivalences.

PART III

COMPARATIVE PERSPECTIVES ON SEMIOSIS

13 Money Walks, People Talk: Systemic and Transactional Dimensions of Palauan Exchange

Go on your way, and let the people talk.

—Marx (1976, 93)

When money stands still, it is no longer money according to its specific value and significance.

—Simmel (1978, 510)

Money is something always moving.

—Ngiraklang Malsol (1979)

Introduction

Most historical and ethnographic sources on Palau (Micronesia) mention the centrality of money (*udoud*) in the social life of the islands. Johann Kubary, the brilliant nineteenth-century ethnographer, notes:

> In political life, every occasion for intercourse between two tribes is based on an exchange of certain money, the value and the amount of which is determined by custom. In social life, everyone is bound by custom to make certain carefully regulated expenditures in relation to his position in the community. Everyone is responsible for his cousins, his children, and his household, and must pay for them. Every act performed for a stranger must be paid for, just as any injury to a stranger must be compensated for in this way. Family life is likewise founded only on the basis of money. (1895, 28)

Semper, a naturalist who lived in Ngerard in the mid-nineteenth century, comments (1982, 49): "It is said that the money originated from the beautiful shining eyes of one of the heavenly beings. . . . Just as they describe a divine origin to the money, so it is, according to them, that the kinds of money live an actual life like the gods in that island." The Japanese artist and ethnographer Hijikata, who lived in Palau for thirteen years starting in 1928, remarks:

> Regarding modern Palau, without an understanding of the economic rela-
> tions involved in the Palauan money, *udoud*, no description can be complete.
> From village to village, house to house, and person to person, *udoud*, Palauan
> money, is always of greatest importance. Therefore the exchange of *udoud* has
> an effect on the rise and fall of a household, as well as on the prosperity or
> destruction of a community. (1993, 218)

Barnett, the leader of a team of researchers who came to Palau just after World
War II, writes:

> The Palauans exhibit an emotional attachment to their money that verges
> upon the mystical. They tend to identify themselves with it and the things that
> are intimately associated with it. . . . Palauan money is essential to social posi-
> tion and it must play a part in every arrangement that testifies to the social or
> political importance of an individual. . . . [The] uses [of Palauan money] ram-
> ify widely in the culture, so widely, in fact, that every individual is necessarily
> affected by the demands for it. Now, as in the past, it is impossible for a Pa-
> lauan to get along without making use of the native type of money to a greater
> or lesser degree." (1949, 51–54; see also Ritzenthaler 1954, 34; Vidich 1949, 54)

Force summarizes that, during the period of his fieldwork from 1954 to 1956,
"the exchange system was a primary integrating force in Palauan culture" (1960,
55). While it is possible that these foreign observers overstate Palau's obsession
with money due to its striking resonances with their own cultural backgrounds,
it would not be inappropriate to borrow a phrase from Simmel's description
of money (1991, 27) in the capitalist world to describe its importance in Palau:
"Money becomes that absolute goal which it is possible in principle to strive for
at any moment."

The analysis presented here is based on two years of ethnographic fieldwork
(1978–1980) in Ngeremlengui, a group of villages on the western side of Babeldaob, the largest island in the Palau archipelago. My principal informants on
money matters were high-ranking titleholders whose traditional knowledge and
significant personal interest in financial dealings led me to devote a substantial
portion of my energies to exploring issues of classification, nomenclature, transactional strategies, and folklore associated with money. I also participated in
many customary events where pieces of money were exchanged or were the topic
of conversation late into the night. (I have only indirect and anecdotal information about changes in the money system over the past twenty years.) All aspects
of these investigations were both facilitated and stimulated by the two publications dealing with Palauan money that are the cornerstones of all subsequent
study: Kubary's classic article "Uber das einheimische Geld auf der Insel Yap
und auf den Pelau-Inseln" (1895) and Ritzenthaler's detailed monograph, *Native
Money of Palau* (1954).

Despite its obvious cultural salience and its rich ethnographic treatment, Palau's complex and changing money system has not—except for a brief reference in a paper by Mauss (1969, 111)—taken its rightful place in the comparative study of "primitive money" (Dalton 1965). While scholars concerned with the cultures of Oceania have examined and reexamined the exchange of *kula* valuables throughout the Massim (Leach and Leach 1983) and the shell valuables of Rossel Island first described by Armstrong (1928; see also Berde 1973; Liep 1983, 1995), few have taken Palau's money system as a matter for comparative analysis. This paper can do little more than use Palauan data to suggest that a semiotic perspective for studying money systems can advance this comparative work. The important tasks of comprehensively describing the social functions of the Palauan money system, of examining the historical changes in the system over the past two hundred years, of analyzing the large corpus of mythological narratives describing the origin of money, and of constructing an etymologically informed inventory of the names and classes of money must await other opportunities.

Money as a Sign

That Palauan money might be considered "symbolic" at first seems improbable when compared with the character of modern financial mechanisms such as paper currency, credit and debit cards, stock certificates, futures trading, and computerized transactions. These instruments have been called symbolic because they are relatively dematerialized (i.e., they do not have an intrinsic material link to the values they represent), depersonalized (i.e., usage does not vary with the personnel involved in the transaction), decontextualized (i.e., calculations of value and modes of exchange are consistent across social space and interactional time), and conventional (i.e., the value of representational tokens is constituted and enforced by some collective authority). But, as Marx (1976) insightfully argues, paper money is a "symbol" of gold only because coins had already become "symbols of themselves." To the degree that a gold coin functions as the circulating medium, passing "from hand to hand," it is no longer regarded by social actors as a material commodity, embodying the social labor required for its production. Money "only needs to lead a symbolic existence. Its functional existence so to speak absorbs its material existence" (1976, 226; see also 1973, 211). (Marx warns against thinking of symbols as purely "imaginary"; even the commodity itself is a symbol in that it is "the material shell of the human labour expended on it" [1976, 185].) On the other hand, Oceanic beads and shells do not seem to fit comfortably into the category of "natural" or "concrete" money, that is, relatively scarce objects (livestock, salt, hides, coppers, etc.) with intrinsic commodity value which, because of some physical properties useful to permanence, countability, and exchangeability, have become standards of value and mediums of exchange. Other than the social indexical function of wearing beads as jewelry and the curative function believed by some to accrue to those touching money pieces, Palauan money has little evident use-value. And yet, as we will see, Palauans consistently speak of the important "work" money accomplishes.

In an almost trivial sense, of course, anything that functions as a substitute or replacement for something else in consciousness or in social interaction can be a "sign," as Foucault (1970, 181) observes: "Coinage can always bring back into the hands of its owners that which has just been exchanged for it, just as, in representation, a sign must be able to recall to thought that which it represents. Money is material memory, a self-duplicating representation, a deferred exchange" (see also Vaughan 1980). Similarly, from a structuralist point of view, anything that moves reciprocally between giver and receiver, whether words, money, sacred offerings, or—as Lévi-Strauss actually argues (1969, 481)—women, takes on the essential semiotic property of "mediation" (Lévi-Strauss 1976, 11; see also Parmentier 1985a).

To explore the "sign" function of money in a more useful way, it would be both too simplistic and yet approximately accurate to condense the contributions of Ferdinand de Saussure and Charles S. Peirce, the twin founders of semiotics, by saying that, for the former, money must be treated as a system of values, and, for the latter, money must be understood as a medium of real-time social transactions (Ahonen 1989a, 1989b; Parmentier 1997b). Money, as Saussure (1966, 115) famously points out, enters into systemic relations along two intersecting axes: first, money can be exchanged for a fixed quantity of a dissimilar thing ($100 buys a wristwatch), and second, the value of a piece of money can be expressed in terms of a certain quantity of money of other denominations as determined by an abstract system of equivalences (a dollar equals a hundred pennies). Money in the Peircean idiom is the medium or middle term in the three-placed relation: the buyer and the seller are brought into a relationship by means of an "intermediating third term, money, which acts first as agent of the seller and then as agent of the buyer" (Shell 1978, 56).

Combining these initial Saussurean and Peircean insights, a fuller "semiotic" approach to money does not dwell on facile evolutionary dichotomies such as between "natural" and "symbolic" currencies (Riegel 1979, 60–70) but seeks a detailed "systemic" (i.e., Saussurean) and "transactional" (i.e., Peircean) account by looking at several typologically critical dimensions. Money's meaningfulness needs to be sought, first, in significant formal or "iconic" association with other cultural objects and practices; this is not limited to the direct or material values it embodies but includes sensory, metaphorical, and aesthetic aspects. Second, its contextual, positional, or "indexical" properties can be discovered by examining ways that, in transactional events and in individual and collective display, money tokens demarcate, mediate, and emblematize social statuses and relations. Third, money's systemic properties flow from the structured properties organizing the total set of exchange valuables into a relatively interlocking, convertible network—of course, in Palauan and other Oceanic systems there is not usually a perfect degree of convertibility. These iconic, indexical, and systemic aspects of money can then be combined to address the more general question of the cultural value of *udoud*. In particular, these systemic and transactional data can be joined by processual and narrative evidence to show that, in Palau, the "naturalization" of money, that is, the ideological construction of money as an entirely nonsocial realm of value, is accomplished by the "talk" of high-ranking leaders whose hierarchical position it expresses, reproduces, and legitimizes.

Palauan Money as a System

A systemic analysis of Palauan money includes accounts of the classification of classes and types of money pieces, of the differentiation of functional usages of these classes and types, of various exchange mechanisms for establishing intra-systemic equivalences, and of the multiple linkages between *udoud* and other material objectifications of value in Palauan historical experience.

The category of objects labeled *udoud* consists of beads and bracelet segments of various shapes, colors, decorations, and material compositions. These pieces are all of foreign manufacture, perhaps from China, India, Malaysia, or the Philippines, and were brought to Palau by voyagers at least several hundred years ago. Basic to the system of *udoud* is the fact that the supply of these beads is fixed; in fact, due to loss, breakage, and devaluation, the number of beads available for exchange is constantly decreasing. Many stories about money mention that, in an effort to conceal their financial resources, people bury money around the house or even in the taro patch; money is frequently lost when a person dies before informing the family of the hiding place. Attempts to make substitutes out of glass, stone, or porcelain are immediately recognized as fakes.

Considerations of value and secrecy obviously limit scholarly attempts to learn the exact physical composition of *udoud* (Barnett 1949, 35–39; Force 1959; Osborne 1966, 477–94). Efforts to identify specific external cultural sources based on comparative archaeological evidence from Asia and the Pacific have met with only modest success. On the basis of a very limited study, Force (1959, 43) concludes that at least one piece of *udoud* (perhaps a piece of glass money called *cheldoech*) and similar pieces from the Philippines have "high indices of refraction, possess considerable hardness, display isotropism, and contain proportions of elements which are not typical of mineral specimens. Moreover, the elongated or drawn bubble patterns and tendencies toward concoidal fracturing indicate the high probability of artificial fusion. The only possible conclusion as to the material from which the Palauan prisms and other opaque bead money is made is that it is glass not stone."

Regularity of linguistic labels, standardized norms of valuation, and consistent local commentary work together to construct an ethno-classification of nine primary classes of *udoud* based on four factors, composition (fired clay, polychrome, glass), color (yellow, red, green, blue), shape (prismatic sections of rings, rounded and cylindrical beads), and differential social function. The first three classes are segments of bracelet rings (*bachel*): (1) *bachel berrak* (yellow fired clay), (2) *bachel mengungau* (reddish fired clay), and (3) *bachel cheldoech* (greenish to bluish glass). The next three classes are rounded beads (*bleob*) of the same composition as the three ring segment classes: (4) *bleob el berrak* (yellow beads), (5) *bleob el mengungau* (reddish beads), and (6) *bleob el cheldoech* (glass beads). The final three classes consist of various other beads of spherical, cylindrical, and oval shapes: (7) *chelbucheb* (large, multicolored, impressed beads), (8) *kluk* (small colored beads with white lines), and (9) *delobech* (beads cut from larger ones). (Illustrations of *udoud* can be found in Etpison, 38–49; Hijikata 1993, 215; Kubary 1895, 3, plate 1; Osborne 1966, frontispiece.) The general term *kldait* is used to refer to any small beads made out of the same material as either *bachel berrak* or *bachel* mengungau. Because of the ease of counterfeiting, the classes of glass money (classes 3 and 6) were largely forced out of circulation by 1921 (Ritzenthaler 1954, 22). Several of the classes of *udoud* are additionally subdivided into named and ranked types, each containing dozens of individual pieces; and the most valuable pieces in the *bachel* and chelbucheb classes are individually named. The most famous pieces normally have some distinctive or irregular feature, such as a crack line, an unusual design, or a unique shape; and in general, the more a piece appears well worn or well-traveled the higher its value. Although several dozen named pieces in the *bachel* and mengungau classes are known to be extremely valuable (*klou el udoud*), this loose set is not internally graded.

Local knowledge of *udoud* is highly stratified. People from lower-ranking houses and young people of all ranks do not have first-hand knowledge of the names and histories of individual pieces, although some understanding of the major classes and corresponding social functions of money is widespread: "Knowledge of the different forms of money and of their respective values is a cultivated art. It is, moreover, a jealously guarded prerogative of the chiefs and of a few others in the limited circle of their supporters upon whose abilities and judgments they can rely" (Barnett 1949, 41). Since senior men control the financial resources of younger members of the family, it is even possible for a person to "own" a piece of money without knowing anything about its history and without having any say in controlling its movement. Holders of important titles largely know the names and values of *udoud* that have passed through their houses and villages, and they try hard to track the future movement of pieces they once held.

Even knowledgeable elders often do not know the names of the *udoud* they see women wearing around their necks every day, since they never have an opportunity to inspect other people's money closely, and it is considered extremely rude to ask direct questions about money. For some negotiations, money experts need to be consulted before the transaction can be approved, but even experts can disagree about the valuation of pieces.

One of my teachers, for example, thought that Targong, who served as Robert Ritzenthaler's principal informant in 1948, made numerous silly mistakes, especially in trying to specify the exact number of the extant pieces of money in various classes and types and in confusing descriptive labels with individual names. This lack of uniform knowledge leads to the widespread use of trickery, deception, and repeated attempts at counterfeiting, though high-ranking men can certainly manipulate the system even when following the "rules"—indeed, many deceptive strategies are subject to proverbial labels.

Semper (1982, 49) comments that the temptation to make counterfeits was shared by Palauans and early Western traders: "The importance of this money in trade has naturally led traders to try and smuggle in pieces of glass, porcelain bits, or imitation pearls; but these efforts are mostly supposed to be failures. It is significant that the Palauans maintain they can easily distinguish the autochthonous money from those introduced in recent times."

Social Functions of Exchange

The exchange of money is a feature of almost every aspect of traditional and modern Palauan social life. *Udoud* can be used to purchase commodities, to pay for labor services, to cement or break off personal friendship and political alliance, to reciprocate affinal food prestations, to make and terminate marriage, to conclude peace between villages, to ward off illness, to elevate a man to a chiefly title, to resolve fines imposed by chiefly councils, to pass inheritance through the generations, and to coerce the spirits. The various classes of *udoud* have well-established focal usages. *Kluk* and *delobech* are used in economic transactions, including purchasing commodities and paying for services. *Bachel* can be used in the affinal exchanges of important families and otherwise play a prominent role in the political relations among chiefly houses and capital villages. And chelbucheb are used primarily in intervillage political relations and for purchasing the chief's meeting house. This section will summarize several traditional uses of money in family life and in the political arena; particular attention will be paid to specialized "strategies" (*rolel a kelulau*) that shed light on the cultural assumptions of money as a system.

While industrious physical labor (fishing, farming, carpentry, making coconut syrup) and persistent gifts of food and services to one's affines in expectation of financial reward were important traditional ways to earn money, for titleholders the more respectable method of obtaining *udoud* was to control the labor, behavior, and marriages of others. Although, in principle, the senior male (*okdemaol*) in a matriline controls the financial dealings of all lineage members, this control is regularly transferred to the husbands of the matriline's women and to the fathers of its children. A woman works hard for her husband and a child for his/her father, however, in the hope that this labor will ultimately attract wealth into the matriline in the form of affinal payments (*orau*) regularly due from husbands to their wives' kin and of the inheritance of money by children at the death of their fathers and mothers. In all these cases, individuals can stimulate the influx of money by energetic or even excessive presentation of food and contribution of labor.

This asymmetrical flow of valuables across the affinal tie (*omeluchel*) is the fundamental exchange pattern in Palau. The husband (and his relatives) gives *udoud* to the wife (and her relatives) in response to her food production and service. A woman who has provided food and service to her spouse has the right to demand payment of *udoud* from her husband at times when this money is required by her brothers.

> It was quite common for a man to secure money merely by asking his sister to obtain it from her husband. Or chiefs might obtain quantities of money as the result of the services of the young women from their village who served as attendants in other villages' clubhouses. . . . Palauans recognized that the women of the clan were a major source of revenue through the patterned financial payments made by their husbands. (Force and Force 1981, 78)

Often this demand is met with hesitation:

> Some women who were expected to give an important valuable to a brother's "custom" used pressure, threats, and tears to win their way. Their husbands or their husbands' kinswomen gave a valuable to preserve the peace and affinal relationship. Moreover, should the H/HZ [husband/husband's sister] not give a valuable, some women secretly borrow from others in order to save their public reputations. When a woman does so, she has obligated her husband to repay the lender for the use of the valuable. She may elect to shame her husband publicly by letting it be known that she has to gain a valuable from a source other than her husband. (Smith 1983, 103)

The women of a matriline are, thus, the ultimate source of its wealth, even though the strategic manipulation of *udoud* rests in the hands of men. Or as Kubary (1873, 229) puts it: "Love between a man and a woman is conducted on a basis of money. The man has to pay for every embrace. For this reason daughters form the wealth of a family." The distribution of certain pieces of money considered to be "house money" (*udoud er a blai*) and certain pieces properly belonging to the title rather than to the person carrying the title are subject to control by the group of senior women of a house.

While the *omeluchel* flow intensifies on certain ceremonial occasions (funerals, death conferences, house payment ceremonies, etc.), it continues on a regular basis in nonceremonial contexts as well, with men carrying food baskets (*telechull*) to their sisters' husbands and these husbands responding with a gift of money (*orau*) to their wives' or mothers' brothers.

> It [*omeluchel*] takes place when a man feels that his obligations are mounting and nothing of importance in his life or in the lives of his children has happened to provide him with a vehicle for disposing of them. Some pressure may also come from his brothers-in-law if they begin to feel that they have outdone themselves and have received nothing in return. They may come to regard their sister's husband as slow in paying. If they are not on very good terms with him they then begin to make unpleasant remarks and circulate damaging rumors about him. At the same time, they urge their sister to nettle her husband until he sees fit to pay his debts. It is far better for a man's domestic relations as well as for the sake of his prestige to keep his accounts in order. (Barnett 1949, 61)

Failure to pay *orau* can lead to a severe loss in social status or to divorce. Although the intensity of the *omeluchel* system has varied greatly over the past hundred years, its inflation and ramification have been difficult to resist, despite the feeling by many young people and women that it imposes unnecessary hardships on them and that it undermines the autonomy of the modern marriage unit.

The pattern of *omeluchel* flow organizes the movement of money from birth to death. At some early point in a young couple's marriage, the husband's father (or other financial sponsor) gives a piece of money as "initial marriage payment" (*bus*) to the wife's father (or, in some cases, older brother or mother's brother). In addition to the marriage-establishing *bus* payment and the periodic presentation of *orau*, a high-ranking woman hopes to be honored at some point in her life by a major payment that is given during a *mur*-feast. When a husband signals his intention to so honor his wife, his in-laws prepare a lavish meal. The husband not only presents *udoud* to his wife's family but also gives smaller pieces of money to the dancers engaged for entertainment. *Mur*-feasts for the highest-ranking families could last as long as a month, with huge outlays of food and the collection of a large number of *udoud* pieces. And funerals are followed several months later by a complex ceremonial "death conference" called *cheldecheduch* (a word that, in nontechnical usage, means any kind of formal talk) that settles the personal, residential, and financial relationships among the survivors. While kin on the wife's side work hard to prepare excessive amounts of food and demonstrate a high level of service, kin on the husband's side gather their resources to prepare two major payments: one or more pieces of money (together with a large quantity of cash, these days) are presented to the deceased wife's brothers and one or more pieces of money are given to her offspring as "children's money" (*ududir a rengalek*).

One of the reasons why the flow of money in the context of kin-based exchanges inflated so dramatically in the twentieth century is that colonial and postcolonial political regimes severely restricted the manipulation of *udoud* at the intervillage and interdistrict levels. (A second reason would be that the availability of foreign currency to nonchiefly wage earners led to the desire of low-ranking families to emulate the financial practices of title-holding families.) The systems of institutional concubinage, headhunting, warfare, and political feasting, all of which involved exchanges of *udoud*, came to an end in the early part of the past century (Parmentier 1987, 79–98). Other political strategies, such as the payment of substantial money (*tichichau*) by a new titleholder's kin in honor of his taking on chiefly responsibilities and the collection of money to finance house construction (*ocheraol*), continue into the contemporary period.

Brief mention needs to be made of several especially revealing uses of money. Precious pieces of money belonging to a family could be kept as "money of the ancestral spirits" (*udoud el bladek*); this money was not used in normal exchanges but was reserved for intrafamily functions such as decorating a woman during pregnancy (*omebael*) or being worn by sick people as a curative talisman. In unusual situations a man can make use of money owned by his wife—in obvious violation of the asymmetrical *omeluchel* flow. A learned elder named Ruluked once used a *bachel mengungau* named Okulamalk owned by his wife. But he died before he could arrange for its return, and it was not until years later that his descendants plotted to gain it back during a "death conference" (*cheldeched-uch*). Marriages among high-ranking (*meteet*) families are carefully evaluated in terms of the potential flow of *udoud*. A woman from a chiefly house who marries "down" into a house with a lesser title or in a lower-ranking village is said to "slip" (*tmorech*), since her chances of acquiring significant valuables for her brothers are diminished. The same term, *tmorech*, is used for pieces of money that have lost prestige because they were "discarded" (usually as the "marriage payment") to a low-ranking house. An informant explained these two kinds of slippage: "*Udoud* is just like a person. It would no longer have any usefulness. It is no longer on the 'list' and we would not include it as money of Idid or Uudes [two chiefly houses]." Money also penetrated the "spiritual" life of traditional Palau. Offerings (*tenget*) of small, even worthless pieces were made to appease or compensate the gods or the individuals thought to be their spokespersons. Captain Edward Barnard, who was shipwrecked on Palau in 1832, witnessed the consultation of a "priestess":

> No business of importance was ever undertaken by them without first consulting with their Priestess. . . . First, the chiefs met in front of the *bai* [meeting house] and after talking over the business, they repaired to the hut of the Priestess on the half bend and seated themselves in silence. In a few moments one of their number would make known their business to her. . . . A curtain

of mats was drawn round to screen her from the gaze of visitors. In about five minutes she would begin to deliver her message as she received it from her gods. At times a few questions were asked. Payment was always made on the spot, generally a glass bead or a piece of stone resembling brimstone. Pale green glass [i.e., *cheldoech*] was not valued. (Barnard 1980, 20)

Kubary (1969, 25) mentions the use of *udoud* in divination: the priest places a piece on the ground and drives in a wooden stake next to it; he then makes an interpretation based on the quality of the disturbed soil.

The group of senior titleholders of a village has the power to impose a monetary fine (*blals*) on individuals who, in their collective opinion, violate customary laws (*llach*). Although in recent times the fine can be paid in cash, the traditional system required the law-breaker's financial sponsor (maternal uncle, father, older brother) to pay a small *udoud* to the titleholders. Serious physical injury and even murder could be compensated by the immediate payment of *udoud*—one *chelebucheb* being the price of a human life. The expression "buried at the house" (*dekllel a olbiil*) refers to the unfortunate situation where a person is forced to expend his last piece of money to pay a fine, leaving him socially impoverished. Stories mention particularly oppressive chiefs who impose a fine on a person with the full knowledge that the required payment will be the *dekllel a olbiil*. A special form of fine is called "question the death of a person" (*oker a mad el chad*). After the murder or accidental death of a person from another village, the members of the men's club from the deceased's village come to accuse the leaders of the village where the death took place and to demand *udoud* as compensation. The chief can avoid further trouble by "discarding" a low-valued chelbucheb—often the very same piece travels around as compensation among allied villages. A high-ranking titleholder explained,

> A person is a precious thing, and so even if a person is not one of our relatives the very same thing will happen. A chief who is skilled at this strategy will send his messenger to the landing place carrying a small piece of money. The messenger will tell them to weigh anchor and go back to where they came from. But if the money is not given the men's club will enter the village and knock down the canoe sheds and cut down betelnut trees.

An implication of this is that the wealthy were free to break laws they can afford to pay for. As one wealthy individual explained to me,

> In earlier times there was very little *udoud* to go around. Simply put, the rich had money and the poor had none at all. If the child of a rich family is fined, the titleholders know that there will be *udoud* available to pay the fine. There is a principle that my father told me. He said that senior people should never reveal their money to younger people. He told my mother not to tell me the amount of *udoud* in the house, because if I knew then I would feel free to break the law. Wait until a person is older to reveal the money in the house.

Or in Kubary's words (1900, 3): "The substitution of a fine for the death penalty put the power to murder in the hands of the rich. This explains the fear which the poor feel for the former, as well as the unbounded greed for native money."

Systemic Equivalence

Given the massive historical changes that have affected the Palauan economic system over the past two hundred years, it would be a worthless exercise to try to establish a single normative set of extrasystemic valuations for various classes and types of *udoud*. In the nineteenth century, two chelbucheb pieces plus several smaller pieces might purchase a war canoe, and a good *kluk* might buy ten baskets of taro. By the early decades of this past century, the construction of a meeting house might cost four *kluk* and twenty *kldait*, while an elaborate tattoo might cost a *kluk*. Far more interesting are the intrasystemic equivalences accomplished in the process of exchange. Recipients in a transaction have some power to reject a particular offered piece as not being of sufficient value, although high-ranking givers can exercise a "take it or leave it" attitude toward receivers of lower social status. But both acceptance and rejection function to fix the value of the *udoud* in question, at least for the purpose of accomplishing similar social functions in the near future.

It is also the case that people from high-ranking houses need more valuable money to accomplish their social goals than lower-ranking people. For example, in 1938 Hisakatsu Hijikata attended the funeral of Ibedul Tem, the paramount high chief of the southern confederacy, the chief of Koror village and head of its first-ranking house, Idid. Several months after the burial, all the relatives of the late Ibedul gathered to settle the financial situation between the elders at Idid and the relatives of his surviving wife, Idellkei. Elaborate food prestations were brought to the ceremony by close relatives of the widow Idellkei, and in return, the deceased chief's relatives paid 150 Japanese yen, 500 ceramic plates, store-bought clothing, and traditional turtleshell plates to her kin. A dispute arose, however, over the payment of *udoud*. The people of Idid first offered a *bachel mengungau* named Mechut (Old), but the wife's side insisted on receiving a more valuable *bachel berrak* named Oliuch or Belalai, two pieces of money that had been treasured by members of Idid house for generations. The refusal of Idid to part with these pieces was well received by the people of Koror village, who said that it was not proper for these pieces to go to a woman from lower-ranking Ngersuul village. But Idellkei, it turns out, had already made plans to acquire these pieces. Earlier, while her husband was ill, she wrote out his will stating that she would receive Belelai or Oliuch as well as two chelbucheb. As soon as Ibedul and his advisors signed and sealed the will, Idellkei buried the two *bachel* pieces. Hijikata notes that the whole matter ended up in the local court, and then adds a telling ethnocentric comment about the affair:

These women (Idellkei and her clan people) are foolish. If we see this in the style of the traditional way, highly valued *udoud*, like Belelai and Oliuch, will not be devalued, and may even become more valuable if they are given to a clan that can compete with the Idid, such as Uudes of Melekeok. Besides, the *udoud* would not be missed. Even if such valuable *udoud* did go to a house in Ngersuul that does not hold a high status, it is nothing but a pity for the *udoud*. Moreover, it would be meaningless, because there is no way for an insignificant house to utilize *udoud* even if they wanted to. The only way they could use them is if they were to take them to the Reklai [chief of Melekeok] or the Ibedul [chief of Koror] and exchange them for smaller *udoud*. Even if they keep it the way it is, they would simply be laughed at. It isn't possible to increase the status of the house with the *udoud*. . . . Instead of asking for *udoud*, she should have requested 1,000 yen by saying that she and her family had spent a lot of money for the feasts the other day. (1993, 265–66)

Systemic equivalence of money pieces is more commonly established during confidential discussions just prior to important customary exchanges and operationalized in three regular transactional modes, "borrowing," "changing," and "exchanging," each of which involves several pieces of money moving in opposite directions. Lacking a required denomination of *udoud*, a person can "borrow" (*omed*) it from a lender to whom he gives in return two other pieces, a security piece (*ulsirs*) of greater value and an interest piece (*ongiakl*) of lesser value. It is usually prohibited to borrow a *bachel*, perhaps because this class of *udoud* is reserved for transactions that do not appear so "commercial" (*kerreker*). When an equivalent replacement has been acquired by earning or exchange, it is repaid to the lender, who keeps the interest piece and returns the security. The loss of the security piece is a serious offense and can result in the imposition of a fine of a *bachel* or even lead to physical violence.

Owners of a large *udoud* often require instead several smaller ones to complete a social obligation, such as giving money to groups of children or to groups of affines. In addition to the set of smaller pieces agreed to be equivalent to the single larger one, an additional piece called "body of the money" (*bedengel a udoud*) is given. This "body," perhaps a small *kldait*, is thought to be a unitary substitute or placeholder for the larger piece (but clearly not a representation of its value). The "body" functions to "respect" the large piece by making the whole transaction take on a noneconomic atmosphere. Narratives of transactions sometimes note that the "body of the money" is not always presented at the moment of the initial transaction. In this event, the recipient of the large *udoud* indicates that the recipients of the "change" pieces have the right to "call in the debt" (*mengeriil*) in the future—the only stricture being that the recipient of the large *udoud* cannot use it in subsequent transactions until its "body" is given.

As I was told, "The reason we change a *bachel* is that we have no smaller pieces of money to use, and the *kluk*, *klsuk* [a low-valued *kldait*], and *kldait* have many uses, lots of work they can do, whereas the *bachel* just sleeps, like a weak child." In the story of Renguldebuul and the money Muchuchuu, the people of Ngchesar took this very valuable piece and made "change" for the people of Ngerechelong. And when the men from Ngchesar in turn tried to change it, Uchormersai insisted on carefully comparing the weight of Muchuchuu and the sum of the smaller pieces being considered as equal change by hanging them from a sapling of the *detimel* vine. Later in the same story, Muchuchuu is evaluated once more by comparing the displacement of water when placed in a small dish with the displacement caused by the change pieces.

Making change can operate in the other direction as well: certain valuable *udoud* pieces can only be acquired by giving several pieces of "change" that add up to an equivalent value. For example, in order to purchase a plot of land with the highly valuable Iteterachel, the purchaser acquired this *udoud* by collecting from his relatives three *kldait*, one chelbucheb, and 400 yen. Conversely, the receipt of a large piece such as a *bachel* by someone or some group with nonchiefly status requires that it be broken down (*okerd*) in a series of exchanges, so that in the end the recipients obtain pieces that could actually be used. A third procedure for matching the right *udoud* to the right social function is called "exchanging" (*olteboid*), in which one piece is given for another of the same value. This might be needed in cases where a person has been specifically asked to contribute a *berrak* but only has access to a *mengungau*. He finds a person with the required money and asks him to inspect the two pieces to judge their equivalence.

Historical Contexts

Although only brief mention can be made here, Palauan money intersects with several other material representations of cultural values. Archaeologists have not been able to say with certainty when *udoud* came to the islands; Osborne (1979, 241) speculates that its arrival during the "Middle Early" period (CE 200–300 to 900) stimulated the development of social hierarchy. Although *udoud* pieces have not been found in test pits, a few stories do mention the use of black fish teeth (*udoud ungelel*) as currency prior to the arrival of *udoud*. The archaeological record contains a few examples of drilled shell beads (Osborne 1979, 25, fig. 9) and shell bracelet fragments (fig. 26). Sacred stones, including burial pavements marking the graves of clan ancestors, monoliths positioned in village centers, and roughly carved "great faces" scattered across the hillsides, share with *udoud* the properties of being hard, permanent "commemorative signs" (*olangch*) of sociohistorical process and of being the subject of countless narratives that record and broadcast the "news" of the significant events, places, and individuals (Parmentier 1985b, 1987; Van Tilburg 1991). One intriguing difference between *udoud* and stones is that the former appears to be ethnographically uniform throughout the islands, while the latter follow no standard template for material, size, or style. A second difference is that sacred stones do not form a coherent hierarchical set of classes and types (although, like money, a few large stones are individually named).

Although money as a political token seems to have replaced the movement of sacred stones, the presentation of a stone in the historical context of the *udoud* system becomes highly marked. A story describes how the powerful village of Koror manufactured money from small stones of various shapes. They then forced people from low-ranking villages such as Ngeremid and Ngerekesoal to accept these stones in payment for food products. Imeiong, the principal village of Ngeremlengui district, for example, gave away its emblematic stone, Imiungs-elbad, to Ngellau in thanks for helping out in Imeiong's efforts to repulse the threats from its oppressing neighbor Uluang village (Parmentier 1987, 168–69; see also Osborne 1979, 173). In an earlier publication (Parmentier 1985b), I argued that money, stone burial markers, and carved monoliths form a coherent system that fuses increasingly encompassing levels of social organization and corresponding modalities of historical time. While I would not now entirely reject this interpretation, I think that money and stones do not form as consistent a set of indexical markers (*olangch*) as I once thought. Exchanges involving money seem to have superseded the movement of stones at all three levels, infusing each level with an aura of hierarchy. The collection of archaic sacred stones by the modern Modekngei movement can be seen as a nonchiefly back-formation from the operation of the money system, the pieces of which they also hoard.

Next to sacred stones, the other valued material objects are the hammered turtleshell plates and implements that function as "women's money" (*toluk*). The pattern of exchange of these tokens of women's wealth parallels, to some degree at least, the *udoud* exchanged by men; they are given to reward women who contribute labor and food at customary events and as heirlooms to children in the matriline (Parmentier 1994c).

For several hundred years at least, Palauan *udoud* has interacted with various foreign currencies introduced by island neighbors, shipwrecked visitors, foreign traders, and colonial administrators. Palau and its nearest island neighbor, Yap, have participated in intercultural exchanges for centuries. Tradition holds that *udoud* was actually first used as money on Yap, and only when the Yapese discovered on Palau a source for mining huge aragonite pieces of stone did they discontinue using beads. In one account, people on Yap thought that their *udoud* was causing massive illness and so they decided to trade it to Palau in payment for the large stones (Hijikata 1993, 216). Kubary (1895) heard that the village of Ngkeklau was founded by Yapese people and that this village became one of the principal sources of *udoud*.

Liep's observation (1983, 507) about the correlation between the increasing "hierarchization" of shell classes and the increasing rivalry over status distinctions on Rossel Island prompts a parallel question about Palau. Did the advent of *udoud* pieces stimulate the development of a system of ranked titles, villages, and political districts, or was this rank system, already firmly in place, in fact challenged by the arrival of tokens of value that constitute a potential alternative path to social power? Significant here as well is the point made by several scholars of Melanesia, that *kula* circulation is independent of ranked political order in the Massim area. Kubary sheds light on this issue of the historical disjunction of status (*meteet*) and wealth (*merau*) in Palau when he remarks (1873, 227) that Koror, clearly the most powerful village in the mid-nineteenth century, once had no money and acquired its riches through warfare.

That a complex and systematic money system was already in operation prior to Western contact means that the incorporation of foreign currencies was "quite compatible" with Palauan traditions (Force and Force 1972, 125). The opportunity for the general population to earn wages in foreign currency during the German, Japanese, and American administrations both stimulated and suppressed the *udoud* system. On the one hand, individuals without access to *udoud* could purchase a piece for currency (Useem 1949, 17), and the development of a commercial economy reinforced the traditional value placed on the acquisition of wealth (65). On the other hand, the presence of foreign currencies replaced *udoud* in certain mundane transactions, especially in situations where the required *udoud* piece (especially, *kluk*) was in scarce supply; or else customary exchanges developed a pattern where currency and *udoud* were both required (Parmentier 1994c). The *kluk* has been consistently valued at 100 units of whatever foreign currency is in use (German Mark, Japanese yen, US dollar) (Ritzenthaler 1954, 18); Krämer (1917–1929, III, 165) mentions a particularly beautiful *bachel berrak* that was valued at 200 Marks and notes that forty buckets of taro sold for one *kluk* or forty Marks. The acquisition of *udoud* by nontitled people in recent decades has prompted legitimate titleholders to carefully distinguish wealth from status, as one elder from Melekeok put it: "If a man is industrious or had Palauan money and had many sisters, he was considered wealthy. A man may have more money than [chiefs] Ibedul and Reklai, but he is still low in status, because what determines your status is birth and not money or bravery."

As the linguist Edward Sapir famously said about grammars, *udoud* as a system "leaks," and along several dimensions. The system changes properties from high value to low value. While the highest-ranking pieces (in the classes *bachel berrak* and *bachel mengungau*) are individually named tokens, recognized by distinguishing design features, reported in narratives, removed from day-to-day economic transactions, and require accompanying "side" pieces when exchanged, the lower-ranking pieces (*kluk* and *delobech*) are members of large sets, characterized by general class characteristics, and used in equivalence exchanges. Also, at the lower end of the continuum of value are many pieces that are not "real money," including various kinds of counterfeit glass beads, intentionally deceptive pieces for offerings, and other natural objects (stones, shells, fish teeth) passed off as money to lower-ranking people. There are multiple factors involved in the valuation of pieces (including size, appearance, and the rank of the persons involved), and these criteria operate differently at different places in the system. For example, a large *bachel* is valued, but a small *kluk* is valued; and much talk about a piece can counter the downward movement of value if the piece passes through a lower-ranking house or is used to accomplish a negatively valued function (divorce payment, payment of a fine). As a result of these leaks, transitive equivalence relations across the system are possible only to a limited degree, first, because each individual's transactional strategies depend on unique social histories, and second, because the value of a given piece is subject to alteration at each transactional moment.

It is recognized that the history of a given piece—who has owned it, what transactions it has figured in, and so on—contribute as much to its value as do many of its intrinsic qualities (Barnett 1949, 43). The functional stratification of classes of *udoud* implies that Palauan money as a "schematic ordering" (Munn 1983, 302) is fundamentally different from Massim *kula* in that, in Palau, a man's exchange career cannot be described as an ascent through the various ranked classes of money. Very wealthy individuals are distinguished by having amassed and expended large numbers of pieces from the more valued classes and types.

Transactional Perspectives

Although it is certainly necessary to analyze *udoud* as a system, more specific ethnographic descriptions of *udoud* at the transactional level are required to uncover the cultural assumptions that motivate individual actors. This section considers two complementary areas of data: cultural associations about money revealed in economic and noneconomic activity, including thematic regularities in narratives about the mythic origin of *udoud* and transactional histories of particular money pieces that illustrate various strategies of use.

In the ethnographic record, in indigenous narratives, and in my fieldwork experience, social action and discourse dealing with money repeat five key themes: money is moving, hidden, beautiful, foreign, and self-attractive. First, *udoud* is in motion (*di merael*): running, traveling, or flying, money in action is money in motion. A story set in Ngebuked village concerns a mythical sea snake named Ngiratei, who took as his bride the human Dilitechocho (formerly the wife of the titleholder Techocho), the banished sister of the chief of Ollei. Angered at Dilitechocho's infidelity, Ngiratei told the children at the chief's residence to strike the floor of the spirit house with coconut fronds: "When the children did as they had been told, all the money inside fled from there. At first, the *klikes* [a small type of money] ran to the canoe and picked up a pole; a few *chelbucheb* followed, then the other money pieces. They poled away from there and landed in Ngebuked" (Krämer 1917–1929, III, 75). While important pieces of money gain "news" by traveling from chiefly house to chiefly house, the very highest-valued pieces are said not to travel at all; that is, they remain firmly lodged in a house or a village. In proverbial expression, *udoud* is likened to the dugong (a marine mammal), which "does not sleep in the shallows," meaning that an important piece should not be discarded to a low-ranking house, even if it is in a major village; rather, like the dugong, money should remain in place, hidden in the deep part of the channel. The resolution of this paradox of motion and stasis seems to be that "news" is the greatest when one of the "sleepy" or "lazy" pieces of distinguished money is dislodged from its home.

The tendency to put money into play, to let it travel along important transactional "paths" (*rael*), is countered by a conservatism that, in some marked and dangerous situations, borders on hoarding. Not only does a man thought to have financial resources who does not commit them when required gain a reputation as being stingy, but the money he does hold will be devalued, since others will not be eager to be financially involved with him. An important theme of the well-known war chant (*kesekes*) of Urdmau (the poetic name for Ngerdmau district) is that this district's leaders (Beouch and Arurang) had substantial resources in the mid-nineteenth century and yet did not spend their money to avoid attacks by the warriors from Koror. And after the destruction of their villages they did not pay for rebuilding the roads, houses, and meeting houses. As the men from Koror mocked:

> Those who made the path paid a *bachel* to Idid. And now are you, Arurang, stupid enough to try a different strategy?
>
> Back then you did not fear to pay a *bachel* and a *kerdeu*, and when they were put in the canoe, Ngarameketii and Ibedul [from Koror] were there to take them.
>
> So now, Urdmau, you cry over cooked taro [i.e., spilled milk], and you, Melaikesuk, are one crazy man trying to prevent payment from Urdmau's people.

Motion and stasis actually imply each other: to generate its exchange value *udoud* must travel, yet to accomplish its maximal work it must be kept long enough in contiguity with some social unit to become identified with it (cf. Breton 1999; Epstein 1979, 161). One of my teachers told me that he often felt that his possession of several chelbucheb pieces made him vulnerable to being "cursed" (*delebeakl*). Anyone who hoards money, who prevents it from moving around doing its "work," is cursed: "[Hoarded] money becomes my personal property, but *udoud* should circle around among people. . . . Rather, if you have a lot of money you can do a lot of work with it and in this way you will gain a reputation."

And yet Kubary (1873, 228) insists that, by the middle of the nineteenth century, several *bachel* and chelbucheb pieces were already out of circulation, kept by the chiefly house of Idid in Koror. This constant tension between motion and stasis makes it impossible to agree with Weiner that a category of "inalienable possessions" is useful outside the Western context—as she herself suggests in her remark that "transferability is essential to their preservation" (1992, 37).

Second, money is hidden from view, concealed in a titleholder's handbag, covered with a betelnut leaf during transactions, buried behind the house, and kept secret from junior relatives. Rich men need simultaneously to keep their money supply secret so that no one else in the game has knowledge of their resources and to display their wealth periodically so that its "news" will continue to circulate. When wives of wealthy men wear their husband's money around their necks (*olbiungel*), they not only index their own well-placed marriage but also point toward the future, since this is the very piece of *udoud* they are hoping to earn, after the termination of the marriage by the death of one of the couple, for their brothers and uncles as "marriage payment." Exchange ceremonies are often filled with strategic "whispering" but also with loud announcements when pieces are distributed. Several stories tell about haughty villages where the men compete with each other by seeing whose money weighs the most or whose collection covers the most space on a stone display table (*oleketokl*).

Third, pieces of *udoud* are said to be, much like Trobriand *kula* valuables, beautiful, strikingly handsome (*meringel*), and youthfully attractive. When the rare opportunity arises for men to inspect a piece, they rub it against their noses to make the surface shine—an ironic twist on Marx's aphorism that "money does not smell" (1976, 205). Semper (1982, 49) makes explicit the association of beauty and authenticity: "It is significant that the Palauans maintain they can easily distinguish the autochthonous money from those introduced in recent times; it has often amused me to see them at the close of a transaction test a piece to see whether it is real or not by holding it up to the light, wiping it with a cloth, and, finally, rubbing it on a cheek or nose." From a more functional point of view, rubbing money in this way polishes the surface so that distinctive identifying marks can be seen. An unusual decorative treatment of *udoud* is mentioned in the story about Rungiil, who brought many valuable pieces of money to Uluang village. In order to impress the people of Uluang. Rungiil displayed his *bachel mengungau* pieces with bird feathers stuck in tiny holes drilled in the ends. Called Olomel Busech ("Planted with Feathers"), these pieces of money were regarded as strikingly beautiful, and Rungiil himself was judged to be a very impressive person.

Fourth, money is of foreign, celestial, or magical origin, coming from distant lands, from visiting ships, from the eyes of the gods in heavens (Krämer 1917–1929, III, 152), or from magical fish from the depths of the sea. The acquisition of beads plays some role in most of the records of historical encounters between Palauans and foreigners. Early visitors were told stories of Palauans trading for beads with sailors from Chinese junks (157). More recent accounts mention a Chinese ship wrecked on the reef near Ngeruangel at the northern tip of the archipelago; the residents of that island took the curtain rings and, with the help of the captain, cut them into four *bachel* segments with tools found on board. The captain gave away two pieces from each ring and kept the other two; he then came ashore and took the Palauan name Ngirabaliau. (A variant places a similar story at Beliliou.) Some stories talk about a group of people actually living on Ngeruangel prior to its sinking into the sea; these people had a large amount of money, which eventually made its way southward. Although still open to scholarly debate, there is a possibility that Drake's *Golden Hind* briefly engaged in barter during the first encounter between Palauans and Europeans mentioned in Western historical records in 1579; "there many Indians came to them with fish, and gave it to them in exchange for beads and other trifles" (quoted in Lessa 1975, 57–58). In 1710 the Spanish ship *Santisima Trinidad* sailed through Palauan waters; when islanders tried to carry off various items from the ship they were given a "string of glass beads" to prevent further mischief (103).

Captain Henry Wilson's East India packet *Antelope* was the first Western ship to stay at Palau for an extended period of time. At the conclusion of his visit in 1783, Wilson took Lebu ("Lee Boo"), son of Koror's chief Ibedul, back to England, where he was the talk of London. This unfortunate young man shortly caught smallpox and on his deathbed in 1784 made a special request that his English patrons remove the "blue glass barrels" from the furniture of the house where he was staying and send them back to his father, the "King" of Palau (Keate 1788, 357). Captain John McCluer (1791, 115) remarked that when a group of islanders came out in canoes to his ship in 1791, they sat quietly until "the appearance of our large china beads roused up the Spirit of invention among them, and industry [i.e., trade] was introduced among them for awhile."

In 1863 the naturalist Semper (1982, 48) witnessed the payment of a *bachel berrak*, "a large piece of the most valuable indigenous money," by Ibedul to the chiefs of Ngebuked village, the capital of Ngerard district. Previously, an allied group of warriors loyal to Ibedul had destroyed Ngebuked. Hoping to avert a massive counterattack from the north, Ibedul came in person to make peace (*meruul a budech*): "Because of the refusal to accept [the money] amounted to a declaration of war and because the people were not well equipped and still somewhat crestfallen they accepted the money and made peace."

The association of money with the heavens is reinforced in transaction ceremonies when pieces are held up toward the sky with outstretched arms and in the offering of (inferior) money pieces to coerce the gods or their earthly representatives. Very numerous are mentions of money emerging from magical animals and plants. Money comes from the magical orange tree, the fingers of Tmekei, the skin of Dilitekuu, the money bird Delarrok, the money-laying chicken Malk, the sea snake Mengerenger, the eyes of the fish Medatumloket, and the eggs of the white tern Sechosech. Not all the narratives of the heavenly origin of money can be enumerated here, but the following brief story about Ngeraod is an excellent example of the genre.

> The *chelid* [spirit or gods] of Ngeraod, the seat of the gods, wanted to hold a feast but did not have the necessary money. He went to a man on Mount Ngulitel and asked his aid. This man answered: "Let me know the day when you want to have the feast and I shall come over to Ngeraod." The *chelid* sent him the required information and the man of Ngulitel (near Keklau) arrived at the time set and brought along a bag of money. The *chelid* accepted it with the assurance that he would pay it all back in the near future. When the time had come for him to return what he had borrowed, the *chelid* took the empty bag and filled it with all the different types of fruit that he could find. They were transformed into money, which was given the names of the fruit, and thus it was possible for the *chelid* to pay his debts. (Krämer 1917–1929, III, 167)

Another story about the magical fish Tmekei accounts for the acquisition of *udoud* by a low-ranking place. Tmekei bore a female child near the island of Ngeaur; fish by night, child by day, she was adopted by the family of her playmates from the house of Ngetelkou. But when she started to grow so excessively large that she required a separate dwelling, her newfound family asked her to leave. As she departed she stroked her swollen fingers and a large number of *bachel* fell to the ground. In another tale, two brothers from a poor family in Ollei tried to conceal their poverty from their sister by hiding money-shaped stones in a bamboo tube. The sister, determined to elevate her family, decided to marry Olungiis, a hideous monster whose swollen testicles contained a vast amount of money. At the *mur*-feast held in her honor, Olungiis distributed *udoud* to all the people of Ollei. Whether from abroad, from the heavens, or from magical fish, *udoud*'s source is placed in a decidedly nonhistorical locus, thus reinforcing its "transcendent" quality appropriate to the noncontingent system of social rank it supports.

Fifth, it is often said that a particular piece of money "wants to return" to its owner or home—like a boomerang, I was told. Any discussion of the "return" of money usually brings up the well-known story of Ngeraod, a mythical large fish that bears an island on its back. A fisherman and his son were blown over to Ngeraod from Ngcheangel atoll, and after landing their canoe they went up to the beach and fell asleep. While his father was still sleeping, the son got up to play. Finding the beach covered with stones, he started tossing them around, and when he would throw a piece it would return and land in his father's canoe. The boy said to his father, "These are very well-behaved stones, since when I threw them they came right back to the boat." The stones turned out to be pieces of *udoud*, and the fisherman took them with him on subsequent exploits in other villages on Babeldaob.

Several strategies can be pursued toward the end of ensuring the return of money. Although marriage within the range of the matriclan (*kebliil*) is prohibited, it is encouraged between more distantly linked houses (*kaukebliil el blai*), particularly if the houses are of high social rank (Parmentier 1984). Indeed, chiefly houses in Palau are linked by networks of affinal relationships that stipulate the frequent exchange of *udoud* as "marriage payment" (*chelebechiil*) and as "money of the children" (*ududir a rengalek*). Parents encourage their daughters to try to marry into a house that has taken a "marriage payment" from them in the recent past. Similarly, unrelated houses on opposite "sides of the mangrove channel" within a single village can arrange marriages so that money goes back and forth. An elderly titleholder told me,

> Money is very scarce and people are clever in thinking about this problem. A woman is going to think carefully about marrying into a high-ranking house (*meteet*), or into a distantly linked house that holds an important piece of money. For example, Ngerebesakl was the money of my father and was the "marriage payment" of Ngitechob, who was the sister of Rengiil Ngirturong. Ngirturong in turn disposed of it at Koror for Bilung Taru. Then the brother of this Bilung married into Ngiual and so the money was disposed of in Ngiual. Then the younger sister of Techereng sought after it and married Chuong Ngirateuid. People said, "They are relatives and married!" But this woman told me, "It is the *udoud* that I want to take." And so when Chuong died they brought the *udoud* back to Koror.

If the return of the specific piece is impossible, high-ranking houses can plot to take a valuable *udoud* from houses that have taken one from them in the past. Okerangel, the chief of Melekeok, sent Muchuchuu to Koror, and so much later a woman named Oribech from Reklai's family in Melekeok married Ibedul Tem in Koror. When Tem ran off with another woman, Oribech's brother brought her back to Melekeok, with Kerdeu still hanging from her neck, saying that this was her "divorce payment" (*olmesumech*). The Kerdeu was like the replacement for Muchuchuu. The payment of *udoud* in certain situations of asymmetries of social rank sometimes results in the more powerful group plotting the return of the spent money. Koror used to oppress the people of Ngeaur; when concubines (*remengol*) from Ngeaur came to Koror to earn *udoud* they would return home only to find that men from Koror had sailed to Ngeaur, the southernmost island in the archipelago, to bind the titleholders with vines (*sengall*) until they would reveal where their money was hidden. Smith (1983, 117) notes a recent case in Melekeok village where a single family arranged three sequential marriages of its women in order to gain back a single valuable piece of money.

All five of these associations—money in motion, hidden, beautiful, foreign, and returning—come into play when Palauans, in conversation and narrative, anthropomorphize *udoud*, saying that a particular piece is "sleeping," "energetic," "dead," "fallen," or "like a person." In fact, in being secretive, energetic, beautiful, and self-seeking, money is nothing less than the epitome of the ideal male Palau-an personality (cf. Breton 1999). Semper recorded a story in 1862 that personifies the various classes of money:

> One day, a boat was drifting about in which seven kinds of money were seated; they had left their island, Ngarutt [Ngeraod?], in search of other, more appealing places. They had been drifting about in the ocean for some time without fulfilling their wishes. At last, they reached Palau. In the harbor, Berrak, who was the highest ranking of them all, was stretched out on a platform, ordered Mengungau, the next in rank, to go ashore and survey the island. Mengungau was just as indolent as his chief, so he ordered Chelebucheb, just below him, to do it; he did not go but assigned it to Cheldoech who told Kluk. Finally the much pestered Olelongel had to go because he had no one to obey him. . . . So, as it happened, Berrak was deserted by his own people and chiefs. He himself, then, went to get them, but the place pleased him so that they all remained and led the lives they were used to. Berrak does nothing but eat, drink, and sleep, the higher always commands the lower. And so it is . . . that, just as it is among us people, so the large pieces sit quietly at home and do nothing, while the smaller pieces busily circulate, doing the work for the more valuable kinds as well as themselves. (1982, 50)

Later Semper incorporates anthropomorphism as a rhetorical trope when he writes, "If only these pieces [of money] would have told us their histories!" He then proceeds to narrate several stories from the point of view of the *udoud*, including one story of how a particular *bachel berrak*, once the not-so-valuable possession of a low-ranking woman, was used to ransom her son, and so passed to the ownership of the wife of the high chief of Ngerard. Semper remarks (1982, 92), "How proud it is here, almost as if some of her dignity had been transferred to itself!" If *udoud* has human characteristics, it can also function as the equivalent of or substitute for human life in certain contexts, as in the story about Madraklai from Ngerard, who saved his life by substituting a *bachel mengungau* which he hung around his neck. A group of chiefs debated who should take this valuable piece, and finally a woman holding the chiefly title in Ngersuul took it for her son Sesilil. One elderly man I talked to said that his grandfather had bathed his feet in water containing pieces of *udoud*; and Krämer (1917–1929, III, 159) mentions a man who made his children drink water that had been in contact with *udoud* in order to facilitate the "path" to richness.

This linkage between money and person was impressed on me when a key informant agreed to narrate his life history on the last day we worked together in 1980. Expecting him to tell me about his economic activities as a commercial fisherman; his political accomplishments as a local magistrate, distinguished title-holder, and representative to several national congresses; and his wives, children, and grandchildren, I was shocked when he proceeded to tell me about the various political machinations ("whispers") he had pulled off by means of *udoud*. The events he chose to relate all dealt with occasions where he expended his personal wealth for the benefit of the village, such as paying off the fines imposed on several young club members, secretly paying the *oker a saker* (a penalty for marital infidelity) so that an important chief would not be exposed to shame, and using *udoud* to convince an angry village leader to return to his civic responsibilities. That this elder would organize his autobiography in terms of his financial dealings strongly supports Barnett's claim (1949, 51) that Palauans "tend to identify themselves with it [money] and the things that are intimately associated with it."

Transactional Histories

To conclude this exposition of the ethnographic perspective on Palauan money, several examples will be cited to illustrate the narrative representation of the strategic aspect of political negotiations using *udoud*, two from the historical record, one from the archival record, and one from my own field tapes.

In 1783 Captain Henry Wilson's ship *Antelope* ran aground at Ulong Island, several miles south of the important village Koror, home of chief Ibedul, whom Wilson mistakenly titled "king" of Palau. Less than two months later, with the assistance of English troops, warriors from several allied villages, and the *Antelope*'s swivel canon, Ibedul conquered Melekeok, a rival capital village on the east coast of Babeldaob Island. The following passage describes a money distribution ceremony that took place shortly after the battle in Imeiong, a village on the west coast of Babeldaob, the home of Ngiraklang, the ranking titleholder (at that time) of Ngeremlengui district.

> The old Rubak [Ngiraklang Chelungel] of the place came down to the raised square pavement, which was at one end of the great house where our people were; he was brought on a board slung with a rope at each end, and carried by four men. After he was seated, a messenger came and spoke to Ibedul, who immediately said something to the *rubak* in the great house, and they all went out on the pavement, and seated themselves with much respect; Ibedul also quitted the house, leaving none but the English in it; yet did not go to the old Rubak, or take any notice of the ceremony carrying on, but sat down under a tree, where he could not be observed, and amused himself in making the handle of a hatchet. After some time spent in conversation, the old Rubak distributed beads to the other *rubak*, in the following manner; the old Rubak gave them to an officer in waiting, who advancing into the middle of the square, and holding them up between his forefinger and thumb, made a short speech, and with a loud voice called out the person's name for whom they were designed, and immediately ran and gave them to him, and then returned in a slow pace to the old Rubak for the next, which was presented in the same manner. Captain Wilson remained in the house observing the ceremony, till the

linguist was sent to him, when he went out, and was directed to a seat near to his friend Rechucher, and soon after two tortoise-shell spoons, and a string of red beads, which were made from a coarse species of cornelian, were brought forward, which the before mentioned officer holding up, called out Englees, and instantly ran and presented them to the Captain. Ibedul's beads, which were glass [Note in original: The beads spoken of were of their own making, being a kind of coloured earth baked; they made them also at Pelew (Ibedul's *beluu* 'village'), but our people had never any opportunity of seeing how they were manufactured. They also considered as beads the glass ones last mentioned, being only bits of broken glass, which they had the art of drilling; some beads they saw of this kind were made of green and white glass, being small pieces of broken bottles which had been got out of the *Antelope*], were given to Rechucher, who personated the king on this occasion. (Keate 1788, 175–76)

The strategy depicted in this passage is easy to misunderstand, especially since the English guests are themselves puzzled by the seeming indifference of "King" Ibedul. After the successful defeat of Melekeok, Ibedul traveled to the villages in his alliance to participate in a series of money distributions (*boketudoud*). Ibedul was already in Imeiong on the day that his "General" Rechucher arrived, accompanied by a group of Wilson's men. When Imeiong's chief Ngiraklang Chelungel distributed money (*omoket*) individually to all the visiting dignitaries, including Captain Wilson, he was reinforcing the political alliances among villages on Koror's "side of heaven." And, more particularly, he was repaying a debt, since warriors from Koror had recently come to Imeiong to save that village from a sudden attack from Melekeok. The reason Ibedul absented himself from the ceremony, one informant familiar with the text (though not with the actual events) in question explained, is that he signals his high rank by letting a lesser titleholder from Koror handle the implementation of the political negotiations (*kelulau*).

Udoud used as tools of political negotiation often required the reciprocal presentation of *udoud*, as the English observed in 1791, when a party of titleholders from Koror (led by their chief Ibedul) arrived at rival Melekeok village, whose titleholders made a presentation of a large *bachel berrak* in order to avert the destruction of his village.

The chief [of Melekeok] gave into the hand of a *rubak* a bead, which he very carefully inclosed in his hands, and then moved slowly toward Ibedul, with his body bent, as is usual on approaching the King [i.e., Ibedul]; he said something in a low tone of voice, that seemed to meet the approbation of the assembly; he then appeared to be in the act of presenting this bead, and Ibedul on the point of receiving it, when he suddenly drew back his hands, and asked, If so rich a present did not entitle the bearer to some reward; the King immediately gave him a China bead of the second size; as soon as the *rubak* had received it, and not till then, he, with great solemnity, resigned the rich present to the hands of Ibedul. (Hockin 1803, 43)

The "second size" is likely the "body of the money," given as a respectful replacement of the valuable piece. When the British asked to inspect the beads, Ibedul instructed them to "be extremely careful, lest he should let it fall to the ground; for if such an accident happened, it could never be taken up" (Hockin 1803, 44). This explicit association of money with spatial elevation (celestial origin, raised position, and insulated carriage) reinforces the "transcendent" role of this hierarchy of value.

In more recent times, the "creative" manipulation of the *udoud* system sometimes ends up bringing the transaction process into the courts. A particularly fascinating case brought to the Palau District High Court in 1966 involved a wealthy individual named Oseked, who in 1947 was entrusted with a *bachel* named Nglalemeaur ("Planted at Ngeaur") as the "children's money" for two young girls. He immediately gave another less valuable *bachel* named Bisech to the uncle of the girls, implying that the actual value of the "children's money" was only a percentage of Nglalemeaur. At some later point Oseked gave Nglalemeaur to another person to fulfill some obligation. Normally a person holding the "children's money" should either keep it or replace it with a more valuable piece, but in 1961 Oseked attempted a "two-for-one" switch by presenting to the girls' father the *bachel* Belelai in payment for food and labor, and he received Ulengiil as "change." He then attempted to declare in a written document that the presentation of Belelai to the girls' father was in fact the "children's money," and that he no longer had an obligation to return Nglalemeaur in the future. The children's uncle brought suit in the court, arguing that Oseked still needed to provide Ngalemeaur or its equivalent as the "children's money" for his two nieces. The court's decision illustrates the complexity of the affair: Oseked was ordered to return Nglalemeaur to the uncle upon the payment by the uncle of Palauan money equal to two-thirds of the value of Bisech, or in the form of another piece of money equal to the value of Nglalemeaur minus two-thirds the value of Bisech (*Trust Territory Reports*, March 31, 1966, p. 153).

Finally, to illustrate the kind of narratives about financial strategies that I collected in the field, I translate here an account of the "news" of Bulong, a famous *bachel mengungau* piece. The story of Bulong provides excellent justification for the need to understand both systemic and transactional dimensions of money. A brief mention of the movement of Bulong is made by Krämer (1917–1929, IV, 69), who was told that the people of Irrai, at the southeastern end of Babeldaob, carried this money on a litter to the "spirit house" of Ngirakiklang Mladrarsoal, the priest of the god Medechiibelau. (Recall that Ngiraklang Chelungel, chief of Imeiong at the time of Captain Wilson's visit, was carried on a litter.) As the piece was being presented, this priest pronounced a solemn warning that the people of Idid, the home of the powerful Ibedul title, "must evacuate your house," meaning that the line of descendants was destined to die out. My informant's account takes up the story at this point, but since the narrative is complicated and presupposes knowledge of general Palauan customs and specific information about people and places, a few explanatory comments are in order. The story traces a single piece of money as it travels across Babeldaob through five political districts: Irrai, Ngeremlengui (the narrator's home), Ngerard, Ngiual, and Melekeok. In Ngeremlengui the first-ranking title is Ngirturong (his house is called Ngerturong), and the second-ranking title is Ngiraklang (his house is Klang). The capital village of this district is divided into rival factions oriented to these two houses. The working-age men of the village form a men's club, with leaders representing the two factions. A lower-ranking hamlet in the district is the house of a man named Techeltoech, the spiritual founder of Modekngei ("Let Us Go Forward Together"), a nativistic and syncretistic religious movement founded in direct response to colonialism, whose rites involve both *udoud* and sacred stones as curative agents.

> Bulong is a very valuable *bachel mengungau*, which I once had in my handbag. A long time ago members of the men's club of Irrai carried Bulong on a wooden litter (*odekoll*) to be an offering to the god Medechiibelau, with many people dancing alongside. Of course the money was very light but they were acting like it is very heavy, and in this way they were deceiving the god. In German times, this money was used to purchase a meeting house, but before that it was the money of the god of Irrai and was kept in the god's house. The [German official] Winkler seized this money from the god's house and used it to purchase a meeting house he had ordered to be built by the men of Ngeremlengui. But when the leaders of the men's club on the "side of Ngertuong" [allied to the first titleholder Ngirturong] and the leader of the men's club on the "side of Klang" [allied to the second titleholder Ngiraklang] received the money they were not able to break it into smaller denominations, so that half could go to one club leader and half to the other club leader. My father was at that time the leader of the men's club on the "side of Klang." The money stayed put until the death of Ngiraklang Recheboi. When they [his wife's relatives] came to take the "marriage payment" for his widow it became a very difficult situation at the "death conference" (*cheldecheduch*) because Bulong was held by Ngerturong house and the money belonging to Klang house was closely hoarded by the women of Klang. Idub, the senior woman from Klang, argued strongly that Omrukl [a money of the class *bachel berrak*] was rightfully the "children's money" of Ngiraklang Recheboi and that it could not be given away. But Rekemesik from Tabliual house argued against this, saying, "No, I have already killed plenty of pigs and carried many bags of rice. Give me Omrukl." Idub at the time was holding some money from Otang, and she tried to give him [Rekemesik] this, but he refused it, saying, "No, give me Omrukl." The meeting went on all day and into the evening. Ngirturong Sulial and all the other titleholders were sitting in the meeting house. At this point someone pointed out to the women of Klang that there was a piece of money currently held at Ngerturong house that was really the possession of the men's

club leaders of both Klang and Ngerturong. Ngirturong said, "Give me a piece of money to exchange with Bulong, and I will give you this Bulong." So they took one chelbucheb and gave it to Ngirturong Sulial, and they took Bulong to Klang. And then the people of Klang gave Bulong as the "marriage payment" of this woman, who was from Tabliual house. The meaning of this is "enter from the back" (*okiu er a rebai*), since the money did not enter by the front door. No *chelebucheb* could possibly be exchanged for such a large *bachel* and come in the front door.

It stayed this way until the wartime and then Techeltoech, the leader of Modekngei [religion], acquired Bulong when one of the men from Tabliual named Rekemesik Ngiraiechol changed it in order to have more small pieces to distribute to members of the family. Techeltoech was a person very interested in changing money and so he encouraged the people of Tabliual to do this. He gave Rekemesik 1,000 yen and one *bachel* as the "body of the money" Bulong. And then Techeltoech spent it to "send back" (*olmesumech*) his wife to Chelab village in Ngerard, so that he could remarry a pretty young woman. Once I said to him, "You and Rekemesik are a crazy to throw this money away." He asked, "Why do you say this?" I told him that money is like a person, and just like when a woman from Imeiong marries a man from a lower-ranking place she "falls." When a piece of money falls, it no longer has any usefulness; it is like it is no longer on the list of money from the house of Idid or Uudes. But there was nothing else he could do since he really wanted to remarry this woman named Bedebii, who was affiliated with Modekngei and had the ability to whistle as if she was a spirit. When the former wife from Ngerard died, there was a young man who had married a woman from Ngiual village, and so later Secharuleong of Melekeok took Bulong as "children's money." But when the wife of Secharuleong died about 1965 Lomisang [Reklai, high chief of Melekeok] took Bulong as the "marriage payment," because one of the younger relatives of Secharuleong had married a person from Uudes [Reklai's house], and when this young man died they took the "marriage payment" of this girl. And so Secharuleong gave it away to Uudes.

Several points need to be highlighted from this involved narrative. The first obvious point is that a single valuable piece of money is the unifying rhetorical thread of the narrative: the actions and motivations of the various characters and social groups (clubs, houses, titleholders, villages, districts) are structured in terms of the movement of Bulong. Of course, the narrator's personification of Bulong reinforces the sense of its agency. Second, in the short space of less than seventy years Bulong was involved in a sequence of radically different transactions: as the deceptive offering to the god of Irrai, as a commercial payment for meeting house construction, as money too valuable to be of use by the men's clubs of Ngeremlengui, as the object of the chiefly strategy of "entering by the back door," as "fallen" money changed for Japanese yen and then given away in a less than honorable divorce, and then finally rescued when taken by the chiefs of high-ranking Uudes house as "marriage payment." Third, the fact that the narrator can rehearse this tangled account in such detail only confirms the "reputation" (*chais*) of Bulong as a piece of money worth bending the rules for. In particular, observe that Ngirturong actually gives up Bulong to his factional rival Ngiraklang, partially out of respect for the work of the men's club leader from Klang but also partly out of the common interest high-ranking houses have in keeping money belonging to their houses out of the hands of people from lower-ranking villages, even if the transaction is momentarily disadvantageous. Techel-toech also gave the money away in a calculated balance of his self-interest; as the leader of Modekngei he was keen on acquiring Palauan money for his religious movement, but he decided that the acquisition of a new wife achieved a higher purpose. Note, finally, that Reklai's acquisition of Bulong was possible only after it had first entered the village through the house of the prominent titleholder Secharuleong, whose possession helped elevate the previously "fallen" money.

At the End of the Path

The two substantive sections above have presented historical and ethnographic evidence to analyze the systemic and transactional dimensions of Palauan money. Only by considering a group of "iconic" resonances between money and related cultural values and by detailing the strategic mechanisms of wealthy titleholders who employ money as an "index" of their position is it possible to see that *udoud* is actually a *creative diagram* of Palau's hierarchical social system. Any system of inherited rank needs to legitimize the underlying principles of hierarchy in powers and reasons that transcend the social system as a historically contingent construction; and in Palau money functions as the anchor of this process in being both the sedimented embodiment of accomplished power and the transactional mechanism for its attainment. By monopolizing the exchange of tokens of value whose origins lie in celestial and natural forces, titleholders in the centuries before Western contact reinforced their privilege with sacred, foreign, and magical authority. During the subsequent colonial periods, the growth of a market economy and the importation of foreign currencies were encompassed by the expansion of *udoud*'s ability to unify economic, religious, and social exchanges. To the extent that high-ranking owners of money continue to be able to "naturalize" the logic of its value, *udoud* will continue to be the material expression of a will to social power. In all these periods the ability to naturalize money requires talk, and so the omnipresent discourse about how "money walks" is more than rhetorical window-dressing on the economic system; it is constitutive of its internal logic.

Note

This paper was originally published as "Money Walks, People Talk: Systemic and Transactional Dimensions of Palauan Exchange," *L'Homme* 162 (2002): 49–80. Reprinted with permission of EHESS.

14 Representing Transcendence: The Semiosis of Real Presence

With Massimo Leone

The *Tao* of which one can speak is not the eternal *Tao*.
—Lao-tzu (quoted in Schwartz 1975b, 65)

There is no place in culture for the illusion of transparence.
—Valeri (1985, xii)

In USING THE phrase "representing transcendence" to focus this supplementary issue of *Signs and Society*, we are interested in socially constructed and historically specific discursive, behavioral, and material forms of signs that express (depict, imply, suggest, problematize, deny, etc.) something *beyond* normal human experience for individuals and groups in day-to-day and specially marked contexts. We are not, that is, primarily interested in the questions raised, for example, by evolutionary psychology about the "naturalness" for all humans or for humans at some defined "age" of cultural history of cognitive representations expressing beliefs in transcendent entities or quests for transcendent experiences. What is at issue, rather, are the semiotic mechanisms and consequences of efforts to represent, in the double sense of *standing in place of* something that is absent and *making present again* that which was previously absent,[1] the "beyond" in some perceptible or imaginable medium while maintaining, at the same time, an ideological (theological or philosophical) stance that these transcendent objects (beings, deities, powers, ideals, universals), by the definition of their very natures, cannot be so represented— because they are, on the one hand, beyond knowing and, on the other hand, anchored in an utterly separate realm. It may well turn out, ironically, that the fact that cultures at different times and places seem to get embroiled in this "paradox" of representation is itself a significant aspect of some long-term evolutionary or historical picture, but, for a journal devoted to semiosis or sign processes, there are always more localized explanations (especially, as we will see, metasemiotic ones) to be found and compared.

What, then, are some of the types of semiotic consequences for cultural systems that postulate a radical and unbridgeable separation between a mundane world of human experience and a supernatural world that, being wholly other, is not a possible object of direct human experience and yet demand, as a result, diverse mediational forms operable by virtue of or in opposition to "regimenting" ideologies of representation? And how are the resulting efficacious potentialities of these materialized representations understood in relation, for example, to less officially valued "magical" or "idolatrous" objects and to the logic of ritual action required to enliven their performativity? Finally, how can we explain the importance of sophisticated or esoteric semiotic ideologies that regiment local understandings of both representations and rituals when the real-time experience of transcendence often seems to demand a phenomenological "suspension" of those same abstract formulations? After some typological and methodological preliminaries, this essay will focus on two cases of the "real presence" of transcendence: cult statues in the ancient world and the eucharistic practices in medieval Christianity.

Semiotic Conventions and Ideologies of Representation

One possible reaction to this confrontation with absolute transcendence would be to systematically abandon (or actually reject) all efforts to represent the transcendent world in humanly constructed forms, insisting that anything "made by human hands" is utterly inadequate or religiously dangerous.[2] Even in such relatively iconophobic or rigidly iconoclastic regimes some representations of transcendence might be allowed if they were believed to be sent to earth by divine powers, were created by some kind of mechanical or automatic replication process, or carefully avoid the direct pictorial depiction of gods in favor of decorative, abstract, or veiled forms (Besançon 2000; Freedberg 1989; Smith 2004). When set in the context of a "semiosphere" that generally favors the representation of gods, iconoclastic movements can arise that work against either an "external" neighboring tradition or an "internal" religious norm demanding "reform" at the levels of both practice and ideology (Leone 2010). Well-documented examples of this would include the ancient Israelite opposition to the surrounding "idolatries" of Canaanite and (later) Roman cults; the so-called "Amarna revolution" during the reign of Akhenaten (ca. 1353–1336 BCE) in eighteenth-dynasty Egypt that removed all statues and images of gods in favor of depicting only the sun disk, the body of the hidden god, and the sun's rays as the remaining indexical linkage between the transcendent and the king; the two short-lived periods (730–787 CE and 815–843 CE) in medieval Byzantine Christianity that rejected the use of icons in liturgical practice and private devotion; and the "stripping of the altars" during the Protestant Reformation in continental Europe and England.

But even more interesting from a semiotic point of view are cases in which a religious tradition simultaneously guards against the worship or reverence of "idols" and permits representations that are themselves exemplars or analogies of "semiotic mediators" grounded in the very nature of divinity (or the cosmos more generally) that have "built in" a duality of immanence and transcendence. A culture might, for example, recognize a special class of "bridges" between this worldly and other worldly orders, along with sophisticated "theological," "philosophical," or "scholastic" reasonings that explain these interventions in terms that actually reinforce or even widen the distance between the natural and the transcendent (e.g., the multiple "embodiments" of ancient Egyptian gods, eucharistic transubstantiation in Catholic Christianity, and ancestor worship in China [Schwartz 1975b, 62]).

A second possibility would be to harness a culture's ideologies of materiality and corresponding iconographic conventions that, denotationally or connotationally, express the "beyondness" (i.e., distant from the here and now), the maximal greatness (in relation to human finitude), the transient or permanent absence, or some other quality (e.g., blinding brightness, eternal stability, unfathomable powers) that distinguishes transcendent referents from everyday objects of experience. In both Greek and Roman antiquity, the colossal size of statues of gods and emperors instilled "an impression of power and divinity, surpassing the human sphere" (von den Hoff 2012, 107). Early medieval texts explain that precious stones used in mosaics representing Christ are a "material analogy" between the brilliant play of light of the image and the pure divinity of Christ. Similarly, colored and translucent cloisonné enamel used in narrative images served "as a concrete analogy of the Word made flesh. . . . In this way, the very material out of which pictures were made complements and reinforces the incarnational meaning of the narrative" (Thunø 2005, 274).

Figural conventions such as the rayed or golden halo or nimbus found in many religious traditions were easily interpretable ways to signal the transcendence or sacrality of the depicted object: the depiction of Christ with a rayed nimbus derives from images associated with the Roman cult of Sol Invictus ("unconquered sun") (Frazer 1979). Cruciform images, especially when enclosed by a circle or wheel (*rota*), were "convenient schemata above all for cosmological diagrams, which expressed divine order and harmony" (Caviness 1983, 103–04). Putting a frame around a portrait (*imago clipeata*) located within a picture was a device used to represent figures not visible to characters in the scene, thus signaling their apotheosis (Kessler 2000). The depiction of silence in an image can serve as a "visual analogy" (Strickland 2007, 107) for aspects of the divine: the closed mouths of angels contrast with the gaping mouths of demons.

Conventionalized pictorial styles can also be understood to signal transcendence. Pasztory (2005, 131) argues that, for both pre-Columbian and

Western European artistic traditions, an "abstract" style, that is, a style that involves the reduction to single lines and the approximation of geometrical forms and that depicts referents not normally observable in the everyday world, can be used to represent the "ideality" of those transcendent objects. While often difficult for modern museum goers to appreciate, Egyptian cult statues were carved with standardized "frontality," that is, in a style with the god's face looking directly forward—toward the ritual action taking place right in front of the statue. Frontality thus signals undivided attention, not stolid immobility (Robins 1994, 151; 2008, 19). The confinement of these statues in rectangular shrines only reinforces this by leaving one frontal opening: the basalt statue of Wahibra in the British Museum depicts the king holding in his lap a miniature *naos* (shrine) which contains a small relief of the god Osiris, also looking straight ahead (Robins 2008, 19).[3]

A third and especially interesting possibility involves representations that work at the level of "metasemiotics," that is, of explicitly depicting some phase, practice, or norm of nonrepresentational semiosis by showing, for example, the failure of the human faculty of sight; the act or process of hiding, making opaque, or covering the transcendent object; the temporal delay caused by the actual movement of the object outside a pictorial frame; or any other semiotic aspect of process involved in perception, communication, or interpretation.

Whether directly dependent on the mystical writings of Pseudo-Dionysus or, as Zinn (1986) contends, the more locally available influence of Richard of St. Victor, Abbot Suger, the force behind the design of St.-Denis outside Paris as well as the author of texts justifying its ornamentation, was careful not just to exemplify the logic of "anagogical" symbolism but to carefully construct an image showing *how* this interpretive logic worked in a particular case. One of the bronze medallions on the door depicts the scene of the disciples on the road to Emmaus, and Zinn (1986, 35) argues that this particular scene was chosen to illustrate a "specific understanding of the way visible reality leads to invisible truth," that is, the failure of humans to perceive the proper relationship between material signs and spiritual realities: without Redemption, no aspect of the created world can lead to the "True Light." Hamburger (2000, 50) gives a parallel example of the *Madonna and Child with Canon George van der Paele*, completed by Jan van Eyck in 1436, which shows the Canon gazing at the holy pair with his spectacles removed, thus signaling that his vision is with his inner or spiritual rather than corporeal eye.

Generalizing across early Mesopotamian civilizations, Winter (2000, 36) reasons that people's "direct and intense visual experience of the sacred" is precisely mirrored (according to contemporary texts) in the affective *impact* of their experience of temples, cult objects, and royal dwellings. This, she argues, is one explanation for the enlarged eyes of statues of the gods, not just to focus the gaze of spectators but to represent their expected response—literally "being struck" by their awe-inspiring nature.[4] A gypsum relief of Atargatis and Hadad from Dura Europos (late second or early third century CE) provides an interesting inversion of the vector of the gaze, according to Lucian, who remarks: "There is another wondrous feature of this statue. If you stand opposite and look directly at it, it looks back at you and as you move its glance follows. If someone else looks at it from another side, it does the same thing to him" (quoted in Elsner 2007, 21).

Valeri's (1985) comprehensive analysis of the ancient Hawaiian sacrificial rite (*luakini*) offers an excellent extended illustration of the metasemiotic role ritual action plays in creating the possibility (and, in this case, the necessity) of an *apperception* of transcendence. In ancient Hawaii the faculty of sight, made possible by the organ of the eye, was thought to be the fundamental source of knowledge, but in order to create a distinction between (individual) sensory experience and (collective) conceptual understanding, the former must be first blocked, covered, or blinded to fully reveal the latter. The *luakini* ritual that accomplishes the installation of the new king involves the construction of an anthropomorphic image of the god (Haku 'ōhi'a) carved out of a particular species of tree growing wild in the forest and then the sacrificial eating of the victim's eye, taken to be a metonym of human consciousness: "By eating the victim's eye, then, the god feeds on human consciousness, or rather on its trans-formation. And indeed the god exists as a result of the transformation of man's consciousness, which moves from empirical vision to intellectual vision, from the particularity of percept to the universality of concept" (Valeri 1985, 324). This transformation of a visual symbol into an invisible reality is equivalent to the construction of a "true god" (*akua maoli*) "by negating man's empirical vision by blocking it with regard to an initially visible manifestation of the god" (324). The Haku 'ōhi'a image, embodying the natural properties associated with maleness—vertical, strong, red—emblematic (for these Hawaiians) of the ideal form of the human species, stands in the center of the *luakini* temple complex, and this wooden image is then ritually transformed into an image of the god, whose very human qualities are revealed—literally—by removing its covering of ferns and vines.

A key player in the ritual action is the Kahōali'i, who as both the human incarnation of the god Kū and the "double" of the king consumes the eye of the sacrificial victim, thereby transferring to the king the "superior vision embodied in that eye" (Valeri 1985, 325). Accordingly, toward the end of the ritual process all except the king and the high priest turn their backs on the Haku 'ōhi'a image: "The 'real gods' just produced by the ritual must now become invisible in or-der to invisibly guide men's actions and their vision of the empirical world. Men can experience the invisible gods only through the visible victims who are the representations of men as they transcend empirical reality through death" (327). By appropriating objects that are, at first, only implicitly symbolic and making them fully symbolic through collective ritual action, those objects are understood to be gods, not merely the products of the collective subject (345).

Semiotic Mediators and "Axial" Issues

In considering these and other modalities of representations of transcendence, a distinction can usefully be made between a person or group *engaging* in some form of semiosis (singing a chant, looking at a stained glass window, participating in a ritual) and reflexively *considering* the operational principles governing these same sign processes. To be sure, an adequate account of "engaging" in semiosis requires understanding the cultural conventions that, for participants, make singing, viewing, or acting meaningful activities; and part of that understanding involves their metasemiotic construal—in real time and after the fact—of signs as coherent "texts" (specifically, what Silverstein [1996] has termed "interactional texts"). But to frame semiosis as semiosis, that is, to develop an esoteric metasemiotic vocabulary and elaborated theoretical discourse about sign processes implies a mode of referential consciousness that cannot be equal to the consciousness of the engaged participants, though such vocabularies and discourse can have a "feedback" relationship with human experience.

It would be, however, a huge error to use this distinction between engaged and reflexive consciousness to characterize entire epochs of human history, to assume, for example, that some cultural traditions are locked into an unreflexive "mythological" consciousness, while others, thanks to brilliant or creative intellectuals, make the "axial breakthrough" so that, for them, the "shadows in the cave are revealed as fake, as not reality but a manipulated simulacrum of reality" (Bellah 2011, 592; cf. Humphreys 1975; Schwartz 1975a; Gauchet 1999; Taylor 1999, 2011). Cross-cultural investigations suggest rather, as a hypothesis, that the greater the assumed unbridgability of the gap between earthly and transcendent realms (diagnostic for some scholars of the presence of "axial" traditions), the more difficult becomes the task of traditional "semiotic mediators" between realms, mediators which can now become increasingly open to intense ideological critique and political attack.

The "statistical" frequency of these mediators cannot, of course, be used analytically to argue for a normative "collapse" between realms, since the necessity of their operation implies the opposite. And while it is surely the case that not all these critiques and attacks are the result of rational, "second-order" reflection (another supposed "axial" diagnostic), these cultural conflicts do, in many cases, lead to the generation of heated discourses—a veritable clash of semiotic ideologies—and to innovative forms of semiosis.

In this vein, Assmann argues that, for both the prophetic reforms in ancient Israel and the growth of philosophical speculation in classical Greece, revolutionary "political theology" that insists on the radical separation of politics from religion "turns into a critical discourse which, in the biblical tradition, is critical of government, and in the Greek tradition is critical of religion" (2004, 151). One of the many ironies of the theorization of "axial age" traditions, then, is that the very conceptualization of the "tension" (rather than a doxic homologous or analogical correspondence) between the mundane and the transcendent necessarily posed the question of the ways in which "the chasm between the transcendental and the mundane could be bridged" (Eisenstadt 1986, 3). Criticism of traditional beliefs could, for example, lead to more complex, self-consciously constructed discursive practices, such as the *allegorization* of stories contained in epic poetry, the *rationalization* of religious beings (so that a god becomes, for Plato, the immaterial cause of the cosmos), and the *ritualization* of commemorative public ceremonies (Humphreys 1986, 98–100). And in certain situations the florescence of image use in rituals could be a logical response to the adoption of certain highly general moral principles, as the development of the doctrine of noninjury to live beings (*asiṃsā*) in post-Vedic India might correspond to the spread of the sacrificial use of images as animal substitutes (Salmond 2004, 24). On the other hand, there is also the analytical irony that the greater the postulation of the absolute and universal transcendence of the gods, the more some analysts point to a "sociological" explanation for this transcendence, as anchored, for example, in the representational analogy from ever-wider sociopolitical units, so that high gods are seen as projections of earthly monarchs—"the entire cosmos functioned exactly as a kingdom" (Bottero 1992, 215), a situation exactly the opposite of purported "axial" civilizations.

First Case Study: Cult Statues

Cult statues in ancient Mesopotamia were made of wood, plated with gold and silver, and clothed in splendid robes (Dick 2005, 47–50). Texts refer to statues as being displayed in ritual processions, repeatedly plundered and destroyed, and periodically in need of physical restoration. Statues of the same god could be located in multiple temples, and the artificial quality of the artisans' craft was minimized in references to the role of the gods in ceremonially "giving birth" to their own statues.

In the ancient Greek world, statues of gods were constructed of materials (wood, plant material, aromatics) specifically appropriate to the divinity involved, were often filled with papyrus texts naming the god, and were empowered by ritual spells. Although, as Haluszka (2008) argues, worshippers might have come to regard the god as being "contained" in the statue, from a semiotic perspective the statue functioned as a Peircean "index," that is, as a "pointer" linking the vivified object to a divinity, whose power is thereby brought into cognitive salience and thus effective action (cf. Bahrani 2008, 53). Price (1999, 57), on the other hand, states that the "anthropomorphism" of Greek statues was a matter of "conventional representation," that is, that worshippers did not think that the "guises" (old or young, male or female) and "attributes" (thunderbolt, trident) of a statue formed a "literally accurate image" of the god.

The crux of the dilemma of representing divinity in ancient Greece involved a tension between the gods' propensity to reveal themselves (as sources of potency and generation) and the danger to humans who might experience, however momentarily, that power. To mitigate this situation, the gods tended to conceal themselves within clouds or behind masks and by impersonating mortals; and humans believed that divinities were, correspondingly, present in various aniconically shaped objects such as pillars, pyramids, and rock piles (Steiner 2001, 81–85): "The installation of images within temples and shrines may have sought to recapitulate the notions expressed in these myths. Just as numinous powers choose to hide themselves, or only to allow a rare glimpse of their epiphanic presences, so the idols that housed the god should properly do the same, conveying something of the divinity's own mode of oblique self-representation and the fleeting quality of his self-display" (87). If not divine creations, cult statues could sometimes be divinely approved, as Pausanias recounts: "Even the god himself bore witness to the art (*techne*) of Pheidias: when the statue [of Zeus] was completely finished, Pheidias prayed to the god to make a sign if the work pleased him, and immediately a flash of lightning struck the pavement at the place where the bronze urn was still standing in my time" (Pausanias, *Description of Greece*, 5.11.9; quoted by Finkelberg 2000, 30)

Vernant (1991) proposes a historical transition (at about the fifth century BCE) from objects that presented or manifested the divine without being in any sense a figuration of divinity to artifacts that represent divinities mimetically by the illusionistic skills of artists.[5] But both sides of this periodization, Vernant claims, respond to the same need to establish real contact with "inaccessible and mysterious" divinity, that is, with its "otherness" (1991, 153). Burkert (1997, 22–30) sees this dichotomy rather differently: in place of the aniconic-iconic sequence of Vernant, he suggests that, across the ancient Mediterranean more generally, a more useful distinction is between "classical" representations of divinities— epitomized in large-scale seated cult statues—and coexisting nonvisual modes of experiencing transcendent powers based, for example, on ecstatic dancing, auditory epiphany, or oracular signs.

In ancient Egypt divine transcendence and absolute hiddenness were strongly linked in texts, architecture, and ritual objects (Assmann 2001, 35–47). Assmann explains that the institution of kingship is the primary focus for the "symbolic mediation" required by the cosmological gap between earthly and transcendent worlds:

> But because the gods are remote, there has to be an institution that ensures contact with the divine world even under conditions of remoteness. From now on, gods will be manifest on earth only through a structure of representation. In their myths the Egyptians describe themselves as inhabiting a disenchanted world; the present state (in both senses of the word) is both the healing of a breach and a compensation for a loss, the loss of corporeal closeness to the gods. Real presence is replaced by representation. By virtue of their symbolic power, state and cult, temples, rites, statues, and images make present the divine and establish an irremediably indirect contact with the gods. . . . The state is the institution of this closeness. The pharaoh rules as the representative of the creator god. (2002, 186–87)

Assmann cites a ritual description of the god Amun: "His hidden all-embracing abundance of essence cannot be apprehended" (2009 [1995], 142).

Cult statues in temples were considered to be the bodies of the gods that serve the function of sacred communication between realms, but only after being submitted to rituals of purification, consecration, and vivification. The gradient sacredness of temple space—the location of the *naos* or niche for the cult statue—was signaled by the decreasing amount of available light toward the far end of sanctuary, which was almost totally dark except for carefully positioned window shafts allowing a sliver of solar rays to penetrate the darkness (Teeter 2011, 41–42). The perspective of the deities reversed that of the officiating priests: descending from heaven to earth, deities (in their *ba* or active essence) entered the temple at the shrine end and, if sufficiently attracted by the beauty and appropriateness of the construction materials used (e.g., silver for bones, gold for flesh, lapis lazuli for hair), entered the statue through the "door of heaven" (Robins 2005, 6–7). Taken out of the shrine's darkness, the statue (or its double), still hidden from view by a protective cloth, was transported in a sacred boat and, closer now to the human realm, could be the source of oracular pronouncements and other performative effects (Hornung 1992, 116).

Assmann (2009 [1995], 174) notes the parallel mediational role of Egyptian hieroglyphs (defined as the "writing of divine speech") that operate in a type-token relationship, with the god Ptah creating the divine types and then filling the world with tokens or material realizations (especially natural phenomena, animal species, and humans beings) of these cosmic models—"a kind of Platonism with an infinite variety of material impressions of a finite set of immaterial ideas" or a set of visible signs that stand for something invisible (Assmann 1992). The god Thoth then "found" or "recorded" the hieroglyphic shapes and linguistic names that are the precise iconic forms of and for these realities. Thus, "writing carries out what is already implicit in the structure of reality" (Assmann 2007, 165).

Scholars disagree about the exact point that the theological rationale (and its poetic expression) for cult statues of gods and king became finalized,[6] but it does seem that an analogy was developed between the cosmic creation by the gods of their various embodiments in the physical universe (ranging from heavenly bodies to animal species to the king) to the cultic *re*-creation by the king (or his priestly substitutes) of temples containing the shrines that house the statues of the gods: "The world as it is today (divided into the Now and the Hereafter, into a divine world that is remote and can be visualized only in images and symbols and into an earthly world administered on behalf of the creator by a deputizing king) is a relatively new establishment" (Assmann 2007, 165). The darkness, stillness, and hiddenness of the shrine recreates, to the degree humanly possible, the initial conditions of creation, while the beauty and preciousness of the material forms of the statue are designed to attract the descending god, who sees the statue as one possible body and who understands the promise, clearly illustrated on the temple walls,[7] of pleasingly appropriate cultic actions (cleansing, feeding, clothing, entertaining, processing, etc.).[8]

Statues of gods (and, by parallel logic, mummified bodies of kings) are, thus, the locus of a two-directional process of semiotic mediation required to connect differentiated yet linked realms.[9] Assmann borrows the concept of "sacramental explanation" from medieval Christian hermeneutics to describe the underlying principle by which the literal sense (*sensus literalis*) of ritual action by cult officiants and public participants (e.g., purification and feeding) are mystically or allegorically interpreted (*sensus mysticus*) as rebirth and ascent in the heavenly realm. Furthermore, "It is not only a matter of explanation, however, but of a genuine transformation. From nourishment, as ascent to the sky comes into being, and from the presentation of the *qnj*-breastplate, an embrace that restores life. Transformation is achieved through the establishment of a relationship between the cultic realm and the realm of the gods: something that happens in the cult is transformed into an event in the divine realm" (Assmann 2005, 351–52).

Second Case Study: Eucharistic Transubstantiation

Following Assmann's "sacramental" lead, we now turn to the second case of the "real presence" of transcendence.[10] Scholarly discussions of the various forms and practices of semiosis in the Christian Middle Ages suggest a potential methodological dilemma involving the kinds of evidence addressed: the *same* evidence for the proliferation of ritualized manifestations and discursive theorizations of semiotic mediation can be used, on the one hand, as evidence for the existence of a standardized norm of "participation," "consubstantiality," "filiation," or "immanence" (Bedos-Rezak 2006) or, on the other hand, as extraordinary attempts to overcome an equally normative separation or "disengagement" of the sacred from the profane (Brown 1975, 135). This methodological ambiguity can be seen in Brown's comment, in the context of his discussion of what he sees as a transformation in religious consciousness starting to occur in the eleventh and twelfth centuries: "For the situation we have seen in the early centuries of the Middle Ages is one where the sacred and the profane can be intermingled because the borderline between the objective and the subjective in human experience is deliberately blurred at every turn" (142). To illustrate this hypothesized distinction between the two medieval periods, Brown contrasts "the squat and bejewelled figure of Sainte Foye," the holy relic at Conques, that could act as an "objective force" on its own "subjective" initiative, and the "heightened majesty" of the eucharistic sacraments as defined by the new rational and speculative theological sensibilities of the twelfth century, according to which "the supernatural was strenuously *defined* as that which was totally discontinuous with the human group" (144) and in which human groups, in turn, were defined in terms of their hierarchically differentiated contact with the supernatural. The point to note is that Brown silently switches from the popular, "blurring" religiosity of pilgrimages to saints' relics to the "defined" decrees of the Lateran Council of 1215.[11]

Kessler (2004, 166–67) contends that it was medieval Christianity's belief in the dual nature of Christ, a mysterious union of human and divine, that provided religious viewers' "inner eye" with a theory of artistic representation in which the physical image and the transcendent prototype are simultaneously distinct (representationally) and united (theologically).

> The old theologians had dealt with the basic question by referring to the common experience of the image and its relation to the person represented. They argued that God had become visible in Christ, as in an image, while the new theologians, as advocates of the image, contended that Christ could become visible in his image. If the invisible God, they said, had become visible in the man Jesus, then the latter could be made visible in images. The reality of Christ's incarnation, a dogma still widely discussed, thus was linked to the possibility of Christ's representation, and the image was thereby promoted to a criterion of orthodoxy. (Belting 1994, 152)

Rather than merely resting on the assumption behind this "theory," medieval artists explicitly represented the transformational moment, for example, depicting the bottom half of Christ's torso as he leaves the earth at the Ascension: "As pictured in the Odbert Gospels [ca. 1000 CE], the Lord's disappearance introduced the fundamental paradox of Christian art: as a man, Christ had been seen and cherished by other humans and therefore could be represented in material images; but his absence had to be asserted as well so that the love engendered by his person could be transferred to his invisible divinity" (Kessler 2004, 168). Still other examples contain explicit wording to remind the viewer not to confuse the pictorial image and the divine reality: "Revere the image of Christ by kneeling before it when you pass by it; but in so doing make sure you do not worship the image but rather him whom it represents" (171).

Thus the Incarnation became a model promoting sacramental signification as "real presence," since the transcendent *res* ("thing") is actualized in the immanent *signum* ("sign"), first of all by not undergoing any change and second of all by virtue of an ontological dualism not dependent on the arbitrariness of linguistic agreement (Bedos-Rezak 2000, 1499). As conceptualized by advocates of the doctrine of transubstantiation, the consecrated elements (the signifying forms) *are* the body and blood of Christ (the signified reality) and at the same time they stand for them. So if the "dual nature" of Christ codified in incarnational theology offered a theory for experiencing transcendence through material representation, the medieval development of eucharistic theology went one step further in reaffirming the immanent presence of divine reality *in* the material signs repeatedly generated at each performance of the liturgy.

Once doctrinally established for the unique case of the Eucharist, however, the argument for the "participation" relationship between sign and reality became generalized: "Thus, although this mode of signification pertained strictly only to the eucharist, the argument for real presence and its principle of immanence ultimately realigned theories of representation, with consequence for society as a whole" (Bedos-Rezak 2010, 177). Sophisticated metasemiotic reflection was, thus, harnessed to explain the consilience between the hermeneutics of the Incarnation and the Eucharist by, for example, the metaphor of sealing as a semiotic process in which the impressed or imprinted image (Son) is consubstantial with the metallic substance (God), while remaining invisible until the incarnational moment: "The notion of image as imprint therefore promoted, like the Eucharist, a form of immanent semiotics whereby the image in actualizing its constitutive relationship to an originating model signified by formulating likeness as a relationship between form and matter, which involved gradations of contact and presence" (Bedos-Rezak 2012, 83)

To this ideological generalization (following the pattern of "secondary elaboration" elucidated by Franz Boas) must be added the other pole of the semiosis of real presence: the experiential responses to images, including but going beyond the eucharistic, that complete the "circle of semiosis." The first example is a story retold by Ginzburg (2001) about a cleric named Bernard d'Angers, who made a pilgrimage in the early eleventh century to Conques to see the famous saint's image located there. Having complained to his fellow pilgrims about the Christian "idols" they had met along the way ("Do you suppose that Jove or Mars would have thought such a statue unworthy of them?"), Bernard continued to show his disdain by comparing the image of Saint Foy to the likeness of Venus or Diana. And yet, Ginzburg explains, by the time Bernard wrote an account of his experience he had changed his mind, after witnessing the miracles performed by Saint Foy.

> In the miraculous tales that Bernard of Angers relates, the image of Saint Foy is regarded in a characteristically ambivalent manner. On the one hand, it aroused hostility and sarcasm among its detractors; on the other, it appeared in the visions of the faithful. The monks carried it in procession so that, in accordance with established practice, it might take possession of a piece of land left to the monastery of which they had been unlawfully deprived. The people of Conques made no distinction between the image of Saint Foy and the saint herself. Bernard's suggestion that the image was an aid to memory—an argument that he put forward to ward off the suspicion of idolatry—would have been acceptable to only a tiny minority of believers. (Ginzburg 2001, 75)

A second example is provided by Rubin's (1991, 109–42) account of late medieval *exempla*, that is, collections of tales (often derived from vernacular preaching) dealing with the experience of the Eucharist. While designed to supplement more "parochial guidelines" to orthodox doctrine, these widely distributed stories challenged the automatically "miraculous" yet invisible moment of transubstantiation by offering "florid . . . sometimes lurid miraculous events that had left a great impression on contemporaries" (112) and only served to reinforce the "miraculous mood" in medieval culture: "Viewing a eucharistic miracle could influence understanding of sacramental claims more than many sermons, and tales abound of shaky belief which was strengthened by a vision, such as that told of the Patarins of Ferrara who were convinced of the faith when a lamb appeared in the host, or that of a northern heretic, Gautier of Flos, who saw a baby in the host during a mass celebrated by St. John of Cantimpré" (113). Rubin documents a number of tale types: tales in which the Eucharist stimulates visions of a bloody, crucified, or childlike Christ; stories involving miraculous effects of the host experienced by skeptical laity and doubting priests; narratives of changes in the course of nature brought about by contact with eucharistic elements; and stories revealing the agency of the host in repelling violations of the liturgical code.

Later medieval depictions of eucharistic transubstantiation continued to face the key theological paradox that this transformation of bread and wine into Christ's body and blood occurred at the level of invisible substance and in the accidents of appearance. The representation of what Bynum (2006, 210–15) calls "a presence beyond"—a "real" presence that was objective (or "real") to laypersons, visionaries, pilgrims, and theologians—could never be justified by appeal to the sensory experience of the eucharistic elements but only to the experiential and testimonial evidence of performative effects in believers and nonbelievers. Bynum (2011, 285) identifies the fundamental paradox for late medieval Christianity, as evidenced in both religious practice and theological discourse, as the "simultaneous intensification of contrary responses" with regard to the difference between a material world of generation, change, and passing away, on the one hand, and a realm of the "eternal changelessness of God," whose nature is eternal, immutable, and unknowable, on the other: "Therefore, I would suggest that behind the resistance to seeing found in so much theological writing of the period is a resistance to change itself, a sense that the fundamental difference between early and divine is that fact that we change, God does not. For becoming visible is *mutatio*. The objections of theologians and diocesan synods to seeing Christ in the host or revering holy relics . . . were not merely fear of superstition or popular piety but efforts to maintain the changelessness and unseeability of God" (2006, 230). The key to understanding these "contrary responses," Bynum proposes, is to realize that instances of the paradoxical admixture of contradictory realms are themselves fleeting, lasting "only a moment," and to appreciate that, in the final analysis, the relationship between "the stuff of the world" and the "beyondness of ultimate meaning" (2011, 286) cannot be spoken of, only lived.

Conclusion: Toward a "Circle of Semiosis"

But, as the two extended case studies above so clearly demonstrate, this is certainly *not* true: "lived" experience is always mediated by available symbolic forms, and that mediation is itself mediated by various modalities of metasemiotic regimentation—both in the forms themselves and in the discursive apprehension of the real-time functioning of those forms. And so what "cannot be spoken of" becomes precisely the focal object of entextualized discourses that claim to know about what cannot be known and to represent what cannot be represented. This way of rethinking the relationship between semiosis as the experience of transcendence and semiosis in entextualized discourse about transcendence in this way suggests, finally, an alternative way to enter into the important debate between Freedberg's *The Power of Images* (1989) and Belting's *Likeness and Presence* (1994). In clarifying his argument against Belting, Freedberg claims that understanding sacred images (or, in his view, any image) requires, first, a reassertion of an "anthropology" (that is, a universal psychological tendency) of apprehending the prototype (the divine referent) as "inhering" in the image, and second, a serious attention to metasemiotic texts (philosophical, theological, etc.) that postulate a specific "ontology" informing the image-prototype relationship. But as his discussion of accounts of Artemidorus's dream reveals, Freedberg gives clear priority to the first over the second of these methodological principles: "But it is worth remembering these textual variations simply as demonstrations of how a complex and general psychological problem [first principle], that of the belief in the inherence of the prototype, illustrated most sharply by the phenomenology of dreams, actually informs and determines the philosophical tradition and the history of a text [second principle]" (1996, 74).

The focus of the present essay has been to reverse these priorities, to see the ("universal") regimenting function of texts as the key to understanding the ("relative") psychological response to semiotic forms such as images. Egyptian cult statues and Christian eucharistic elements look very similar in terms of the semiosis of real presence—their "sacramental" dimension, to recall Assmann's usage— not because of an "anthropological" tendency but because of the historically contingent regimenting operation of parallel metasemiotic texts.

Notes

This paper was originally published as "Representing Transcendence: The Semiosis of Real Presence," *Signs and Society* 2, no. S1 (2014): 1–22. Semiosis Research Center, Hankuk University of Foreign Studies.

    1. Marin explains the difference between "mimetic" and "spectacular" representation: "To represent" signifies first of all to substitute something present for something absent (which is of course the most general structure of signs). This type of substitution is, as we know, governed by a mimetic economy: it is authorized by a postulated similarity between the present thing and the absent thing. But in other respects, to represent means to show, to exhibit something present. In this case, the very act of presenting constructs the identity of what is represented, identifies the thing represented as such. On the one hand, a mimetic operation between presence and absence allows the entity that is present to function in the place of the absent one. On the other hand, a spectacular operation, a self-presentation, constitutes an entity and a property by giving the representation legitimate value. (2001b, 352)

    2. Camille (1989) notes that the positive value attached, in many traditions, to images that showed no evidence of being created by human hands reflects the general theological principle that humans should not "usurp God's role as artificers of man and the universe" (33) as well as the widespread attitude "that human labor is degrading and ignoble," resulting in the "displacement of production to somewhere outside human space and time" (30).

    3. Although Akhenaten's "religion of light" temporarily eliminated the cultic use of statues of the gods, depictions of the sun's disk and rays continue the convention of frontality as expressing the "greatest possible effectiveness" (Hornung 1999, 78). Rather than showing the face-to-face interaction between the king and the god, as was typical prior to the Amarna Revolution, the king and his family are depicted as the exclusive recipients of life-giving rays descending from the solar disk above, itself depicted frontally.

    4. Gaifman (2006, 266) notes a similar depiction of astonishment on a Greek *krater* resembling Athena Parthenos.

    5. Price (1999, 57) warns against restricting the Greek term *xoana* to aniconic statues, quoting an inscription from 197–196 BCE describing a procession carrying images (*xoana*) of twelve gods "attired as beautifully as possible" (175). And Vegetti (1995, 261) adds the important point that figural conventions of statues can be seen as iconographic supplements to the traditional imagery of epic poetry.

    6. Compare, for instance, Assmann (2005, 109), Dunand and Zivie-Coche (2004, 14–18), Frankfort (1948, 7–8), Hornung (1982, 136), Meskell (2004), Morenz (1973, 153–55), Quirke (1992, 75–76), and Teeter (2011, 46–51).

7. The ubiquitous illustration of cultic activities on Egyptian temple walls contrasts sharply with the (almost—the Parthenon being the notable exception) absence of such pictures on the walls of Greek temples (Price 1999, 32), although they are frequent on other media such as amphora. In both cases the parallel interpretive question arises: Are these images representations of the gods "themselves" or of their "representations"? On this general problem of "divine reflexivity" see Patton (2009).

8. In the temples constructed at his new capital Akhetaten ("Horizon of the Sun-Disk"), Akhenaten removed the roofs so that sunlight could illuminate the cultic objects and activities within. While revolutionary in the Egyptian context, this use of light was in fact the norm in Mesopotamia and other ancient traditions, as Winter explains:

> Texts record special value accorded the attribute of light and/or radiance. Temples are described as being endowed with interiors of silver and gold—not merely as signs of material wealth, but as indications of divine presence—the logic being that if radiance is an attribute of the divine, then that which shines has been touched *by* the divine. Indeed, this use of light in a symbolic way to indicate the sacred unites Mesopotamian temples and liturgical objects with early Christian churches and objects, and provides links as well across the divide between the pre-Islamic and Islamic Near East, as well as with the rest of Asia. (2002, 13)

On the impact of "dazzle" in Late Antique Christianity, see Miller (2009, 77–81).

9. Assmann notes that the "beyond" realm increasingly becomes the ideal destiny of people (especially pharaohs) for whom immortality shifted from being a matter of social memory (secured through monumental architecture) to a quest for permanent residence in "a radically other sphere, beyond human reach, the realm of Osiris" (2004, 142). This required the exercise of the divine authority of Osiris's "court of judgment" and led ultimately to the emergence of concepts of internal consciousness ("heart") and personal decision making as being themselves "transcendental" (2004, 138–42).

10. The following discussion follows the programmatic analytical approach set out by Bedos-Rezak (2000, 1491), especially taking to heart her warning not to assume or even seek "conformity" between semiotic ideology and semiotic practice. Helpful sources for the discussion include Stock (1983), Rubin (1991), Kobialka (1999), Radding and Newton (2003), and Bynum (2007).

11. This methodological difficulty parallels a similar problem in evaluating the relationship between "regimenting" proscriptions and common practices—for example, that Queen Elizabeth's royal proclamation of 1559 against all things "superstitious," including among other things shrines, pictures, paintings, tables, candlesticks, and other "monuments" of miracles, pilgrimages, and idolatries, implies in fact the widespread and fervent use of *just these semiotic forms* and practices (Davidson 1988, 37; Frankfurter 2008, 139). Indeed, as Duffy (2005, 570) notes, subsequent to these injunctions, many churches attempted to avoid the destruction of their images by placing them in private households, and many parishioners hoped for a speedy return to the old, Catholic ways.

15 The "Savvy Interpreter": Performance and Interpretation in Pindar's Victory Odes

With Nancy Felson

> I am no statue maker, to fashion delightful objects that stand idle on their bases; but on every merchant ship and every skiff, sweet song, go forth, spreading the news from Aegina.
>
> —Pindar, *Nemean* 5.1–3

> All Greek literature—song, poetry, prose—originates in *kleos*, the act of praising famous deeds, and never entirely loses that focus.
>
> —Nagy (1990a, 9)

> The pragmatic process of interpretation is not an empirical accident of the text *qua* text, but is a structural element of its generative process.
>
> —Eco (1979, 9)

ONE OF CHARLES S. Peirce's fundamental contributions to the study of sign processes is to provide an analytic vocabulary for describing the intersecting vectors involved in all semiosis, a vector of the "representation" of some object by expressive signs that stand for it and a vector of "determination" of this sign relationship by subsequent interpreting signs, what he called "interpretants." One way to visualize the temporal linkage of these two vectors is to consider how the same interpretants look "backward" at the signs that determine them, especially as they creatively construe or apprehend the original sign relation as having a typologically specifiable *kind* of relation—though not always the actual character of that original sign relation (Parmentier 1994b, 4–10)—and look "forward" to the future sign productions they will, in turn, generate—perhaps a verbal reply, an artistic imitation, a physical response, or a logical consequent. All varieties of verbal art considered as performances are especially interesting illustrations of the temporal movements of these two vectors, since, as Bauman (2014) has most effectively argued, they combine *both* a highly structured or "marked" pattern of organizational coherence and a projected goal of performative effectiveness. While the former's focus on poetic form tends to "decontextualize" discourse—that is, delimit or constrain the role of indexical linkages—the latter entrusts the audience (or hearers) with the responsibility for understanding, evaluating, and acting on the performed words, which in effect leads to further "recontextualization" of the original discourse. In this paper we are concerned with a particular genre of verbal performance called in archaic Greek culture "epinician" or praise poetry, in which the commissioned poet composes in the written register semantically dense, traditionally allusive, and organizationally complex choral odes that, when properly "entextualized" by the audience present at the event celebrating athletic victory, demand future reperformance in order to maximally continue the chain of praise. Thus, the interpretant of each performance of the ode involves the generation of "recontextualized" sign processes (i.e., looking forward) by virtue of the intended entextualization (i.e., looking backward).

And what if the "pragmatics" of a performed poetic text, that is, the connection between the linguistic forms as fashioned by the poet and the context of its performative effectiveness, requires that the text itself be replicated, or at least be replicable, at future times and at distant places? And what if this recontextualization demands, further, advanced interpretive skills on the part of the original listeners, who must overcome stylistic and compositional challenges intentionally posed by the poet, in order to construct a "metapragmatic" reading, that is, an account of the pragmatics of the text, encompassing this form/context linkage? And what if, finally, the poet claims to model both an ideal poet's compositional skill and an ideal audience's interpretive success on an extended metaphor or analogy that links this artistic skill to the victors' athletic triumphs celebrated in the poems, tying them together as the path to the widening glory or fame (*kleos*) of both poet and victor? These are precisely the challenges set by Pindar (518–c. 438 BCE), a Greek lyric poet composing in the first half of the fifth century BCE. His *epinikia* (victory odes, praise poems) are deictically anchored to their token-level performance contexts—a set of indexical relations—by virtue of their capacity to enable hearers to make complex interpretive constructions, that is, type-level texts that function as Peircean interpretants. These interpretants are inherently "metasemiotic" (Eco 1979, 189), since they stand for or "represent" some other semiotic relation, and because, as we will argue, the interpretants of epinician poetry represent (and are designed to represent) a pragmatic "rules of use" (Silverstein 1976, 43) for the production of *kleos*, we can more specifically call them "metapragmatic interpretants."

The completion of this pragmatic sequence, from the moment of athletic triumph to the wide circulation of *kleos*, makes names re-*sound* through time (Ford

2002, 120).[1] It requires the successful interpretation of the poem by its hearers/ readers, something that the poet, as *ego*, can directly describe, predict, and facilitate but cannot guarantee. But since the circulation of *kleos* is the intended interpretant of the Pindaric odes, the poet must compose the poem to be an "indexical icon" of this desired interpretive process. That is, the ode's structure must both provide a clear diagram or model (the iconic part) of the interpretive process and be itself, in its contextual performance, an exemplary instance of praise-making (the indexical part). And this, in turn, requires that potentially "savvy interpreters" (*sophoi* or *sunetoi*) be trained to be even more so when they are finally equipped with the needed interpretive tools. Any text can, of course, describe (and thus regiment) its model interpretant, but only the regular reperformance of a text can affirm this as a predictable accomplishment. And if the proof of the circulation of the victor's *kleos* lies in the reperformance of the poem itself, then, thanks to the analogy between poetry and athletics so carefully developed in both of the odes under study here and a common trope in many Pindaric odes, this is also to proclaim the poet's own *kleos* (Lefkowitz 1977, 212; 1980, 33). As Nagy (1990a, 16) explains this "double-use" of *kleos*: "The patron gets fame from the praise of the poet, whose own fame depends on the fame of his patron in the here-and-now."

So the genre of epinician poetry—the parameters of which were largely constructed by Pindar—is defined by the movement from momentary praise to eternal renown. Our analytic task, as critics, is not simply to collate all explicit passages in the odes that refer to the goal of the circulation of *kleos* or to list all the places where Pindar develops the analogy between athletic prowess and poetic genius. Rather, we will describe the complex construction of what we will call "textual modalities" in our sample odes; and we will treat the intended entextualization by the ideal audience as a metapragmatic interpretant. The notion of "entextualization" (Bauman and Briggs 1990, 73; see also Silverstein and Urban 1996, 15) is not to be limited to the writing down of some stretch of discourse but specifies the more general "process of rendering discourse extractable . . . of making a stretch of linguistic production into a unit—a *text*—that can be lifted out of its interactional setting." This process is especially remarkable in the case of performed poetry, where the powerful deictic forces that anchor or center the "text" must be overcome, that is, decontextualized, in order to allow recontextualization in future performance contexts. In arguing for the primacy of this pragmatic rule—that *kleos* fundamentally involves recontextualization—we acknowledge that other artistic and ideological functions are also in play; but these other functions do not account for the poetic particulars of Pindar's odes. Indeed, the poetic dimension of Pindar's epinician odes can never be separated from the political dimension since the movement from praise to renown is itself fundamental to the—perhaps historically threatened—value structure of the elite Greek culture of the period, especially as this system is grounded in the analogical parallelism between athletic triumph and artistic skill (Rose 1992, 157, 164). As Detienne (1999, 52) describes this linkage between politics and poetry: "In Mycenean society the poet seems to have played the role of an officiating priest or acolyte of the sovereign who collaborated in imposing order on the world. In the archaic period, even after this liturgical function disappeared along with the function of sovereignty, the poet remained an all-powerful figure for the warrior and aristocratic nobility. He alone could confer or withhold memory. It was in his speech that men could recognize themselves."

Performing Exemplarity

Pindar constructs his victory odes to reach out beyond the particulars most salient to the local audiences at each premiere, beyond the particular here-and-now.[2] As a traveling poet born and home-based in Thebes, he navigates astutely between his own native identity and that of the athletic victor whom he is commissioned to extol. First performed at a public event within a geographically restricted community that included the victor, his relatives, and the fellow citizens attending the public premiere, the victory odes could subsequently circulate beyond that local community. Thus there were two types of activity, public performance and the circulation of a script (Hubbard 1985).[3] Even readers, remote in time and space, can to some degree imaginatively identify with the original audiences and understand the odes in their original settings. They can strive to emulate the activities of exemplary figures, both mythological and contemporary, whose efforts transcend the limits of the human condition through the practice of *aretê* 'excellence' or 'virtue'. Far from narrowly focusing on elite athletic competitions, the rhetoric of each ode encourages all interpreters, by practicing excellence, to experience in their own lives "a gleam of splendor given of heaven" (*Pythian* 8.98).

Pindaric odes invite listeners to join an elite category of savvy interpreters who listen or read virtuously, with *aretê*, and who discern the complex and subtle meanings of his notoriously difficult poetry.[4] The savvy interpreters Pindar imagines and occasionally calls "wise" or "discerning"[5] (line 86: συνετοῖσιν) are not individuals or groups that he could possibly preselect; rather, his odes themselves help "train" all inherently competent and receptive members of his audiences and readership to join a community of excellence that transcends time and space. They do so, in part, through the exemplary activities of *ego*. Thus, despite the facts that the odes came into existence to satisfy wealthy patrons from around the Greek-speaking world and that the poet Pindar presents his projected self, his *ego*, as someone engaged in the economy of aristocratic gift exchange,[6] this wider community of interpreters is not "gated," that is, not restricted to interpreters within aristocratic lineages. The odes welcome anyone who combines "natural talent" (*phua*) with "hard work" (*ponos*), especially under the tutelage of an expert guide.

Fränkel describes Pindar's world of universal values, the *Wertwelt* that the poet creates when praising the victor's momentary and transitory heroism: "Pindar's poetry is concerned with the noble, the great, the good, and the godly/divine—in a single word, with value; and indeed so exclusively that everything is ignored that has no positive or negative connection to values."[7] Other scholars since Fränkel have tried to explain the far-reaching appeal of these praise-poems beyond the original occasion of their first performance. Morgan, for example, attributes to Pindar a "self-sufficient and totalizing poetic discourse that throws the excellence of his song into relief by subsuming all aspects of the present revel, the poetry of the past, and the performative context of the future" (1993, 14–15).[8] This discourse, she adds, will absorb all other forms of victory celebration and song. In an inspirational essay Young writes:

> Poetry of the present can interest people of the future only if it brings its occasional subjects into relation with larger, enduring questions. Myth is the major means by which Pindar places his athletes' achievements in the timeless makeup of the world. There is a reciprocal process. By itself, neither the present nor the past implies a general truth. But by holding his contemporaries up against figures from mythology, Pindar affirms the permanence of the heroic past and its relevance to the present. Conversely, by connecting his occasional topics to mythological examples, Pindar validates their participation in a recognized pattern of human life. (1982, 161–62)

In semiotic terms, Pindar translates particular "token" victors into general "types" (Peirce 1998, 480) by linking the present performance to the mythological past and thereby creating a palette of exemplarity.

As he draws on the world of values—Fränkel's *Wertwelt*—Pindar develops elaborate correspondences between and among the activities of characters of the mythical and contemporary worlds. Mythological heroes and heroines populate thirty-seven of the forty-five epinician odes. They exist alongside the victor, his immediate family, and his illustrious ancestors, and alongside the figure of the poet himself, invoked by the first-person pronoun *ego*. Mythical and contemporary characters who transgress or fall short of excellence also populate the odes, highlighting, by contrast, the excellence of those who succeed. Triumphs in multiple domains, including the composition of victory odes in the language-based sphere of making poetry, become metaphors for one another and lead, on the basis of this parallelism of athletic and poetic prowess, to important generalizations and abstractions. When *ego* utters the embedded exemplary maxims, he seems to stand on a higher plane, from which he is able to see patterns governing humankind. This constitutes one Pindaric strategy for inviting interpreters to appropriate moral lessons and overcome comparable challenges and obstacles in their own particular domains and spheres.

The odes have the power to inculcate heroic (both athletic and poetic) values in all willing receivers and thus to become public, just like acclaim won by victors at the four Panhellenic games held at Olympia, Delphi, Nemea, and the Isthmus. Fundamentally invitational, these stories of triumph and failure are accessible to those who can absorb the generalizations into their own conceptual and experiential framework. These values are not a closed set that one can simply list; they help define the optimal human life, given that mortals are, in Pindar's words, "creatures for a day" (*Pythian* 8.95–100):

> ἐπάμεροι· τί δέ τις; τί δ' οὔ τις; σκιᾶς ὄναρ
> ἄνθρωπος. ἀλλ' ὅταν αἴγλα διόσδοτος ἔλθῃ,
> λαμπρὸν φέγγος ἔπεστιν ἀνδρῶν καὶ μείλιχος αἰών.
> [Creatures of a day! What is a man?
> What is he not?
> A shadow's dream is humankind. But when the gleam that Zeus dispenses comes,
> then brilliant light rests over men and life is kindly.]
> (Trans. Miller 1996)

Textual Modalities and Their Construction

It is useful to distinguish five textual modalities, or ways of being texts, in Pindar's victory odes based on a combination of features intersecting at different semiotic levels. Criteria for differentiating these textual modalities include: the nature of their extratextual historical references, the selection and combination of foregrounded deictic devices (especially the relative location of the poetic *ego* and the deictic anchor or *origo*), the characteristic poetic or metrical style, the typical position within the rhetorical flow of the poem (e.g., prologue, digression, transition, conclusion), the severity of the interpretive demands placed on the audience, and their "ontological" status as text (e.g., as performed, as quoted, as replicated, or as projected into the future). In some cases these modalities occupy clearly segmentable parts of the ode, but Pindar frequently makes this segmentability extremely opaque.[9] The following five modalities will be useful in the analyses below: (1) the "narrator's text" anchored by reference to Pindar's home city of Thebes and to the poetic *ego*; (2) the "victor's text" relating to the victor's athletic triumph and the subsequent celebration in the victory's home city; (3) the "mythological text" fashioned by the poet out of tradition to provide models or exempla, frequently placed in parallels or sequences, and often requiring esoteric or specialized knowledge; (4) the "gnomic text" (*gnomai*) stating or alluding to some general universalizing moral principle or maxim that the poet intends to apply to the "participants in the performance of the song in which they occur"

(Wells 2009, 68);[10] and (5) the overarching "metapragmatic text" intended by the poet to be, ideally, constructible by original and future audiences whose achieved understanding of the poem as a work of verbal art is the key to its accomplishing its praise function.[11]

It is important to think of these five textual modalities as essentially pragmatically constructed or entextualized discourse, and not as segmentable parts of the odes as they are printed today nor as conventionally attested speech-acts definable by a degree of coherence between the poet's metalanguage and some assumed linguistic function.[12] Rather, the concept of modalities is designed to identify the distinct components that the poet defines, instructs, and challenges the hearers to integrate into a comprehensive reading or interpretation of the ode as performed, not just as a (potentially) diagrammable structure (e.g., a ring structure) but as a pragmatic artefact, one that demands "recontextualization" as an essential feature of its structure. In other words, textual modalities are the building blocks (1 through 4) and the final interpretant (5) of what savvy interpreters *do*.

Nearly all Pindaric victory odes celebrate historic victors in a variety of athletic events held at one of the four Panhellenic games.[13] Competitors came from all over Greece to compete in the Olympian, Pythian, Nemean, and Isthmian Games, even from as far away as the Greek-colonized island of Sicily and from colonies in southern Italy and North Africa. Each ode premiered in live performance, most often soon after the victor's return to his homeland from the Games. A chorus usually of fellow citizens,[14] often trained by Pindar himself, who would have traveled to the performance site, or by a surrogate,[15] would sing and dance its words and rhythms, accompanied by music. The "narrative" and "victor" textual modalities of the odes usually contain materials carefully selected from an array of historical referents or happenings in the real world, although, like the historian, the poet is not constrained to follow a linear sequence that reflects either historical chronology or causation. The seven most salient features of these two constructed modalities are: (1) an athlete wins at a Panhellenic game; (2) the athlete or a member of his family commissions Pindar to celebrate the victory with an ode (*chreos* [the poet's] 'task or obligation'); (3) to complete his task and fulfill his obligation, the poet finds inspiration, usually in his native town of Thebes; (4) the poet composes his *epinikion*, pays a chorus to perform it, and may direct its performance (certainly, if the site is in his native land); (5) the poet exports/sends/accompanies his completed ode to its destination (journey); (6) a chorus of citizens from the victor's homeland performs the ode in song and dance; and (7) the poet and victor, and their respective homelands, win lasting *kleos*, which is reactivated each time the ode is reperformed or eventually read and reread. These privileged or selected events often appear discontinuously, leaving gaps to be filled in by the interpreter.

Capable interpreters who are knowledgeable about the features that anchor and define the epinician genre can construct, as the first approximation of the ultimate "metapragmatic text," a sequential storyline having its own narrative logic and starring its character-narrator, *ego*. It begins with the athletic victory and includes the composition and performance of the victory ode and a nod to its final outcome, namely the acquisition of lasting glory. Note, crucially, that the narrative description (to the degree provided explicitly by the poet) and the audience's coherent understanding (given their newly acquired skill) both construct the ideal pragmatic trajectory of this genre, which is itself a necessary but not sufficient guarantee of the poem's effectiveness. An ability to construct this storyline is, additionally, a prerequisite for admission into the virtual community of savvy interpreters of Pindaric verse. But savvy interpretation, as we will see, requires much more integrative skill at the level of narrative;[16] that is, the interpreter must ascend the heights *with* the Pindaric *ego* and view his or her own activity with a god's-eye view, to the extent possible.

We will show how, by constructing a coherent text integrating all these modalities, interpreters first gain access to one victorious story of talent, hard work, and eventual "splendor given of heaven" and then, by identifying with *ego* and appropriating his insights, they reframe what is useful and possibly universal in his enactment of poetic triumph, that is, the poem understood in its fullest pragmatics. Moreover, by prompting interpreters to engage with his odes and to overcome comparable challenges and obstacles in their own particular domains and spheres, *ego* in a sense ensures his own perpetuity.

In sum, Pindar's victory odes provide an optimistic and aesthetically satisfying closure to challenging endeavors. Though composed to celebrate specific victors at a specific time, they uplift and transport interpreters and impart timeless wisdom.[17] In addition, readers' difficulty in understanding a Pindaric ode can be seen as itself an "athletic" struggle, itself requiring *aretê* and deserving of praise.

The Poetics of Deixis

Having established the overall pragmatic challenges for interpreting Pindaric odes, we need now to pinpoint at a more technical level the essential role of deixis in Pindar's poetic technique—without losing sight of the more general goal of linking these "here and now" anchors to Pindar's quest for a far more universalizing textual trajectory. In particular, we will be concerned with Pindar's manipulation of the poetic *ego* (especially fundamental to the narrator's text) and with the various ways he engages with his audience in the mutual task of linking the "victor's text" to the more illusory mythological text and still more puzzling gnomic text.[18]

We can define deixis (<*deiknumi* 'point to or at') as "the relation of reference to the point of origin of the utterance" (Grundy 2000, 22), expressed in terms of person, space, and time. The coincidence of I-here-now creates a center of energy, called an origo or "deictic center," that listeners or readers can occupy as they experience a prolonged moment of engagement.[19] The study of deixis in literary texts received impetus from Bühler's (1990, 138–40) distinction between "ocular deixis" (*demonstratio ad oculos*) and "imagination-oriented" deixis (*deixis am Phantasma*).[20] Ocular deixis, that is, straightforward visual pointing, is most familiar in oral contexts, while imagination-oriented deixis, *that is, pointing to* (or speaking of) an imagined object in, for example, a fictional universe, has the surprising effect of bringing that object into existence in an interpreter's mind's eye. Deictic reference is, thus, fundamentally egocentric. As a consequence, to disambiguate deictics requires that one identify the origo of the speaker, whether for an oral or a written utterance, by recognizing his or her spatio-temporal coordinates. In the case of Pindar's performance poetry, because we have lost the full context, all nonoriginal interpreters have to construct an imaginary situation of utterance wherein deictic expressions are anchored in relation to a fictional speaker, ego (Semino 1992).

In narratological terms, deixis depends on a primary narrator-focalizer, that is, a figure who sees and narrates.[21] Interpreters accompanying that figure wherever he travels, sometimes experiencing a full "vicarious transport," sometimes a mere shift in orientation.[22] In Pindaric victory odes, the poet locates the primary *origo* with *ego* most explicitly in the modality we are calling the narrator's text, and speaks using "proximal deixis" (relatively near to the speaker) in designating the coordinates of space and time in which *ego* operates. In the modality we are calling the "victor's text," he uses "distal deixis" (relatively far from the speaker) for recounting the victor's achievement in the third person and as a past event, even though at the premiere he and the victor regularly occupy the same space and time. He places the exploits of mythical heroes at a further remove from the *origo*, in the distant past; and yet, by design, these heroes often occupy the same space as the site of the premiere in the victor's homeland.

To illustrate Pindar's use of poetic deixis, we turn to epinician myth, which sometimes includes quoted prayers, prophecies, or exchanges between characters. In mythical exchanges we find full speech contexts, with a full set of mythical speakers and addressees, along with an audience of onlookers. Under such circumstances, the deictic pronouns, adjectives, adverbs, and verbs are fully intelligible and transparent, and so an analysis of these features in the mythological text helps us understand the workings of deixis in the more fragmentary, more disjointed narrative of the victor's text.[23]

In a passage from *Isthmian* 6, for example, Herakles, clad in a lion's skin, arrives at King Telamon's wedding banquet. There, in the presence of his host and an assemblage of banqueters, he prays that Telamon and his bride will have a son (44–7):

νῦν σε, νῦν εὐχαῖς ὑπὸ θεσπεσίαις
λίσσομαι παῖδα θρασὺν ἐξ Ἐριβοίας
ἀνδρὶ τῷδε, ξεῖνον ἁμὸν μοιρίδιον τελέσαι,
τὸν μὲν ἄρρηκτον φυάν, ὥσπερ τόδε δέρμα με νῦν περιπλανᾶται
θηρός, ὃν πάμπρωτον ἄθλων κτεῖνά ποτ᾽ ἐν Νεμέᾳ· θυμὸς δ᾽ ἐπέσθω.’
[Right now, now, with heavenly prayers
I beg that from Eriboia you bring to term,
in due time, a child—a bold son for this
man here and a fated guest-friend for me!
Make his nature impervious, like this pelt that
enwraps me, won from the beast that I killed in the first of the
contests at Nemea, and let his courage correspond!]
     (Trans. Burnett 2010, adapted)

This passage illustrates Pindar's use of ocular deixis, as Herakles points to the time ("now") and the addressee ("you" [Zeus]) and designates his host ("this man here") and the lion-skin ("this pelt"). The host and the pelt are visible to the audience at the banquet. For savvy interpreters, once they reimagine this contextualized speech-act, the deictic system is indeed intelligible and transparent.

Another, quite different example of secondary deixis comes from the epinician myth found in *Olympian* 1.25–88. Pelops, a youth who has recently been returned to earth by Poseidon after his father's transgression, is about to compete in a chariot race for the hand of Hippodameia. He asks his divine patron for the swiftest of all chariots. In his prayer, Pelops delivers a maxim about heroic action and then applies it to himself:

Great risk does not place its hold on cowards.
Since we must die, why sit in darkness
and to no purpose coddle an inglorious old age,
without a share of all that is noble? But for me, this contest is a task I
must undertake; may you bring to fulfillment what I hold dear.
     (Trans. Miller 1996)

Pelops' self-exhortation, *ego* tells us, was not without effect: he won the race and the bride. As an epinician mythical speaker, Pelops, like *ego*, uses language efficaciously: after he changes direction and takes up the task, he gets immediate results. (This example will be revisited in our discussion below of *Pythian* 3.)

We have discussed the fundamental egocentricity of all first-person narrations and the need for interpreters to reimagine the situation of utterance where the deictic expressions are anchored to the fictional speaker. In Pindaric epinicians, the first-person pronoun implicitly or explicitly refers to "I, Pindar of Thebes," the creator of the verse, but can also refer to members of the chorus as they perform the ode and utter the word "*ego*" (Bakker 2010; Bonifazi 2004a; Felson 1999, 2004a). We can consider this a form of "staging" (D'Alessio 1994, 279). Each time a trained chorus performs impersonating *ego*, they reactivate the composition story. Within a single ode, Pindar makes the poet salient at one moment, the chorus at the next; but he keeps the less-salient referent of *ego* nonetheless present in the background. Paradoxically, the authorial identification of *ego* does not detract from the perception at the premiere that first-person references point as well to the bodies, *ad oculos*, of the citizen performers. In a sense, Pindar is offering a puzzle to his interpreters whenever a chorus performing the ode utters "I." Savvy interpreters can, of course, experience this sleight of hand as a source of interpretive pleasure.[24]

Pindar offers, in both narrator's modality and victor's modality, the deictic construction of *ego* as a paradigm for other achievements, both athletic and heroic. At other times he animates distant mythical triumphs and catastrophes and invites interpreters to draw inferences by analogy. And through gnomic maxims that impart nuggets of aristocratic wisdom—values like "don't strive to be Zeus," "don't stay at home by your mother's side," "be among the front runners," "avoid excess," "practice moderation"—he further generalizes and even universalizes these mythical lives. In so doing, he sometimes places *ego* on a higher plane than the other characters, surveying space and time from above, as if from the vantage point of the Olympian gods. At such moments, *ego* assumes "a god's-eye view," from which he exhibits impartial, prophetic vision, based on his broad knowledge of life-stories that have occurred and are occurring across space and time. These glimpses from above help transform time-bound events into a timeless narrative that will win everlasting fame (*kleos*) for the victor and the poet.

The important point to note is that Pindar uses a full range of similar deictic techniques, many organized by spatial and temporal oppositions, across the various textual modalities as a unifying poetic device. One way that he forges correspondences or parallelisms among the inspired and creative poet, the triumphant and now praised victor, and the exemplary mythological heroes is by emphasizing the homeland of each, a spatially grounded indexical sign of the inhabitants.[25] While praise of the victor's homeland is a standard and well-examined feature of every epinician ode, scholars have paid too little attention to the frequent mention of Pindar's own homeland and of Theban events and themes.[26] Linking the figure of *ego* with Thebes reinforces its reference to the poet-creator. "Pindar of Thebes" is an identifiable entity, comparable, say, to real or fictional characters such as Theron of Akragas or Telesikrates of Kyrene or Herakles of Thebes. The particulars of Pindar's historical identity, as refracted in the ode, do not lessen the possibility of identifying with him; instead, they invite identification: like all of us, he is a person from a specific place.

Robust representations of *ego* across the various modalities give interpreters the access they need to involve themselves in *ego*'s struggle for victory and acclaim. Egocentric, proximal deixis thus ironically enlarges their horizons and inspires them to want to follow *ego*'s example and succeed.

The chorus's impersonation of the poet from Thebes is one kind of imaginative deixis.[27] Another is what comes across as a pretense, namely, Pindar's representation of the compositional activities that took place *before* the performance as if they are happening in the here-and-now. Pindar seems to stage his songs as impromptu performances. The deictic positioning of *ego* as he "weaves" his composition gives the illusion of spontaneity, which some scholars have called "pseudo-spontaneity" (Carey 1981, 52; Scodel 1995) or "oral subterfuge" (Miller 1993).[28] From one point of view, that of the token-level performed text, *ego* is indeed an extemporizing speaker, creating the illusion of the ode as "emergent." His discourse includes such features as impulsiveness, digressiveness, false stops and starts, and self-corrections. Of course, members of the audience know the poet has already completed his ode and taught it to a chorus, who are in the process of performing it. But they pretend that he is in the throes of formulating his thoughts and arranging his heterogeneous materials. So, too, do later readers, imagining the ode's delivery at its premiere. Of course, Pindar, as he composed, perhaps back in Thebes, was savvy enough to anticipate how the text would be perceived at performance and even, most likely, how it would be read in the distant future. By conflating his Theban here-and-now (D'Alessio's "coding time") and the time of performance, he cleverly manipulates these two deictic systems. Hence, there is no disadvantage to using terms like *pseudo-spontaneity* or *oral subterfuge*. This ploy allows Pindar to take his audiences into the creative process of composition, with all its obstacles and triumphs, and to give them an enduring point of access to his eternal themes.[29]

First Case Study: *Olympian 3*

This ode celebrates the victory of Theron of Akragas, son of Ainesidamos, in a chariot race of 476 BCE. [30] The three-triad *epinikion* begins with *ego*'s wish to please (ἀδεῖν) the Tyndarids—the Dioskouroi Twins, Kastor and Pollux, and their sister Helen, and it returns to the Twins at its conclusion.[31] In it, Pindar ingeniously fashions *ego* as a savvy interpreter in action and invites his interpreters, emulating *ego*, to engage in interpretation of a similarly high quality.

In stating his goal of pleasing the Twins and Helen, *ego* emphasizes poetic innovation, for which he uses two verbs of joining with two sets of direct objects: (1) "as I search out a new-fashioned way to yoke (ἐναρμόξαι) Dorian dance (beat, meter) with voices that celebrate triumph"; (2) "my ritual duty of suitably co-mingling (συμμεῖξαι πρεπόντως) the elegant tones of the lyre with a shout from the pipe and a placement of words in due praise of Ainesidamos' son!" Innovation, then, with the Muse standing somewhere (ποι) nearby, will determine *ego*'s success. In the lines quoted above, two hapaxes (one-time occurrences), νεοσίγαλον (4) and ἀγλαόκωμον (6), the latter further emphasized through enjambment, imply a positive outcome, as do the intricate parallels to winners. Clearly, to succeed in this ritual task (τοῦτο θεόδματον χρέος, literally, "godbuilt task") of praising the victor and perpetuating his renown will require the ultimate poetic skill and technique.

In an interlude (9–13), *ego* generalizes the practice of crowning victors with an olive wreath and describes how victory odes, *epinikia*, travel outward from Olympia. The mythological text that follows (13b–38) begins at the end of epode A with τὰν ποτε ("which once"), taking us back in time to the founding of the Olympic Games by Herakles, here the son of Amphitryon (13b) and of Zeus (21: πατρὶ and 31: πατρόθεν). His achievements culminate in his final apotheosis and provide a paradigm for all who strive to succeed.

Herakles in the mythic text resembles other triumphant figures in the ode, but particularly Theron and *ego*, analogies that imply that *ego* too will succeed in his venture—to complete the ode and please the Tyndarids. Pleasing the Tyndarids may seem like a limited goal, but its prominence aligns *ego* with Theron and his tribe of Emmenids, who have already earned the Twins' favor—as demonstrated by their gift of the current victory in a chariot race (38b–39b) and their reciprocal relationship with them (40). It is as if *ego*, too, about to embark on his own "course around the racetrack," will reach the finish line and earn his crown.

That the myth demands hard work from interpreters is evident from the extensive scholarship on its problematic passages. Among the various conundrums are the questions of how many trips Herakles made to the land of the Hyperboreans (14) and, if two, why they seem to be conflated into one. Clearly, Herakles takes two journeys, the first in the service of Eurystheus (26b–32), the second self-motivated but beginning "as a mere thought, caught as it flashed through the hero's mind," inspired by his recollection of the olive trees he spotted on his first journey. *Ego* never describes the course of the second; instead, Herakles's first journey supplies its missing elements. The close formal connection between the two trips requires that interpreters combine the reports and fill in the gaps.

In conflating the two strands of myth, *ego* bedazzles the interpreter to experience the reduplicated journeys as a single event, with Olympia as the point of departure and return. Olympia is also the site of the poet's god-sent songs (θεόμοροι . . . ἀοιδαί) and the native soil for the adornment of olive placed on the victor's brow (9b–13b). By metonymy, Olympia links the poet to Herakles, a connection reinforced by the use of θυμός 'heart', as the motivator for the hero's second journey (25) and the poet's song of praise (38b). Interlocking the two journeys has an additional poetic effect: the textual order of events makes it seem as if Herakles has won the olive trees (31–34) as a prize for outrunning the Hind (25 and 30–32).[32]

Other sleights of hand present challenges to interpreters. The sudden darting back and forth between the initial and the second trip renders shifts between the two journeys almost imperceptible; but an interpreter can unravel these strands and assign elements either to the first, mandated journey—a Heraklean Labor under the orders of Eurystheus—or to the second, a self-imposed task (χρέος) that his heart set in motion at that very time (25, δὴ τότ') when the garden seemed to him defenseless (ἔδοξεν γυμνὸς αὐτῷ) against the sun's sharp rays.[33]

Herakles's remembrance of the olive trees he spotted on his first journey pulls *ego* and the savvy interpreters to the very place where the hero first encountered and marveled at these trees. The adverb ἔνθα 'where' (26) provides the gateway to this change of location, and the directional (deictic) verb δέχομαι 'receive, welcome', along with ἐλθόντ' 'coming,' 'when he came,' accentuates this new location: "where Leto's daughter once had received him when he came." The "where" clause orients interpreters from the *origo* at the Ister (Danube). Artemis *appears* to be welcoming the hero on the second trip, since line 26 follows closely upon Herakles's focalization at Olympia (24); but, surprisingly, the narrative spins back to the hero's initial journey, mandated not by his heart (25, θυμός) but under compulsion from his father (28, ἀνάγκα).

Such deictic shifts bring about vicarious transport of *ego*.[34] As the myth's narrator, *ego* seems to accompany its protagonist twice to the land of the Hyperboreans, to see what Herakles sees and remember what Herakles remembers.[35] His identification with Herakles as he moves into his space through vicarious transport invites interpreters to participate in the hero's subjective cognitive activity in that far-off land, along with *ego*. They too experience the hero's bold adventure; his ordeal becomes, in a sense, their own.

In *Olympian* 3 Pindar aligns five ritual events that all provide occasions for interactions between the divine and human worlds: (1) the Games at Olympia founded in Zeus's honor on the banks of the Alpheus River (19; 21–22); (2) the reenactment of the original event each time the Games are held, each time the Aetolian judge crowns a victor (11; 19–22); (3) the Twins' preservation of the ancient (Olympic) rites (41: φυλάσσοντες μακάρων τελετάς); (4) Herakles's and the Twins' attendance at the festival at Olympia[36] at the time when Herakles appointed them to supervise the Games (36); and (5) the Twins' habitual presence (cf. θαμά 'often') in Akragas at *theoxenia* in their honor—that is, at banquets hosted for the gods.

Theoxenia in Akragas attest to the habitual piety of the Emmenids and of Theron in particular. We cannot assume that a *theoxenion* in Akragas was literally the setting for the premiere, since there is no trace of deictic markers pointing to such an event at Akragas in the here-and-now (Krummen 2014 [1990], 253–61).[37] Instead, we take the poem's language of hosting gods at a *theoxenion* as a metaphor that makes the audiences *imagine* a first performance at a theoxeny and that captures the intimacy and reciprocity between striving humans and the powers that be, intimacy that enables an athlete, hero, or poet to succeed.

Coming full thematic circle, the ode for Theron ends with a return to the here-and-now of *ego*'s ongoing poetic task, with the implication that the Twins, who honored Theron by delivering the Olympic victory in the four-horse chariot race to him (38–40), will favor *ego* as well. To satisfy the Twins and promote the success of this *epinikion*, Pindar has *ego* both state and practice the principle of "nothing too much":

> If water is best, gold the most honored of all man's possessions, so it is
> Theron who reaches the outermost edge of success, moving from home to
> Herakles' pillars! No wise man goes further, nor even the
> unwise. I'll not attempt it—I'd be a fool!

The maxim warns all interpreters, and *ego* himself, not to go too far, not to exceed the Pillars of Herakles, an extreme terminus, the outermost limits of the known world. Though *ego* is always at risk of misusing his poetic talent (τέχνη), his ensuing "action" puts into practice exemplary poetic behavior that avoids *hubris*. Like Theron, who grasps the Pillars of Herakles "from his home" (οἴκοθεν), *ego* ends his *epinikion* just in time and thereby becomes the very model of self-restraint. Thus he demonstrates that, having understood the maxim, he has complied with the principle that travel beyond the Pillars of Herakles is forbidden (lit., ἄβατον 'impassable') for the wise and the unwise.[38] Pindar has fulfilled his ritual obligation (11), and the Muse indeed has stood beside him as he invented (6–7). Like the successful travelers Herakles and Theron, he completes his poetic journey and thematically returns home. He pushes limits, goes from center to periphery, nearly transgresses, but finally stops short.[39] He uses his own poetic journey to provide an additional and especially vivid paradigm of "not staying at home" but instead venturing out as a hero, to the benefit of his immediate audiences and future readers. The fact that he travels to a limit and not beyond will resonate, as we shall see next, with the counterfactuals of *Pythian* 3.

Second Case Study: *Pythian* 3

Pythian 3 celebrates the victory of Hieron of Syracuse in a single-horse race, the κέλης, of 478 or 476 BCE.[40] In it, Pindar consoles Hieron who is suffering from an illness, probably gallstones.[41] The substantial composition narrative of *Pythian* 3 invites the interpreter to draw analogies between *ego*, the victor, and the hero Herakles, whose two round-trip journeys between Olympia and the northernmost land of the Hyperboreans, signified by the Ister (Danube) River, provide a paradigm for other journeys in the composition narrative: of the victor, the poet, and even the crown of olive.

This ode is an atypical *epinikion*, since there is no mention of a commission, the poet's task, the ode's reception and performance, or lasting glory (*kleos*); its content and metrical form imply that it was sent to be publicly performed at the Syracusan palace.[42] Yet the narrator's text once again features *ego* developing into an exemplary figure, worthy of emulation; but in stark contrast to *ego*'s behavior in *Olympian* 3, in *Pythian* 3 he remains situated at Thebes, unable, for unspecified reasons, to journey to Syracuse, homeland of the victorious equestrian, Hieron.

Through a variety of complex compositional strategies, *ego* undergoes a change of state that happens in spurts in the course of the poem. Triggering this change, we infer, are lessons *ego* gleans from the mythical figures whose lives he narrates to Hieron. As the ode moves forward, these lessons *change* the poet's own composition tactics: from piling up exuberant unattainable wishes and counterfactuals, to yearning for what is distant and impossible, he finally prays to Mother Cybele in the indicative mood, respectful of limits and enjoying what is near at hand. We see *ego* hard at work, practicing the very value he affirms in the ode's final line: "for few among humans is attainment easy." In his final, completed state, *ego* epitomizes the virtuous and skillful creator of poetry who appreciates and learns from song. *Pythian* 3 is about undertaking challenges, enduring hardship, and embracing poetic wisdom. *Ego* practices what he urges Hieron to do, and since Hieron, in time, becomes a stand-in for others who are in dire circumstances, the lessons seep into the larger public.

Pindar begins the ode with a deliberately tentative, unattainable wish—or a counterfactual, depending on whether you read the missing verb in the protasis as the imperfect ἦν or, with Pelliccia and Currie, as present tense εἰμι.[43] Subsequent *bona fide* counterfactuals in the poem clarify this initial and probably intentional syntactic ambiguity, so that, as the ode unfolds, a live audience hears the counterfactuals (retroactively or cumulatively) as a set. As a set, the counterfactuals are an important structural component of the ode that contribute, as we shall see, to the meaning of this *epinikion*.

The extensive mythical text (5–58) recounts the story of Chiron, the philanthropic centaur, his tutoring of Asklepios, son of Apollo, and his pupil's punishment for misusing his medical skill. The phrase οἷος ἐὼν, "being such a one," modifying Chiron, provides the transition into the mythical text and the transport to the time when the centaur reared Asklepios and taught him the art of healing.

The myth is presented in two parallel segments, each ending in a cataclysm at the hands of an offended god. In the first, Koronis, a Thessalian princess, enrages Apollo when she sleeps with a stranger (Ischys of Arcadia), though pregnant with the seed of the god. In addition to her sexual transgression, Koronis violates a ritual injunction by not waiting to hear the hymeneals or marriage songs at a wedding feast (16–19), an insensitivity to ritual that makes her the antithesis of an appreciator of poetic song. In a maxim (21–23) *ego* associates her sexual and social misbehavior with a whole class (φῦλον) of humans who do not seek what is at hand but yearn for the distant; their outcome is disastrous. By Apollo's designs (τέχναις Ἀπόλλωνος), Artemis destroys her, but Apollo, in an act of clemency, rescues his son from the pyre and from the womb of the dying Koronis. His speech on this occasion is quoted in direct discourse, bringing interpreters into proximity with the mythic event.

The rescue of Asklepios from the dire destiny of his mother inaugurates the second segment: Apollo takes Asklepios to the wise centaur for his medical education. There Asklepios practices all manner of healing, but eventually, lured by gold, he resuscitates a dead man, thus enraging Zeus, who thunderbolts them both.

Though each segment emphasizes the negative outcome of a human transgression, in each there is some reprieve. When Koronis dies, her relatives place her on a funeral pyre and give her a proper burial, suggesting that she is still part of her community. Apollo rescues his infant son, and for a time, Asklepios practices his trade as a physician. Once he is thunderbolted, no reprieve is mentioned; but one scholar views his violent death as an occasion for cult, a kind of immortality.[44]

Pindar depicts the narrator of this doubly calamitous myth, *ego*, as changing his speech behavior as a result of his own narration. First he pronounces a maxim (59–60) that endorses the value of living in the here-and-now. The maxim sums up the lesson he extracts from the myth: "We must, with mortal minds, seek from the gods such things as are befitting,/knowing what lies before our feet (τὸ πὰρ ποδός), what destiny is ours" (60). Then *ego* applies the maxim to himself by admonishing his own soul not to "strive for the life of the immortals but exhaust the practical means at your disposal" (μή, φίλα ψυχά, βίον ἀθάνατον/σπεῦδε, τὰν δ' ἔμπρακτον ἄντλει μαχανάν) (61). Thereupon *ego* modifies his diction: from using exorbitant counterfactuals, piled one upon another, he will eventually pray in the indicative mood (74)—a more sober practice. But first he returns to his earlier wish, the theme of the opening strophe, this time using a clear counterfactual (63–67):

> Yes, if wise Chiron dwelt still in his cave, and if
> the honeyed discourse of my songs had power
> to charm his will, long since I would have won from him a healer . . .
> for worthy men who now live prey to feverish ills.

Ego proceeds to pile more counterfactuals on top of the previous ones (72–6), prolonging the fantasy of his trip to Syracuse.

> If to him I had brought the twofold joy
> of golden health and a revel song
> to cast a brightness on the Pythian wreaths

which the triumphant Pherenikos garnered once at Kirrha,
I would, I say, have dawned
upon him as a light outblazing any star in heaven, passing over that deep sea.

The entire series of counterfactuals saves *ego* from the plight of Koronis and Asklepios, that is, from verbal *hubris* and the misuse of a link to the gods (Koronis) or of one's art (τέχνη) (Asklepios). The use of this sustained syntactic device (61–70) allows *ego* to express his wish with impunity, as he imagines arriving at the fountain of Arethousa at the palace of his Syracusan host. In this fictive scenario he *is* Hieron's far-shining light, though in the "real" world of the poem, he remains at the very doorstep of his Theban home, where he listens to the maidens who often sing to the Mother, along with Pan, that is, to Kybele, a holy goddess (79).[45]

In epode Δ, when *ego* proclaims, "But as it is, my wish is first to offer prayer/ to the great Mother" (74: ἀλλ' ἐπεύξασθαι μὲν ἐγὼν ἐθέλω . . .), he finally embraces, for the first time in the entire ode, the indicative mood. Pindar's *ego* is a frequent audience and host, his house a site of rituals, and he himself a connoisseur of ritual music. When he tells Hieron, "Yours is a happy lot: upon a king,/leader of hosts, great Destiny casts smiles/as on no other man" (84–86), *ego* aligns the Syracusan king, in his lifetime, with Theban Kadmos and Aiakid Peleus[46]—models for enduring adversity whose traditions illustrate the universal principle of braving life's vicissitudes (86–99). All three connoisseurs of music— Hieron, Kadmos, and Peleus—may be taken as exemplary savvy interpreters of song: while Kadmos and Peleus hear the Muses singing, Hieron hears *Pythian* 3.[47] In their interpretive expertise (*sophia*), they differ markedly from Koronis, who does not appreciate even her own wedding hymn. And *ego*, too, as one who often (θαμά) hears music at his doorstep, partakes of the high status of the privileged auditor and interpreter.

By building up the figure of *ego* as Hieron's consoler and counselor—indeed, as his far-shining light and thus his benefactor—the stay-at-home poet achieves what he would have wished to accomplish had he crossed the sea to Sicily. His emphasis on his own credentials as a Theban poet with expertise in Theban myth and cult helps legitimize his offering of solace to the Syracusan tyrant and increases the value of his poetic gift. As Kadmos of Thebes and Peleus the descendant of Aiakos are paired in a mythological exemplum, so too are *ego* and Hieron, though they remain separated by the sea. By representing *ego*'s activity in Thebes vividly, Pindar entices Hieron to come to Thebes, to hear a chorus of Theban maidens sing to the Mother; in short, to be his guest. As a center of Theban hospitality to song, his house resembles the description of Hieron's palace in *Olympian* 1.14–7, where the Syracusan ruler is frequently (θαμά) glorified by the choice of music, "such as we poets perform in play around his welcoming table." This makes the two characters equals, in a sense, despite Hieron's status as a patron of the arts and the ruler of Syracuse.

We have traced *ego*'s "development" from risky speech-acts to moderation in his use of syntactic forms (from conditionals to indicatives), his choice of words, and his selection and arrangement of happenings as he interweaves the various textual modalities. The "personality" of *ego* that eventually emerges is exemplary and worthy of emulation. The *epinikion*, publicly performed in Syracuse as its metrical choral form suggests, explores the theme of reception of wisdom through poetic song. The consolation offered here to the ailing Hieron supplants the typical victory narrative; yet this atypicality sharply illustrates Pindar's practice of offering *ego*'s poetic behavior as a vivid example of how to proceed in *any* domain of life. When this offer is repeatedly accepted, an epinikion comes ever closer to acquiring lasting *kleos*.

Conclusion: Recontextualization in Performance

As we have seen in the two case studies discussed above, Pindar is vitally concerned with the relationship between the narrative *ego* and the local audience as an essential aspect of the poetic process itself. In both *Olympian* 3 and *Pythian* 3 Pindar presents *ego* responding to the mythical lessons he imparts and, with a few verbal gestures, directing them also to himself as a creative and adaptive poet. The moralizing language that he deploys in his maxims—about vicissitudes, turning the best outward, and striving for what is near at hand—causes him to alter his course. He approaches the finish line of his victory odes with renewed verbal mastery (*aretê*) and also with clarity and poetic wisdom (*sophia*). *Ego* obviously stars in those narrative modalities that appear to be unfolding in the here-and-now. It is their pseudo-spontaneity that beckons to savvy interpreters, making available to all of us the *aretê* and *sophia* that *ego* enacts before our mind's eyes. This is what is meant by "imaginative deixis": traveling with *ego*, even when he is accompanying mythical characters like Herakles and the Dioscouroi, or Koronis and Asklepios, we interpreters take vicarious journeys. In doing so, we appropriate the challenges and triumphs of the heroes, athletes, and, most importantly, *ego* himself. Our special challenge, however, is to decipher poetic enigmas that Pindar purposefully places in his odes. Like *ego* and others who succeed, we must supplement our natural talent (*phua*) with solid labor—filling in gaps, retrieving a coherent storyline, lining up complex and often imperfect parallelisms, and linking various series of "translated" material symbols.

In *Pythian* 3, by use of the pragmatic analogy between Asklepios's curing by medicine and the poet's healing by his own consoling words, Pindar asserts the general principle that it is only through the genius of "skilled craftsmen of song" that we know the archaic stories upon which we can model our behavior and anticipate our fate. Grounded in these exempla from the mythological texts and the corresponding maxims from the gnomic texts, we, as listeners, can trust in the regularity of this process of textual replication thanks to the efforts of poets.

But, as we have noted, this guarantee always involves risk, as clearly outlined in the sudden reversals and partial remediations narrated in the ode's mythological texts. Pindar closes this ode with his usual twist: if you think that being virtuous is difficult, consider how difficult it is to *compose* the praise poetry that renders virtue knowable into the future: "It is radiant poetry that makes virtue long-lived, but for few is the making easy" (115).

In addition to this stated difficulty of the poetic task, a task Pindar performatively proclaims his outstanding competence to accomplish, the conclusion of this ode indirectly suggests that the projected complete interpretation of the composition, including a sophisticated metapragmatic grasp of the relationship among the multiple textual modalities, is equally difficult, though accomplishable by a select group of savvy interpreters, those "few" for whom "the making"—that is, the virtual metapragmatic interpretant—is "easy." And when we do succeed, inspired and trained by Pindar, wiser (we hope) and more virtuous, we bring together the occasional and the timeless and join an ever-growing community of savvy interpreters of the victory odes.

The recent turn toward the study of performance in classical scholarship on Homeric epic and choral lyric poetry has naturally focused attention on the historical transition from oral to written registers (Nagy 1990b). At issue in this paper, in contrast, is not so much the actual diachrony of entextualization (Parmentier 2012, 195) subsequent to the performance event—whether reperformed on the occasion of celebrations within the same family of additional athletic victories, in subsequent symposia (Kurke 1991, 5), edited in written form by later redactors, or even inscribed in golden letters at the temple of Athena on Rhodes (Walker 2000, 193).[48] Rather, we argue that the expectations generated in the original event itself—crucially, about the linkage between present praise and future renown—break the bonds of the here-and-now and that the interpretations of first audiences must engage this insight as a pragmatic rule constitutive of their understanding of the genre (Hubbard 2004, 72). Our insistence on the pragmatic rule of recontextualization as fundamental to the metapragmatic interpretant in the context of performance is echoed in Nagy's (2011) discussion of the praise poems of Bacchylides, where the poet sets up a metonymic sequence of reenacted ritual acts, including the "overall ritual act of performing the victory ode" (199). (Nagy, in fact, points to a direct comparison with Pindar's *Nemean* 5.50–1.) And our argument can be seen as the inverse of that of Pfeijffer (as cited in Morrison 2012, 113n), who claims that Pindar's focus was fully on the "encomiastic aims in the context of the first performance" and that subsequent reperformances that might occur decrease in importance proportional to their distance from the first event (Carey 2007, 199).

Ledbetter (2002) points out Pindar's careful meta-attention to the nature of poetic inspiration and creativity—especially in portraying the poet as the correct interpreter of the Muse's oracle and the poem itself as an "intrinsically meaning-ful interpretation of [that] inspiration" (66). In this way, each of Pindar's praise poems is another instance of the Muse's singing. More interesting for our pur-poses, however, is Ledbetter's passing comment that, in inviting the gods them-selves to join the audience for the "*current* performance" (75, emphasis in origi-nal), "Pindar imposes a standard for human responses to his poem, as it elevates its human auditors." In our terms, Pindar as interpreter models his audiences as equally savvy interpreters.

Wells (2009, 28) is certainly correct in arguing that, as performances, Pin-dar's victory odes are "open-ended," in the sense that all verbal performances are "emergent" or "risky," since their final textual shape is never completely fixed in advance. (Think, for example, of relying only on the prepared text of Martin Luther King Jr.'s "I Have a Dream" speech to understand what happened at the Lincoln Memorial in 1963.) Pragmatic outcome is never guaranteed, and there is always the potential for "backfiring" if contextual parameters conspire against the performative success.[49] But, from our perspective of focusing on textual mo-dalities, Pindar does his best to direct, with skill and assurance, the audiences' final interpretant; and so, in this sense, the victory odes are "closed texts," to use Eco's (1979) notion. But note that citing Eco's idea of closed texts does not imply that the process of interpretation itself is fixed or comes to a sudden halt; in fact, what *is* "closed" in Pindar is the specificity of what Peirce calls the "determina-tion" (*EP* 2, 392–93) of the rule of interpretation.

In arguing that Pindar's odes specify pragmatic rules demanding wide-spread reperformance, we are suggesting that scholars who stress the paucity of references to their performance parameters (Herington 1985, 30) might see this, rather, as one means for Pindar to facilitate recontextualization with different pa-rameters (solo voice, limited instruments, no dancing). In a detailed discussion of deixis in *Pythian* 1, Athanassaki (2009, 250) provides another corrective to the "paucity" argument, citing the parallelism drawn between the "eternally recur-rent" divine performances by the gods on Olympus and the diachrony of human reperformance at public festivals.

Comparative ethnographic experience and common sense combine to sug-gest that it would be practically impossible for the original audience, hearing a recently composed praise song for the first time, to come to a complete grasp of the relationship among the component textual modalities, that is, to entextual-ize the metapragmatic interpretant in the context of the original performance. Thomas (2012), citing recent scholarship on Pindar and comparative evidence of praise poetry in Africa, summarizes possible ways that "difficulty" (e.g., sudden transitions and break-offs, obscure allusions, and compressed style) might *in-crease* the audience's understanding: density makes the poem more memorable; elaboration elevates the sense of occasion; difficulty is read as profundity; risk only increases excitement; political relevance encourages extreme concentration; spontaneity keeps the audience on "tenterhooks"; and ambiguity encourages postperformance discussion.

But it is not unreasonable for audiences to understand that their role *as interpreters* is crucial for starting the song—and thus the *kleos* of the *laudandus* (meaning, the one who is being praised)—on its far-flung "journey." As Thomas (2007, 148) points out, citing in particular *Nemean* 5.1–15 and *Isthmian* 2.44–6, the metaphor of movement is used to convey the sense "that the 'news'— and the 'song'—will travel far in the present and far into the future." In fact, overcoming difficulties in interpretation, just like overcoming challenges in athletic competition, is not something to be avoided: it is the whole point of the genre which so skillfully identifies its referent—the immediate glory of the victor's triumph—with its future interpretant—immortality achieved through poetic creativity.[50]

Silk (2007; cf. 1998, 65–66) envisions the relationship between the token-level of "momentary events" and the type-level of aristocratic values, poetic conventions, and mythological traditions as forming an "inverted pyramid," in which the bulk of the type-level material "enacted" in the odes balances precariously on the point of "praise" performance: "Poetic life, life as conveyed, or created, by this poetry, is—if not sweet—at least possibly glorious, or gloriously possible, but only so long as the oh-so-precarious inverted pyramid stays in its place. Cough skeptically at any of Pindar's connectings and enactings, and the whole construction seems to wobble" (196). In order for this balance to remain unchallenged, interpreters, both contemporary hearers and modern readers, need to be "attuned to a configuration—of the physical, cultural, symbolic, and poetic—within which the mere thought of a cough has no place." But Silk's image needs to be corrected in two respects. First, we need to clarify the connection between indexical relations (that is, signs to contiguous objects) and type-token relations (that is, instantiation of generals in instances): cultures consist of indexical types (and, of course, iconic types), what Peirce calls "indexical legisigns," that is, regularities of pragmatic functioning.[51] And, as we have argued, *kleos* is the key pragmatic rule in Pindar's odes. Second, in postulating an image of a static inverted pyramid, Silk downplays the temporal dimension, namely, the constant theme in the odes that momentary "praise" really isn't praise at all: the glory of victory needs to spread widely in space and time by means of the interpreted ode as its travelling vessel. The poetic celebration is, thus, of a different semiological order than is the athletic victory: the former is an enactable type while the latter is only a referred-to event. That is, while the *laudandus*'s victory can be placed in a sequence of similar events (including mythological exempla and the performance celebration itself), this semiotic construal is only ratified if the interpreters construct interpretants of the ode's "configuration"[52] in such a way that realizes that it is the overarching pragmatic rule of recontextualization that propels the poetic ship on its journey

(Currie 2004, 50). That the poet has this inspired and creative ability to render an event-token into an event-type is at once an authorization and a model for savvy interpreters to continue the generativity that Peirce so wisely judged to be the essence of all fully "symbolic" relations.

Appendix A: *Olympian* 3

I pray to please the guest-loving Tyndarids, golden-haired Helen, too,
while I pay honor to famous Akragas and
rouse up for Theron the hymn of Olympian victory owed to the tireless
hooves of his team! Once more the Muse stands at my side somewhere as I search out a
new-fashioned way to yoke Dorian dance with

voices that celebrate triumph. Crowns fixed in my hair mark a
ritual duty of suitably co-mingling the elegant
tones of the lyre with a shout from the pipe and a placement of words in due praise of
Hagesidamos' son, and Pisa commands me as well. From there
songs travel, god-sent and destined for

each upon whose brow the strict Elian judge,
following Herakles' ancient rule, places a wreath of grey olive to
bind in his hair, from the tree which once Amphitryon's
son brought from the shadowy sources of the Ister[53] to serve as best
emblem of games at Olympia, once his

B

words had persuaded the men of Apollo who live beyond the Boreas.
He made his plea in good faith, wanting a
tree for the famed grove of Zeus, as shade to be shared by the crowd and as a badge of
valiant success. For, with his father's altars already hallowed, the eye of the midmonth
moon had shone full upon him from her golden

hair as on Alpheos' banks he established a sacred judging of games and a
festival, every four years, but no splendid
trees as yet grew in that field by the Kronian Hill—Pelops' domain. To him the
precinct seemed naked, enslaved to the sharp rays of the sun, and in that
moment his heart had urged him to go

back to the Istrian land where Orthosia,
horse-driving daughter of Leto, had earlier met him, come from Arkadia's
ridges and glens, forced by commands of Eurystheus (and by the oath of this father) to
bring back the hind whose horns were of gold, the gift that Taygeta
offered to Artemis with her inscription.

Γ

Chasing that doe, he'd glimpsed the land that lies back of the chill winds of
Boreas and he had stood there in silence,

stunned by the trees. A sweet longing to plant just such trees at the turn of his twelve-lap
course later seized him, and now he is glad as he visits that Elean
festival, joining the twin sons of Leda!

To them, when he went to Olympos, he left the care of his glorious
contests of muscle and chariot skills.
My heart commands me say that these same horse-loving Tyndarids now bring
glory to Theron and to the Emmenid tribe, who, of all men, have most frequently
welcomed these heroes at their friendly feasts,

piously keeping the rites of the Blessed. If
water is best, gold the most honored of all man's possessions, so it is
Theron who reaches the outermost edge of success, moving from home to
Herakles' pillars! No wise man goes further, nor even the
unwise. I'll not attempt it—I'd be a fool!

> —Trans. Burnett (2010), adapted

Appendix B: *Pythian 3*

A

Would that Chiron, Philyra's son—
if it is right that from my lips
this common prayer should fall—
he that is dead and gone, were living still,
offspring of sky-born Kronos, wide in stewardship,
and ruling in the glens of Pelion, that beast of wood and field
whose mind was warm toward mankind, as when once
he reared the craftsman of mild remedies for pain, Asklepios, whose hero's hands
warded from weary bodies all disease.

Before the daughter of knightly Phlegyas
could bring him with Eleithyia's aid to birth, she was laid low by golden
arrows loosed from the bow of Artemis
and sank from bedchamber to Hades' house,
Apollo so contriving it: the wrath of Zeus's children
proves far from futile. She, adrift from sense,
made light of it and welcomed a second union secret from her father,
though she had lain before with Phoibos of the unshorn locks

and bore the god's pure seed within her.
She would not wait to join the bridal feast
nor hear the clear full sound of marriage hymns, such as
young girls, age-mates and friends, delight
to sing at dusk with soft endearments. No, instead
she lusted for what was distant. Many have done so.
There is a kind among human beings, random, rash,
who scorn all things at hand and gaze afar,
stalking illusions out of empty hopes.

B

Such dire infatuation seized the will
of Koronis in her lovely robes: she bedded with a stranger
who came from Arkadia,
but not unnoticed by one watcher: Loxias,
the lord of Pytho rich in sacred sheep, heard news within his temple,
persuaded into judgment by the surest confidant, his all-knowing mind.
He lays no hand on lies, and neither god
nor mortal man can cheat his vigilance in act or thought.

So now, knowing that Ischys, Eilatos' son,
lay as a stranger in her arms, an act of impious deceit, he sent his sister
raging with irresistible might
to Lakereia, since it was there beside the shores of Boibias
that the girl had her home. A hostile power,
swerving to evil, laid her low, and neighbors too
reaped woe, and with her many died. So, on a mountain, from one seed of flame,
fire leaps upon wide woods and pulls them down to dust.

But when on towering logs her kinsmen had
laid the dead girl, and around her licked and roared
Hephaistos' hungry brightness, then Apollo said: "No longer
shall I endure at heart to make my son's destruction
a piteous incidental to his mother's heavy doom."
Thus he spoke, and within one stride was there, and from the corpse
ripped out the infant, standing in parted flame.
He took the child to the Centaur in Magnesia, to be taught
the art of healing mankind's many ills.

Γ

Some came afflicted by spontaneous sores,
some with limbs gashed by hoary bronze, or bruised
by stones slung from a distance;
others, their frames despoiled by summer's fire
or wintry cold. Releasing each from his own ailment,
he drew them into ease, attending some with smooth
incantatory words, or gentle potions; others he bound with poultices
or with the knife set upright on their feet.

But greed holds even the rarest skill in bondage.
Turned by a lordly wage, the gleam of gold in hand,
he dared to fetch from death
a man already captive. Zeus then struck down both,
snatched from the breast of each his very breath
with instant speed: the thunderbolt flashed forth and brought down havoc.
We must, with mortal minds, seek from the gods such things as are befitting,
knowing what lies before our feet, what destiny is ours.

Do not, my soul, pursue the life of gods
with longing, but exhaust all practicable means.

Yes, if wise Chiron dwelt still in his cave, and if
the honeyed discourse of my songs had power
to charm his will, long since I would have won from him a healer
for worthy men who now live prey to feverish ills
some son of Leto's son or of his father—
and would have sailed, cutting the Ionian sea,
to Arethousa's spring and Aitna's lord, my host and friend,

Δ

who in his rule at Syracuse is mild to townsfolk,
bears the nobility no grudge, and is revered by strangers as a father.
If to him I had brought the twofold joy
of golden health and a revel song
to cast a brightness on the Pythian wreaths
which the triumphant Pherenikos garnered once at Kirrha,
I would, I say, have dawned upon him as a light outblazing any star
in heaven, passing over that deep sea.

But as it is, my wish is first to offer prayer
to the great Mother, whom by night before my door girls often celebrate,
with Pan, in dance and song, that reverend goddess.
Next, Hieron, since you know how from old tales to glean
essential truth, you have learned this lesson well:
the gods apportion mortal kind two griefs for every good.
Children and fools cannot endure such odds with grace or steadfastness;
the noble do so, turning the fair side ever outward.

Yours is a happy lot: upon a king,
leader of hosts, great Destiny casts smiles
as on no other man. Yet life without sharp change
was granted neither Peleus, Aiakos' son,
nor godlike Kadmos, though they say these two
prospered beyond all mortals, having heard the hymns
with which, upon the mountain and in seven-gated Thebes,
the Muses blessed them when the one wed lovely-eyed Harmonia,
the other, glorious Thetis, daughter of the deep-sea sage.

E

The gods joined both in feasting;
they saw the royal sons of Kronos throned in gold, and won
from each a bridal gift. So Zeus, through grace set
releasing them from former anguish,
their hearts upright in cheer. In time, however,
the bitter sufferings of three daughters wrenched from Kadmos
a share of happiness; and yet the fourth, Thyone of white arms,
drew by her loveliness great Zeus, the king and father, to her bed.

And Peleus' child, the only one to whom immortal
Thetis gave birth in Phthia, yielding up his life in war to bow shot,

roused lamentation from the Greeks
about his blazing pyre. If a man holds in his mind
the truth's straight course, he will, when kindly handled by
the Blessed, be content. The winds at different times veer from above
now this way and now that. For men, prosperity does not long remain
secure, when it attends them weighted with abundance.

Small amid small things, great among things great
my state shall be. Whatever momentary shifts
fortune may bring me I shall honor to the limits of my means.
If heaven should hand me wealth and its delight,
I hope to earn through aftertime high fame
of Nestor and Lykian Sarpedon, names still on all tongues,
only resounding verses shaped by skillful craftsmen give
us knowledge. Excellence confirmed in song
endures; to few is such achievement easy.

　　　　　—Trans. Miller (1996)

Notes

This paper was originally published as "The 'Savvy Interpreter': Performance and Interpretation in Pindar's Victory Odes," *Signs and Society* 3, no. 2 (2015): 261–305. Semiosis Research Center, Hankuk University of Foreign Studies.

　　1. Svenbro (1993, 14–25) explains the fundamentally acoustic nature of *kleos*: "For in truth, 'fame' is not a very satisfactory translation for *kléos*. In the first place, *kléos* is the technical term for what the poet bestows on individuals who have accomplished something remarkable, as we know from the studies of Marcel Detienne and Gregory Nagy. Second, *kléos* belongs entirely to the world of sounds. . . . If *kléos* is not acoustic, it is not *kléos*."

　　2. Four books of victory odes have survived virtually intact and are arranged according to the various athletic festivals for which they were written—Olympic, Pythian, Nemean, and Isthmian. In Alexandrian times Pindar's works took up seventeen books and comprised all the major choral genres: hymns, paeans, dithyrambs, victory odes, maiden songs, and encomiums.

　　3. Kurke (1991, 8), citing the sociologist Pierre Bourdieu (1977), suggests that the *epinikion* can be viewed as a "marketplace of symbolic capital," that is, as the locus of series of social exchanges involving the "stock of honor and prestige," which is a "precious commodity" for the victor's city or household. Morrison (2011, 326–27) echoes this: that the "preservation and re-activation of symbolic capital is one driving-force behind the performance and re-performance of epinicians in Aegina (as elsewhere in the Greek world) and that its importance implies audiences usually encompassing those outside as well within the victor's close family or wider *patra*."

　　4. In doing so, these listeners understand what the poet, who is wise by nature like the eagle of Zeus (*Olympian* 2.88), announces to them. Most (1986), in a persuasive reading of *Olympian* 2.83–90, takes the noun ἑρμηνέων (86), making its first appearance in this ode, as designating not Pindar's interpreters (as most scholars think) but poets who know many things and do not keep them hidden in their quiver but speak them forth. Such poets, when they release the arrows from their quiver, perform an act of translation for those with understanding (the

sunetoi). As one such poet, *ego* bids his spirit: "aim your bow at the target" (89–90). (We thank Kathryn Morgan for pointing out the relevance of Most's insight to our argument.)

5. For a rich history of *sophia* see Kurke (2010, 95–102). Slater (2012), s.v. *sophia*, lists (*a*) in general, art, wisdom; (*b*) especially poetic skill, art; and (*c*) of other arts or skills (such as medicine). On the range of Pindaric usage, see also Hubbard (1985, 117 and n. 43). Similarly, the less common synonym, *sunesis* (with its adj. *sunetos*), can mean (*a*) understanding in general and (*b*) understanding of poetry in particular, as in *Olympian* 2.84–6.

6. At the very least, Pindar regularly represents his commission from the victor and his family as a gift exchange or debtor's obligation (*chreos, tethmos*).

7. Cf. Fränkel (1975, 554 and 558); for a discussion, see Patten (2009, 54–59).

8. Morgan (1993, 15) concludes that, by depicting himself as a professional poet and an expert and universalizing singer, Pindar "submerges the choral into a virtually monadic personality." This notion of "submergence" relates to our view of the composition story as framing other narratives. On frame narratives, see Wolf (2006, 181).

9. Pfeijffer (2004) suggests that this intentional obscuring of the boundaries of the various textual modalities is one way Pindar generates a "fictional mimesis of extempore speech" (215): the poet conceals not only the contractual arrangements behind the performance but also the fact of its written composition.

10. Wells (2009, 73) also notes that these *gnomai* are frequently metalingual (metapragmatic in our terms) in that they refer to "rules for appropriate speech." For a general discussion of *gnomai* in Pindar, see Boeke (2007, 24–27); she cites in particular *Pythian* 3.80–3, where the narrator praises Hieron for understanding "the true point of sayings," namely, for applying ancient wisdom to current life situations.

11. A possible sixth type of textual modality would be the "intertextual" construction by the audience of a cycle of odes. For example, Clay (2011, 341) discusses the possibility that audiences might notice that the set of *Olympian* 1, 2, and 3 are framed by metaphors of "gold" and "water"; if so, their memories might have been aided by entextualized versions of the previous odes.

12. Wells (2009) might want to add to our list of textual modalities the explicit and implicit "prayers" that Pindar frequently includes in the odes. But on this logic it would be hard not to include a much longer list of such "speech-acts" as swearing, requesting, entreating, etc.

13. The exceptions are the final three *Nemean* odes, which celebrate victories at Sicyon (*Nemean* 9), Argos (*Nemean* 10), and Tenedos (*Nemean* 11).

14. This is clearly the case in Aeginetan and Theban odes, and probably in Sicilian odes as well.

15. Our one example of a trainer who is named is Aineas in *Olympian* 6.87ff.

16. Standard features include a list of prior victories, details about the most recent victory, homeland praise, praise of the victor's family, and self-conscious statements about the poetic process. Scholars since Schadewaldt (1928) have assigned these features to the *Programme*. Hamilton (1974) gives a history of the term and its uses.

17. Fränkel (1975, 514, Index A 2.2-5) sees Greek lyric as "an address to others, on things that are of importance to others as well as to oneself. Thus the person who experiences is often meant not as an individual but as a type, and the person who judges does not express individual views or feelings, but tells us how we ought to judge or feel."

18. Lefkowitz (1963, 180) observes that occurrences of the first-person "bardic ego" often serve to mark transitions from one textual modality to another.

19. We follow Bühler (1990 [1965]) in calling this intersection the "*origo*" and Duchan et al. (1995) in calling the "deictic center." This is what Lyons (1995 [1977]) refers to as "the zero-point of utterance."

20. See also Danielewicz (1990, 16–17). As an example of *deixis am Phantasma*, Athanassaki (2011, 256) discusses the possibility that many in the audience for reperformances of *Pythian* 7 in Athens would be able to imagine details of the temple of Apollo at Delphi, the site of the original celebratory performance of the ode.

21. On focalization, cf. Bal (1997); Schmid (2010) reviews and critiques the concept.

22. On the distinction between vicarious transport and a mere shift in orientation, see Felson (1999, 2004b).

23. Ocular deixis includes references to "this city here" and "this festival here" or a place "over there," as well as deictic verbs such as *arrive, welcome, receive*—verbs that point to objects or activities in the here-and-now of a first performance. For later interpreters, such deictics are difficult to decipher. Cf., among others, Bonifazi (2004b).

24. Perhaps this experience resembles the suspension of disbelief at a dramatic performance, where the audience acclimates to the ruse. In Pindar's odes, though, the shifts would rupture such an acclimation.

25. For a definition of indexical signs, based on spatial and/or temporal contiguity between the sign and its object, see Peirce (*EP* 2, 274–77).

26. The mythological centrality of Thebes enables the Theban poet to ground his poetic authority in his own homeland, which he represents as rich in tradition, despite the Thebans' unheroic Medizing during the Persian War. Currie (2012, 289–90) describes Pindar's use of Thebes as "the epinician variant of the 'reference to the narrator's own space' motif"; Bacchylides's self-designation at the end of ode 3 as "the nightingale from Keos" is another example.

27. Instead of the text representing itself as either an impromptu composition or impromptu performance, D'Alessio (2004, 278–80) prefers to emphasize how the text easily embeds metatextual descriptive elements in itself, enclosing information about its own (real, or more frequently represented) "history." He rejects the view of Carey (1981, 5) that Pindar "creates and sustains the impression of *ex tempore* composition," but is less critical of Carey's later formulation (1989, 552): Pindar "speaks as though he were meditating on the contents or shape of his song prior to or during composition, whereas of course the ode is complete by the time of performance."

28. For a critique of the term "oral subterfuge," see Bonifazi (2000).

29. Cf. D'Alessio (2009) and Gentili (1988). Svenbro (1976, 8–21) comments on audience interference in *Odyssey* 1.325–44, prompted by a song of ongoing events—namely, the homecomings from Troy. Scodel (1995, 66) sees "a strong cultural bias in favor of unprepared song, or song which presents itself as unprepared even if it is not, even where originality may be valued."

30. For the text in English translation of *Olympian* 3, see app. A. In a full discussion, Krummen (2014 [1990], 253–315) reviews the scholarly literature on *Olympian* 3 up to 1989; for more recent treatments of the myth, see especially Shelmerdine (1987), Sfyroeras (2003), Pavlou (2010), and Ferrari (2012).

31. On the ritual significance of the Dioskouroi and Helen in the ode, see Krummen (2014 [1990], 301–24).

32. Krummen (2014 [1990]), 282–83 and 313–40.

33. Kurke (1991). The first clue to those who would unravel the two trips is the use of the imperfect ἔθαλλεν 'it was blossoming', after a short series of aorists, ἀντέφλεξε (20) and θῆκε (22). By combining a participle with an imperfect in θάμβαινε σταθείς (31–2), *ego* lingers over the hero's recollection and slows the narrative down. In so doing, he invites interpreters to experience the prolonged activity of Herakles's recollection. "The garden seemed to him" captures Herakles's focalization, and this too is invitational. With the next line, we are suddenly

back at Olympia at the moment after Herakles notices the absence of trees and reimagines his first sighting of them.

34. The substantial composition narrative invites the interpreter to draw analogies between *ego*, the victor, and the hero Herakles, whose two round-trip journeys between Olympia and the Ister River provide a paradigm for other journeys in the composition narrative, not only of the victor and the poet but even of the crown of olive.

35. The Twins, keepers of the Games, are masters of the round-trip journey around the race-track. Their mention in the two passages provides a poetic frame (or ring) that emulates the race-course, where the athlete journeys to the *sêma* 'turning post', and then returns to the starting place. The figure of the round trip is built into the contest itself, especially for a chariot or foot race; it resonates with the road imagery that Kurke (1991, 15–34) calls the "loop" of *nostos*. Youths in Greek culture take such round-trip journeys as they come of age: Jason, Telemakhos, Orestes, Bellerophon, to name a few that appear in epinician myth.

36. Krummen (2014 [1990], 272–78) follows Fränkel (1975, 162, 494 n. 18; Eng. trans. 434 n. 18) in rejecting the scholiast's idea that καί νυν ἐς ταύταν ἑορτὰν, "now to this festival," refers to Akragas in the here-and-now. She takes ταύταν as anaphoric and not demonstrative (deixis *ad oculos*). Thus ἑορτὰν 'festival' is a synonym for ἀγῶνα 'contest'. Indeed, the single marker of the here-and-now in *Olympian* 3 is νῦν δὲ 'now truly' (43), which introduces Theron's attainment of the pillars of Herakles through his victory in the chariot race.

37. For a different view, see Ferrari (2012, 161), who follows Krummen in concluding that Theron's victory celebration must have been a *theoxenion*, given the central role of the Twins and Helen in the ode, their invocation with the cult title φιλόξεινοι, "hospitable to strangers," and their reciprocal relation with the Emmenids.

38. The phrase "For the wise and the unwise" is what Bundy (1986 [1962], 24 and n. 56) calls a "universalizing doublet" due to its inclusivity.

39. Though Scholia B glosses *oikothen* as "through his native virtues," it is best to take the adverb as marking the starting point of the round-trip journey (cf. Kurke 1991, 23, 24, and n. 27). The journey is outward, the return (*nostos*) left open.

40. Pindar's use of ποτέ 'once', in an elaborate counterfactual that refers to Hieron's triumph once at Delphi, allows for the victory to antedate the ode, as Young (1983) argues. Others point to the identification of Hieron as Aitna's lord (69: Αἰτναῖον ξένον, literally, "the Aitnaian host") as evidence for dating the ode to 476 BCE, the year Hieron founded Aitna, or thereafter.

41. See Scholia, *Inscriptions* a, b. Hieron dies in 467 BCE, eleven years after the performance of *Pythian* 3.

42. On the controversy as to the genre of *Pythian* 3, *epinikion* vs. epistolary consolation, see especially Young (1983, 42), who attacks the notion that the poem belongs to the genre "poetic epistle," for which there is no example at this date. Morgan (2015, 268–72), after reviewing the scholarship, argues that "rather than agonizing over whether an ode is or is not a 'normal' epinician, we need perhaps to expand our notion of epinician" (271) and recognize that consolatory *topoi* fit well in an ode celebrating victory, where pain is transformed into triumph. Morgan also notes, correctly, that the metrical form of *Pythian* 3 suggests public choral performance.

43. In oral delivery, such syntactic ambiguity would engage the interpreter, who might take the notion of Chiron still being alive as an unattainable wish (Pelliccia 1987, 40–46; Morgan 2015, 273, n. 17) or as a counterfactual that turns most of the ode into a *recusatio* (Young 1968, 28, 33–34).

44. Currie (2005, 360–63) offers an elaborate though ultimately unconvincing argument for the ability of the ode to confer literal immortality on Hieron—that is, to rescue him from

death. He sees immortalization through fire as a major theme of the ode and views being struck by Zeus's thunderbolt as a positive event in that it leads to heroization and immortalization. Compare Apollo's rescue of Asklepios with Zeus's rescue of Dionysus from the womb of Semele, with similar implications of being selected and privileged and, explicitly in Dionysus's case, "twice-born."

45. Cf. *Dithyramb* 2.

46. An Aiakid is a descendant of the hero Aiakos of Aegina, father of Telamon and Peleus.

47. Moreover, we know of Nestor and Sarpedon because of Homer's song. Cf. Morgan (2015, 289, 299) on the juxtaposition of divine and human song.

48. Hornblower (2012, 103) finds evidence for the reperformance of odes by descendants of the original victors' families "into the fourth- and even third-century Epirus."

49. See Parmentier (1994b, 96–97) for an ethnographic example of this backfiring.

50. Currie (2005) reviews the debate over the inclusionary or exclusionary nature of *kleos*, that is, whether or not immortality for humans consists only in "renown" created by the poet's song. Currie cites *Isthmian* 4.35–42, where the poet draws an explicit comparison between the reperformance of Homer by rhapsodes and the role of his own odes as "the same beacon of song." (76).

51. For Peirce (*EP* 2, 294–95), these come in two classes, "rhematic indexical legisigns" (e.g., demonstrative pronouns) and "dicent indexical legisigns" (e.g., the vendor's street cry, "Ice cream!"), each requiring *instantiations* in their respective semiotic modality, as "rhematic indexical sinsigns" and "dicent indexical sinsigns," in order to enter the realm of human experience.

52. Writing specifically about *Olympian* 12, one of the shortest odes, Silk's (2007) list of the features of its configurational "architectonics" includes antithetical patterns, ring-form, exact parallelism, chiastic sequence, successive cola, mirror image, and highly elaborate style.

53. The Ister River, the Danube, is a synecdoche for the land of the Hyperboreans.

References

Abu-Lughod, Lila. 1991. "Writing Against Culture." In *Recapturing Anthropology: Working in the Present*, edited by Richard Fox, 137–62. Santa Fe, NM: School of American Research.

Ahonen, Pertii. 1989a. "The Meaning of Money: Comparing a Peircean and Saussurean Perspective." *Law and Semiotics* 3: 13–29.

———. 1989b. "Tracing the Meaning of Money." *Signs of Humanity* 1: 100–12.

Almeder, Robert. 1983. "Peirce on Meaning." In *The Relevance of Charles Peirce*, edited by Eugene Freeman, 328–47. La Salle, IL: The Hegeler Institute.

Alston, William P. 1956–1957. "Pragmatism and the Theory of Signs in Peirce." *Philosophy and Phenomenological Research* 17: 79–88.

Apel, Karl-Otto. 1981. *Charles S. Peirce: From Pragmatism to Pragmaticism*. Translated by John Michael Krois. Amherst: University of Massachusetts Press.

———. 1989. "Linguistic Meaning and Intentionality: The Compatibility of the Linguistic Turn and the Pragmatic Turn of Meaning-Theory within the Framework of a Transcendental Semiotics." In *Semiotics and Pragmatics: Proceedings of the Perpignan Symposium*, edited by Gérard Deledalle, 19–70. Amsterdam: John Benjamins.

———. 1995. "Transcendental Semeiotic and Hypothetical Metaphysics of Evolution: A Peircean or Quasi-Peircean Answer to the Recurrent Problem of Post-Kantian Philosophy." In *Peirce and Contemporary Thought: Philosophical Inquiries*, edited by K. L. Ketner, 366–97. New York: Fordham University Press.

Appadurai, Arjun. 1991. "Global Ethnoscapes: Notes and Queries for a Transnational Anthropology." In *Recapturing Anthropology: Working in the Present*, edited by Richard Fox, 199–210. Santa Fe, NM: School of American Research.

Arendt, Hannah. 1977. *Between Past and Future: Eight Exercises in Political Thought*. New York: Penguin Books.

Armstrong, W. E. 1928. *Rossel Island*. Cambridge: Cambridge University Press.

Assmann, Jan. 1992. "Semiosis and Interpretation in Ancient Egyptian Ritual." In *Interpretation in Religion*, edited by Shlomo Biderman and Ben-Ami Scharfstein, 87–109. Leiden, Netherlands: Brill.

———. 2001. *The Search for God in Ancient Egypt*. Translated by David Lorton. Ithaca, NY: Cornell University Press.

———. 2002. *The Mind of Egypt: History and Meaning in the Time of the Pharaohs*. Translated by Andrew Jenkins. Cambridge, MA: Harvard University Press.

———. 2004. "Axial 'Breakthroughs' and Semantic 'Relocations' in Ancient Egypt and Israel." In *Axial Civilizations and World History*, edited by Johann P. Arnason, S. N. Eisenstadt, and Björn Wittrock, 133–56. Leiden, Netherlands: Brill.

———. 2005. *Death and Salvation in Ancient Egypt*. Translated by David Lorton. Ithaca, NY: Cornell University Press.

———. 2007. "Creation through Hieroglyphs: The Cosmic Grammatology of Ancient Egypt." In *Poetics of Grammar and the Metaphysics of Sound and Sign*, edited by S. La Porta and D. Shulman, 17–34. Leiden, Netherlands: Brill.

———. 2009 [1995]. *Egyptian Solar Religion in the New Kingdom: Re, Amun, and the Crisis of Polytheism*. New York: Routledge.

Athanassaki, Lucia. 2009. "Narratology, Deixis, and the Performance of Choral Lyric: On Pindar's *First Pythian Ode*." In *Narratology and Interpretation: The Content of Narrative Form in Ancient Literature*, edited by Jonas Grethlein and Antonios Rengakos, 241–73. Berlin: de Gruyter.

———. 2011. "Song, Politics, and Cultural Memory: Pindar's *Pythian 7* and the Alcmaeonid Temple of Apollo." In *Archaic and Classical Choral Song: Performance, Politics, and Dissemination*, edited by Lucia Athanassaki and Ewen Bowie, 235–68. Berlin: de Gruyter.

Auer, Peter. 1995. "Context and Contextualization." In *Handbook of Pragmatics*, edited by Jef Verschueren, Jan-Ola Österman, and Jan Blommaert, 1–19. Amsterdam: Benjamins.

Babcock, Barbara A. 1978. "Two Many, Too Few: Ritual Modes of Signification." *Semiotica* 23 (3/4): 291–302.

Bahrani, Zainab. 2008. *Rituals of War: The Body and Violence in Mesopotamia*. New York: Zone Books.

Bakhtin, M. M. 1981. *The Dialogic Imagination: Four Essays*. Translated by C. Emerson and M. Holquist. Austin: University of Texas Press.

———. 1986 [1979]. "The Problem of the Text in Linguistics, Philology, and the Human Sciences: An Experiment in Philosophical Analysis." In *Speech Genres and Other Late Essays*, edited by C. Emerson and M. Holquist, translated by Verne W. McGee, 103–31. Austin: University of Texas Press.

Bakker, Egbert J. 2010. *A Companion to the Ancient Greek Language*. Chichester: Blackwell.

Bal, Mieke. 1997. *Narratology*. Toronto: University of Toronto Press.

Barnard, Edward C. 1980. *Naked and a Prisoner: Captain Edward C. Barnard's Narrative of Shipwreck in Palau, 1832–1833*. Edited by Kenneth R. Martin. Sharon, MA: The Kendall Whaling Museum.

Barnett, Homer. 1949. *Palauan Society: A Study of Contemporary Native Life in the Palau Islands*. Eugene: University of Oregon Publications.

Battaglia, Debbora. 1999. "Toward an Ethics of the Open Subject: Writing Culture in Good Conscience." In *Anthropological Theory Today*, edited by Henrietta L. Moore, 114–50. Malden, MA: Polity Press.

Bauman, Richard. 2004. *A World of Other's Words: Cross-Cultural Perspectives on Intertextuality*. London: Wiley-Blackwell.

———. 2014. "Performance." In *A Companion to Folklore,* edited by Regina F. Bendix and Galit Hasan-Rokem, 94–118. New York: Wiley-Blackwell.

Bauman, Richard, and Charles Briggs. 1990. "Poetics and Performance as Cultural Perspectives on Language and Social Life." *Annual Reviews of Anthropology* 19: 59–88.

Bednarik, Robert G. 1992. "Palaeoart and Archaeological Myths." *Cambridge Archaeological Journal* 2 (1): 27–57.

Bedos-Rezak, Brigitte Miriam. 1992. "Ritual in the Royal Chancery: Text, Image, and the Representation of Kingship in Medieval French Diplomas 700–1200." In

European Monarchy: Its Evolution and Practice from Roman Antiquity to Modern Times, edited by Heinz Duchhardt, Richard A. Jackson, and David Sturdy, 27–40. Stuttgart: Franz Steiner Verlag.

———. 1993. *Form and Order in Medieval France: Studies in Social and Quantitative Sigillography*. Aldershot: Variorum.

———. 2000. "Medieval Identity: A Sign and a Concept." *American Historical Review* 105: 1489–1533.

———. 2006. "Replica: Images of Identity and the Identity of Images in Prescholastic France." In *The Mind's Eye: Art and Theological Argument in the Middle Ages*, edited by J. F. Hamburger and A.-M. Bouché, 46–64. Princeton, NJ: Princeton University Press.

———. 2010. *When Ego Was Imago: Signs of Identity in the Middle Ages*. Leiden, Netherlands: Brill.

———. 2012. "Were Jews Made in the Image of God? Christian Perspectives and Jewish Existence in Medieval Europe." In *Studies in Medieval Jewish Intellectual and Social History*, edited by David Engel, Lawrence H. Schiffman, and Elliot R. Wolfson, 63–96. Leiden, Netherlands: Brill.

Bell, David N. 1984. *The Image and Likeness: The Augustinian Spirituality of William of St. Thierry*. Kalamazoo, MI: Cistercian Publications.

Bellah, Robert N. 2011. *Religion in Human Evolution: From the Paleolithic to the Axial Age*. Cambridge: Belknap Press of the Harvard University Press.

Belting, Hans. 1994. *Likeness and Presence: A History of the Image before the Era of Art*. Translated by Edmund Jephcott. Chicago: University of Chicago Press.

Berde, Stuart. 1973. "Contemporary Notes on Rossel Island Valuables." *Journal of the Polynesian Society* 82: 188–205.

Berger, Harry, Jr. 1968. "Ecology of the Medieval Imagination: An Introductory Overview." *Centennial Review* 12: 278–313.

Berndt, Ronald M. 1983. "Images of God in Aboriginal Australia." In *Representations of God*, edited by H. G. Kippenberg, L. P. van den Bosch, L. Leertouwer, and H. A. Witte, 14–39. Leiden, Netherlands: Brill.

Besançon, Alain. 2000. *The Forbidden Image: An Intellectual History of Iconoclasm*. Translated by Jane Marie Todd. Chicago: University of Chicago Press.

Bloch, R. Howard. 1983. *Etymologies and Genealogies: A Literary Anthropology of the French Middle Ages*. Chicago: University of Chicago Press.

Boeke, Hanna. 2007. "Gnomai as a Source of Cosmological Reflection." In *Value of Victory in Pindar's Odes: Gnomai, Cosmology and the Role of the Poet*, 11–28. Boston: Brill.

Bogatyrev, P. 1971. *The Functions of Folk Costume in Moravian Slovakia*. The Hague: Mouton.

———. 1976a. "Costume as a Sign." In *Semiotics of Art: Prague School Contributions*, edited by L. Matejka, and I. R. Titunik, 13–19. Cambridge, MA: MIT Press.

———. 1976b. "Semiotics in Folk Theater." In *Semiotics of Art: Prague School Contributions*, edited by L. Matejka and I. R. Titunik, 33–50. Cambridge, MA: MIT Press.

Bogatyrev, P., and Roman Jakobson. 1982. "Folklore as a Special Form of Creativity." In *The Prague School: Selected Writings, 1929–1946*, edited by Peter Steiner, 32–46. Austin: University of Texas Press.

Bonifazi, Anna. 2000. "Sull'idea di sotterfugio orale negli epinici Pindarici." *Quaderni Urbinati di Cultura Classica* 95: 69–86.

———. 2004a. "Communication in Pindar's Deictic Acts." *Arethusa* 37: 391–414.

———. 2004b. "Relative Pronouns and Memory: Pindar beyond Syntax." *Harvard Studies in Classical Philology* 102: 41–68.

Bottero, Jean. 1992. *Mesopotamia: Writing, Reasoning, and the Gods*. Translated by Zainab Bahrani and Marc van de Mieroop. Chicago: University of Chicago Press.

Bouissac, Paul. 1998. "Converging Parallels: Semiotics and Psychology in Evolutionary Perspective." *Theory & Psychology* 8 (6): 731–53.

———. 2000. "Can Semiotics Progress?" *American Journal of Semiotics* 15/16: 7–26.

Bourdieu, Pierre. 1977. *Outline of a Theory of Practice*. Translated by Richard Nice. New York: Cambridge University Press.

———. 1990 [1980]. *The Logic of Practice*. Translated by Richard Nice. Stanford, CA: Stanford University Press.

Boyer, Pascal. 1990. *Tradition as Truth and Communication: A Cognitive Description of Traditional Discourse*. Cambridge: Cambridge University Press.

Brandt, Per Aage. 2000. "Grounding Iconicity." In *Iconicity: A Fundamental Problem in Semiotics*, edited by B. Brogaard, T. D. Johansson, and M. Skov, 145–67. Aarhus, Denmark: NSU Press.

Brent, Joseph. 1993. *Charles Sanders Peirce: A Life*. Bloomington: Indiana University Press.

———. 1996. "Pursuing Peirce." *Synthese* 106: 301–22.

———. 1998. *Charles Sanders Peirce: A Life*, enlarged edition. Bloomington: Indiana University Press.

Breton, Stéphane. 1999. "Social Body and Icon of the Person: A Symbolic Analysis of Shell-Money among the Wodani, Western Highlands of Irian Jaya." *American Ethnologist* 26: 558–82.

Briggs, Charles L. 1993. "Generic versus Metapragmatic Dimensions of Warau Narratives: Who Regiments Performance?" In *Reflexive Language: Reported Speech and Metapragmatics*, edited by John Lucy, 179–212. Cambridge: Cambridge University Press.

Brock, Jarrett E. 1981. "An Introduction to Peirce's Theory of Speech Acts." *Transactions of the Charles S. Peirce Society* 17: 319–26.

Brooke, Rosalind, and Christopher Brooke. 1984. *Popular Religion in the Middle Ages*. London: Thames and Hudson.

Brown, Peter. 1975. "Society and the Supernatural: A Medieval Change." *Daedalus* 104 (2): 133–51.

Bühler, Karl. 1990 [1965]. *Theory of Language: The Representational Function of Language*. Translated by Donald Fraser Goodwin. Amsterdam: Benjamins.

Bundy, Elroy L. 1986 [1962]. *Studia Pindarica*. Berkeley: University of California Press.

Burkert, Walter. 1997. "From Epiphany to Cult Statue: Early Greek *Theos*." In *What Is God? Studies in the Nature of Greek Divinity*, edited by Alan B. Lloyd, 15–34. London: Duckworth.

Burnett, Anne Pippin. 2010. *Odes for Victorious Athletes*. Baltimore: Johns Hopkins University Press.

Buytaert, E. M. 1974. "Abelard's Trinitarian Doctrine." In *Peter Abelard*, edited by E. M. Buytaert, 127–52. Leuven, Belgium: Leuven University Press.

Bynum, Caroline Walker. 1991. *Fragmentation and Redemption: Essays on Gender and the Human Body in Medieval Religion*. New York: Zone Books.

———. 2006. "Seeing and Seeing Beyond: The Mass of St. Gregory in the Fifteenth Century." In *The Mind's Eye: Art and Theological Argument in the Middle Ages*, edited by Jeffrey F. Hamburger and Anne-Marie Bouché, 208–40. Princeton, NJ: Princeton University Press.

———. 2007. *Wonderful Blood: Theology and Practice in Late Medieval Northern Germany and Beyond*. Philadelphia: University of Pennsylvania Press.

———. 2011. *Christian Materiality: An Essay on Religion in Late Medieval Europe*. New York: Zone Books.

Camille, Michael. 1989. *The Gothic Idol: Ideology and Image-Making in Medieval Art*. Cambridge: Cambridge University Press.

Carey, Christopher. 1981. *A Commentary on Five Odes of Pindar: Pythian 2, Pythian 9, Nemean 1, Nemean 7, Isthmian 8*. New York: Arno Press.

———. 1989. "The Performance of the Victory Ode." *The American Journal of Philology* 110: 545–65.

———. 2007. "Pindar, Place, and Performance." In *Pindar's Poetry, Patrons, and Festivals: From Archaic Greece to the Roman Empire*, edited by Simon Hornblower and Catherine Morgan, 198–210. Oxford: Oxford University Press.

Carruthers, Mary. 2008. *The Book of Memory: A Study of Memory in Medieval Culture*. Cambridge: Cambridge University Press.

Caton, Steven C. 1993. "The Importance of Reflexive Language in George H. Mead's Theory of Self and Communication." In *Reflexive Language: Reported Speech and Metapragmatics*, edited by John Lucy, 315–38. Cambridge: Cambridge University Press.

Caviness, Madeline H. 1983. "Images of Divine Order and the Third Mode of Seeing." *Gesta* 22 (2): 99–120.

Chenu, M.-D. 1968. *Nature, Man, and Society in the Twelfth Century*. Translated by Jerome Taylor and Lester K. Little. Chicago: University of Chicago Press.

Clay, Jenny Strauss. 2011. "*Olympians* 1–3: A Song Cycle?" In *Archaic and Classical Choral Song: Performance, Politics, and Dissemination*, edited by Lucia Athanassaki and Ewen Bowie, 337–45. Berlin: de Gruyter.

Cohn, Bernard. 1961. "The Pasts of an Indian Village." *Comparative Studies in Society and History* 3 (3): 241–49.

Colish, Maria L. 1983. *The Mirror of Language: A Study in the Medieval Theory of Knowledge*. Lincoln: University of Nebraska Press.

———. 1988. "Systematic Theology and Theological Renewal in the Twelfth Century." *Journal of Medieval and Renaissance Studies* 18 (2): 135–56.

Currie, Bruno. 2004. "Reperformance Scenarios for Pindar's Odes." In *Oral Performance and Its Contexts*, edited by C. J. Mackie, 49–70. Leiden, Netherlands: Brill.

———. 2005. *Pindar and the Cult of Heroes*. Oxford: Oxford University Press.

———. 2012. "Pindar and Bacchylides." In *Space in Ancient Greek Literature: Studies in Ancient Greek Narrative*, edited by Irene J. F. de Jong, 285–303. Leiden, Netherlands: Brill.

D'Alessio, Giovan Battista. 1994. "First-Person Problems in Pindar." *BICS* 39: 117–39.

———. 2004. "Past Future and Present Past: Temporal Deixis in Greek Archaic Lyric." *Arethusa* 37: 267–94.

———. 2009. "Defining Local Identities in Greek Lyric Poetry." In *Wandering Poetics in Ancient Greek Culture: Travel, Locality and Pan-Hellenism*, edited by Richard Hunter and Ian Rutherford, 137–67. New York: Cambridge University Press.

Dalton, George. 1965. "Primitive Money." *American Anthropologist* 67: 44–65.

Danesi, Marcel, and Paul Perron. 1999. *Analyzing Cultures: An Introduction and Handbook*. Bloomington: Indiana University Press.

Daniel, E. Valentine. 1987. *Fluid Signs: Being a Person in the Tamil Way*. Berkeley: University of California Press.

———. 1998. "The Limits of Culture." In *In Near Ruins: Culture Theory at the End of the Century*, edited by Nicholas B. Dirks, 67-91. Minneapolis: University of Minnesota Press.

Danielewicz, Jerzy. 1990. "'Deixis' in Greek Choral Lyric." *Quaderni Urbinati di Cultura Classica* 34 (1): 7–17.

Danielsson, Bengt. 1952. *Raroia: Happy Island of the South Seas*. Chicago: Rand McNally.

Danto, Arthur. 1997. *After the End of Art: Contemporary Art and the Pale of History*, Bollingen Series XXXV: 44. Princeton, NJ: Princeton University Press.

Davidson, Clifford. 1988. "The Anti-Visual Prejudice." In *Iconoclasm vs. Art and Drama*, edited by Clifford Davidson and Ann Eljenholm Nichols, 33–46. Kalamazoo, MI: Medieval Institute Publications, Western Michigan University.

Davidson, Deanna. 2007. "East Spaces in West Times: Deictic Reference and Political Self-Positioning in a Post-Socialist East German Chronotope." *Language & Communication* 27: 212–26.

Davis, Whitney. 1986. "The Origins of Image Making." *Current Anthropology* 27 (3): 193–215.

Deacon, Terence. 1997. *The Symbolic Species: The Co-evolution of Language and the Human Brain*. London: Allen Lane.

———. "Editorial: Memes as Signs: The Trouble with Memes and What to Do about It." *The Semiotic Review of Books* 10 (3): 10–13.

Deledalle, Gérard. 2000. *Charles Peirce's Philosophy of Signs: Essays in Comparative Semiotics*. Bloomington: Indiana University Press.

Dening, Greg. 1986. *Islands and Beaches*. Honolulu: University of Hawaii Press.

Detienne, Marcel. 1999. *The Masters of Truth in Archaic Greece*. Translated by Janet Lloyd. New York: Zone Books.

Dick, Michael B. 2005. "The Mesopotamian Cult Statue: A Sacramental Encounter with Divinity." In *Cult Image and Divine Representation in the Ancient Near East*, edited by Neal H. Walls, 43–67. Boston: American School of Oriental Research.

Duby, Georges. 1980. *The Three Orders: Feudal Society Imagined*. Translated by Arthur Goldhammer. Chicago: University of Chicago Press.

———. 1981. *The Age of Cathedrals: Art and Society, 980–1420*. Translated by Eleanor Levieux and Barbara Thompson. Chicago: University of Chicago Press.

Duchan, Judith F., Gail A. Bruder, and Lynne E. Hewitt, eds. 1995. *Deixis in Narrative: A Cognitive Science Perspective*. Hillsdale, NJ: Erlbaum.

Duffy, Eamond. 2005. *The Stripping of the Altars: Traditional Religion in England 1400–1580*, 2nd ed. New Haven, CT: Yale University Press.

Dunand, Françoise, and Christiane Zivie-Coche. 2004. *Gods and Men in Egypt: 3000 BCE to 395 CE*. Translated by David Lorton. Ithaca, NY: Cornell University Press.

Eco, Umberto. 1979. *The Role of the Reader: Explorations in the Semiotics of Texts*. Bloomington: Indiana University Press.

———. 1981. "Peirce's Analysis of Meaning." In *Proceedings of the C. S. Peirce Bicentennial International Congress*, edited by Kenneth L. Ketner, Joseph M. Ransdell, Carolyn Eisele, Max H. Fisch, and Charles S. Hardwick, 179–93. Lubbock: Texas Tech Press.

———. 1986. *Art and Beauty in the Middle Ages*. Translated by Hugh Bredin. New Haven, CT: Yale University Press.

———. 1995. "Unlimited Semeiosis and Drift: Pragmaticism vs. 'Pragmatism'." In *Peirce and Contemporary Thought: Philosophical Inquiries*, edited by Kenneth L. Ketner, 205–21. New York: Fordham University Press.

Eisenstadt, S. N. 1986. "Introduction: The Axial Breakthrough—Their Characteristics and Origins." In *The Origins and Diversity of Axial Age Civilizations*, edited by S. N. Eisenstadt, 1–25. Albany: State University of New York Press.

Elsner, Jaś. 2007. *Roman Eyes: Visuality and Subjectivity in Art and Text*. Princeton, NJ: Princeton University Press.

Epstein, A. L. 1979. "Tambu: The Shell-Money of the Tolai." In *Fantasy and Symbol*, edited by R. H. Hook, 149–205. London: Academic Press.

Etpison, Mandy T. *Palau: Portrait of Paradise*. Koror, Palau: NECO Marine Corp.

Fabian, Johannes. 1985. "Culture, Time, and the Object of Anthropology." *Berkshire Review* 20: 7–23.

Felson, Nancy. 1999. "Vicarious Transport: Fictive Deixis in Pindar's *Pythian* Four." *Harvard Studies in Classical Philology* 99: 1–31.

———. 2004a. "Introduction." *Arethusa* 37 (3): 253–66.

———. 2004b. "The Poetic Effects of Deixis in Pindar's Ninth *Pythian* Ode." *Arethusa* 37 (3): 365–89.

Ferrari, Franco. 2012. "Representations of Cult in Epinician Poetry." In *Reading the Victory Ode*, edited by Peter Agócs, Chris Carey, and Richard Rawles, 158–72. Cambridge: Cambridge University Press.

Finkelberg, Margalit. 2000. "Two Kinds of Representations in Greek Art." In *Representation in Religion: Studies in Honor of Moshe Barasch*, edited by Jan Assmann and Albert I. Baumgarten, 27–41. Leiden. Netherlands: Brill.

Fisch, Max H. 1986. *Peirce, Semeiotic, and Pragmatism*. Bloomington: Indiana University Press.

Fisch, Max H., and Jackson I. Cope. 1952. "Peirce at the Johns Hopkins University." In *Studies in the Philosophy of Charles Sanders Peirce*, edited by Philip P. Wiener and Frederic H. Young, 277–311. Cambridge, MA: Harvard University Press.

Fitzgerald, John J. 1996. "Peirce's Doctrine of Symbol." In *Peirce's Doctrine of Signs: Theory, Application, and Connections*, edited by Vincent M. Colapietro and Thomas Olshewsky, 161–72. Berlin: Mouton de Gruyter.

Foley, James Miles. 1999. *Homer's Traditional Art*. University Park: Pennsylvania State University Press.

Force, Maryanne T., and Roland W. Force. 1972. *Just One House: A Description and Analysis of Kinship in the Palau Islands*. Bernice P. Bishop Museum Bulletin no. 235. Honolulu: Bishop Museum Press.

———. 1981. "The Persistence of Traditional Exchange Patterns in the Palau Islands, Micronesia." In *Persistence and Exchange*, edited by Roland W. Force and Brenda Bishop, 77–89. Honolulu: Pacific Science Association.

Force, Roland W. 1959. "Palauan Money: Some Preliminary Comments on Material and Origins." *Journal of the Polynesian Society* 68: 40–44.

———. 1960. *Leadership and Culture Change in Palau.* Fieldiana Publications in Anthropology no. 50. Chicago: Chicago Natural History Museum.

Ford, Andrew. 2002. *The Origins of Criticism: Literary Culture and Poetic Theory in Classical Greece.* Princeton, NJ: Princeton University Press.

Foucault, Michel. 1970 [1966]. *The Order of Things: An Archaeology of the Human Sciences.* New York: Vintage Books.

Fox, J. J. 1977. "Roman Jakobson and the Comparative Study of Parallelism." In *Roman Jakobson: Echoes of His Scholarship,* edited by D. Armstrong and C. H. van Schooneveld, 58–90. Lisse, Netherlands: Peter de Ridder Press.

Fränkel, Hermann. 1975. *Early Greek Poetry and Philosophy: A History of Greek Epic, Lyric, and Prose to the Middle of the Fifth Century.* Translated by Moses Hadas and James Willis. Oxford: Blackwell.

Frankfort, Henri. 1948. *Ancient Egyptian Religion.* New York: Columbia University Press.

Frankfurter, David. 2008. "Iconoclasm and Christianization in Late Antique Egypt: Christian Treatments of Space and Image." In *From Temple to Church: Destruction and Renewal of Local Cultic Topography in Late Antiquity,* edited by Johannes Hahn, Stephen Emmel, and Ulrich Gotter, 135–59. Leiden, Netherlands: Brill.

Frazer, Margaret E. 1979. "Iconic Representations." In *The Age of Spirituality: Late Antique and Early Christian Art, Third to Seventh Century,* edited by Kurt Weitzmann, 513–16. New York: Metropolitan Museum of Art.

Freedberg, David. 1989. *The Power of Images: Studies in the History and Theory of Response.* Chicago: University of Chicago Press.

———. 1996. "Holy Images and Other Images." In *The Art of Interpreting,* edited by Susan C. Scott, 69–80. University Park: Pennsylvania State University Press.

French, Roger K., and Andrew Cunningham. 1996. *Before Science: The Invention of the Friars' Natural Philosophy.* Brookfield, Vermont: Scholars Press.

Friedrich, Paul. 1988. "Eerie Chaos and Eerier Order." *Journal of Anthropological Research* 44: 435–44.

Gaifman, Milette. 2006. "State, Cult and Reproduction." *Art History* 29 (2): 258–79.

Gal, Susan. 1998. "Multiplicity and Contention among Language Ideologies: A Commentary. In *Language Ideologies: Practice and Theory,* edited by B. B. Schieffelin, K. A. Woolard, and P. V. Kroskrity, 317–31. Oxford: Oxford University Press.

Gallie, W. B. 1952. "Peirce's Pragmatism." In *Studies in the Philosophy of Charles Sanders Peirce,* edited by Philip P. Wiener and Frederic H. Young, 61–74. Cambridge, MA: Harvard University Press.

Garcia-Acosta, Virginia. 2002. "Historical Disaster Research." In *Catastrophe & Culture: The Anthropology of Disaster,* edited by S. M. Hoffman and A. Oliver-Smith, 49–66. Santa Fe, NM: SAR Press.

Gauchet, Marcel. 1999. "The Dynamics of Transcendence." In *The Disenchantment of the World: A Political History of Religion,* translated by Oscar Burge, 47–66. Princeton, NJ: Princeton University Press.

Geertz, Armin W. 2000. "Global Perspectives on Methodology in the Study of Religion." *Method and Theory in the Study of Religion* 12 (1): 49–73.

Geertz, Clifford. 1973. *The Interpretation of Cultures.* New York: Basic Books.

Gellrich, Jessie M. 1985. *The Idea of the Book in the Middle Ages: Language Theory, Mythology, and Fiction.* Ithaca, NY: Cornell University Press.

Gentili, Bruno. 1988. *Poetry and Its Public in Ancient Greece: From Homer to the Fifth Century.* Baltimore: Johns Hopkins University Press.

Gero, Stephen. 1973. "The Libri Carolini and the Image Controversy." *The Greek Orthodox Theological Review* 18: 7–35.

Ginzburg, Carlo. 1992. "Clues: Roots of an Evidential Paradigm." Translated by John Tedeschi. In *Clues, Myths, and the Historical Method*, 96–125. Baltimore: Johns Hopkins University Press.

———. 2001. *Wooden Eyes: Nine Reflections on Distance.* New York: Columbia University Press.

Gladwin, Thomas, and Seymour B. Sarason. 1953. *Truk: Man in Paradise.* New York: Wenner-Gren Foundation for Anthropological Research.

Glidden, David. 1983. "Skeptic Semiotics." *Phronesis* 28: 213–55.

Goodenough, E. R. 1965. *The Psychology of Religious Experience.* New York: Basic Books.

———. 1967. "A Historian of Religion Tries to Define Religion." *Zygon* 2 (1): 7–22.

Goodenough, Ward H. 1951. *Property, Kin, and Community on Truk.* No. 46. New Haven, CT: Yale University Publications in Anthropology.

———. 1956. "Componential Analysis and the Study of Meaning." *Language* 21: 195–216.

———. 1970a. *Description and Comparison in Cultural Anthropology.* Chicago: Aldine.

———. 1970b. "The Evolution of Pastoralism and Indo-European Origins." In *Indo-European and Indo-Europeans,* edited by George Cardona, Henry M. Hoenigswald, and Alfred Senn, 253–66. Philadelphia: University of Pennsylvania Press.

———. 1974. "Toward an Anthropologically Useful Definition of Religion." In *Changing Perspectives in the Scientific Study of Religion,* edited by Allan W. Eister, 165–84. New York; John Wiley & Sons.

———. 1981a. *Culture, Language, and Society.* Menlo Park, CA: Benjamin/Cummings Publications.

———. 1981b. "On Describing Religion in Truk: An Anthropological Dilemma." *Proceedings of the American Philosophical Society* 125 (6), 411–15.

———. 1983 [1963]. *Cooperation in Change: An Anthropological Approach to Community Development.* New York: Russell Sage Foundation.

———. 1986. "Sky World and This World: The Place of *Kachaw* in Micronesian Cosmology." *American Anthropologist* 88: 551–68.

———. 1988. "Self-Maintenance as a Religious Concern." *Zygon* 23: 117–28.

———. 1990. "Evolution of the Human Capacity for Beliefs." *American Anthropologist* 92 (3): 597–612.

———. 1992. "Belief, Practice, and Religion." *Zygon* 27: 83–114.

———. 1997. "Philogenetically Related Cultural Traditions." *Cross-Cultural Research* 31: 16–26.

———. 1999. "Being Religious: Working at Self-Maintenance and Self-Transformation." *Zygon* 34 (2): 273–82.

———. 2002. *Under Heaven's Brow: Pre-Christian Religious Tradition in Chuuk.* Philadelphia: American Philosophical Society.

Goodenough, Ward H., and Hiroshi Sugita. 1980. *Trukese-English Dictionary.* Philadelphia: American Philosophical Society.

Gose, Peter. 1993. "Segmentary State Formation and the Ritual Control of Water under the Incas." *Comparative Studies in Society and History* 35: 480–514.

Grant, Edward. 2001. *God and Reason in the Middle Ages*. Cambridge: Cambridge University Press.

Gregory, Tullio. 1988. "The Platonic Inheritance." In *A History of Twelfth-Century Western Philosophy*, edited by Peter Dronke, 54–80. Cambridge: Cambridge University Press.

Grundy, Peter. 2000. *Doing Pragmatics*, 2nd ed. London: Routledge.

Guilfoy, Kevin. 2004. "Mind and Cognition." *The Cambridge Companion to Abelard*, edited by Kenneth E, Brower and Kevin Guilfoy, 200–222.

Gupta, Akhil, and James Ferguson. 1992. "Beyond Culture: Space, Identity, and the Politics of Difference." *Cultural Anthropology* 7: 6–23.

Gurevich, Aaron. 1985. *Categories of Medieval Culture*. Translated by G. L. Campbell. London: Routledge & Kegan Paul.

———. 1992. *Historical Anthropology of the Middle Ages*. Chicago: University of Chicago Press.

Habermas, Jürgen. 1995. "Peirce and Communication." In *Peirce and Contemporary Thought: Philosophical Inquiries*, edited by K. L. Ketner, 243–66. New York: Fordham University Press.

Halbertal, Moshe. 1998. *Idolatry*. Cambridge, MA: Harvard University Press.

Halpinen, Risto. 1995. "Peirce on Language and Reference." In *Peirce and Contemporary Thought: Philosophical Inquiries*, edited by K. L. Ketner, 272–303. New York: Fordham University Press.

Haluszka, Adria. 2008. "Sacred Signified: The Semiotics of Statues in the Greek Magical Papyri." *Arethusa* 41 (3): 479–94.

Hamburger, Jeffrey F. 2000. "Seeing and Believing: The Suspicion of Sight and the Authentication of Vision in Late Medieval Art and Devotion." In *Imagination und Wirklichkeit*, edited by Klaus Kruger and Alessandro Nova, 47–62. Mainz, Germany: von Zabern.

Hamilton, Richard. 1974. *Epinikion: General Form in the Odes of Pindar*. The Hague: Mouton.

Hannerz, Ulf. 1989. "When Culture Is Everywhere: Reflections on a Favorite Concept." *Ethnos* 58: 96–111.

Hardwick, C. S., ed. 1977. *Semiotic and Significs: The Correspondence between Charles S. Peirce and Victoria Lady Welby*. Bloomington: Indiana University Press.

Hatten, Robert S. 1994. *Musical Meaning in Beethoven: Markedness, Correlation, and Interpretation*. Bloomington: Indiana University Press.

Hendrick, Clyde. 1993. "The Relevance of Peirce for Psychology." In *Charles S. Peirce and the Philosophy of Science*, edited by E. C. Moore, 333–49. Tuscaloosa: University of Alabama Press.

Herington, John. 1985. *Poetry into Drama: Early Tragedy and the Greek Poetic Tradition*. Berkeley: University of California Press.

Herzfeld, Michael. 1986. "On Some Rhetorical Uses of Iconicity in Cultural Ideologies." In *Iconicity: Essays on the Nature of Culture*, edited by P. Bouissac, M. Herzfeld, and R. Posner, 401–20. Tübingen, Germany: Stauffenburg.

———. 1992. "Metapatterns: Archaeology and the Uses of Evidential Scarcity." In *Representations in Archaeology*, edited by J.-C. Gardin and C. S. Peebles, 66–86. Bloomington: Indiana University Press.

Hezel, Francis X. 1973. "The Beginnings of Foreign Contact with Truk." *Journal of Pacific History* 8: 51–73.

Hijikata, Hisakatsu. 1993 [1942]. "Currency of the Palau Islands." In *Collective Works of Hijikata Hisakatsu: Society and Life in Palau*, edited by E. Hisashi, 215–21. Tokyo: Sasakawa Peace Foundation.

Hill, Jonathan D. 1996. "Ethnogenesis in the Northwest Amazon: An Emerging Regional Picture." In *History, Power, and Identity: Ethnogenesis in the Americas, 1492–1992*, edited by J. D. Hill, 142–60. Iowa City: University of Iowa Press.

Hockin, John P. 1803. *A Supplement to the Account of the Pelew Islands*. London: G. and W. Nichol.

Hornblower, Simon. 2012. "What Happened Later to the Families of Pindaric Patrons— and to Epinician Poetry?" In *Reading the Victory Ode*, edited by Peter Agócs, Chris Carey, and Richard Rawles, 93–110. Cambridge: Cambridge University Press.

Hornung, Erik. 1982. *Conceptions of God in Ancient Egypt*. Translated by John Baines. Ithaca, NY: Cornell University Press.

———. 1992. *Idea into Image: Essays on Ancient Egyptian Thought*. Translated by Elizabeth Bredeck. New York: Timken.

———. 1999. *Akhenaten and the Religion of Light*. Translated by David Lorton. Ithaca, NY: Cornell University Press.

Hubbard, Thomas. 1985. *The Pindaric Mind*. Leiden, Netherlands: Brill.

———. 2004. "The Dissemination of Epinician Lyric: Pan-Hellenism, Reperformance, Written Text." In *Oral Performance and Its Contexts*, edited by C. J. Mackie, 71–94. Leiden, Netherlands: Brill.

Humphreys, S. C. 1975. "'Transcendence' and Intellectual Roles: The Ancient Greek Case." *Daedalus* 104 (2): 91–118.

———. 1986. "Dynamics of the Greek Breakthrough: The Dialogue between Philosophy and Religion." In *The Origins and Diversity of Axial Age Civilizations*, edited by S. N. Eisenstadt, 92–110. Albany: State University of New York Press.

Inoue, M. 2004. "What Does Language Remember? Indexical Inversion and Naturalized History of Japanese Women." *Journal of Linguistic Anthropology* 141: 39–56.

Irvine, Judith T. 1996. "Shadow Conversations: The Indeterminacy of Participant Roles." In *Natural Histories of Discourse*, edited by Michael Silverstein and Greg Urban, 131–59. Chicago: University of Chicago Press.

———. 2004. "Say When: Temporalities in Language Ideology." *Journal of Linguistic Anthropology* 14 (1): 99–109.

Irvine, Judith T., and Susan Gal. 2000. "Language Ideology and Linguistic Differentiation." In *Regimes of Language: Ideologies, Polities, and Identities*, edited by P. V. Kroskrity, 35–83. Santa Fe, NM: SAR Press.

Jaeger, C. Stephen. 1994. *The Envy of Angels: Cathedral Schools and Social Ideals in Medieval Europe, 950–1200*. Philadelphia: University of Pennsylvania Press.

Jakobson, Roman. 1971. "Results of a Joint Conference of Anthropologists and Linguists." In *Selected Writings*. Vol. 2, *Word and Language*, 593–602. The Hague: Mouton.

———. 1976. "Signum et signatum." In *Semiotics of Art: Prague School Contributions*, edited by L. Matejka and I. R. Titunik, 176–87. Cambridge, MA: MIT Press.

———. 1980. "A Few Remarks on Peirce, Pathfinder in the Science of Language." In *The Framework of Language*, 31–38. Ann Arbor: Michigan Studies in the Humanities.

———. 1985. "Sign and System of Language: A Reassessment of Saussure's Doctrine." In *Verbal Art, Verbal Sign, Verbal Time*, 28–33. Minneapolis: University of Minnesota Press.

Jakobson, Roman, S. Karcevskij, and V. Mathesius. 1982 [1929]. "Theses Presented to the First Congress of Slavic Philologists in Prague, 1929." In *The Prague School: Selected Writings, 1929–1946*, edited by P. Steiner, 4–31. Translated by John Burbank. Austin: University of Texas.

Jakobson, Roman, and Krystyna Pomorska. 1983. *Dialogues*. Cambridge, MA: MIT Press.

James, William. 1967 [1898]. "Philosophical Conceptions and Practical Results." *The Writings of William James: A Comprehensive Edition*, edited by J. J. McDermott, 345–61. New York: Random House.

———. 1975 [1907]. *Pragmatism*. Cambridge, MA: Harvard University Press.

Janowitz, Naomi. 2002. *Icons of Power: Ritual Practices in Late Antiquity*. University Park: Pennsylvania State University Press.

Joseph, John E. 2012. *Saussure*. Oxford: Oxford University Press.

Keane, Webb. 1997. *Signs of Recognition: Power and Hazards of Representation in Indonesian Society*. Berkeley: University of California Press.

———. 2003. "Semiotics and the Social Analysis of Material Things." *Language & Communication* 23: 409–25.

Keate, George. 1788. *An Account of the Pelew Islands*. London: Nicol.

Keeler, Mary A. 1990. "Investigating Transparency in the Conditions of Mediation from a Semiotic Point of View." *Semiotica* 82 (1/2): 15–41.

Kessler, Herbert L. 2000. *Spiritual Seeing: Picturing God's Invisibility in Medieval Art*. Philadelphia: University of Pennsylvania Press.

———. 2004. *Seeing Medieval Art*. Toronto: Broadview Press.

Ketner, Kenneth Laine. 1993. "Novel Science: Or, How Contemporary Social Science Is Not Well and Why Literature and Semeiotic Provide a Cure." *Semiotica* 93 (1/2): 33–59.

Kitzinger, Ernst. 1954. "The Cult of Images in the Age before Iconoclasm." *Dumbarton Oaks Papers* 8: 83–150.

Kobialka, Michal. 1999. *This Is My Body: Representational Practices in the Early Middle Ages*. Ann Arbor: University of Michigan Press.

Koselleck, Reinhart. 1985. "History, Histories, and Formal Structures in Time." Translated by Keith Tribe. In *Futures Past: On the Semantics of Historical Time*, 92–104. Cambridge, MA: MIT Press.

Krämer, Augustin. 1917–1929. *Palau*. 5 vols. In *Ergebnisse der Südsee-Expedition, 1908–1910*, edited by G. Thilenius. Hamburg: Friederichsen.

Kremer-Marietti, Angele. 1994. "Peirce's Epistemology as a Generalized Theory of Language." In *Living Doubt: Essays Concerning the Epistemology of Charles Sanders Peirce*, edited by G. Debrock and M. Hulswit, 109–22. Dordrecht, Netherlands: Kluwer Academic Publishers.

Krummen, Eveline. 2014 [1990]. *Cult, Myth, and Occasion in Pindar's Victory Odes: A Study of Isthmian 4, Pythian 5, Olympian 1, and Olympian 3*. Classical and Medieval Texts, Papers and Monographs 52. Prenton, UK: Francis Cairns.

Kubary, Johann S. 1873. "Die Palau-Inseln in der Südsee." *Journal des Museum Godeffroy* 1: 177–238.

———. 1895. "Uber das einheimische Geld auf der Insel Yap und auf den Pelau-Inseln." In *Ethnographische Beitrage zur Kenntnis des Karolinen Archipels*, 1–28. Leiden, Netherlands: P. W. M. Trap.

———. 1900. "Das Verbrechen und das Strafverfahren auf den Pelau-Inseln." In *Die Mikronesischen Colonien aus ethnologischen Gesichtspunkten*, edited by A. Bastian II, 1–36. Berlin: Mittler.

———. 1969 [1888]. *The Religion of the Palauans*. Woodstock, MD.: Micronesian Seminar.

Kuijt, Ian. 1997. "Meaningful Masks: Death, Social Memory, and Levantine Neolithic Community Identity." Paper delivered at the Annual Meeting of the American Anthropological Association, Washington, DC.

Kurke, Leslie. 1991. *The Traffic in Praise: Pindar and the Poetics of Social Economy*. Ithaca, NY: Cornell University Press.

———. 2010. *Aesopic Conversations: Popular Tradition, Cultural Dialogue, and the Invention of Greek Prose*. Princeton, NJ: Princeton University Press.

Kuryłowicz, Jerzy. 1949. "La nature de procès dits 'analogiques'." *Acta Linguistica* 5: 121–38.

Ladner, Gerhart B. 1953. "The Concept of the Image in the Greek Fathers and the Byzantine Iconoclastic Controversy." *Dumbarton Oaks Papers* 7: 1–34.

Lansing, J. Stephen. 1983. *The Three World of Bali*. New York: Praeger.

Leach, Jerry W., and Edmund Leach, eds. 1983. *The Kula: New Perspectives on Massim Exchange*. Cambridge: Cambridge University Press.

Ledbetter, Grace M. 2002. "Pindar: The Poet as Interpreter." In *Poetics before Plato: Interpretation and Authority in Early Greek Theories of Poetry*, 62–77. Princeton, NJ: Princeton University Press.

Lefkowitz, Mary. 1963. "Τω και εγω: The First-Person in Pindar." *Harvard Studies in Classical Philology* 67: 177–253.

———. 1977. "Pindar's *Pythian 8*." *The Classical Journal* 72 (3): 209–21.

———. 1980. "Autobiographical Fiction in Pindar." *Harvard Studies in Classical Philology* 84: 29–49.

Le Goff, Jacques. 1989. "Head or Heart? The Political Use of Bodily Metaphors in the Middle Ages." In *Fragments for the History of the Human Body, Part 3*, edited by Michel Feher, 12–27. Translated by Patricia Ranun. New York: Zone Books.

Lempert, Michael. 2007. "Conspicuously Past: Distressed Discourse and Diagrammatic Embedding in a Tibetan Represented Speech Style." *Language & Communication* 27: 258–71.

Leone, Massimo. 2010. "The Sacred, (In)visibility, and Communication: An Inter-Religious Dialogue between Goethe and Hāfez." *Islam and Christian-Muslim Relations* 21 (4): 373–84.

Leone, Massimo, and Richard J. Parmentier. 2014. "Representing Transcendence: The Semiosis of Real Presence." *Signs and Society* 2 (S1): S1–S22.

Leroi-Gourhan, Andre. 1986. "The Religion of the Caves: Magic or Metaphysics." Translated by Annette Michelson. *October* 37: 7–17.

Lessa, William A. 1975. *Drake's Island of Thieves: Ethnological Sleuthing*. Honolulu: University Press of Hawaii.

Leupin, Alexandre. 1989. *Barbarolexis: Medieval Writing and Sexuality*. Translated by Kate M. Cooper. Cambridge, MA: Harvard University Press.

Lévi-Strauss, Claude. 1969. *The Elementary Structures of Kinship.* Translated by J. H. Bell and J. R. von Sturmer. Boston: Beacon Press.

———. 1974. "The Structural Study of Myth." In *Structural Anthropology,* 206–31. New York: Basic Books.

———. 1976 [1960]. "The Scope of Anthropology." Translated by Monique Layton. In *Structural Anthropology II,* 3–32. New York: Basic Books.

———. 1978. "Preface." In Roman Jakobson, *Six Lectures on Sound and Meaning,* xi–xxvi. Cambridge, MA: MIT Press.

Liep, John. 1983. "Ranked Exchange on Yela, Rossel Island." In *The Kula: New Perspectives on Massim Exchange,* edited by J. W. Leach and E. Leach, 503–25. Cambridge: Cambridge University Press.

———. 1995. "Rossel Island Valuables Revisited." *Journal of the Polynesian Society* 104 (2): 159–80.

Lincoln, Bruce. 2000 [1996]. "Reflections on 'Theses on Method.'" In *Secular Theories on Religion: Current Perspectives,* edited by Tim Jensen and Mikael Rothstein, 119–22. Copenhagen: Museum Tusculanum Press.

Linenthal, Edward. 2003. *The Unfinished Bombing: Oklahoma City in American Memory.* New York: Oxford University Press.

Lotman, Yuri M. 1979. "The Origin of Plot in the Light of Typology." *Poetics Today* 1: 161–84.

———. 1990. *Universe of the Mind: A Semiotic Theory of Culture.* Translated by A. Shukman. Bloomington: Indiana University Press.

Lotman, Yuri M., and Boris Uspenskij. 1978. "Myth-Name-Culture." *Semiotica* 22 (3/4): 211–33.

Lotman, Yuri M., B. A. Uspenskij, V. V. Ivanov, V. N. Toporov, and A. M. Pjatigorskij. 1973. "Theses on the Semiotic Study of Culture as Applied to Slavic Texts." In *Structure of Texts and Semiotics of Culture,* edited by J. van der Eng and M. Grygar, 57–83. The Hague: Mouton.

Luscombe, D. E. 1992. "Peter Abelard." In *A History of Twelfth-Century Western Philosophy,* edited by P. Dronke, 279–307. Cambridge: Cambridge University Press.

Lyons, John. 1995 [1977]. *Linguistic Semantics: An Introduction.* New York: Cambridge.

Malinowski, Bronislaw. 1938. "The Problem of Meaning in Primitive Languages." In *The Meaning of Meaning: A Study of the Influence of Language upon Thought and of the Science of Symbolism,* edited by C. K. Ogden and I. A. Richards, 296–336. New York: Harcourt, Brace.

Manetti, Giovanni. 1993. *Theories of the Sign in Classical Antiquity.* Translated by Christine Richardson. Bloomington: Indiana University Press.

Marin, Louis. 2001a. "Depositing Time in Painted Representations." In *On Representation,* translated by Catherine Porter, 285–305. Stanford, CA: Stanford University Press.

———. 2001b. "The Frame of Representation and Some of Its Figures." In *On Representation,* translated by Catherine Porter, 352–72. Stanford, CA: Stanford University Press.

Martens, Ekkehard. 1981. "C. S. Peirce on Speech Acts." In *Proceedings of the C. S. Peirce Bicentennial International Congress,* edited by Kenneth L. Ketner, Joseph M. Ransdell, Carolyn Eisele, Max H. Fisch, and Charles S. Hardwick, 289–92. Lubbock: Texas Tech Press.

Martin, Richard P. 1998. "The Seven Sages as Performers of Wisdom." In *Cultural Poetics in Archaic Greece: Cult, Performance, Politics*, edited by C. Dougherty and L. Kurke, 108–28. New York: Oxford University Press.

Marx, Karl. 1904. *A Contribution to the Critique of Political Economy*. Translated by N. I. Stone. New York: International Library Publishing

———. 1963 [1846–1847]. *The Poverty of Philosophy*. New York: International Publishers.

———. 1964 [1844]. *The Economic and Philosophic Manuscripts of 1844*. Edited by D. J. Stuik, translated by Martin Milligan. New York: International Publishers.

———. 1973 [1857–1858]. *Grundrisse: Foundations of the Critique of Political Economy*. Translated by Martin Nicolaus. New York: Vintage Books.

———. 1976 [1867]. *Capital: A Critique of Political Economy*. Vol. 1. Translated by Ben Fowkes. New York: Vintage Books.

———. 1981 [1894]. *Capital: A Critique of Political Economy*. Vol. 3. Translated by David Fernbach. London: Penguin.

———. 1989 [1881]. "Drafts of a Letter to Vera Zasulich." In *Marx and Engels Collected Works*, vol. 24, 346–69. London: Lawrence & Wishart.

———. 1994 [1861–1863]. "Economic Manuscripts of 1861–63." Translated by Ben Fowkes. In *Marx and Engels Collected Works*, vol. 34. London: Lawrence & Wishart.

———. 2010a [1879–1880]. "[Marginal Notes on Adolph Wagner's *Lehrbuch der Politischen Oekonomie*.]" In *Marx and Engels Collected Works*, vol. 24, 531–59. London: Lawrence & Wishart.

———. 2010b [1837]. "[Marx to His Father]." In *Marx and Engels Collected Works*, vol. 1, 10–21. London: Lawrence & Wishart.

Marx, Karl, and Frederick Engels. 1970 [1845–1846]. *The German Ideology*. Edited by C. J. Arthur. New York: International Publishers.

———. 2002 [1848]. *The Communist Manifesto*. Translated by Samuel Moore. London: Penguin.

Mauss, Marcel. 1969 [1914]. "Les origines de la notion de monnaie." In *Oeuvres*, vol. 2, edited by Viktor Karady, 106–12. Paris: Editiones de Minuit.

McCluer, John. 1791. "Voyage to the Pelew Islands in the H. C. Snow Panther." Typescript in Palau Museum Library. Original manuscript in British Library.

McDowell, Nancy. 1988. "A Note on Cargo Cults and Cultural Constructions of Change." *Pacific Studies* 11 (2): 121–43.

McKeon, Richard, ed. 1930. *Selections from Medieval Philosophers*. 2 vols. New York: Charles Scribner's Sons.

Mead, Margaret. 1964. "Vicissitudes of the Study of the Total Communication Process." In *Approaches to Semiotics: Cultural Anthropology, Education, Linguistics, Psychiatry, Psychology*, edited by T. A. Sebeok, A. S. Hayes, and M. C. Bateson, 277–87. The Hague: Mouton.

Merrell, Floyd. 1997. *Peirce, Signs, and Meaning*. Toronto: University of Toronto Press.

Mertz, Elizabeth. 1985. "Beyond Symbolic Anthropology: Introducing Semiotic Mediation." In *Semiotic Mediation: Sociocultural and Psychological Perspectives*, edited by Elizabeth Mertz and Richard J. Parmentier, 1–22. Orlando: Academic Press.

———. 1996. "Recontextualization as Socialization: Text and Pragmatics in the Law School Classroom." In *Natural Histories of Discourse*, edited by Michael Silverstein and Greg Urban, 229–52. Chicago: University of Chicago Press.

Mertz, Elizabeth, and Richard J. Parmentier, eds. 1985. *Semiotic Mediation: Sociocultural and Psychological Perspectives*. Orlando: Academic Press.

Meskell, Lynn. 2004. "Statue Worlds and Divine Things." In *Object Worlds in Ancient Egypt: Material Biographies Past and Present*, 87–116. Oxford: Berg.

Miller, Andrew M. 1993. "Pindaric Mimesis: The Associative Mode," *The Classical Journal* 89 (1): 21–53.

———. 1996. *Greek Lyric: An Anthology in Translation*. Indianapolis: Hackett.

Miller, Patricia Cox. 2009. "Dazzling Bodies." In *The Corporeal Imagination: Signifying the Holy in Late Antique Christianity*, 62–81. Philadelphia: University of Pennsylvania Press.

Monelle, Raymond. 1991. "Music and the Peircean Trichotomies." *International Review of the Aesthetics and Sociology of Music* 22 (1): 99–108.

Moore, Edward C., ed. 1993. *Charles S. Peirce and the Philosophy of Science*. Tuscaloosa: University of Alabama Press.

Morenz, Siegfried. 1973. *Egyptian Religion*. Translated by Ann E. Keep. Ithaca, NY: Cornell University Press.

Morgan, Kathryn A. 1993. "Pindar the Professional and the Rhetoric of the ΚΩΜΟΣ." *Classical Philology* 88 (1): 1–15.

———. 2015. *Pindar and the Construction of Syracusan Monarchy in the 5th Century B.C.* Oxford: Oxford University Press.

Morris, Charles. 1939. "Esthetics and the Theory of Signs." *Erkenntnis* 8: 131–50.

Morrison, A. D. 2011. "Pindar and the Aeginetan *Patrai*: Pindar's Intersecting Audiences." In *Archaic and Classical Choral Song: Performance, Politics, and Dissemination*, edited by Lucia Athanassaki and Ewen Bowie, 311–35. Berlin: de Gruyter.

———. 2012. "Performance, Re-Performance, and Pindar's Audiences." In *Reading the Victory Ode*, edited by Peter Agócs, Chris Carey, and Richard Rawles, 111–33. Cambridge: Cambridge University Press.

Morrison, Karl F. 1990. *History as a Visual Art in the Twelfth Century Renaissance*. Princeton, NJ: Princeton University Press.

Most, Glenn W. 1986. "Pindar, *O.* 2.83–90." *The Classical Quarterly* 36 (2): 304–16.

Muellner, Leonard. 1996. *The Anger of Achilles: Mênis in Greek Epic*. Ithaca, NY: Cornell University Press.

Mukařovský, Jan. 1979. *Aesthetic Function, Norm and Value as Social Facts*. Translated by M. E. Suino. Ann Arbor: Michigan Slavic Contributions.

Munn, Nancy. 1983. "Gawan Kula: Spatiotemporal Control and the Symbolism of Influence." In *The Kula: New Perspectives on Massim Exchange*, edited by J. A. Leach and E. Leach, 277–308. Cambridge: Cambridge University Press.

Murphey, Murray G. 1961. *The Development of Peirce's Philosophy*. Cambridge: Harvard University Press.

Nagy, Gregory. 1979. *The Best of the Achaeans: Concepts of the Hero in Ancient Greek Poetry*. Baltimore: Johns Hopkins University Press.

———. 1990a. "Early Greek Views of Poets and Poetry." In *The Cambridge History of Literary Criticism*. Vol. 1, *Classical Criticism*, edited by George Alexander Kennedy, 1–77. Cambridge: Cambridge University Press.

———. 1990b. *Pindar's Homer: The Lyric Possession of an Epic Past*. Baltimore: Johns Hopkins University Press.

———. 1990c. "Sema and Nóēsis: The Hero's Tomb and the 'Reading' of Symbols in Homer and Hesiod." In *Greek Mythology and Poetics*, 202–22. Ithaca, NY: Cornell University Press.

———. 1992. "Homeric Questions." *Transactions of the American Philological Association* 122: 17–60.

———. 1995. "An Evolutionary Model for the Making of Homeric Poetry: Comparative Perspectives." In *The Ages of Homer*, edited by J. B. Carter and S. P. Morris, 163–80. Austin: University of Texas Press.

———. 1996. "Mimesis of Homer and Beyond." In *Poetry as Performance: Homer and Beyond*, 59–86. Cambridge: Cambridge University Press.

———. 1997. "Ellipsis in Homer." In *Written Voices, Spoken Signs: Tradition, Performance, and the Epic Text*, 167–89. Washington, DC: Center for Hellenic Studies.

———. 2001. "Homeric Poetry and Problems of Multiformity: The 'Panathenaic Bottleneck.'" *Classical Philology* 96 (2): 109–19.

———. 2002. *Plato's Rhapsody and Homer's Music: The Poetics of the Panathenaic Festival in Classical Athens*. Washington, DC: Center for Hellenic Studies.

———. 2003. "Homeric Rhapsodes and the Concept of Diachronic Skewing." In *Homeric Responses*, 39–48. Austin: University of Texas Press.

———. 2004. "Transmission of Archaic Greek Sympotic Songs: From Lesbos to Alexandria." *Critical Inquiry* 31: 26–48.

———. 2011. "A Second Look at the Poetics of Re-enactment in *Ode* 13 of Bacchylides." In *Archaic and Classical Choral Song: Performance, Politics, and Dissemination*, edited by Lucia Athanassaki and Ewen Bowie, 173–206. Berlin: de Gruyter.

Nash, June. 1997. "Gendered Deities and the Survival of Culture." *History of Religions* 36: 333–56.

Newfield, Madeleine, and Linda R. Waugh. 1991. "Invariance and Markedness in Grammatical Categories." In *New Vistas in Grammar: Invariance and Variation*, edited by L. R. Waugh and S. Rudy, 221–38. Amsterdam: John Benjamins.

Nichols, Stephen G., Jr. 1983. *Romanesque Signs: Early Medieval Narrative and Iconography*. New Haven, CT: Yale University Press.

Nisetich, F. J. 1980. *Pindar's Victory Songs*. Baltimore: Johns Hopkins University Press.

Ogden, C. K., and I. A. Richards. 1938 [1923]. *The Meaning of Meaning: A Study of the Influence of Language upon Thought and of the Science of Symbolism*. New York: Harcourt, Brace.

Ortner, Sherry. 1995. "Resistance and the Problem of Ethnographic Refusal." *Comparative Studies in Society and History* 37: 173–93.

Osborne, Douglas. 1966. *The Archaeology of the Palau Islands: An Intensive Survey*. Bernice P. Bishop Museum Bulletin no. 230. Honolulu: Bishop Museum Press.

———. 1979. *Archaeological Test Excavations, Palau Islands, 1968–1969*. *Micronesica* Supplement 1. Agana, Guam: University of Guam.

Panofsky, Erwin. 1979. *Abbot Suger on the Abbey Church of St.-Denis and Its Art Treasures*. Princeton, NJ: Princeton University Press.

Pape, Helmut. 1996. "Object and Final Cause in Peirce's Semeiotic." In *Peirce's Doctrine of Signs: Theory, Application, and Connections*, edited by V. M. Colapietro and T. M. Olshewsky, 103–18. Berlin: Mouton de Gruyter.

———. 1999. "Why We Mean Always More and Sometimes Less Than We Say: Context-Dependence and Vagueness in Peirce's Semiotics." In *Proceedings of the International Colloquium on Language and Peircean Sign Theory*, edited by M. Shapiro and M. Haley, 590–621. New York: Berghahn.

Paris, Matthew. 1986. *Chronicles of Matthew Paris: Monastic Life in the Thirteenth Century*. Translated by Richard Vaughan. New York: St. Martin's Press.

Parmentier, Richard J. 1984. "House Affiliation System in Belau." *American Ethnologist* 11: 656–76.

———. 1985a. "Signs' Place *in medias res*: Peirce's Concept of Semiotic Mediation." In *Semiotic Mediation: Sociocultural and Psychological Perspective*, edited by Elizabeth Mertz and Richard J. Parmentier, 23–48. Orlando: Academic Press.

———. 1985b. "Times of the Signs: Modalities of History and Levels of Social Structure in Belau." In *Semiotic Mediation: Sociocultural and Psychological Perspectives*, edited by Elizabeth Mertz and Richard J. Parmentier, 131–54. Orlando: Academic Press.

———. 1987. *The Sacred Remains: Myth, History, and Polity in Belau*. Chicago: University of Chicago Press.

———. 1994a. "Comment on Byers, Symboling and the Middle-Upper Palaeolithic Transition." *Current Anthropology* 35: 388–89.

———. 1994b. "Naturalization of Convention." In *Signs in Society: Studies in Semiotic Anthropology*, 175–92. Bloomington: Indiana University Press.

———. 1994c. *Signs in Society: Studies in Semiotic Anthropology*. Bloomington: Indiana University Press.

———. 1994d. "Transactional Symbolism in Belauan Mortuary Rites." In *Signs in Society: Studies in Semiotic Anthropology*, 47–69. Bloomington: Indiana University Press.

———. 1997a. "Charles S. Peirce." In *Handbook of Pragmatics*, edited by Jef Verschueren, Jan-Ola Östman, and Jan Blommaert, 1–18. Amsterdam: John Benjamins.

———. 1997b. "The Pragmatic Semiotics of Cultures." *Semiotica*, 116–21.

———. 2009. "Troubles with Trichotomies: Reflections on the Utility of Peirce's Sign Trichotomies for Social Analysis." *Semiotica* 177: 139–56.

———. 2012. "Anthropological Encounters of a Semiotic Kind." *RS/SI* 32: 187–99.

———. 2014. "Semiotic Degeneracy of Social Life: Prolegomenon to a Human Science of Semiosis." *Semiotica* 202: 1–20.

Parret, Herman. 1983. "The Homologation of Semiotics and Pragmatics." In *Semiotics and Pragmatics: An Evaluative Comparison of Conceptual Frameworks*. Amsterdam: Benjamins.

———. 1986. "Pragmatics." In *Encyclopedic Dictionary of Semiotics*, edited by T. A. Sebeok, 751–60. Berlin: Mouton de Gruyter.

Pasztory, Esther. 2005. *Thinking with Things: Toward a New Vision of Art*. Austin: University of Texas Press.

Patten, Glenn. 2009. *Pindar's Metaphors: A Study in Rhetoric and Meaning*. Heidelberg: Winter.

Patton, Kimberley Christine. 2009. "The Problem Defined and a Proposed Solution: Divine Reflexivity in Ritual Representation." In *Religion of the Gods: Ritual, Paradox, and Reflexivity*, 161–80. New York: Oxford University Press.

Pavlou, Maria. 2010. "Pindar *Olympian* 3: Mapping Acragas on the Periphery of the Earth." *Classical Quarterly* 60 (2): 313–26.

Peirce, Charles S. 1865–1909. *MS* 339. "Logic." (Peirce manuscripts as identified in Robin [1967]).

———. c. 1902. *MS* 599. "Reason's Rules." (Peirce manuscripts as identified in Robin [1967]).

———. c. 1903. *MS* 7. "On the Foundations of Mathematics." (Peirce manuscripts as identified in Robin [1967]).

———. 1906. *MS* 793. "On Signs." (Peirce manuscripts as identified in Robin [1967]).

———. 1907. *MS* 318. "Pragmatism." (Peirce manuscripts as identified in Robin [1967]).

———. 1909. *MS* 637. (Peirce manuscripts as identified in Robin [1967]).

———. 1909. MS 634. "Preface." (Peirce manuscripts as identified in Robin [1967]).

———. 1910. *MS* 654. "Essays." (Peirce manuscripts as identified in Robin [1967]).

———. 1912. *MS* 12. "Notes Preparatory to a Criticism of Bertrand Russell's Principles of Mathematics." (Peirce manuscripts as identified in Robin [1967]).

———. 1931–1966. *Collected Papers of Charles Sanders Peirce.* 8 vols. Edited by Charles Hartshorne, Paul Weiss, and A. W. Burks. Cambridge, MA: Harvard University Press. [cited as *CP*].

———. 1933. *Collected Papers of Charles Sanders Peirce.* Vol. 3, *Exact Logic (Published Papers)* Edited by Charles Hartshorne and Paul Weiss. Cambridge, MA: Belknap Press of Harvard University Press. [cited as *CP* 3].

———. 1934. *Collected Papers of Charles Sanders Peirce.* Vol. 5, *Pragmatism and Pragmaticism.* Edited by Charles Hartshorne and Paul Weiss. Cambridge, MA: Belknap Press of Harvard University Press. [cited as *CP* 5].

———. 1975–1979. *Charles Sanders Peirce: Contributions to* The Nation. 3 vols. Edited by Kenneth Laine Ketner and James Edward Cook. Lubbock: Texas Tech Press. [cited as *N*].

———. 1976. *The New Elements of Mathematics.* 4 vols. Edited by Carolyn Eisele. The Hague: Mouton. [cited as *NEM*].

———. 1978 [1894]. Unsigned review of Thomas H. Huxley, "Method and Results: Essays." In *Charles Sanders Peirce: Contributions to* The Nation: *1894–1900* (vol. 2), edited by Kenneth Laine Ketner and James Edward Cook, 19–23. Lubbock: Texas Tech Press.

———. 1982–2010. *Writings of Charles S. Peirce: A Chronological Edition.* 8 vols. Edited by the Peirce Edition Project. Bloomington: Indiana University Press. [cited as *W*].

———. 1986 [1873]. "On Representation." In *Writings of Charles S. Peirce: A Chronological Edition, 1872–1878*, vol. 3, edited by Christian J. W. Kloesel, 62–75. Bloomington: Indiana University Press.

———. 1992 [1898]. *Reasoning and the Logic of Things.* Edited by K. L. Ketner. Cambridge: Harvard University Press. [cited as *RLT*].

———. 1998. *The Essential Peirce: Selected Philosophical Writings.* Vol. 2. Edited by the Peirce Edition Project. Bloomington: Indiana University Press. [cited as *EP* 2].

———. 2000. *Writings of Charles S. Peirce: A Chronological Edition, 1886–1890*, vol. 6, edited by the Peirce Edition Project. Bloomington: Indiana University Press.

———. 2010. *Writings of Charles S. Peirce: A Chronological Edition, 1890–1892*, vol. 8, edited by the Peirce Edition Project. Bloomington: Indiana University Press.

———. *MS* 693. [Peirce manuscripts as identified in Robin (1967)]

Pelliccia, Hayden. 1987. "Pindarus Homericus: *Pythian* 3.1–80." *Harvard Studies in Classical Philology* 91: 39–63.

Perrino, Sabina. 2007. "Cross-Chronotope Alignment in Senegalese Oral Narrative." *Language & Communication* 27: 227–44.

Petrucci, Armando. 1995. *Writers and Readers in Medieval Italy: Studies in the History of Written Culture.* Translated by Charles M. Radding. New Haven, CT: Yale University Press.

Pfeijffer, I. L. 2004. "Pindar and Bacchylids." In *Narrators, Narratees, and Narratives in Ancient Greek Literature: Studies in Ancient Greek Narrative,* edited by Irene F. J. de Jong, 213–32. Leiden, Netherlands: Brill.

Piltz, Anders. 1981. *The World of Medieval Learning.* Translated by David Jones. London: Blackwell.

Porter Poole, Fitz John. 1994. "The Reason of Myth and the Rationality of History: The Logic of the Mythic in Bimin-Kuskusmin Modes of Thought." In *Religion and Practical Reason: New Essays in the Comparative Philosophy of Religions,* edited by F. E. Reynolds and D. Tracy, 263–326. Albany: SUNY Press.

Portis-Winner, Irene. 1986. "Semiotics of Culture." In *Frontiers in Semiotics,* edited by J. Deely, B. Williams, and F. E. Kruse, 181–84. Bloomington: Indiana University Press.

———. 2002. *Semiotics of Peasants in Transition: Slovene Villagers and their Ethnic Relatives.* Durham, NC: Duke University Press.

Potter, Vincent G. 1996. "Peirce's Pragmatic Maxim: Realist or Nominalist?" In *Peirce's Philosophical Perspectives,* edited by Vincent M. Colapietro, 91–102. New York: Fordham University Press.

Preston, James J. 1985. "Creation of the Sacred Image: Apotheosis and Destruction in Hinduism." In *Gods of Flesh, Gods of Stone,* edited by J. P. Waghorne and N. Cutler, 8–30. Chambersburg, PA: Anima.

Preucel, Robert W. 2006. *Archaeological Semiotics.* Malden, MA: Blackwell.

Price, Simon. 1999. *Religions of the Ancient Greeks.* Cambridge: Cambridge University Press.

Quirke, Stephen. 1992. *Ancient Egyptian Religion.* New York: Dover.

Radding, Charles M., and Francis Newton. 2003. *Theology, Rhetoric, and Politics in the Eucharistic Controversy 1078–1079: Alberic of Monte Cassino against Berengar of Tours.* New York: Columbia University Press.

Rappaport, Roy. 1999. *Ritual and Religion in the Making of Humanity.* Cambridge, MA: Cambridge University Press.

Rethore, Joelle. 1994. "A Survey of the Use and Usefulness of Peirce in Linguistics, in France in Particular." In *Living Doubt: Essays Concerning the Epistemology of Charles Sanders Peirce,* edited by G. Debrock, and M. Hulswit, 275–88. Dordrecht, Netherlands: Kluwer Academic Publishers.

Ricoeur, Paul. 1971. "The Model of the Text: Meaningful Action Considered as a Text." *Social Research* 38 (3): 529–62.

Riegel, Klaus F. 1979. *Foundations of Dialectical Psychology.* New York: Academic Press.

Ritzenthaler, Robert E. 1954. *Native Money of Palau.* Publications in Anthropology No. l. Milwaukee: Milwaukee Public Museum.

Robin, Richard S. 1967. *Annotated Catalogue of the Papers of Charles S. Peirce.* Amherst: University of Massachusetts Press.

———. 1997. "Classical Pragmatism and Pragmatism's Proof." In *The Rule of Reason: The Philosophy of Charles Sanders Peirce,* edited by J. Brunning and P. Forster, 139–52. Toronto: University of Toronto Press.

Robins, Gay. 1994. *Proportion and Style in Ancient Egyptian Art*. Austin: University of Texas Press.

———. 2005. "Cult Statues in Ancient Egypt." In *Cult Image and Divine Representation in the Ancient Near East*, edited by Neal H. Walls, 1–12. Boston: American School of Oriental Research.

———. 2008. *The Art of Ancient Egypt*. Rev. ed. Cambridge, MA: Harvard University Press.

Rose, Peter W. 1992. *Sons of the Gods, Children of Earth: Ideology and Literary Form in Ancient Greece*. Ithaca, NY: Cornell University Press.

Rosenthal, Sandra B. 1994. *Charles Peirce's Pragmatic Pluralism*. Albany: SUNY Press.

Rossi-Landi, Ferruccio. 1973. "Commodities as Messages." In *Recherches sur les Systéme Signifiants*, edited by J. Rey-Debove, 625–31. Paris: Mouton.

———. 1983. *Language as Work and Play: A Semiotic Homology for Linguistics and Economics*. South Hadley, MA: Bergin.

Rubin, Miri. 1991. *Corpus Christi: The Eucharist in Late Medieval Culture*. Cambridge: Cambridge University Press.

Sahlins, Marshall D. 1981. *Historical Metaphors and Mythical Realities: Structure in the Early History of the Sandwich Islands Kingdom*. Ann Arbor: University of Michigan Press.

———. 1985. *Islands of History*. Chicago: University of Chicago Press.

Salmond, Noel A. 2004. *Hindu Iconoclasts: Rammohun Roy, Dayananda Sarasvati, and Nineteenth-Century Polemics against Idolatry*. Waterloo, CAN: Wilfrid Laurier University Press.

Sarangi, Srikant. 1995. "Culture." In *Handbook of Pragmatics*, edited by J. Verschueren, Jan-Ola Östman, and Jan Blommaert, 1–30. Amsterdam: John Benjamins.

Saussure, Ferdinand de. 1959 [1915]. *Course in General Linguistics*. Translated by Wade Baskin. New York: McGraw-Hill.

———. 2006 [2002]. *Writings in General Linguistics*. Edited by Simon Bouquet and Rudolf Engler, translated by Carol Sanders and Matthew Pires. Oxford: Oxford University Press.

Savan, David. 1987. *An Introduction to C. S. Peirce's Full System of Semiotic*. Monographs Series of the Toronto Semiotic Circle l. Toronto: Victoria College.

Schadewaldt, Wolfgang. 1928. *Der Aufbau des Pindarischen Epinikion*. Halle (Saale), Germany: Niemeyer.

Schmid, Wolf. 2010. *Narratology: An Introduction*. Berlin: Walter de Gruyter.

Schneider, David. 1976. "Notes toward a Theory of Culture." In *Meaning in Anthropology*, edited by K. H. Basso and H. A. Selby, 196–220. Albuquerque: University of New Mexico Press.

Schwartz, Benjamin I. 1975a. "The Age of Transcendence." *Daedalus* 104 (2): 1–8.

———. 1975b. "Transcendence in Ancient China." *Daedalus* 104 (2): 57–68.

Schwimmer, Erik. 1969. *Cultural Consequences of a Volcanic Eruption Experienced by the Mount Lamington Orokaiva*. Eugene: University of Oregon, Department of Anthropology.

———. 1986. "Icons of Identity." In *Iconicity: Essays on the Nature of Culture*, edited by P. Bouissac, M. Herzfeld, and R. Posner, 359–84. Tübingen, Germany: Stauffenburg Verlag.

———. 1990. "The Anthropology of the Ritual Arts." In *Art and Identity in Oceania*, edited by F. A. Hanson, 6–14. Honolulu: University of Hawaii Press.

Scodel, Ruth. 1995. "Self-Correction, Spontaneity, and Orality in Archaic Poetry." In *Voice into Text*, edited by Ian Worthington, 59–80. *Mnemosyne-Supplementum*. Leiden, Netherlands: Brill.

Sebeok, Thomas A. 1995a. "Indexicality." In *Peirce and Contemporary Thought: Philosophical Inquiries*, edited by K. L. Ketner, 222–43. New York: Fordham University Press.

———. 1995b. "Semiotics and the Biological Sciences: Initial Conditions." Keynote address, First Annual Conference of the Semiotics Research Unit of the University of Toronto.

———. 1997. "Global Semiotics." In *Semiotics around the World*, edited by I. Rauch and G. F. Carr, 105–30. Berlin: Mouton de Gruyter.

Sebeok, Thomas A., and Marcel Danesi. 2000. *The Forms of Meaning: Modeling Systems Theory and Semiotic Analysis*. Berlin: Mouton de Gruyter.

Sebeok, Thomas A., Alfred S. Hayes, and Mary Catherine Bateson, eds. 1964. *Approaches to Semiotics: Cultural Anthropology, Education, Linguistics, Psychiatry, Psychology*. The Hague: Mouton.

Semino, Elena. 1992. "Building on Keith Green's 'Deixis and the Poetic Persona': Further Reflections on Deixis in Poetry." *Language and Literature* 1 (2): 135–40.

Semper, Karl. 1982 [1873]. *The Palau Islands in the Pacific Ocean*. Translated by Mark L. Berg. Agana, Guam: University of Guam, Micronesian Area Research Center.

Sfyroeras, P. 2003. "Olive Trees, North Wind, and Time: A Symbol in Pindar, *Olympian* 3." *Mouseion: Journal of the Classical Association of Canada* 3 (3): 313–24.

Shapiro, Michael. 1981. "Peirce's Interpretant from the Perspective of Linguistic Theory." In *Proceedings of the C. S. Peirce Bicentennial International Conference*, edited by Kenneth L. Ketner, Joseph M. Ransdell, Carolyn Eisele, Max H. Fisch, and Charles S. Hardwick, 313–18. Lubbock: Texas Tech Press.

Shell, Marc. 1978. *The Economy of Literature*. Baltimore: Johns Hopkins University Press.

Shelmerdine, Susan C. 1987. "Pindaric Praise and the Third *Olympian*." *Harvard Studies in Classical Philology* 91: 65–81.

Short, T. L. 1989. "Why We Prefer Peirce to Saussure." In *Semiotics 1988*, edited by T. Prewitt, J. Deely, and K. Haworth, 124–30. Lanham, MD: University Press of America.

———. 2004. "The Development of Peirce's Theory of Signs." In *The Cambridge Companion to Peirce*, edited by C. Misak, 214–39. Cambridge: Cambridge University Press.

Silk, Michael. 1998. "Pindar's Poetry and the Obligatory Crux: *Isthmian* 5:55–63, Text and Interpretation." *Transactions of the American Philological Association* 128: 25–88.

———. 2007. "Pindar's Poetry as Poetry: A Literary Commentary on *Olympian* 12." In *Pindar's Poetry, Patrons, and Festivals: From Archaic Greece to the Roman Empire*, edited by Simon Hornblower and Catherine Morgan, 177–98. Oxford: Oxford University Press.

Silverstein, Michael. 1975. "La sémiotique Jakobsonienne et l'anthropologie sociale." *L'Arc* 60: 45–49.

———. 1976. "Shifters, Linguistic Categories, and Cultural Description." In *Meaning in Anthropology*, edited by K. H. Basso and H. A. Selby, 11–55. Albuquerque: University of New Mexico Press.

———. 1981. "Metaforces of Power in Traditional Oratory." Unpublished lecture.

———. 1985. "The Functional Stratification of Language and Ontogenesis." In *Culture, Communication, and Cognition: Vygotskian Perspectives*, edited by J. W. Wertsch, 205–35. Cambridge: Cambridge University Press.

———. 1992. "The Indeterminacy of Contextualization: When Is Enough Enough?" In *The Contextualization of Language*, edited by P. Auer and A. Di Luzio, 55–76. Amsterdam: John Benjamins.

———. 1993. "Metapragmatic Discourse and Metapragmatic Function." In *Reflexive Language: Reported Speech and Metapragmatics,* edited by J. Lucy, 33–58. Cambridge: Cambridge University Press.

———. 1996. "The Secret Life of Texts." In *Natural Histories of Discourse*, edited by Michael Silverstein and Greg Urban, 81–105. Chicago: University of Chicago Press.

———. 1997. "Commentary: Achieving Adequacy and Commitment in Pragmatics." *Pragmatics* 7: 625–33.

———. 2003. "Indexical Order and the Dialectics of Sociolinguistic Life." *Language & Communication* 23: 193–229.

———. 2005. "Axes of Evals: Token versus Type Interdiscursivity." *Journal of Linguistic Anthropology* 15 (1): 6–22.

Silverstein, Michael, and Greg Urban. 1996. "Natural Histories of Discourse." In *Natural Histories of Discourse*, edited by Michael Silverstein and Greg Urban, 1–17. Chicago: University of Chicago Press.

Simmel, Georg. 1978 [1900]. *The Philosophy of Money*. Translated by Tom Bottomore and David Frisby. Boston: Routledge & Kegan Paul.

———. 1991. "Money in Modern Culture." Translated by Mark Ritter and Sam Whimster. *Theory, Culture & Society* 9: 17–31.

Singer, Milton. 1984. *Man's Glassy Essence: Explorations in Semiotic Anthropology*. Bloomington: Indiana University Press.

Slater, William J. 2012. *Lexicon to Pindar*. Berlin: de Gruyter.

Smith, DeVerne Reed. 1983. *Palauan Social Structure*. New Brunswick, NJ: Rutgers University Press.

Smith, Jonathan Z. 1976. "A Pearl of Great Price and a Cargo of Yams: A Study in Situational Incongruity." *History of Religions* 40: 1–19.

———. 1993 [1978]. *Map Is Not Territory: Studies in the History of Religions*. Chicago: University of Chicago Press.

———. 2001. "A Twice-Told Tale: The History of the History of Religions' History." *Numen* 48 (2): 131–46.

Smith, Mark S. 2004. *The Memoirs of God: History, Memory, and the Experience of the Divine in Ancient Israel*. Minneapolis: Fortress Press.

Snodgrass, Anthony. 1980. *Archaic Greece: The Age of Experiment*. Berkeley: University of California Press.

Southern, R. W. 1995. *Scholastic Humanism and the Unification of Europe*. Vol. 1: *Foundations*. Oxford: Blackwell.

Spinks, C. W. 1991. *Peirce and Triadomania: A Walk in the Semiotic Wilderness*. Berlin: Mouton de Gruyter.

Steiner, Deborah Tarn. 2001. *Images in Mind: Statues in Archaic and Classical Greek Literature and Thought*. Princeton, NJ: Princeton University Press.

Stock, Brian. 1973. *Myth and Science in the Twelfth Century: A Study of Bernard Silvester*. Princeton, NJ: Princeton University Press.

———. 1983. *The Implications of Literacy: Written Language and Models of Interpretation in the Eleventh and Twelfth Centuries.* Princeton, NJ: Princeton University Press.

Stocking, George W., Jr., ed. 1974. *A Franz Boas Reader: The Shaping of American Anthropology, 1883–1911.* Chicago: University of Chicago Press.

Strickland, Debra Higgs. 2007. "The Holy and the Unholy: Analogies for the Numinous in Later Medieval Art." In *Images of Medieval Sanctity: Essays in Honour of Gary Dickson*, edited by D. H. Strickland, 101–20. Leiden, Netherlands: Brill.

Struck, Peter T. 2004. *Birth of the Symbol: Ancient Readers at the Limits of Their Texts.* Princeton, NJ: Princeton University Press.

Stürzenhofecker, Gabriele. 1998. *Times Emeshed: Gender, Space, and History among the Duna of Papua New Guinea.* Stanford, CA: Stanford University Press.

Svenbro, Jesper. 1976. *Le Parole et le marbre: Aux origines de la poétique grecque.* Lund, Sweden: Studentlitteratur.

———. 1993. *Phrasikleia: An Anthropology of Reading in Ancient Greece.* Translated by Janet Lloyd. Ithaca, NY: Cornell University Press.

Tambiah, Stanley Jeyaraja. 1984. *The Buddhist Saints of the Forest and the Cult of Amulets: A Study in Charisma, Hagiography, Sectarianism and Millennial Buddhism.* Cambridge: Cambridge University Press.

Tarasti, Eero. 2002. "From *Mastersingers* to Bororo Indians: On the Semiosis of Improvisation." In *Signs in Music: A Guide to Musical Semiotics*, 161–78. Berlin: Mouton de Gruyter.

Taussig, Michael. 1980. *The Devil and Commodity Fetishism in South America.* Chapel Hill: University of North Carolina Press.

Taylor, Charles. 1999. "Forward." In Marcel Gauchet, *The Disenchantment of the World: A Political History of Religion*, ix–xv. Princeton, NJ: Princeton University Press.

———. 2011. "What Was the Axial Revolution?" In *Dilemmas and Connections: Selected Essays*, 367–79. Cambridge, MA: Belknap Press of Harvard University Press.

Teeter, Emily. 2011. *Religion and Ritual in Ancient Egypt.* Cambridge: Cambridge University Press.

Thayer, H. S. 1968. *Meaning and Action: A Critical History of Pragmatism.* Indianapolis: Bobbs-Merrill.

Thomas, Rosalind. 2007. "Fame, Memorial, and Choral Poetry: The Origins of Epinikian Poetry—An Historical Study." In *Pindar's Poetry, Patrons, and Festivals: From Archaic Greece to the Roman Empire*, edited by Simon Hornblower and Catherine Morgan, 141–60. Oxford: Oxford University Press.

———. 2012. "Pindar's 'Difficulty' and the Performance of Epinician Poetry: Some Suggestions from Ethnography." In *Reading the Victory Ode*, edited by Peter Agócs, Chris Carey, and Richard Rawles, 224–48. Cambridge: Cambridge University Press.

Thunø, Erik. 2005. "Materializing the Invisible in Early Medieval Art: The Mosaics of Santa Maria in Domnica in Rome." In *Seeing the Invisible in Late Antiquity and the Early Middle Ages*, edited by Giselle de Nie and Karl F.Morrison, 265–89. Turnhout, Belgium: Brepols.

Turner, Terence. 1988. "History, Myth, and Social Consciousness among the Kayapó of Central Brazil." In *Rethinking History and Myth: Indigenous South American Perspectives on the Past*, edited by J. D. Hill, 195–213. Urbana: University of Illinois Press.

Tweedale, Martin M. 1976. *Abailard on Universals.* Amsterdam: Elsevier.

Urban, Greg. 1985. "The Semiotics of Two Speech Styles in Shokleng." In *Semiotic Mediation: Sociocultural and Psychological Perspectives*, edited by Elizabeth Mertz and Richard J. Parmentier, 311–29. Orlando: Academic Press.

———. 1986. "Semiotic Functions of Macro-parallelism in the Shokleng Origin Myth." In *Native South American Discourses*, edited by Joel Sherzer and Greg Urban, 15–57. Berlin: Mouton de Gruyter.

Urban, Greg, and Kristin Smith. 1998. "The Sunny Tropics of Dialogue?" *Semiotica* 121 (3/4): 263–81.

Useem, John. 1949. *Report on Palau*. Coordinated Investigations in Micronesian Anthropology Report no. 21. Washington, DC: Pacific Science Board.

Valeri, Valerio. 1985. *Kingship and Sacrifice: Ritual and Society in Ancient Hawaii*. Translated by Paula Wissing. Chicago: University of Chicago Press.

Vance, Eugene. 1986. *Mervelous Signals: Poetics and Sign Theory in the Middle Ages*. Lincoln: University of Nebraska Press.

———. 1987. *From Topic to Tale: Logic and Narrativity in the Middle Ages*. Minneapolis: University of Minnesota Press.

Van Dijk, Jacobus. 2002. "The Amarna Period and the Late New Kingdom c. 1352–1069 BC." In *The Oxford History of Egypt*, edited by I. Shaw, 265–307. New York: Oxford University Press.

Van Tilburg, Jo Anne. 1991. "Anthropomorphic Stone Monoliths on the Islands of Koror and Babeldaob, Republic of Belau Palau, Micronesia." *Bishop Museum Occasional Papers* 31: 3–62.

Vaughan, Genevieve. 1980. "Communication and Exchange." *Semiotica* 29 (1/2): 113–43.

Vegetti, Mario. 1995. "The Greeks and Their Gods." In *The Greeks*, edited by Jean-Pierre Vernant, 254–84, translated by Charles Lambert and Teresa Lavender Fagan. Chicago: University of Chicago Press.

Vernant, Jean-Pierre. 1991. *Mortals and Immortals: Collected Essays*. Edited by Froma I. Zeitlin. Princeton, NJ: Princeton University Press.

Vidich, Arthur J. 1949. *Political Factionalism in Palau: Its Rise and Development*. Coordinated Investigations in Micronesian Anthropology Report no. 23. Washington, DC: Pacific Science Board.

Vikan, Gary. 1989. "Ruminations on Edible Icons: Originals and Copies in the Art of Byzantium." In *Retaining the Original: Multiple Originals, Copies, and Reproductions. Studies in the History of Art*, edited by Kathleen Preciado, 20. Washington, DC: National Gallery of Art.

Von den Hoff, Ralf. 2012. "Horror and Amazement: Colossal Mythological Statue Groups and the New Rhetoric of the Image in Late Second and Early Third Century Rome." In *Paidea: The World of the Second Sophistic*, edited by Barbara E. Borg, 105–129. Berlin: de Gruyter.

Walker, Jeffrey. 2000. "A 'Truest Paradigm of Western Lyric': Pindar, *Isthmian* 3, and *Olympian* 1." In *Rhetoric and Poetics in Antiquity*, 185–207. Oxford: Oxford University Press.

Watt, W. C. 1984. "Signs of the Times." *Semiotica* 50 (1/2): 97–155.

Waugh, Linda. 1982. "Marked and Unmarked: A Choice between Unequals in Semiotic Structure." *Semiotica* 38 (3/4): 299–318.

———. 1992. "Let's Take the Con Out of Iconicity: Constraints on Iconicity in the Lexicon." *American Journal of Semiotics* 9: 7–48.

Weiner, Annette B. 1992. *Inalienable Possessions: The Paradox of Keeping-While-Giving* Berkeley: University of California Press.

———. 1994. "Cultural Difference and the Density of Objects." *American Ethnologist* 21: 391–401.

Wells, James Bradley. 2009. *Pindar's Verbal Art: An Ethnographic Study of Epinician Style*. Washington, DC: Center for Hellenic Studies.

West, Cornel. 1989. *The American Evasion of Philosophy: A Genealogy of Pragmatism*. Madison: University of Wisconsin Press.

Winter, Irene J. 1992. "Idols of the King: Royal Images as Recipients of Ritual Action in Ancient Mesopotamia." *Journal of Ritual Studies* 6: 13–42.

———. 2000. "The Eyes Have It: Votive Statuary, Gilgamesh's Axe, and Cathected Viewing in the Ancient Near East." In *Visuality Before and Beyond the Renaissance*, edited by Robert S. Nelson, 22–44. Cambridge: Cambridge University Press.

———. 2002. "Defining 'Aesthetics' for Non-Western Studies: The Case of Ancient Mesopotamia." In *Art History, Aesthetics, Visual Studies*, edited by Michael Ann Holly and Keith Moxey, 3–28. Williamstown, MA: Sterling and Francine Clark Art Institute.

Wirtz, Kristina. 2007. "Enregistered Memory and Afro-Cuban Historicity in Santería Ritual Speech." *Language & Communication* 27: 245–57.

Wolf, Werner. 2006. "Framing Borders in Frame Stories." In *Framing Borders in Literature and Media*, edited by Werner Wolf and W. Bernhart, 179–206. Amsterdam: Rodopi.

Wu, Yunqiu. 1994. "Peirce's Arguments for His Pragmaticist Maxim." In *Living Doubt: Essays Concerning the Epistemology of Charles Sanders Peirce*, edited by G. Debrock and M. Hulswit, 67–77. Dordrecht, Netherlands: Kluwer Academic Publishers.

Young, David C. 1968. *Three Odes of Pindar: A Literary Study of* Pythian 2, Pythian 3, *and* Olympian 7. Leiden, Netherlands: Brill.

———. 1982. "Pindar." In *Ancient Writers: Greece and Rome*, vol. 1, *Homer to Caesar*, edited by Y. J. Luce, 157–77. New York: Scribner's.

———. 1983. "Pindar *Pythians* 2 and 3: Inscriptional ποτέ and the 'Poetic Epistle.'" *Harvard Studies in Classical Philology* 87: 31–48.

Zinn, Grover A., Jr. 1986. "Suger, Theology, and the Pseudo-Dionysian Tradition." In *Abbot Suger and Saint-Denis: A Symposium*, edited by Paula Lieber Gerson, 33–40. New York: Metropolitan Museum of Art.

Index

Affinal exchange, 9, 169–70
Anagogical symbolism, 195
Aniconic representation, 14, 119
Arbitrariness, 5, 9, 11, 21, 38, 95, 203
Archaeology, 58–60
Aristotle, 4, 25, 86, 140
Assmann, Jan, 198–201
Axial Age, 119, 197–98

Bedos-Rezak, Brigitte Miriam, 58, 96–99,
    127–30
Benveniste, Emile, 123
Boas, Franz, 76, 127, 132, 263
Bogatyrev, Petr, 6–7
Bourdieu, Pierre, 54, 88, 136

Chuuk (Micronesia), 107–10, 113–19
Circle of semiosis, 203, 205
Collateral acquaintance, 34–35
Commodity form, 145–54, 157–59
Comparison, 18, 70–71, 99, 110–16, 119, 158, 227
Complexity, 19, 53–55, 94
Conventionality, 4, 53, 58, 106
Cultural text, 17–18, 20, 135

Daniel, E. Valentine, 14
Deixis, 34, 99, 123, 215–17, 219, 228
Degeneracy, 54, 63–77
Denotational text, 124–26
Diachronic skewing, 127, 134–35
Diachrony, 7, 10, 21, 135, 228
Dialogue, 33, 66

Emic/etic, 111–12, 118–19, 145, 158
Entextualization, 15, 40, 105, 123, 125, 128, 133–34,
    209–10, 227
Ethnosemiotics, 17, 22, 61, 129, 134,
Exchange, 9, 21, 53, 95, 106, 150–51, 164–72, 177
Exchange-value, 146–57, 180

Felson, Nancy, 90–92, 99
Fetishism, 152–53, 156
Functional universals, 118–19, 112–14

Goodenough, Ward, 106–19

Herzfeld, Michael, 17, 21, 85–86

Icons, indexical, 60, of identity, 14; religious, 5,
    7, 52, 57–58, 97–98, 193
Iconicity, 17, 29, 34, 52, 57, 59
Iconoclasm, 58
Ideology, 15–16, 60, 95, 97, 135, 140, 156, 158; of
    history, 103–104. *See also* semiotic ideology
Idolatry, 51, 54
Indexicality, 11–12, 13–17, 21, 24, 34, 52, 55–59,
    87–88, 124; creative, 125
Interactional text, 124–26, 197
Interpretant, 4, 14, 21, 29, 31–32, 39, 46, 48, 53–58,
    68, 71, 122–24; metapragmatic, 227–28
Interpretation, 15, 24, 29, 34–37, 40, 51, 55–58,
    65–67, 87, 94, 112, 215, 227–29
Intertextuality, 92, 121, 134

Jakobson, Roman, 6–8, 10–11, 24, 89, 123
James, William, 25

Lévi-Strauss, Claude, 8, 14, 95, 166
Lotman, Yuri, 18–20, 83, 89

Malinowski, Bronislaw, 8
Marked/unmarked. *See* markedness
Markedness, 15, 88–89, 123–26, 192, 209
Marriage payment, 171–72, 181, 184, 189–90
Marx, Karl, 137
Material signs, 16, 58–60, 95, 195, 203
Materiality, 57, 62, 98, 194. *See also* material
    signs
Meaning, as translation, 11, 24; pragmatic, 12;
    propositional, 30; symbolic, 15–16
Metapragmatic function, 125
Metapragmatics, 12, 52, 91–93, 124
Metasemiotics, 12, 15–19, 58, 92, 94, 99, 129, 195–97
Mead, Margaret, 3, 38
Money, 149–56, 163–65, 167–99
Motivation, relative, 37–39
Moscow-Tartu School, 17, 19, 83

Nagy, Gregory, 127, 132–35, 227
Naturalization, 53–54, 167

Objectification, 15, 87, 139, 153, 167

Palau, disharmonic regime, 103; ethnosemiotic models, 23; hierarchical, 191; historical markers, 23, 122. *See also* money
Parallelism, 7–8, 15–16, 20, 89, 95, 125–26, 144, 211, 226
Peirce, Charles S., 21, 24–36, 39, 42–44, 48–60, 68–71, 166; and Saussure, 4–5, 38, 42, 45; on language, 27–28, 42, 45, 56; on signs, 29
Performance, 3, 86, 91, 127, 133, 192, 209
Phylogenetic relationship, 110–11, 118–21
Poetic form, 7, 32, 34, 93, 126, 209
Portis-Winner, Irene, 19–20
Proverbs, 92–93
Pragmatic maxim, 26–32, 35
Pragmatic rule, 88, 210, 227–29
Pragmatics, 12, 25–27, 35, 93, 135, 215; of language, 33, 35, 122; of texts, 134, 209
Pragmatism, 24–26, 29
Prague Linguistic Circle, 6–7, 19, 89, 105, 123
Precapitalist society, 141–44, 155–56
Preucel, Robert, 58–60

Reciprocal delimitation, 40, 46
Recontextualization, 209–210, 214, 227–29
Reflexivity, 132
Regimentation, 12, 32, 37, 40, 85, 94, 134, 205–206
Religion, 106, 145, 198, definition, 118–18; domain, 113, 152
Replica, 13, 29, 49, 51, 57–78, 62, 67–68, 86–88, 95, 129
Replication, 49, 57–59, 68, 87, 95–99, 193
Representation, 36–37, 69, 71–72, 77, 84, 98, 122, 166, 176, 192–97
Rhematization, 17, 53
Ritual, 108, 114, 116–18, 145, 198

Sacrifice, 196, 198
Sahlins, Marshall D., 21, 23, 101
Saussure, Ferdinand de, 5–14, 21, 37–39, 43; on linguistic sign, 44; on value, 21, 38
Sebeok, Thomas A., 45, 94
Secondary elaboration, 132, 205

Secondary modeling system, 18
Semiosis, 4–5, 16, 28, 34–37, 39, 46, 50, 53, 63, 65, 69, 77, 84, 94, 99, 122, 195–97, 201–203
Semiotic anthropology, as a subdiscipline, 3–5, 12–13, 21; of Middle Ages, 127
Semiotic ideology, 16–17, 56
Semiotic mediation, 16, 33, 64, 94–95, 128, 131, 201
Semiotics, history of, 166; meaning of term, 3
Shifters, 11, 16, 23–24, 91, 123
Sign classes, 48–51, 53–55, 58, 60–62
Signs of history/signs in history, 23, 121–22, 126–28
Signification, 13, 15, 38, 43, 72, 87, 97, 130; sacramental, 203
Silverstein, Michael, 11–12, 24, 52–53, 83, 87, 94, 124, 134
Singer, Milton, 12–13
Sinsign, 21, 48–49, 60, 67–68, 85–86, 130
Social change, 20, 22, 27, 101–6
Speech acts, 21, 28–29, 134, 214, 217, 226
Statues, 36, 51–52, 56, 97, 193–94, 198–201, 206
Style, 14, 50, 60, 62, 85, 97, 177, 195, 213, 228
Surplus value, 145, 153–54, 157
Symbol, 4–5, 9, 11, 19, 24, 29, 37–39, 44, 48, 53, 70–73, 85, 106, 122, 165, 230
Synchrony, 7, 46, 52, 123

Temporality, 17, 34, 45, 59, 90, 102–3, 122–23, 126,
Text, 19, 65, 77, 90; closed, 228. *See also* textuality
Textual modality, 210, 213–16, 218, 226–28
Textuality, 21, 127, 134
Thirdness, 15–16, 27, 48, 53–54, 56, 63, 70–71, 94, 134
Transcendence, 131, 193–95, 198–99, 203, 205
Transparency, 32, 46, 54, 90, 126
Transubstantiation, 194, 203–4
Trichotomies, of signs, 4, 9, 14, 24, 39, 48–54, 61
Type/token, 5, 9, 16, 21–23, 29, 49, 52, 57, 85–86, 97, 200, 229
Typology, 119, 123, 205; of signs, 60

Valeri, Valerio, 196

Use-value, 139, 146–52, 154, 166

RICHARD J. PARMENTIER is Professor of Anthropology at Brandeis University. He is the author of *The Sacred Remains: Myth, History, and Polity in Belau*; *Signs in Society: Studies in Semiotic Anthropology*; and *The Pragmatic Semiotics of Cultures*. With Elizabeth Mertz, he coedited *Semiotic Mediation: Sociocultural and Psychological Perspectives*. He is editor-in-chief of *Signs and Society*; affiliated researcher, Hankuk University of Foreign Studies (Korea); and foreign member, doctoral program in humanities, University of Turin (Italy).

.